Deep and Shallow

Providing an essential and unique bridge between the theories of signal processing, machine learning, and artificial intelligence (AI) in music, this book provides a holistic overview of foundational ideas in music, from the physical and mathematical properties of sound to symbolic representations. Combining signals and language models in one place, this book explores how sound may be represented and manipulated by computer systems, and how our devices may come to recognize particular sonic patterns as musically meaningful or creative through the lens of information theory.

Introducing popular fundamental ideas in AI at a comfortable pace, more complex discussions around implementations and implications in musical creativity are gradually incorporated as the book progresses. Each chapter is accompanied by guided programming activities designed to familiarize readers with practical implications of discussed theory, without the frustrations of free-form coding.

Surveying state-of-the-art methods in applications of deep neural networks to audio and sound computing, as well as offering a research perspective that suggests future challenges in music and AI research, this book appeals to both students of AI and music, as well as industry professionals in the fields of machine learning, music, and AI.

Shlomo Dubnov is a Professor in the Music Department and Affiliate Professor in Computer Science and Engineering at the University of California, San Diego. He is best known for his research on poly-spectral analysis of musical timbre and inventing the method of Music Information Dynamics with applications in Computer Audition and Machine improvisation. His previous books on *The Structure of Style: Algorithmic Approaches to Understanding Manner and Meaning* and *Cross-Cultural Multimedia Computing: Semantic and Aesthetic Modeling* were published by Springer.

Ross Greer is a PhD Candidate in Electrical & Computer Engineering at the University of California, San Diego, where he conducts research at the intersection of artificial intelligence and human agent interaction. Beyond exploring technological approaches to musical expression, Ross creates music as a conductor and orchestrator for instrumental ensembles. Ross received his B.S. and B.A. degrees in EECS, Engineering Physics, and Music from UC Berkeley, and an M.S. in Electrical & Computer Engineering from UC San Diego.

Chapman & Hall/CRC Machine Learning & Pattern Recognition

For more information on this series please visit: https://www.routledge.com/Chapman--Hall-CRC-Machine-Learning--Pattern-Recognition/book-series/CRCMACLEAPAT

Deep and Shallow
Machine Learning in Music and Audio

Shlomo Dubnov and Ross Greer

CRC Press
Taylor & Francis Group
Boca Raton London New York

CRC Press is an imprint of the
Taylor & Francis Group, an **informa** business

A CHAPMAN & HALL BOOK

Cover Credit: Erik Jepsen

First edition published 2024
by CRC Press
6000 Broken Sound Parkway NW, Suite 300, Boca Raton, FL 33487-2742

and by CRC Press
4 Park Square, Milton Park, Abingdon, Oxon, OX14 4RN

CRC Press is an imprint of Taylor & Francis Group, LLC

© 2024 Shlomo Dubnov and Ross Greer

ISBN: 978-1-032-14618-8 (hbk)
ISBN: 978-1-032-13391-1 (pbk)
ISBN: 978-1-003-24019-8 (ebk)

DOI: 10.1201/9781003240198

Typeset in font Nimbus
by KnowledgeWorks Global Ltd.

Publisher's note: This book has been prepared from camera-ready copy provided by the authors.

Dedication

To our families and friends, for your unwavering support, and to our teachers, students, and peers, for endless inspiration.

הרבה למדתי מרבותי ומחברי יותר מרבותי ומתלמידי יותר מכולן

"I have learned much from my teachers, more from my colleagues, and the most from my students."

Rabbi Hanina, Babylonian Talmud

Contents

Preface

This book complements a largely missing textbook for a popular and growing in demand field of Machine Learning for Music and Audio. One of the difficulties in covering this subject is the interdisciplinary nature of domain knowledge that creates a barrier to entry to this field, which combines background in signal processing, symbolic sequence processing, statistical analysis, classical machine learning, and more recently the quickly growing field of deep neural networks. As a result of the breadth of the required background, students or practitioners who are interested in learning about the field have to look for relevant information across multiple disciplines. Moreover, the focus of the book is on generative methods, which are usually considered as more advanced subjects in machine learning that are often not explained in introductory or basic-level courses on machine learning.

The book is intended for upper-division undergraduate- or graduate-level courses, with basic understanding of statistics and Python programming. Music concepts and basic concepts in analysis of audio signals will be covered in the book, providing a one-stop reference to questions of musical representation and feature extraction, without assuming extensive prior musical and acoustics knowledge.

Starting with representation aspects in audio and symbolic music in Chapter 1, the second chapter goes immediately into stochastic aspects in both music and audio, addressing the conceptual premise of thinking about the relations between noise and structure. The idea of composition using random dice with lookup tables, or so-called "Mozart Dice Game", shows early on how the concepts are related, also providing historical context and relation to later formal algorithmic methods.

Although symbolic music versus audio signals are capturing sound data at different timescales and levels of detail, the parallels between the two domains are demonstrated throughout the book by considering aspects of anticipation both in the perceptual (sound versus noise) and cognitive (events surprisal) realms. In Chapter 2, we introduce a unifying analysis framework called "Music Information Dynamics" that stems from conceptual formulation of music and audio modeling and understanding as a problem of information processing. Introducing Markov models as basic statistical models for text and music, we proceed to consider information dynamics for the case of Markov models, relating it to questions of what type of random processes generates music that are more or less interesting to a predictive listener.

Accordingly, concepts from information theory and Shannon's laws are covered in Chapter 3. The central idea of thinking about music as an information source forms the basis to the way this book approaches and represents the musical machine learning problem. Using "off the shelf" data compression methods, one can build efficient representations of musical style. We demonstrate how style learning and continuation of musical phrases in a particular style can be accomplished by traversing a codebook that was derived from the famous Lempel-Ziv compression method.

In Chapter 4, we look deeper into the properties of audio signals by introducing the basic mathematical tools of digital signal processing. After briefly introducing the concepts of sampling, we talk about frequency analysis and conditions for short-time Fourier transform (STFT) prefect reconstruction. Such signal reconstruction is not possible when only the magnitude of STFT is available, so we cover the Griffin-Lim phase reconstruction that is often used for generating audio (also called vocoding) from magnitude spectrograms. We conclude the chapter with discussion of source-filter models and their application to speech modeling. Finally, we use the concept of spectral analysis and, in particular, the idea of spectral flatness to distinguish noise versus structure in audio, relating it to questions of prediction and information dynamics.

More advance information theory concepts are developed in Chapter 5, as part of concatenative and recombinant audio generative methods. Using a symbolization process that renders audio into a sequence of symbolic representation, known as Audio Oracle, we demonstrate the use of Variable-Memory Markov models and string-matching compression algorithms for creating new sequences of audio features or audio descriptors. These new symbolic sequences are then rendered back into audio using the concatenative method. The problem of finding repetitions in audio data and the use of recopying for compression and prediction are also linked to questions of computational aesthetics, namely the aesthetics measures of Birkhoff and Bense as ratios of order and complexity, as well as ethical aspects of reuse of existing music in training generative models.

Chapter 6 serves as a bridge between the signal processing and statistical methods of earlier chapters and the materials in later chapters that are dealing with deep neural networks for music and audio. After introducing the basic building blocks of artificial neural networks, we discuss aspects of representation learning by looking into similarities and differences between auto-encoder and a classical statistical data reduction and representation method known as principal components analysis (PCA). Specifically, the use of a PCA-like method for finding an optimal transform of audio signals, known as Krahunen-Loeve transform, is demonstrated in the context of noise removal.

Chapters 7–10 cover deep neural network approaches to music, starting in Chapter 7 with the question of unsupervised representation learning using sequence and image models that use Recurrent Neural Networks (RNN) and Convolutional Neural Networks (CNN). The idea of tokenization is basic to the ability of capturing the complex sequential structures in music into a neural recurrent representation. Relations across both time and pitch or frequency are captured using the CNN approach.

In Chapter 8, we return to the fundamental concept of turning noise into structure through the notion of neural networks that imagine. The concept of generative models is introduced by extending the previously discussed autoencoder into a Variational Autoencoder (VAE) that allows probabilistic approximation and representation. In this view, the random seed or input to the generative networks results in generation of variable replicas or samples from the same statistical model of music that was learned by the neural network. This chapter also covers Generative Adversarial

Networks, tying representation learning of the VAE to broader generative tasks, and also introducing conditional generation methods similar to style transfer in images. Such methods are important for specifying constraints on the generative processes in order to produce music or audio that correspond to user specifications or other contextual input.

Chapter 9 covers the recently extremely successful Transformers models, relating them to the problem of finding repetition and memory structures that were encountered earlier in the Variable Markov Oracle (VMO) of Chapter 5 and RNN in Chapter 7. Several state-of-the-art transformer models are surveyed here both in audio and symbolic representations.

The book concludes by reviewing and summarizing the broad problem of viewing music as a communication process in Chapter 10. By relating the phenomena of music understanding and creation to the models of music information dynamics, we are able to discuss the future of AI in music in terms of building new compositional tools that operate by learning musical structures from examples and generating novel music according to higher level meta-creative specifications, approaching novel levels of man-machine co-creative interaction.

Interactive code exercises are an important feature of this book. Instructor solutions are available by request through the publisher's book website. Referenced code will be available as Jupyter Notebooks at:

https://github.com/deep-and-shallow/notebooks

The authors provide the following possible suggestions for the curriculum of an introductory and advanced course on Machine Learning for Music and Audio. The focus of the first course is an introduction to the basic concept of music and audio representation, modeling music as a probabilistic information source, music information dynamics, and an introduction to representation learning and sequence modeling using neural networks.

- Class 1: Representation of Sound and Music Data (MIDI, audio), Audio features, MFCC, Chroma
- Class 2: Aleatoric music, stochastic processes in music and sound (Mozart Dice Game), Noise and Electronic Music
- Class 3: Sampling, Spectral Analysis, Fourier transform, FFT, Spectral Flatness
- Class 4: Short-Time Fourier Analysis, Perfect Reconstruction (COLA), Griffith-Lim phase reconstruction,
- Class 5: Information Theory and Music, String Matching, Universal Compression and Prediction
- Class 6: Markov Models for Text and Music, Lempel-Ziv Algorithm for Motif Continuation
- Class 7: Introduction to Neural Networks, Neural Network Models of Music
- Class 8: Autoencoder (AE) and PCA, Representation Learning
- Class 9: Neural Language Models, Recurrent Neural Network for Music
- Class 10: Introduction to Generative Models and next course overview

The advanced second course dives deeper into signal processing of speech signals and vocoders, generative neural networks for audio and music with focus on variational methods, and return to information theory for deep musical information dynamics with possible implications toward understanding creativity in neural networks.

- Class 1: Review of Music and Audio Representation, Short-Time Fourier Analysis
- Class 2: Linear Filters and Convolution Theorem, Pole-Zero Plots
- Class 3: History of the voder/vocoder, Source-Filter Models, and Linear Prediction
- Class 4: Concatenative Synthesis, Variable Markov Oracle (VMO), Symbolization, and Information Dynamics
- Class 5: Review of Neural Networks, AutoEncoders and RNN
- Class 6: Convolutional NN for Music and Audio (U-Net) for Genre Classification and Source Separation
- Class 7: Variational AE, ELBO, Generating Music with VAE
- Class 8: Generative Adversarial Networks, W-GAN, MuseGAN, CycleGAN
- Class 9: Attention and Transformers, MuseNet, Audio Spectrogram Transformer
- Class 10: Information Theory Models of NN, Deep Music Information Dynamics

Including extra time for quizzes, projects, and exams, these course contents should suffice for a semester-long course each, or as two quarters of instruction followed by a quarter of practical projects. Overall, we estimate that with additional practical and theoretical assignments, the materials of the book represent about one year of academic study that is needed for students with focus on AI and music or a concentration in machine learning with specialization in music and audio. It is our hope that the current text would help establish this as a field of study.

1 Introduction to Sounds of Music

Music is a particular form of art that is particularly hard to grasp, define, or put in a mold. In many respects, music deals with shaping air vibrations into meaningful sound perceptions, and each type of music, depending on culture, style, period, or location, has its own particular ways of expression that might be grounded in practices that are close to the hearts of some and meaningless to others. In this book, we are trying to understand music from the artificial intelligence (AI) and machine learning (ML) perspectives. To make the question about the meaning of music even more acute, we may ask ourselves – what does it take to make music meaningful to a machine? If we desire to build artificial agents that can compose music or engage creatively in real time with musicians in a process of improvisation, we hope that these interactions will convey to the intelligent machine the same significance we ascribe to the music.

1.1 FROM SOUND TO FEATURES

Broadly speaking, the meaning of music is established by human musicians themselves who have the creative intent of producing particular types of sound structures, and by their listeners who engage with these sounds to experience them in interesting and exciting ways. Music, in many ways, is the most abstract art, devoid of a particular reference to the outside world. It may excite us or calm us down, affect our mood or be simply regarded as an intricate fabric of sound structures, where the pleasure can be found in the act of listening itself. Accordingly, asking the question of what establishes meaning in sounds is a formidable problem to which we unfortunately will not be able to give a definite answer.

In our journey from physical sounds to musical meaning, we need to go through several intermediate stages. The first step is choosing the palette of music sounds at our disposal, which can be later organized in time into a complete musical piece. Since one person's music may be another person's noise, the challenge for the machine is very much same as that of the uninitiated listener: to first of all distinguish noise from music or find the structure in sounds that makes it musical. In our journey into creative musical machines, we start with sound structures that are most common in music, namely notes, rhythms, and scales. The most elementary musical sounds, often called "tones" comprise duration (length), frequency (pitch), amplitude (loudness), and timbre (sound quality). Tones are organized in patterns, where the times and lengths of their appearances (onsets and durations) are organized into rhythm; selection of allowed frequencies is organized into scales and tonalities; multiple notes playing together create harmonies; and so on. Each of these aspects can

DOI: 10.1201/9781003240198-1

be considered as a musical representation; it summarizes a physical phenomena –
sound – into few essential properties that are considered musical. Since this is not
a music theory book, we will not go into elaborate theories of how music is represented or the "rules" for musical composition that depend also on the musical style
and culture, but will rather stay as close as possible to examples in representation related to common Western music notation[1] and representations that can be extracted
from a sound recording before further processing to discover statistical relations by
ML methods. Accordingly, we may summarize the basic sound properties or features
as follows:

- **Pitch** is a perceptual phenomenon which encapsulates the relationship between
  the frequency generated by an instrument and the frequency perceived by the
  listener. As an example, when musicians in a modern orchestra tune to concert
  pitch, they typically listen to an oboe play the pitch A4. This pitch is produced
  at a frequency of 440 Hertz[2]. Slight changes in frequency have little effect on
  perceived pitch. The perception of pitch varies logarithmically with the generated
  frequency; that is, to hear the same pitch at a higher octave, the frequency of the
  sound must be doubled.

  Tuning systems explore the problem of mapping a discrete number of possible
  notes to the continuous frequency space. For example, a piano has a limited number of keys spanning an octave, but there are an infinite number of frequencies
  which theoretically exist between any set of notes. Western music traditionally
  uses a 12-tone equal-tempered scale. In an *equal-tempered scale*, every pair of
  adjacent notes has an identical frequency ratio. Thus, each octave is divided into
  12 logarithmically equal parts.

Example: Notes on a Keyboard

Musical Instrument Digital Interface, or MIDI, is a protocol for recording
and playing music on computers. The lowest note on a standard acoustic
piano, named A0, is pitch number 21 in MIDI convention. The highest
note on a keyboard, named C8, is pitch number 108 in MIDI. By defining
the note named A4 (MIDI pitch 69) to be the reference pitch at 440 Hz,
we can define the following relationship between any MIDI pitch number
p and its corresponding frequency:

$$F_{pitch}(p) = 2^{(p-69)/12} \times 440 \qquad (1.1)$$

To interpret this equation, note that the exponential term effectively counts
how many steps of an 12-step-octave the input note is from the reference pitch, then uses this as the (fractional) power due to the logarithmic

---

[1]Note that many of these techniques can be applied to analysis in other music notation schemes, given appropriate methods of tokenization and abstraction.

[2]Hertz is the unit used to measure frequency, referring to occurrences per second of any periodic phenomena.

relationship between perceived notes and requisite frequency. This coefficient is then used as a multiple to the reference pitch of 440 Hz. We can see that a pitch located 12 *half steps*[a] above the reference pitch would create an exponent of one, allowing for the resulting doubling of the frequency, as would be expected for a note found an octave above the reference. Every n steps away from the reference pitch on an equally tempered keyboard corresponds to a multiplication of the reference frequency by the twelfth-root of two, n times.

---

[a] Here, we must acknowledge some possible confusion in terminology: though the octave is divided into 12 portions, musicians refer to these portions as *half steps*. Two half steps span a *whole step*, and sequential combinations of half and whole steps are used to define different *scales*. The musical term *flat* refers to a pitch one half step below the reference, while the term *sharp* refers to a pitch one half step above the reference. This provides a variety of possible descriptors for the same pitch, referred to as an *enharmonic* relationship; for example, C♯ (C-sharp) and D♭ (D-flat) refer to the same pitch. Nuances in use of these symbols can provide context to a performer about special tuning to play within a particular modes or harmony, but for the sake of our examples, we can consider these pitches equivalent and thus must be careful that our schemes for abstracting these pitches do not mistakenly contain two possible table entries for the same pitch.

- **Timbre**, also referred to as tone quality or tone color, is the quality of musical sound that distinguishes different types of sound production, such as different voices or instruments. When you hear the same note played at the same volume and same duration first by one instrument and then by another, the difference you hear is due to timbre. Physically, this property depends on the energy distribution in the harmonics and relationships between the constituent sinusoids, phenomena which will be introduced in Chapter 4.

As a prototype of sound, consider a sinusoidal wave (that is, a wave with a fixed frequency, phase, and amplitude). The period is the time it takes for the wave cycle to repeat and can be measured using successive peaks in the wave (unit: seconds), and is the inverse of frequency (unit: Hertz). The amplitude is one-half the pressure difference between the high and low points (often measured in micro Pascals).

1.1.1 LOUDNESS

Loudness is the subjective perception of sound pressure, meaning that loudness is a combination of not only the physical attributes of a sound but also physiological and psychological phenomena.

Torben Poulsen [1] shows that the physical aspect of loudness is related to sound pressure level, frequency content, and sound duration. **Sound pressure level** is used to measure the effective pressure of a sound relative to a reference pressure value (often 20 µPa, a canonical threshold for human hearing). Sound pressure level is described by the formula

$$20\log_{10}\frac{p}{p_0}, \tag{1.2}$$

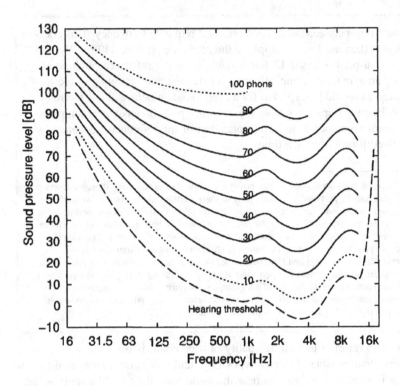

Figure 1.1   The equal-loudness graph created by Suzuki and Takeshima [2] shows that different frequencies create the same perceived loudness at different sound pressure levels. Following any one curve on the graph provides frequency-SPL pairs which were found to create the same perceived loudness.

where p is the measured sound pressure and p_0 is the reference pressure, giving a unit of decibels (dB).

Steven's power law, formulated as $\Psi(I) = kI^a$, connects sound pressure levels I to the perceived loudness of a single tone; that is, it defines the relationship between a change in the stimulus sound pressure level and the corresponding increase in perceived sensation. Steven's power law typically uses an exponent α of 0.67, and this exponent and scalar constant k are empirically sourced approximations; accordingly, there exist other methods and models to relate sound pressure levels to perception. Another interesting perceptual phenomena is the relationship between stimulus frequency and perceived loudness, portrayed by a so-called *equal-loudness graph* as shown in Figure 1.1.

1.1.2 MFCC

In the field of timbral analysis, or in other words, extracting sound properties that are unrelated to pitch, duration, or loudness, the Mel-Frequency Cepstral Coefficients (MFCC) became the "go-to" method for capturing the overall shape of frequency distribution, also called the *spectral envelope*. The spectral envelope may characterize the color of the sound that is independent of the specific note an instrument plays, which is useful in distinguishing between different types of instruments. MFCCs have historically been the dominant features in speech recognition since they are invariant to pitch or loudness of the speech and rather capture the broad shape of the energy distribution of the voice (that comprises so-called "speech formants"[3]). Moreover, MFCC analysis has been applied to complex music such as polyphonic music (multiple voices or multiple instruments, such as orchestra) to characterize the distribution of energies at different frequencies. For example, they were used in music retrieval systems, music summarization, and musical audio analysis toolboxes[4].

A detailed description of MFCC requires technical terms that assume knowledge of spectral analysis, which is using Fourier transforms to discover the underlying frequency components in a sound signal. While Fourier analysis will be introduced in the next chapter, what is important to note at this point is that each step in the process of MFCC computation is motivated by perceptual or computational considerations. Briefly, it first converts the Fourier analysis, which is linear in frequency, to a Mel-scale that is perceptually scaled according to human judgments of pitches being equal distance from each other. This means that when comparing distances between any two points on the Mel scale, the same distance should correspond to the same perceived change in pitch. Within the linear frequency scale, this relationship is not preserved since the relationship of frequency to perceived pitch is logarithmic. A common formula for relating Mel[5] to the frequency in Hertz (Hz) is $m = 2595 \log_{10}\left(1 + \frac{f}{700}\right)$. After that, a technique called "cepstral analysis" is applied to the scaled spectrum. The idea of cepstral analysis is to separate short-time structure versus longer period repetitions in sounds by assuming a "source-filter" model. By looking at the spectral analysis of a sound, one notices that there are the harmonics, or partials showing as individual peaks, and an overall "spectral envelope" that shapes the spectrum in terms of broad areas of resonances. In the source-filter view, the spectral peaks of the harmonics originate from the repetitions of the excitation source, such as flapping of the vocal chords in speech or vibrations of reed or string in a musical instrument. The broad shape of the spectrum is attributed to the filter, representing the resonance of the body of the instrument or speech formants in a vocal tract. As we will see in the following chapters, operation of a filter on another signal amounts to an operation of multiplication in the frequency domain between the filter's and signal's spectra, respectively. In cepstral analysis, a log function is applied

---

[3]The voice as a combination of speech formants will be introduced in Chapter 4.

[4]Musical audio analysis toolboxes such as Librosa will be introduced in Appendix B.

[5]A unit whose name is derived from "melody" [3].

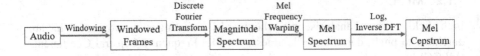

Figure 1.2 Main steps in calculation of MFCC.

to the log of amplitude-spectrum, and then a Fourier analysis is applied to split it into low-order and high-order components. The idea of cepstral analysis is that the log operation, at least approximately, separates the aspects of source and filter into two additive components, one that contains the harmonics without the spectral envelope and the other that captures the envelope. Then by applying the Fourier transform the result is rendered back into time-like units, called "Quefrency". By going back to a time-like domain, the spectral envelope is translated into the lower cepstral coefficients (low quefrency), while the harmonic structure due to pitch shows up the peaks at higher quefrencies. Eventually, only the lower cepstral coefficients (the filter characteristics) are kept as features, as they capture the broad shape of the spectrum, removing the spectral shape of the harmonics due to the pitch (source). Formally written, cepstral analysis is defined as follows:

$$C(q) = \left| \mathcal{F}^{-1} \left\{ \log \left(|\mathcal{F}\{x(t)\}|^2 \right) \right\} \right|^2 \tag{1.3}$$

with $C(q)$ being the cepstrum and different quefrencies, $x(t)$ the original time signal, and $\mathcal{F}$ and $\mathcal{F}^{-1}$ being the Fourier and inverse Fourier transforms, respectively. A diagram of MFCC analysis is shown in Figure 1.2. To obtain a frequency scale that better corresponds to human hearing, a mel-scale is used instead of linear frequency spacing. Moreover, since sound properties change over time, MFCC analysis is applied to short instances of sound by applying a windowing function that extracts a portion of a signal in time. It should be noted that the total energy or overall loudness of the sound is captured by the first cepstral coefficient and is often disregarded too[6]. An investigation suggests that MFCC are approximately optimal representations, at least for the case of speech and song, as they approximate a statistically optimal basis [7], derived by Principal Component Analysis (PCA) applied to a Mel-Spectra correlation matrix. The technical method of PCA will be described in Chapter 6. To summarize, the vector of MFCC is a timbral feature that captures the overall spectral

---

[6]Since Fourier transform performs and integral operation over a signal multiplied by a phasor at each frequency, Fourier analysis at zero frequency is simply an integral over the whole signal, which in the case of Equation 1.3 is an integral over the log of energy at all frequencies, thus giving the total log-energy of the signal. We will cover Fourier transform in later chapters.

[7]PCA finds basis vectors that optimally represent randomly distributed vectors, such as sound features, in a way that is both decorrelated and sorted according to the amount of variance they capture in the original signal. A basis is a set of vectors that can be combined in multiples to construct any other vector within a defined vector space.

shape of a sound in its lower coefficients, independent of aspects of pitch or energy, in approximately optimal and independent manner.

1.1.3 CHROMA

Chromatic features of sound refer to the phenomenon that doubling or halving the frequency of the sound results in a similar perceived sound, just higher or lower. A musical example of this *octave* phenomenon is shown in Figure 1.3.

This chromatic feature is best visualized with the *chromagram*, shown in Figure 1.4. There is a property of chromatic invariance between pitches separated by one or more octaves; as you move up or down the helix of the chromagram, the projection of position onto the chromatic wheel provides the chroma perceived, while the height indicates how "high" or "low" the sound is perceived. The distance between any point and the point directly above is equal to one octave (that is, the next time the same chroma will occur). Thus, every frequency can be constructed as a combination of height and chroma:

$$f = 2^{h+c}, \tag{1.4}$$

Figure 1.3 The third movement of Beethoven's ninth Symphony famously begins with octave jumps in the strings. Each set of notes begins at a high pitch, then drops an octave. From a physical standpoint, the frequency of the string's vibration is halved. Listen to a recording of this scherzo to hear the remarkable similarity between pitches spaced an octave apart; this similarity is described as the *chroma* feature.

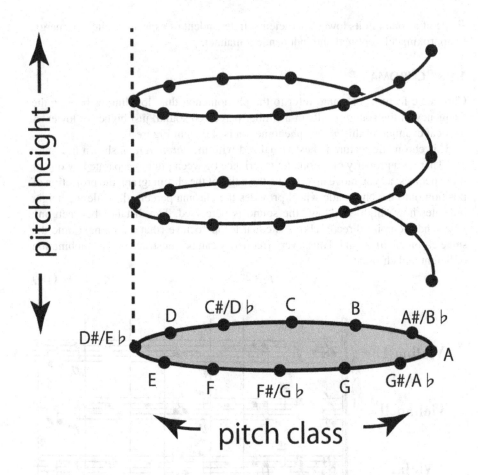

Figure 1.4 The helix pattern of the chromagram. Projections onto the circle at the base provide the chroma perceived, while the height provides reference to the general frequency level associated with the pitch.

where height h is a natural number and chroma c is in the range $[0, 1)$. Similarly, chroma itself can be thought of as the "carry" after subtracting the nearest height level from the frequency:

$$c = \log 2f - \lfloor \log 2f \rfloor. \tag{1.5}$$

Having an understanding of these properties and features of sound will be a useful frame for the analysis of music, especially in relation to musical events we perceive as consonant or dissonant, to which we may ascribe the musical significance we seek to represent and recreate in our models.

1.2 REPRESENTATION OF SOUND AND MUSIC DATA

1.2.1 SYMBOLIC REPRESENTATIONS

Though we may never answer our classic question of "What *is* music?", here we hope to make discussion of some ways we may *represent* music.

If music is composed of sounds, we might consider Western music notation to be an example of *symbolic representation* of sounds. Note that while this system of symbols is capable of representing creative ideas, this music notation is incomplete in its ability to represent every possible sound and is of course subject to interpretation by its time and cultural context. This incompleteness is a property we will see across representations, even in our "best" audio encodings. We are always limited by the number of bits[8] available to represent the sonic information, so a representation which allows for perfect reconstruction of the physical sound is a near-impossible task. Of course, we can come close, adopting representations which can encode information to the resolution and rate of human hearing.

Though a trivial statement, we note here that the representation scheme offered by Western music notation is, in general, sufficient to represent Western music. So, here we define some of its common structures and features used to describe common musical expressions, as we will use these structures as the building blocks for composing similar music.

- A **note** describes a pitch and duration. A very brief introduction to Western music notation is provided in Figure 1.5.
- A **chord** is the combination of two or more notes sounding simultaneously.
- A **melody** is a sequence of notes.
- **Rhythm** is the timing pattern assigned to a set of notes.

Symbolic representation relates abstract symbols to the continuous-time sound waves (audio) we perceive or imagine, when respectively listening or composing. However, it can be difficult to precisely derive these features from the audio. You can explore the associated challenges by trying the provided *Introduction to Music Representation* programming exercises, where we explore a means of converting a symbolic representation to a pseudo-physical representation (audio), then transcribing this generated audio back to a symbolic representation.

Most musicians may be especially familiar with the symbolic representation of music as a printed notation system. Consider the first five bars of the famous fifth Symphony of Beethoven, shown in Figure 1.6. This is a graphical notation form which indicates which notes are to be played, and for what duration. This representation relies on an agreed upon convention of understanding, and can be considered a set of performance instructions. These instructions are translated by a musician and

---

[8] A *bit* (binary digit) is the smallest unit of information that can be represented by a computer; conceptually, the unit is an entity that can take one of two states, which can be imagined as "on" or "off", 1 or 0, "True" or "False", etc.

Figure 1.5 This excerpt from Tchaikovsky's Overture to Romeo & Juliet illustrates the characteristic symbols used to notate Western music. Each note has a **head** (shown in blue) which sits on a position within the **staff** (the name given to each series of five horizontal lines). The placement of the head on the staff indicates the pitch relative to some reference, provided by the **clef** (symbol sitting in the left-most position of the staff, indicated in green). Flags, beams, and stems (boxed in red) are used to indicate note durations. A brief catalog of some note and rest durations is shown in this excerpt, ranging from whole (entire measure of time) to sixteenth (one-sixteenth of the measure duration). The top staff contains whole notes, the second staff half notes, the third staff sixteenth notes, the fourth staff eighth notes, and the bottom staff quarter notes. Similarly, the third staff contains a half rest, the fourth staff an eighth rest, and the bottom staff a quarter rest (all boxed in yellow). While this fractional notation of duration is in theory unbounded, beyond a certain limit (thirty-second notes or so), the smaller the fraction the more rare its occurrence in commonly performed music.

their instrument into the physical vibrations of air, forming the acoustic signal we hear. In fact, the performance instructions we are used to reading draw from a very limited set of possible sounds when we consider the noise that surrounds us every day (speaking voices, chirping birds, clanging machinery, etc.). In this section, we will introduce some common symbolic notation systems adopted by digital devices.

1.2.1.1 MIDI

How might a computer represent symbolic music? Considering the first violin line of Figure 1.6, the information communicated to the performer is the sequences of pitches to be played (silence, then a series of three Gs, then an E-flat), and the duration for these pitches or silence (eighth notes, at a tempo of Allegro con brio, a rate of 108 beats per minute; in the case of this piece, each beat comprises a measure of four eighth notes).

Figure 1.6 The score depicting the well-known motif which opens Beethoven's fifth Symphony[9].

There are some challenges to translate this to a computer instruction, explored in Exercise 2 at the end of the chapter. First, though the three notes are given in direct sequence, there must be some brief (and unmeasured) separation between them, which is conventionally understood by the performer; without this, we would hear sequential notes performed as a continuous tone. In other words, the sound must not be sustained between the three notes since the separation defines the note length. The MIDI [Musical Instrument Digital Interface] standard requires the definition of PPQ (pulses per quarter note) and tempo (measured as microseconds per quarter note). Using these rates, we can set durations (measured in ticks) for each note, with appropriate pauses in between, resulting in the memory table illustrated in Figure 1.7. In addition to the duration of each note, we must also communicate which pitch is to be played (in this case, a G4), which we map to the MIDI index standard (reference pitch C4 = Note Number 60) to determine G4 = Note Number 67. Having covered pitch and duration, the remaining information available in a score is the relative volume at which the notes are played, often reflected in the parameter of Velocity in MIDI, which can indicate the power at which a note is struck or released [4]. The MIDI table is therefore a sequence of these parameters, given as instructions to turn the given note ON or OFF for the given duration at the given velocity.

---

[9]Technically, we're missing the clarinets from this figure (and the many instruments which are resting), but the motif is clear and should spark the intended musical memory.

Time (Ticks)	Message	Note Number	Velocity
55	NOTE ON	67	100
5	NOTE OFF	67	0
55	NOTE ON	67	100
5	NOTE OFF	67	0
55	NOTE ON	67	100
5	NOTE OFF	67	0
240	NOTE ON	63	100

Figure 1.7 A table representing the MIDI instructions for the first violin of Beethoven 5.

1.2.1.2 Piano Roll

Similar to Western music notation, the **piano roll** notation system uses a horizontal time axis and a vertical pitch axis. Notes are represented by activation of a point on the piano roll, indicating the pitch should be sounded at that time. Original piano rolls were perforated paper, with the perforations read be a player piano to activate a particular keypress. You may also be familiar with piano roll as a popular visualization of keyboard music on YouTube[10] (though note that sometimes the time and pitch axes are interchanged). Figure 1.8 shows our continued example of the opening of Beethoven 5, this time in piano roll notation.

1.2.1.3 Note-Tuple Representation

The MusPy package[11] reads music in note-tuple representation, where music is framed as a sequence of (pitch, time, duration, velocity) tuples. If we want to encode the beginning of Beethoven 5 for a violin part, we would could use the chart in Figure 1.7:

- (67, 0, 55, 100)
- (67, 60, 55, 100)
- (67, 120, 55, 100)
- (63, 180, 240, 100)

Note that events are represented with an intial onset time and duration, rather than a set of note-on and note-off instructions.

---

[10]Check out a great variety of piano roll notation examples, the first example being a true piano roll:

- https://www.youtube.com/watch?v=TgrqjkWqhE8
- https://www.youtube.com/watch?v=IAOKJ14Zaoo
- https://www.youtube.com/watch?v=8QorZ9fcg3o

[11]Introduced in Appendix B.

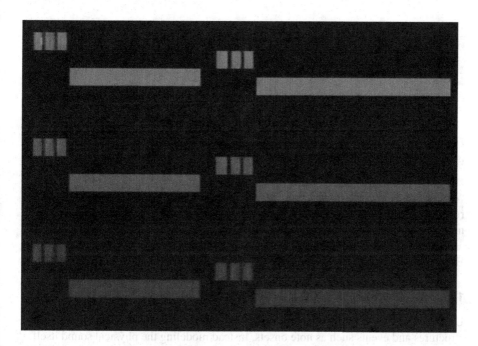

Figure 1.8 Notice the similarities between the notated score, MIDI representation, and now piano roll representation of the first bars of Beethoven's fifth Symphony. Quantized cells are highlighted to indicate activation; as the reader scrolls through the piano roll, these pitches will be sounded as the cursor (whether a reader's eyes, a computer scan, or a turning mechanism) passes over the respective column.

1.2.1.4 ABC Notation

ABC notation[12] (stylized "abc") was designed to notate folk tunes (that is, single melodies of one stave) in plain text format. Since its inception by Chris Walshaw in 1993 and subsequent popularization, features have expanded to allow for multiple voices, articulation, dynamics, and more. The eighth note is given unit length, so Beethoven 5 could be written as [|zGGG|_E4|]; check out the coding scheme included on the ABC notation reference site to understand how different notes, rests, and durations are encoded.

1.2.1.5 Music Macro Language

Music Macro Language (MML) is another text-based language, similar to abc notation. Many variations have developed with different use cases; one distinguishing feature is the use of operators that change parser state while parsing notes (such as an

---

[12]https://abcnotation.com/

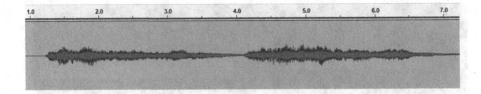

Figure 1.9 Visualization of a recording of the opening of Beethoven 5. The horizontal axis is time (seconds), and the vertical axis is amplitude.

"octave up" or "octave down" symbol which reads continually in a new octave until reset). Our usual Beethoven example might be notated as "pg8g8g8e-2" (but please note that this would be preceded in an MML file by some global parameters such as default note length, tempo, etc.). A description of modern MML can be found in Byrd et al.'s reference handbook [5].

1.2.2 AUDIO REPRESENTATIONS

Unlike symbolic representations of music, *audio* does not explicitly specify musical structures and events such as note onsets, instead modeling the physical sound itself. for the purposes of our discussion, when considering audio representation, we are referring to the digital representation of physical sonic information, as opposed to the coding schemes and data-structures used to format such information into "files". In other words, when we speak of audio, we are speaking of the vector of values that correspond to pressure amplitudes perceived by the microphone, and not to the specific encoding formats (such as "WAV", "MP3", etc.) used to represent this information.

When we record an orchestra playing the score from Figure 1.6, the microphones record the air pressure patterns in the form of digial audio, depicted in Figure 1.9. Digital audio, at its finest level, represents the sound encoded as a series of binary numbers. The wave-like nature of the sound is not apparent due to the physically compressed viewing window, so a zoomed-in view is offered in Figure 1.10.

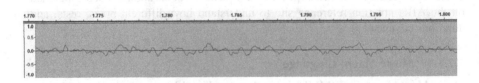

Figure 1.10 Zoomed-in visualization of a recording of one of the first three notes of Beethoven 5 (orchestra playing G2, G3, and G4 simultaneously). The horizontal axis is time (seconds), and the vertical axis is amplitude. As we zoom in on the audio signal, the wave-like nature may be more clear.

These visualizations are generated by the free audio software Audacity, introduced in Appendix C.

The basic process of capturing an audio file is recording acoustic vibration using some sort of a sound-capturing mechanism, normally a mechanically driven microphone that translates air pressure changes to electrical signals. We will not discuss microphone and recording techniques in this book. Moreover, since we are dealing with computational methods, we will also skip the analog ways of recording and storing sounds, such as magnetic tapes or vinyl records. In the next chapter, we will immediately move to discussion of digitizing sounds, also called analog-to-digital conversion (ADC) which is a process of sampling a continuous sound at fixed, albeit very short or fast-paced intervals. Understanding the theory of sampling and reconstruction of analog signals from their digital version, called digital-to-analog conversion (DAC), is important for assuring that the quality of the digital sound will be equal to its analog version, or in other words, to assure perfect reconstruction of the acoustic waveform to prevent distortion due to the sampling process.

Considering representation of audio from the content perspective, there are also multiple levels of analysis that must be addressed. The immediate level is the conversion of audio signal information initially represented as a sequence of numbers in time, to a collection of frequencies that change over time. This type of representation change, or transformation of the audio data from one format to another is purely technical or mathematical and is actually a common technique in audio processing which can be quite revealing. Note that we will also call a digital sound a waveform, even though it is in fact a time series or an array of numbers,

Sound can be framed as a superposition of sinusoids (called *Fourier analysis*). The notes produced by a musical instrument are a complex superposition of pure tones, as well as other noise-like components. *Harmonics* are integer-multiples of the fundamental frequency which produces the sound.

Example: Harmonics and Overtones

If we begin with a fundamental frequency of 440 Hz, the first integer multiple of the frequency ($2 \times 440 = 880$Hz) is referred to as the first harmonic. The second integer multiple of the frequency ($3 \times 440 = 1320$Hz) is referred to as the second harmonic.

How are these harmonics generated? When we energize a physical oscillator (pluck a string, strike a drum), the medium has several modes of vibration possible, and it is usually the case that multiple modes will vibrate simultaneously. These additional modes beyond the fundamental generate *overtones*, additional pitches present (usually with lower energy than the fundamental) when an instrument produces a sound. Because these overtones often fall very close to the harmonic series, they are often referred to as *harmonics*.

At the next abstracted level of audio representation, more and more complex features can be extracted. One immediate caveat of moving up in the hierarchy of features is that in order to get deeper insight into the sound we also need to discard some information. For instance, we might want to consider the sinusoidal amplitude or energies at different frequency bands, rather then preserve the exact detail about timing of the sinusoids, thus discarding their phase information. This immediately causes the representation to be non-invertible, or in other words, the original waveform cannot be directly reconstructed from the features. Pitch, loudness, MFCC and Chroma features that were discussed earlier in this chapter are considered to be higher level representation of audio. The general term applied to such representation is "audio descriptors", which can vary in the granularity in time or extent of sound events that it represents. The general study of such features belongs to a relatively young field of **Music Information Retrieval** (MIR) since one of the immediate uses of such features is classification or recognition of music that can be used for various retrieval applications.

One might consider **transcription**, the process of converting music from an audio representation to a symbolic notation, as the ultimate representation task. Some musicians transcribe by ear to handwritten notation; likewise, researchers explore methods of computer transcription. Many commercial software applications offer their solutions toward automatic transcription as a tool for composers and performers, but there is still much to be improved in these systems, much like an auto-captioning system may make mistakes while transcribing spoken language to text. To understand the complexity of the transcription task, in our computer exercises we provide an example of matching MIDI piano roll representation to an acoustic representation called Constant-Q Transform (CQT). The difficulty in finding such match depends on the complexity of the sounds performing the MIDI score, or in other words, the timbre of the instrument performing the music complicates the frequency contents of the signal. Today, state of the art transcription methods such as the MT3 system [6] use neural networks especially trained to recognize the different musical instruments, significantly outperforming the traditional signal-processing-based methods.

1.3   ACOUSTICS AND BASICS OF NOTES

One of the basic tenets of applying machine learning to music is that acoustic signals that we consider musical have a certain common structure and organization that can be captured by a machine, if it is exposed to a rich variety of examples. There is an inherent trade-off or tension between randomness and rules in music. We expect music to be exciting, changing, and dynamic, but at the same time predictable enough to make sense, be recognizable, and provide engagement. On the most rudimentary level, we might consider musical acoustics from the perspective of periodicity versus noise. After all, all musical cultures have selected from the infinite possibilities of sounds two large categories – musical tones, which are sound phenomena that have a relatively clear perception of pitch or musical height (i.e., notes), and percussive events that have sharp transitory sounds, where the main structuring element and characteristic would be organization into rhythms. Other types of sounds, such as many natural sounds and sound effects (think about sounds of water in a river sound or splashing waves, animal calls in a jungle, or industrial noises) have came into use only recently, with the invention of recording technology and electronic sound synthesis. Such sounds are much more difficulty to categorize, organize, and compose. The fascination with such sounds was a driving force behind many modern music experimental practices (a term used to denote music innovations of the twentieth century), as well as instrumental music innovations till this day.

Keeping in mind the broad distinction between structure and randomness, we will deal first with the question of periodicity versus noise on the short term acoustic level. Broadly speaking we will distinguish between

- periodic or almost periodic signals
- noise or a-periodic signals

The framework we will use to consider such signals is so-called "random processes", which considers random signals as signals whose instantaneous values are largely unknown, but can still be predicted with a certain level of probability. Moreover, we largely divide random signals into stationary and non-stationary, where stationary signals retain their statistical characteristics in the long run, which can be either done by long enough observation of the signal statistics that do not change, or by repeated independent observations of the signal on different occasions. Strictly speaking, this equivalence of long observation or many short independent observations is called the "ergodic" property, which is a common assumption in stochastic analysis. As an example, every time you pluck a string on a guitar or blow air into a flute, the exact vibrations of the air waves will be different, but if you repeat it many times, you will be able to observe (or hear) all such variations. In practice, most audio signals, and formidably music, is non-stationary. We play different notes, and express different sounds when we speak (vowels, consonants, change in intonation). Even machinery that keeps running in the same manner (think about a car engine), will have different sounds depending on changes in the way it works (you press the gas pedal). We will separately deal with non-stationary sounds when we will try to segment audio recording into frames of short-time sound events, or treat notes as an abstraction of a short-term fixed event, which in practice will be synthesized or rendered into sound slightly differently every time. Each note will be characterized by some typical periodic property, such as the name or MIDI number of the note being played. These tones are periodic, but we need to define periodicity first.

Periodic signals are considered random signals having some repeated property or phenomena that is the same after a particular time. Periodic phenomena do not need to be exact repetitions. Periodic signals return approximately to their previous values after a specified time interval, an effect that can be statistically captured by computing *correlation* or other statistical similarities.

Correlation

In the interest of creating machine learning models which generate audio that is similar to existing audio, it is important that we have a means of measuring the similarity of two audio signals.

Consider a sine wave, shown in red in the figure. The sine wave is offset from the cosine wave (in blue on the same plot), unless given a delay of half its period, at which point the two signals perfectly align.

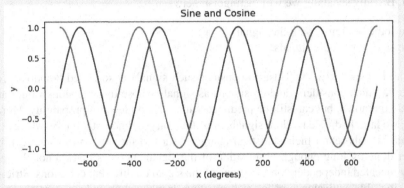

Because of this, it is difficult to produce exactly one number that captures the strength of similarity between the two signals – there is a natural dependence on the amount of the delay.

The correlation function accounts for this, providing a measure of similarity (or coherence) as a function of the signals' relative delay n:

$$(f \star g)[n] = \sum_{m=-\infty}^{\infty} \overline{f[m]}g[m+n], \tag{1.6}$$

where f and g are two signals being compared. Here, the bar over $f[m]$ refers to the complex conjugate; multiplying a conjugate term with a non-conjugated term gives a value which increases when the two complex numbers are in near phase angles.

Readers interested in understanding the mathematics behind cross-correlation and similar topics of autocorrelation and convolution are encouraged to visit the resources in signal processing provided in Chapter 4. For now, we recommend two primary takeaways:

- Similarity between signals is an important property that we seek to quantify as a tool for training machine learning models.

> • A product between two signal samples, then summed over all possible steps through the signal, will be a recurring theme in both signal processing and neural network architectures, giving networks their ability to extract features from the signal they act upon.

In the following we will use so-called "Fourier Analysis" to compare the signal to idea repeating signals which are sinusoidal wave-forms. When multiple sinusoidal wave-forms can be found in a signal, we call these constituents "partials" or "harmonics". For a signal to be periodic, its partials have to be related by integer ratios, which is a reason for calling them "harmonics". One can show this by applying a so-called convolution theorem that we already mentioned before that states that convolution (or filtering operation) in time is multiplication in freqeuncy and vice versa. For a time-domain signal to be periodic, in need to repeat the same block of signal every period. Such periodic signal can be expressed as a short basic waveform comprising of a single period waveshape convolved with a Dirac comb. Thus, its Fourier transform will be the Fourier transform of the basic waveform multiplied by the Fourier transform of a Dirac comb, which turn to be another Dirac comb, thus resulting in a signal that is non-zero at discrete frequencies. Another way to prove why periodic signals have discrete frequencies is to think about the physics of standing waves. Since the boundary conditions of a vibrating string or pressure levels for a sound wave propagating along a pipe are fixed, the only waves that can exist are standing waves that respect these boundary conditions. From geometric considerations (or by looking at solutions of the wave equation) one can see that the basic frequency is the lowest period that satisfies the boundary conditions, but then other waves are possible too, but they always will need to be multiples of the basic frequency to satisfy the boundary conditions.

Sounds can be in-harmonic (such as bell sounds) that have multiple periods that sound more like musical chords then a single note with well defined pitch. The period of the note is often called "fundamental frequency" and is closely related to a perception of pitch. To be precise, pitch is a perception of note height, while its fundamental frequency is the mathematical property of the lowest partial in a harmonic signal (and sometimes the perceived pitch is higher than the fundamental frequency).

Analysis of sound into its sinusoidal constituents is also known as spectral analysis since the individual partials are considered as the equivalent of a specific color or spectral line in the visual domain. Figure 1.11 schematically demonstrates this effect of splitting white light into its constituent colors by a prism. The light analogy should be carried with some caution since the underlying prism phenomena occurs due to physical effect called diffraction that causes bending of light when it passes from one material to another. When the diffraction depends on frequency, this causes different colors to land at different angles. A much more interesting physical decomposition of sound into constituent frequencies happens in the ear, when due to the specific geometry of the cohlea standing waves occur at different positions on the basilar membrane, which are then captured by hair cells and transmitted to the brain according to position and time of firing that contains information about the magnitude and

Figure 1.11 Prism splits lights according to colors.

relative phase of each frequency. The details of auditory processing happening in the cohlea are beyond the scope of this book, and interested readers are referred to a beautiful animation by Howard Hughes Medical Institute[13].

So the same way spectral analysis of visual signals or even electromagnetic radiation tries to separate the signal into individual spectral lines, Fourier analysis does that to audio signals. On the opposite side of periodic signal stands the noise. Mathematically speaking, noise does not have spectral lines. Its spectral analysis comprises broad spectral bands, or continuous spectrum.

An interesting relation exists between periodicity and information. One common property of signals, musical or not (think about radio waves), is its ability to carry information. Encoding information into a physical signal and later extracting it from the signal (a process known as *decoding*) requires extracting or recognizing salient properties of the signal. For instance, when fluctuation in air pressure from a sound reaches the eardrum, this signal is converted into electrical impulses that are sent to the brain, which is later interpreted as something "meaningful" or something carrying or containing information. Later we will define the concept of information as a relation between the incoming signal and expectations or predictions of the decoder. This subtle, and somewhat confusing term, is very important. It basically says that

---

[13]https://www.youtube.com/watch?v=dyenMluFaUw

information is carried between two random phenomena, and the ability to decode or extract information is related to the reduction in uncertainty about the incoming signal done in our brain, or by a model that a computer has learned. A signal's decoding (as well as perception, from an information-theoretic view) allows the information aspects of the signal to be removed from any specific physical nature of that signal, such as current, voltage, or amplitude of an acoustic wave. In this view, noise is the unpredictable or disturbing element that prevents or makes it more difficult to extract useful information from a signal. The mathematical model of the signal is some function that often has the ability to capture the essential structure, such as periodicity of the signal, and distinguish it from noise. In our discussion, our focus will be not on physical models, but rather predictive or information-theoretical models.

1.4 PERCEPTION AND COGNITION: ANTICIPATION AND PRINCIPLES OF MUSIC INFORMATION DYNAMICS

Same as in the case of representation, the question of music perception and cognition exists on various levels: it deals with the physical transduction of acoustic phenomena to nerve impulses, the translation of these impulses to perception of sound in the auditory cortex, the segmentation and segregation of the audio flow into sound events and their recognition, all the way to cognitive models dealing with expectation, emotions, and feelings of surprise versus familiarity of the incoming sound stream– including enculturation and entrainment of specific musical styles and learning of normative sound expressions. One should note that dealing with music understanding will often require us to consider the questions of perception and cognition in rather abstract terms. Unlike speech or natural or man-made sound events, such as understanding the spoken word, recognizing a bird chirp or detecting a submarine from a clutter of sonar blips, music as an art form often does not have a concrete or specific denotation with a universally agreed meaning. Moreover, different musical cultures use different methods for structuring sounds into music – some may put more emphasis on structuring notes in harmonies, tonalities, and long-term structure, while others may exhibit more sensibilities to subtle variations in sound or emotional inflections of the sound production itself, while allowing more freedom or deviations in terms of tuning, or molding voice relations into strict harmonic relations.

Relating computer modeling and machine learning methods to human perception and cognition is a formidable task that is beyond the scope of this book. The way we may relate the statistical and machine learning models to aspects of human perception is through identifying and naming different types of musical data on the continuum of acoustics-perception-cognition. As such, we will make a distinction between musical timbre, or quality of the sound itself, musical texture, which is a relatively short-term aggregation of musical elements governed by common statistics, and musical structure that deals with organization of shorted musical elements into longer repetitions, such as chorus-verse or other formal arrangements of musical repetitions with variations, comprising so-called musical form.

In our approach, expectancies will be playing a central role in shaping the experience of musical structure. An idea put forward many years ago by music theorists such as Meyer and Narmour states that listening to music consists of forming expectations and continual fulfillment or denial thereof [7], [8]. Information-theoretic measures of audio structure have been proposed in attempt to characterize musical contents according to its predictive structure [9], [10], [11], [12]. These measures consider statistical relations between past, present and future in signals, such as predictive information that measures the mutual information between limited past and the complete future, information rate that measures information between unlimited past and the immediate present, and predictive information rate that tries to combine past and future in view of a known present. Additional models of musical expectancy structure build upon short-long-term-memory neural networks introduced in Chapter 7 and predictive properties that are local to a single piece versus broader knowledge collected through corpus-based analysis. Later models also include use of more elaborate and sophisticated neural network models, such as WaveNet, SampleRNN, Transformers and more, covered in Chapters 7 and 9. One common property of such models is that they assume that some hidden or *latent* representation exists that is capable of capturing a great variety of music in one model. Such mapping is often termed encoder-decoder to emphasize the information communicated by the system, where a mapping of the musical notes or acoustic data (sometimes referred to as musical surface or foreground) into its latent representation (also called background or reduction) is done in terms of probabilistic model. When time aspects are taken into account, such musical processes are broadly analyzed in terms of changes in information called "Music Information Dynamics". The underlying assumption in investigation of Musical Information Dynamics (MID) is that the changes in information content, which could be measured in terms of statistical properties such as entropy and mutual information, correlate with musically significant events, which in parallel could be captured by cognitive processes related to music perception and acquired through exposure and learning of regularities present in a corpus of music in a certain style. These models may provide an explanation for the inverted-U relationship proposed by Daniel Berlyne that is often found between simple measures of complexity and judgments of aesthetic value [13]. When applied to music and its predictive properties, we will see that very simple music, though predictable, has less MID effect since the relative reduction in complexity through prediction is not significant. Very complex music that is hardly predictable has also small MID since the complexity before and after prediction remain high. The "sweet-spot", according to MID theory is when music appears complex initially, but by careful listening and prediction, the complexity is drastically reduced. In other ways, the ability of the listener to "explain out" a lot of the music complexity by active listening has an important effect on their enjoyment of music, which is captured by MID in terms of relative reduction of complexity through prediction.

1.5 EXERCISES

1. Assuming an twelve tone equal tempered tuning (TTET), calculate the change in percent in frequency of two adjacent notes (keys on a keyboard).
   Hint: The change in frequency is multiplicative and equal between all adjacent notes so that after 12 steps you reach an octave, i.e. your double the frequency.
2. Given a standard tuning of an A note as 440Hz, what is the frequency of a C three semitones above?
3. In Pythagorean and other earlier "pure" tunings, an interval of a fifth (7 semitones) was tuned to be frequency ratio of 3:2. Compared to equal temperament, what is the percent error between pure tuning and twelve-tone equal temperament tuning for the fifth interval?
4. You have designed a special keyboard, tuned in 12-tone equal temperament with A0 as the reference pitch. However, the piano maker was running low on black keys, so they gave you a keyboard with only the white keys in place [14]. You would like to explore which frequencies this piano can produce. Write a Python function which takes a number n as input, and gives as output the frequency of a note found n whole steps above the reference pitch.
5. Consider the musical example shown in Figure 1.6. At a tempo of 108 beats per minute, where each measure is assigned a one-beat duration, how many seconds does each eighth note occupy? How many ticks of a general MIDI clock would be used to represent this duration? Since the tick count for each instruction must be discrete, is it possible to perfectly reconstruct this tempo? If each eighth note is given the calculated tick duration, will the rendered audio sound similar to natural phrasing?
6. Consider the pitch G4, the highest pitch played by the orchestra in the audio visualized in Figure 1.10. Considering a pure sine wave of pitch G4, how many periods of this wave would occur in 0.5 seconds of audio?
7. Using the definition of Sound Pressure Level, explain why most people cannot hear a sound at 0 dB.
8. Why must the partials of a periodic signal be related by integer ratios?

Additional questions and programming exercises are found in the **Introduction to Music Representation** notebook at `https://github.com/deep-and-shallow/notebooks`.

---

[14]Curious? Search for the "Sinhakken" model from the 2014 Musical Instruments Fair in Japan.

2 Noise: The Hidden Dynamics of Music

Noise has always played a central role in music. As sound production, noise often serves as the initial source of energy in musical instruments that "carve out" notes from a pluck of a string or from a turbulent air stream blown into a pipe. We have seen in the previous chapter how an unvoiced hiss or pulses of a glottal buzz are shaped into speech sound via a source-filter voice model. Filters and resonances help turn the flat frequency response of an impulse or of a continuous noise into a periodic, more predictable sound structure. As an idea generator, noise is driving the musical choices during the composition process. As much as music theory tells us how choices of notes need to be done according to certain rules, the role of noise is in creating uncertainties and ambiguities that are an essential component in the music listening experience. Random methods, often called "aleatoric" music in contemporary practice, have been used historically to trigger and drive the process of music creation by generating initial musical choices, which were further constrained and shaped during later stages of composition. Moreover, on a broad cultural and historical perspective, Attali's book *Noise: The Political Economy of Music* examines the relations of music to the political-economic structure of societies through noise. Although such social-science and economic investigations of music are outside of the scope of this book, a consideration of what Attali understands by the term "Music" might be appropriate for our discussion. For Attali music is the organization of noise, and the entirety of the evolution of Western knowledge through development of scientific, technical, and market tools is viewed through the lens of shaping and controlling noise:

> "The world is not for beholding, it is for hearing. Our science has desired to monitor, measure, abstract and castrate meaning, forgetting that life is full of noise and that death alone is silent. Nothing essential happens in the absence of noise."

2.1 NOISE, ALEATORIC MUSIC, AND GENERATIVE PROCESSES IN MUSIC

We continue our journey of music by considering generative processes that turn randomness into structure. In previous chapters we considered two main data formats for music: one is as a sound recording captured into an audio file, the other is a sequence of performance actions captures as notes in a symbolic MIDI or music sheet format. To understand better the structures present in these two data types, we introduced various features that allow more meaningful representations by extracting

DOI: 10.1201/9781003240198-2

salient aspects of sound, going back and forth between signals and symbols. Music is a unique human endeavor: it comprises deliberate and intentional selection of sounds from infinite possibilities of air vibrations, narrowed into a much smaller palette of musical instruments producing notes from periodic vibrations. These notes are further organized into scales, tonalities, melodies, and chords, building progressions and repetition of themes arranged into verse, chorus, and other musical forms. The fact that all of these constructions are deliberate human choices is often taken for granted. Different cultures follow different musical rules, and when musical styles evolve and instruments change, the type of music expression may drastically change. It takes a while to get used to and find beauty in unfamiliar music, or come up with new ways of sonic expression or break existing musical rules to create artistic novelty and impact.

As listeners, or even as composers, we often do not think about such formal aspects of musical evolution or change, but when the challenge of finding or generating meaning in musical data is given to the machine, we need to revisit the basic premises of what makes musical sounds meaningful in order to be able to program musical algorithms or build musical learning machines. Music can be defined as *Organization of Sounds to Create an Experience*. In this most abstract and general way of defining music, we capture some of the fundamental principles for a formal study of music. First, a selection of sounds is made, representing them as latent variables or features extracted from the sound data. Their organization assumes certain temporal and sequential relations that could be further established by learning the dynamics of these latent variables. And finally, creating an experience requires including the listener as part of the model.

2.1.1   MUSIC AS COMMUNICATION

Understanding music requires both a sender and a receiver, or encoder and a decoder that communicate information. But unlike in vision, speech, or computer communications, where a typical inference task is one of recognizing a particular shape, transcribing speech, or executing a command, the effect of musical information is one of eliciting an emotional or aesthetic response. Such response assumes an active listening framework that triggers a wide variety of reactions, some of which might be innate or pre-wired, and others learned from exposure to existing musical cultures. Can such structures be learned by a machine in a so-called end-to-end fashion by feeding it with music data paired with a desired target output? Can novel applications and unheard musical style be created by going outside of statistical models of existing styles or emerge through machine interaction with a human?

In our journey of machine learning in music we will find the concept of noise particularly useful. On the signal level, spectral analysis allows distinguishing acoustic noise from periodic sounds. Noise, in its "purest" physical or engineering sense, is a signal characterized by a white spectrum (i.e., composed of equal or almost-equal energies in all frequencies). Mathematically, to qualify as a random or stochastic process, the probability density of the signal frequency components must have a continuous spectrum, whereas periodic components that are more predictable present themselves in frequency domain as spectral lines, i.e sharp and narrow spectral peaks. Moreover, in terms of its musical use, noise does not allow much structural manipulation or organization. In contrast to noise, notes are commonly the basic building blocks of larger sound phenomena that we call music, and as such could be considered as elements of sonic "structure". On the symbolic level, noise is more closely related to predictability of a sequence of elements, often encoded into tokens. When applying language models to music, noise refers to uncertainty or variability of the next token as possible continuations to past sequence of tokens. Although seemingly unrelated, these two aspects of noise have common mathematical foundations that are related by the signal information contents measured in terms of residual uncertainty passed in a signal over time. The better our prediction about the future becomes, the smaller the prediction error will be, and the overall uncertainty will be reduced. In this chapter we take a new look at the relations between randomness and structure in both symbolic and audio signals. In order to do so, we consider the meaning of randomness as a phenomena that has an aspect of uncertainty and surprise to it. This is contrasted with *structure*, an aspect of the data that is more predictable, rule-based, or even deterministic.

From the listener perspective, acoustic noise belongs to the perceptual domain, while perception of musical organization belongs to the cognitive domain. The two domains are bridged by the Prediction Coding framework in cognitive science that is centered around the idea that organisms represent the world by constantly predicting their own internal states. Comparisons between predictions and bottom-up signals occur in a hierarchical manner, where the "error signal" corresponds to the unpredicted aspect of the input that passes across various stages of representation and processing. The core framework posited by such theories is one of deep generative models that can be understood both in terms of Bayesian theories of cognition that consider perception as a hypothesis-testing mechanism, and as a simulation model that considers signal representation in terms of statistical models that incorporate signal uncertainty as part of their generative structure. Such fundamental questions about mental representations are outside the scope of this book, but similar concerns emerge in design of musical applications where practical issues of structural representation are often given by more historically mainstream accounts of music theories, and later extended through statistical-probabilistic structures that are designed to bear musically relevant similarity to some musical goal or idea. Such similarity can vary from stylistic imitation, sometimes called "deep fake" models of existing music, to experimental practices that explore novel musical ideas and possibilities for creative interaction with machines.

Throughout the book, we will often refer to a particular approach to musical modeling that views anticipation as the key to understanding music, planning its structure, and a possible way of understanding the effects that music has on the listener's mind. We already mentioned anticipation in the previous chapter where we introduced the concept of Musical Information Dynamics as a generic framework for modeling processes in terms of changes in its information contents. But before exploring further the statistical tools that are needed in order to extract and quantify information in music and sound, it helps to see anticipation in the context of the historical developments that led to contemporary ways of music modeling and formalization.

2.2 HISTORY OF MATHEMATICAL THEORY OF MUSIC AND COMPOSITIONAL ALGORITHMS

Continuing our discussion of noise from the historical perspective, it is important to note that creation of music has been always linked to certain technical tools, namely musical instruments, that enabled the creation of sounds and determined their structuring principles. As such, randomness and uncertainty in sound production has always been linked to its production and composition methods.

The ancient Greek philosopher Pythagoras (570-495 B.C.) is generally credited with having discovered the mathematical relations of musical intervals which result in a sensation of consonance. Such relations are deeply rooted in the acoustics of string and wind instruments, and the human voice, which are highly harmonic. In Pythagorean tuning, the frequency ratios of the notes are all derived from the number ratio 3:2, which is called an interval of a *fifth* in music theory.

> In musical terms, an **interval** is the difference in pitch between two notes. In a physical sense, the interval is a ratio of frequencies between the two notes. Different tuning systems may assign different frequency ratios to intervals of the same name. In Western music, intervals are usually described by a number (unison, second, third, fourth, fifth, etc.) and a quality (perfect, major, minor, augmented, or diminished). In general, the number indicates the spacing, while the quality indicates some further tuning on a smaller scale than represented by the number.

When two notes are played in a fifth, this music interval produces a combined sound where most of the partials overlap, thus creating a seamless blending and a highly coherent precept. Using the fifth and moving along the circle of fifths (see Figure 2.1) results in pentatonic and diatonic scales (taking 5 and 7 steps, accordingly) that are common in Western music. Although this tuning was adjusted later on in history to accommodate for more complex chromatic musical styles, the idea that music sensations can be related to mathematical proportions and rules had been rooted deeply in music theory. Moreover, cultures that use different musical instruments, such as metallophones (metalic percussion instruments) dominant in Gamelan music, result in different tuning system, such as Pelog and Slendro, where the preferred intervals are such that different tones optimally blend by maximising the overlap between the partials of their respective timbres.

In terms of composition practices, probably the best known early example of using formal rules for writing music can be attributed to Guido d'Arezzo who, around 1026, set text to music by assigning pitches to different vowels. According to this method a melody was created according to the vowels present in the text. In the fourteen and fifteenth centuries isorhythmic techniques were used to create repeated

Figure 2.1 The circle of fifths is a helpful construct for musicians to relate patterns in key signatures, harmonic progressions, and other uses of the chromatic scale. Each step clockwise around the circle represents a note an interval of a perfect fifth above the previous.

rhythmic cycles (talea), which were often juxtaposed with melodic cycles of different length to create long varying musical structures. Dufay's motet Nuper Rosarum Flores (1436) used repetition of talea patterns at different speeds in four sections according to length ratios 6:4:2:3, which some claim were taken from the proportions of the nave, the crossing, the apse, and the height of the arch of Florence Cathedral or from the dimensions of the Temple of Solomon given in Kings 6:120. Formal manipulations such as retrograde (backward motion) or inversion (inverting the direction of intervals in a melody) are found in the music of J.S. Bach and became the basis for the twentieth century twelve-tone (dodecaphonic) serial techniques of Arnold Schoenberg (1874-1951). Exploiting the recombinant structure of harmonic progression, Mozart devised his Musikalisches Wurfelspiel ("Musical Dice Game")

(1767[1]) that uses the outcomes of a dice throw and a table of pre-composed musical fragments to create a Minuet. There are 176 possible Minuet measures and 96 possible Trio measures to choose from. Two six-sided dice are used to determine each of the 16 Minuet measures and one six-sided die is used to determine each of the 16 Trio measures. This provides an early example of a stochastic process driving musical output, a theme we will see later in the Variational Autoencoder and other examples. In this case, compositional blocks are defined in a discrete codebook, but in later cases, we will find these constituent pieces to be learned from bodies of musical data.

The search for formal composition techniques took on a life of its own in post-World War II academic music. In a trend which is sometimes attributed to the desire to break away from the stylistic confines and associations of late Romanticism, mathematical rules such as serialism were sought in order to construct musical materials that sounded both new and alien to traditional tonal and rhythmical musical languages. One such feeling was expressed by the Czech novelist Milan Kundera in his writing about the music of the Greek composer and microsound theorist Iannis Xenakis (1922–2001) – "Music has played an integral and decisive part in the ongoing process of sentimentalization. But it can happen at a certain moment (in the life of a person or of a civilization) that sentimentality (previously considered as a humanizing force, softening the coldness of reason) becomes unmasked as 'the supra-structure of a brutality'. ... Xenakis opposes the whole of the European history of music. His point of departure is elsewhere; not in an artificial sound isolated from nature in order to express a subjectivity, but in an earthly 'objective' sound, in a mass of sound which does not rise from the human heart, but which approaches us from the outside, like raindrops or the voice of wind" [14].

The use of automation or process is the common thread in the above examples. Composers have increasingly allowed portions of their musical decision-making to be controlled according to processes and algorithms. In the age of computer technology, this trend has grown exponentially. Before going into more technical aspects of musical modeling with computers, it is helpful to compare these experimental academic music approaches to those in the non-academic musical world. To gain this perspective requires briefly surveying the different stylistic approaches for using computers in popular music making.

2.2.1 GENERATIVE MUSIC IN POPULAR MUSIC PRACTICES

One particular genre of generative music that has become popular among the general listening public is *ambient music*. Governed by recombinant processes of chords and melodies, ambient music emphasizes mood and texture over directionality and contrast, blending with the environment in which it is heard. This music often lacks the dramatic or sentimental design of classical and popular music. Unlike generative methods in the academic experimental genres, such as Xenakis's exploration of

---

[1]Though this game is attributed to Mozart, earlier examples have been discovered, including Johann Kirnberger's 1757 *Der allezeit fertige Menuetten- und Polonaisencomponist*.

masses of sounds and processes in opposition to Western music tradition, the ambient genre centers around familiar and often pleasant sounds drawn either from tonal harmonic language or from recordings of environmental sounds that blend into each other with no particular larger scale form or intention.

Perhaps the first explicit notion of ambient music comes from Erik Satie's concept of *musique d'amebulement*, translated as "furniture music". Satie's music is often built from large blocks of static harmony, and creates a sense of timelessness and undirected sound, but this was music which was meant not to be listened to, only to be heard as background to some other event [15]. There is arguably no composer more associated with ambient and environmental sound than John Cage, the twentieth-century experimentalist who redefined the materials and procedures of musical composition. Throughout his career, Cage explored the outer limits of sonic experience, but his most notorious work is the famous "silent piece", 4'33", composed in 1952. Instead of defining musical materials, Cage defined a musical structure, and allowed the ambient sounds of the concert environment to fill the structure [16]. His other groundbreaking approaches to music included reliance on chance operations, or so-called indetedeminate or "aleatoric techniques" for its random selection of notes. In his *Music of Changes* the Chineese I-Ching book technique was used to select note pitches and durations. I-Ching is also used to determine how many layers should there be in a given phrase to create different densities of musical voices. These chance operations were done independently of previous outcome. When selection of next notes are done in ways that are dependent on already generated events, this induces so-called Markov property to the chance operaions. Lejaren Hiller and Leonard Isaacson's 1957 Illiac Suite used Markov chains to selected consecutive intervals for each instrument according to greatest weight to consonant versus smallest intervals. In 1959, Iannis Xenakis wrote several works in which he used many simultaneous Markov chains, which he called "screens", to control successions of large-scale events in which some number of elementary "grains" of sound may occur.

The late twentieth century saw an explosion of musical styles which challenged traditional notions of musical experience and experimented with the ways in which sound can communicate space, place, and location. "Soundscape" composition and the use of field recordings help to create a sense of a real or imagined place, while genres of electronic dance music like chill-out are often associated with specific club environments. Some artists have also bridged the gap between contemporary visual and installation art and music, and "sound art" is now commonplace. These artists often deal with psychoacoustic phenomena and relationships between visual and auditory media, often work with multiple forms of media, and take influence from minimalism, electronic music, conceptual art, and other trends in twentieth-century art.

Most importantly for our discussion is the way in which composers of ambient and related genres often delegate high-level aspects of their work to algorithmic processes or generative procedures – or in the case of field-recording work, to features of the sound materials themselves. Techniques which originated in the most avant-garde and experimental traditions, such as looping, automated mixing, and complex signal processing, are increasingly used in popular music and are now commonly found in commercial, off-the-shelf music production software.

Brian Eno's Ambient 1: Music for Airports (1978) provides the template for many later works: repetitive, with an absence of abrasive or abrupt attacks, and using long decays, the harmony and melody seem to continue indefinitely. During the compositional process, Eno constructed tape loops of differing lengths out of various instrumental fragments [17]. As these loops played, the sounds and melodies moved in and out of phase, producing shifting textures and patterns. The studio configuration itself became a generative instrument. In 1996 Brian Eno released the title "Generative Music 1" with SSEYO Koan Software. The software, published in 1994, won the 2001 Interactive Entertainment BAFTA[2] Award for Technical Innovation. Koan was discontinued in 2007, and the following year a new program was released. Noatikl "Inmo" – or "in the moment" ("inmo") – Generative Music Lab was released by Intermorphic ltd. as a spiritual successor to Koan. The software had new generative music and lyric engines, and the creators of the software claimed that

> "...learning to sit-back and delegate responsibility for small details to a generative engine is extremely liberating. ... Yes, you can focus on details in Noatikl, but you can also take more of a gardener's view to creating music: casting musical idea seeds on the ground, and selecting those ideas which blossom and discarding those that don't appeal."

Electronic dance music producers, like the English duo Autechre, often embrace the most avant-garde trends and techniques, while still producing music which remains accessible and maintains a level of popular success. Autechre have often employed generative procedures in their music-making, using self-programmed software and complex hardware routings to produce endless variations on and transformations between thematic materials. In a recent interview, Rob Brown spoke of attempting to algorithmically model their own style:

> "Algorithms are a great way of compressing your style. ...if you can't go back to that spark or moment where you've created something new and reverse-engineer it, it can be lost to that moment... It has always been important to us to be able to reduce something that happened manually into something that is contained in an algorithm." [18]

Commercial digital audio workstations (DAWs) – computer software for recording, mixing, and editing music and sound – often support various types of generative procedures. For example, the "Follow" function in Ableton Live, a popular DAW, allows composers to create Markov chain-like transitions between clips. One of the typical uses of this is to add naturalness to a clip. Instead of having a single, fixed

---

[2]British Academy of Film and Television Arts

loop, one records multiple variations or adds effects, such as cuts, amplitude envelopes or pitch changes, to a single loop and uses "Follow" to sequence the clips randomly. This allows variations both in terms of the musical materials contents and their expressive inflections that breaks away from mechanical regularity and synthetic feel often associated with loop-based musical production.

In the field of computer and video games, composers and sound designers, with the help of custom software (often called music middle-ware), frequently make use of generative and procedural music and audio in their work. Advantages of procedural audio include interactivity, variety, and adaptation [19]. Karen Collins provides a good overview of procedural music techniques [20]. Collins describes the challenges faced by game composers, who must create music which both supports and reacts to an unpredictable series of events, often within constraints imposed by video game hardware and/or storage. In fact, Collins points out that a contributing factor to the use of generative strategies in video games was the need to fit a large amount of music into a small amount of storage. Generative techniques allow for the creation of large amounts of music with smaller amounts of data. Some strategies for this kind of composition can include:

- Simple transformations: changes in tempo, restructuring of largely pre-composed materials, conditional repeats of material based on in-game activities.
- Probabilistic models for organizing large numbers of small musical fragments.
- Changes in instrumentation of music based on the presence of specific in-game characters.
- Generation of new materials within melodic / rhythmic constraints.
- Re-sequencing, also known as horizontal remixing, allowing non-linear playback of pre-recorded music
- Remixing, or vertical remixing, which operates by adding or muting parallel simultaneous musical tracks

2.3 COMPUTER MODELING OF MUSICAL STYLE AND MACHINE IMPROVISATION

On August 09, 1956 the "Illiac Suite" by Lejaren Hiller and Leonard Isaacson, named after the computer used to program the composition, saw its world premiere at the University of Illinois [21]. The work, though performed by a traditional string quartet, was composed using a computer program, and employed a handful of algorithmic composition techniques. This work, together with the work of Xenakis described in *Formalized Music*, marks the beginning of modern mathematical and computational approaches to representing, modeling, and generating music. Among the most prominent algorithmic composition techniques are stochastic or random modeling approaches, formal grammars, and dynamical systems that consider fractals and chaos theory, as well as genetic algorithms and cellular automata for generation and evolution of musical materials. More recently, advanced machine learning techniques such as neural networks, hidden Markov models, dynamic texture models, and deep learning are being actively researched for music retrieval, and to a somewhat lesser extent, also for creative or generative applications. With the advent of machine learning methods, the models could be trained to capture statistics of existing music, imitate musical styles, or produce novel operations in computer-aided composition systems. With these developments, the goals and motivation behind using random operations for composing has changed from thinking about mass events with densities and texture, to capturing fine details of musical style that were not previously amenable to probabilistic modeling.

Markov models are probably one of the best-established paradigms of algorithmic composition, both in the experimental and the style learning domains. In this approach, a piece of music is represented by a sequence of events or states, which correspond to symbolic music elements such as notes or note combinations, or sequences of signal features extracted from a recording. Markov sources are random processes that produce new symbols depending on a certain number of past symbols. In other words, the whole process of music generation from a Markov model has some kind of "memory" whose effect is that new symbols are produced in a manner dependent on its past. In other words, old symbols influence new symbols by determining the probability of generating certain continuations. Markov chains are statistical models of random sequences that assume that the probability for generating the next symbol depends only on a limited past. A Markov model establishes a sequence of states and transition probabilities, which are extracted by counting the statistics of events and their continuations from a musical corpus. The length of the context (the number of previous elements in the musical sequence used for the calculation of the next continuation) is called the *order* of the Markov model. Markov sources can have different orders: simple independent random sequences are considered as Markov of order zero, then processes of a memory of a single symbol are Markov of order one, of a memory of length two are Markov of order two, and so on. Since higher order models produce sequences that are more similar to the corpus, but are harder to estimate and may also have disadvantageous effects in terms of the model's ability to deal with variations, several researchers have turned their attention to predictive models that use variable memory length models, dictionary models, and style-specific lexicons for music recognition and generation. See [22] for a survey of music generation from statistical models and [23] for comparison of several predictive models for learning musical style and stylistic imitation.

Generative grammars are another well-established and powerful formalism for the generation of musical structure. Generative grammars function through the specification of rewriting rules of different expressiveness. The study of grammars in music in many ways paralleled that of natural language. Chomsky erroneously believed that grammatical sentence production cannot be achieved by finite state methods, because they cannot capture dependencies between non-adjacent words in sentences or model the recursive embedding of phrase structure found in natural language [24]. Since such complex grammars could not be easily "learned" by a machine, this belief limited the types of music handled by grammar models to those that could be coded by experts in terms of rules and logic operations. This approach is sometimes called an *expert system* or *knowledge engineering*. Although these methods achieve impressive results, they are labor intensive as they require explicit formulation of musical knowledge in terms that are often less than intuitive.

Some more specific models, such as Transition Networks ([25]) and Petri Nets ([26], [27]) have been suggested for modeling musical structure. These are usually used to address higher levels of description such as repetition of musical objects, causality relations among them, concurrency among voices, parts, sections, and so on. David Cope's work describes an interesting compromise between formal grammar and pattern-based approaches. Cope uses a grammatical-generation system combined with what he calls "signatures": melodic micro-gestures typical of individual composers [28]. By identifying and reusing such signatures, Cope reproduced the style of past composers and preserved a sense of naturalness in the computer-generated music.

In the following we will describe some of the research on learning musical structure that begins by attempting to build a model by discovering phrases or patterns which are idiomatic to a certain style or performer. This is done automatically, and in an **unsupervised** manner. This model is then assigned stochastic generation rules for creating new materials that have similar stylistic characteristics to the learning example. One of the main challenges in this approach is formulating the rules for generation of new materials that would obey aesthetic rules or take into account perceptual and cognitive constraints on music making and listening that would render pleasing music materials.

A learning process is **unsupervised** if the process learns patterns in data without being provided additional expected output. By contrast, **supervised** methods rely on an expected, defined output (commonly referred to as *ground truth*) to drive learning. Supervised and unsupervised methods are applied to different types of problems based on what can be learned in the absence (or presence) of ground truth (i.e., known labels or answers to the question at hand). For example, the problem of *classification* (predicting the class associated with a data instance) can be addressed with supervised learning, given a collection of datum-class pairs. On the other hand, without knowing explicit class membership for each data instance, the process becomes unsupervised – but we can still learn associations between like-data-points, a problem known as *clustering*.

Another interesting field of research is machine improvisation, wherein a computer program is designed to function as an improvisational partner to an instrumentalist. The software receives musical input from the instrumentalist, in the form of MIDI or audio, and responds appropriately according to some stylistic model or other algorithm. An important early work in this style is George Lewis's *Voyager* (1988), a "virtual improvising orchestra." The *Voyager* software receives MIDI input derived from an instrumental audio signal, analyzes it, and produces output with one of a set of many timbres [29]. The input data is analyzed in terms of average pitch, velocity, probability of note activity, and spacing between notes. In response, *Voyager*

is capable of both producing variations on input material and generating completely
new material according to musical parameters such as tempo (speed), probability of
playing a note, the spacing between notes, melodic interval width, choice of pitch
material based on the last several notes received, octave range, microtonal transpo-
sition, and volume. Due to the coarse statistical nature of both the analysis and generative mechanisms, the type of music produced by the system is limited to abstract
free improvisation style.

Another family of "virtual improvisor" software will be introduced in later chapter, inclduing PyOracle and VMO [3], and musical improvisation systems OMax and
SOMax [4]. These programs use sequence matching based on an algorithm called Factor Oracle, to create a model of the repetition structure specific to the incoming music material both for audio or MIDI input. By recombining carefully selected segments of the original recording according to this repetition structure, the programs
can produce new variations on the input, while maintaining close resemblance to
the original musical style. Although essentially a procedural remixing method, once
the determination of the next musical step is performed by chance operations that
are governed by probability of continuations of motifs of variable length as found
in a training corpus, this improvisation process can be considered as an extension
of Markov approach to variable memory length models. In the next section we will
introduce the mathematical foundation for Markov models that are the tool of trade
for modeling sequences of data, notably in the domain of text and natural language
modeling. This will allow a more profound look into concepts of entropy, uncertainty
and information, paving the road to understanding musical creation and listening as
a communication process.

2.4   MARKOV MODELS AND LANGUAGE MODELS FOR MUSIC

Let us assume that we have a sequence of notes (a melody). If the notes are generated
in an independent manner (such as in John Cage's "Music of Changes" mentioned
earlier), the best description of that music could be in terms of frequencies of appearance of different notes. Claude Shannon, considered to be the father of information
theory, suggested that if we look at large blocks of symbols (long sequences), this
information around frequency of appearance "reveals itself" without any need to
calculate probabilities. This property (called the asymptotic equipartition property
or AEP, discussed in the next chapter) basically says that if we look at a long enough
sequence, we will see only the "typical" messages. The entropy of the source defines
the amount of the typical messages. That is why a completely random (aleatoric) sequence, where all the notes appear with equal probability, has maximal entropy: the
number of typical sequences is equal to all possible sequences. On the other hand,

---

[3] https://github.com/wangsix/vmo

[4] https://forum.ircam.fr/collections/detail/improvisation-et-generativite/

the more structure a sequence has, the less will be the number of typical sequences. The exponential rate of growth of the number of typical sequences, relative to the number of all possible sequences of the same length, is the **entropy**, introduced in the next section. Thus, looking at longer blocks of symbols we approach the "true" statistics of the source.

2.4.1   ENTROPY, UNCERTAINTY, AND INFORMATION

Dealing with noise as a driving force of music, we learn that not all noise is created equal. In the process of throwing dice or passing an acoustic noise through a filter, we are shaping it into sounds and music structures by making choices of note sequences, some being more probable then others, distinguishing between more probable and more surprising events. Can we measure such surprises? Formally, *entropy* is defined as a measure of uncertainty of a random variable x when it is drawn from a distribution $x \sim P(x)$:

$$H(x) = -\sum_{x} P(x) \log_2 P(x) \qquad (2.1)$$

where the sum is over all possible outcomes of x. It can be shown that $H(x)$ is non-negative, with entropy being equal to 0 when x is deterministic, i.e. when only one of the outcomes x is possible, say x^*, so that $P(x = x^*) = 1$ and $P(x \neq x^*) = 0$ otherwise. Maximal entropy is achieved when all outcomes are equally probable. One can easily show that for x taking values over a set of size N (also understood as alphabet of size N or cardinality of x), then $H(X) = \log_2(N)$, which is, up to integer constraints, the number of bits needed to represent symbols in alphabet of that size.

Example: Entropy of a Binary Variable

For a binary variable, with $x \in \{0, 1\}$, with probability $p, (1 - p)$ respectively, the entropy is

$$H(X) = -p \log_2 p - (1 - p) \log_2(1 - p). \qquad (2.2)$$

This entropy is shown graphically in Figure 2.2.

Entropy can be considered as a functional, which is a function that accepts another function and returns a number. In our case, the function that the entropy expression operates on is the probability distribution, and it summarizes the whole probability distribution into a single number that gives a sense of the overall uncertainty of that distribution.

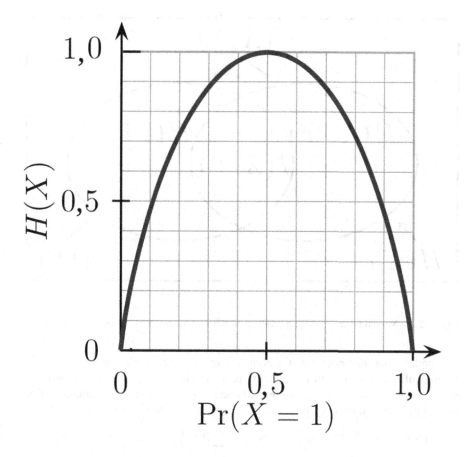

Figure 2.2 Binary entropy as a function of probability p.

Example: Chromatic Entropy

As an example musical application, entropy can be considered as a measure of uncertainty in note distributions. Given 12 notes of a musical chromatic scale, it is possible to measure the uncertainty of notes when assuming that each note is drawn independently from a scale. Tonal profiles were found by musicologists (Krumhansl and Schmuckler) [30] to determine a scale in terms of probability of notes, with most probable notes being the fifth (dominant) and first (tonic) note of a scale. Of course, the basic units of music do not have to be individual notes. These could be pairs of notes, or longer sequences, and growing the length of the melodies leads to increasingly more complex distributions. A Markov model is one such modeling approach that tries to account for such complexity.

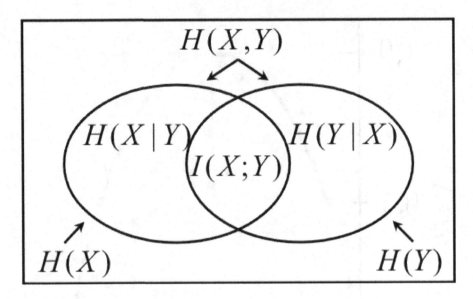

Figure 2.3 Mutual information as a cross-section between entropies of two variables.

Another important notion that is built "on top" of entropy is *mutual information.* Mutual information measures the relative reduction in uncertainty between two random variables X and Y, when outcome of one of them is know. To be able to define mutual information we need first to define *conditional entropy*, which is

$$H(X|Y) = -\sum_{x,y} P(x,y) \log_2 P(x|y) = -\sum_{y} P(y) \sum_{x} P(x|y) \log_2 P(x|y) \quad (2.3)$$

Note that the probabilities appearing in the two components in conditional entropy expression are non the same. The logarithm contains conditional probability only, that is averaged both over x and y. In other words, conditional entropy estimates the entropy of x for each possible conditioning value of y, averaged over all possible ys.

Thus, mutual information, the difference in uncertainty about one variable when the other is known, can be written as:

$$I(X,Y) = H(X) - H(X|Y) = H(Y) - H(Y|X) = H(X) + H(Y) - H(X,Y). \quad (2.4)$$

Mutual information can be visualized as the intersection or overlap between the entropies of the variables X and Y, as represented in the Venn diagram in Figure 2.3.

In the following we will apply the notion of mutual information to time series, as a way to quantify the amount of information passing between the past and the present in a musical sequence. Thus, instead of considering long sequences, we will focus on the entropy of a single symbol in a sequence given its past. This entropy is in fact representing the uncertainly of continuation. By exploiting an implicit knowledge of how to complete unfinisihed phrases, Shannon played his famous game of having human subjects guess successive characters in a string of text selected at random from various sources [31]. Shannon recorded the probability of taking r guesses until the correct letter is guessed and showed that these statistics can be effectively used as a bound on the entropy of English. One of the main problems with the application of Markov theory "as is" is that the true order of the process is unknown. Accordingly, when N-gram models are used to capture the dependence of the next symbol on the past N symbols, N needs to being fixed as a model parameter of choice. The main difficulty in Markov modeling is handling large orders, or even more interestingly, dealing with sources of variable-length memory. In music it is reasonable to assume that the memory length is variable since musical structures sometimes use short melodic figuration, sometimes longer motives, and sometimes rather long phrases can repeat, often with some variations. Shannon's experiment establishes several interesting relations between language complexity and its continuation statistics. Since only certain pairs, triplets and higher N-grams tend to appear together, the amount of guesses needed to predict the next letter is drastically reduced for longer patterns. Moreover, it shows that one can obtain an efficient representation of language by encoding only the continuation choices. This representation, that Shannon called a *reduced text*, can be used to recover the original text, but requiring less storage. Later in the book we will use text compression schemes that encode letter continuations for larger and larger blocks of symbols as an effective way to capture variable memory Markov models in music and use then for generating novel musical sequences.

2.4.2 NATURAL LANGUAGE MODELS

Natural Languages are often characterized by long structured relations between their words, arranged into sequences of letters or words arranged into dictionary entries. In following chapters, we will consider statistical modeling of sequences that is based on information theory and deep neural network learning. In both cases, the goal of the modeling is to create a probability representation of long sequences of symbols or audio units that can be used for inference (finding the probability of a sequences for classification purpose) or generation (producing more sequences of the same kind). In this way, modeling music becomes a similar task to modeling natural language.

As a motivation and perspective about Markov and future models, we discuss briefly the general problem of modeling long temporal sequences, known as Neural Language models.

In general, a language model is a probability distribution over sequences of tokens. Traditionally, languages were represented using formal grammars, or learning the equivalent automata that can generate specific strings that obey the language rules. In modern approaches, the problem in language modeling became one of learning a language model from examples, such as a model of English sentences from a large corpus of sentences.

Mathematically speaking, let $P(w_1, w_2, \ldots, w_n)$ denote the probability of a sequence $(w_1, w_2, \ldots, w_n)$ of tokens. The aim of learning is to learn such probabilities from a training set of sequences.

Consider the related problem of predicting the next token of a sequence. We model this as $P(w_n|w_1, w_2, \ldots, w_{n-1})$. Note that if we can accurately predict the probabilities $P(w_n|w_1, w_2, \ldots, w_{n-1})$, we can chain them together using the rules of conditional probability to get

$$P(w_1, w_2, \ldots, w_n) = P(w_1)P(w_2|w_1)P(w_3|w_1, w_2)P(w_n|w_1, w_2, \ldots, w_{n-1}) \quad (2.5)$$

Most learning approaches target language modeling as the "next token" prediction problem, where the learning system learns a mapping of $(w_1, w_2, \ldots, w_{n-1})$ input to w_n output. Such learning can be considered supervised learning, though there is no need to meticulously label datasets since future provides the target "label". When done statistically, the output of such system is a probability distribution over the various values that w_n could take. Such output could be a high-dimensional probability vector, with hundreds of thousands to millions of options for a language model on English sentences.

Moreover, in the case of language, the input is not a fixed-length vector. The next token is often determined or largely depends on a long phrase, or in the case of music, a motif that comprises a sequence of length n that varies. This phenomena is sometimes called "variable memory length" and is one of the primary factors that make language, and music modeling, difficult.

Statistical approaches to estimating $P(w_n|w_1, w_2, \ldots, w_{n-1})$ when n is large must make some assumptions to make the problem tractable. Even with an alphabet of just two symbols, 0 and 1, the minimal training set size to reliably estimate $P(w_n|w_1, w_2, \ldots, w_{n-1})$ is of the order 2^n. Such a big dataset is required in order to reliably visit or sample all possible input combinations in order to be able to predict the next token reasonably in each case.

The most widely made assumption in statistical approaches is Markovian. Specifically,

$$P(w_n|w_1, w_2, \ldots, w_{n-1}) \quad (2.6)$$

is approximated by a limited k-tuple,

$$P(w_n|w_{n-k}, \ldots, w_{n-1}). \quad (2.7)$$

This assumes that the next token probabilities depend only on the last k tokens. Most often k is a small number of order 1 or 2. This vastly simplifies the modeling and estimation problem at the cost of not being able to model long-range influences.

The early neural network approach to learning temporal predictions is the so-called Recurrent Neural Network that will be covered in a later chapter. Such models combine two important aspects that are made possible through end-to-end optimization approaches that are the hallmark of deep learning – they learn distributed representations for input tokens, and at the same time they learns the dependencies or relations between these representation in time. Distributed representations, more commonly called word *embeddings*, map the input onto a d-dimensional numeric space. One of the motivations for such embeddings is that semantically related tokens (words in language, piano-roll slices, or signal vectors), will be near each other in this space. Implicitly, this maps probabilities or likelihoods of appearance to distances in some, often non-euclidean geometry, but we will not go into the fascinating field of information geometry that actually tries to formalize this connection in rigorous mathematical ways.

In this chapter we consider a simple Markov transition probability model that begins with a set of discrete events (or states), into which all observations (e.g., notes or sound units or features) can be aggregated. Suppose there are R discrete categories into which all observations can be ordered. We can define a transition matrix $P = [p_{ij}]$ as a matrix of probabilities showing the likelihood of a sound token staying unchanged or moving to any of the other $R - 1$ categories over a given time horizon. Each element of the matrix, p_{ij}, shows the probability of event i in period $t - 1$ moving or transitioning to event j in period t. We impose a simple Markov structure on the transition probabilities, and restrict our attention to first-order stationary Markov processes, for simplicity.

Estimating a transition matrix is a relatively straightforward process, if we can observe the sequence of states for each individual unit of observation (i.e., if the individual transitions are observed). For example, if we observe a sequence of musical chords in a corpus of music,then we can estimate the probability of moving from one chord to another. The probability of a chord change is given by the simple ratio of the number of times a chord appeared in different songs with the same chord label and transitioned to another (or same) chord label. In such case, we identify the chord labels with states, but more sophisticated state-token mappings could be defined. More generally, we can let n_{ij} denote the number of chord appearances who were in state i in period $t - 1$ and are in state j in period t. We can estimate the probability using the following formula:

$$P_{ij} = \frac{n_{ij}}{\sum_j n_{ij}} \tag{2.8}$$

Thus the probability of transition from any given state i is equal to the proportion of chord changes that started in state i and ended in state j as a proportion of all chords that started in state i. (In the exercises, you will prove that the estimator given in the above equation is a maximum-likelihood estimator that is consistent but biased, with the bias tending toward zero as the sample size increases. Thus, it is possible to estimate a consistent transition matrix with a large enough sample. A *consistent* estimator converges in probability to the true parameter value, and may be *biased* for small sample size, meaning that the estimator's expected value differs from the true parameter value.)

As a demonstration of the concept of Markov chains applied to music, it is interesting to note that a representation of chord progressions as a state machine is often used for teaching music composition. One such example is provided in Figure 2.4. One can think of Markov models as a probabilistic extension of Finite State Automata (FSA) that can be learned from data [32] instead of being manually designed from music theory rules.

Major

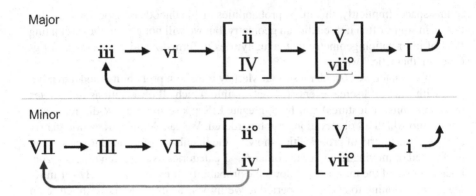

Minor

Figure 2.4 This diagram illustrates harmonic progression patterns common to Western music, where each Roman numeral indicates a triad built from the scale degree corresponding to the numeral. A base chord (I or i for major and minor, respectively) can transition to any chord. Subsequent chords tend to follow a pattern toward what are known as "pre-dominant" and "dominant" functions, leading back to the base chord (or "tonic"). From a mathematical perspective, such models can be formally considered Finite State Automata, with transition probabilities learned from data. From this, it becomes possible to teach machines to compose chord progressions by creating and using such a transition map.

2.5 MUSIC INFORMATION DYNAMICS

In our previous discussion of music perception and cognition in Chapter 1, we introduced the concept of Music Information Dynamics as a generic framework for analysis of predictive structure in music, relating it to a sense of anticipation by the listener who actively performs predictions during the audition process. The underlying assumption in the MID framework is that musical signals, from audio level to higher level symbolic structures, carry changing amounts of information that can be measured using appropriate information theoretical tools. In terms of cognitive or computational processes, the information is measured as a relative reduction in uncertainty about music events that is allowed through the process of anticipation. As we have seen in the previous section, the definition of mutual information basically says that information is carried between two random phenomena, and the ability to decode or extract information is related to the reduction in uncertainty about one signal from another. In the MID approach we consider the musical past as one of the random signals, and the present instance of sound or music section as the second random variable. The information is measured as a difference between the entropy of the second variable and its conditional entropy give the past. Moreover, it is important to note that conditional information of a random variable given its past is equivalent to the *entropy rate* of that variable. Accordingly, information dynamics is a measure of information passing from the past to the present measured by the difference in signal entropy before and after prediction, or equivalently the difference between signal entropy and its entropy rate. In the next two sections we will show now how MIR can be measured for symbolic sequences modeled by a Markov process, and for an acoustic signal whose structure and predictive properties are captured by its spectrum.

2.5.1 INFORMATION RATE IN MUSICAL MARKOV PROCESSES

Equipped with basic knowledge of predictive modeling, it is interesting to consider the case of Markov processes in music in terms of its anticipation structure. More formally, we will consider the notion of information passing from past to present that we call Information Rate (IR) and characterize the reduction in uncertainty when a Markov predictor is applied to reduce the uncertainty in the next instance of the symbolic sequence. Moreover, the same principle of information rate can be used for characterizing the amount of structure versus noise in acoustic signals. What differs between the IR algorithms for the two domains are their statistical models which in turn are used to estimate the uncertainty, or entropy of the signal based on its past.

We assume a Markov chain with a finite state space $S = s_1, ..., s_N$ and transition matrix $P(s_{t+1} = i | s_t = j) = a_{ij}$, which gives the probability of moving from a state i at some point in time t to another state j at the next step in time $t + 1$. When a Markov process is started from a random initial state, after many iterations a stationary distribution emerges. Denoting the stationary distribution as π, the meaning of such stationary state is that the probability of visiting any state remains unchanged for additional transition steps, which is mathematically expressed as $\pi_{t+1} = A\pi_t$, where A is the transitions matrix $A = [a_{ij}]$. Calculating the entropy of the stationary distribution and the entropy rate is given by the following expressions

$$H(S) = H(\pi) = -\sum_{i=1}^{N} \pi_i \log_2(\pi_i)$$

$$H_r(S) = H_r(A) = -\sum_{i=1}^{N} \pi_i \sum_{i=j}^{N} a_{ij} \log_2(a_{ij})$$

Using these expressions, IR can be simply obtained as the difference between the entropy of the stationary distribution and the entropy rate.

$$IR(S) = I(S_{t+1}; S_t) = H(\pi) - H_r(A) \tag{2.9}$$

For example, consider a Markov chain that moves repeatedly from state 1 to N, with negligible probability for jumping between non-adjacent states. Such a situation can be described by matrix A that is nearly diagonal (the non-diagonal elements will be very small). One can verify that for such a matrix, $H_r(A) \approx 0$ and IR will be close to the entropy of the stationary state $IR \approx \log_2(N)$. This is the maximal information rate for such process, showing that such a very predictable process has high amount of dependency on its past. If on the contrary the matrix A is fully mixing, with $a_{i,j} \approx \frac{1}{N}$, then the stationary distribution will be $\pi \approx \frac{1}{N}$ and the entropy and the entropy rate will be the same $H(S) = H_r(A) = log_2(N)$. This results in IR close to zero, meaning that knowledge of the previous step tell close to nothing about the next step. Such process is very unpredictable. Applying the notion of IR to Markov processes can guide the choice of Markov processes in terms of the anticipation or average suprisal that such a process creates.

A more sophisticated measure was proposed by [12] that takes a separate consideration of the past, present, and the next future step. Termed *Predictive Information Rate* (PIR), the measure is given as

$$PIR(S) \triangleq I(S_{t+1}; S_t | S_{t-1})$$
$$= I(S_{t+1}; (S_t, S_{t-1})) - I(S_{t+1}; S_{t-1})$$
$$= H_r(A^2) - H_r(A)$$

The first line is the definition of PIR. Second line is derived by using the definition of mutual information with a conditional variable and adding a subtracting $H(S_{t+1})$

$$I(S_{t+1}; S_t | S_{t-1}) = H(S_{t+1} | S_{t-1}) - H(S_{t+1} | S_t, S_{t-1})$$
$$= H(S_{t+1} | S_{t-1}) - H(S_{t+1} + H(S_{t+1} - H(S_{t+1} | S_t, S_{t-1}))$$
$$= -I(S_{t+1}; S_{t-1}) + I(S_{t+1}; (S_{t-1}, S_{t+1}))$$

The last line is derived from entropy rate expressions of Markov process, where the conditional entropy is used one time for a single step between S_{t+1} and S_t without S_{t-1} due to Markov property, and second time for two steps between S_{t+1} and S_{t-1}. Given a transition matrix $A = [a_{ij}]$

$$H(S_t) = H(\pi) = -\Sigma_i \pi_i \log(\pi_i)$$
$$H(S_{t+1} | S_t, S_{t-1}) = H(S_{t+1} | S_t)$$
$$= H_r(A) = -\Sigma_i \pi_i \Sigma_j a_{ij} \log(a_{ij})$$
$$H(S_{t+1} | S_{t-1}) = H_r(A^2)$$
$$= -\Sigma_i \pi_i \Sigma_j a_{ij}^2 \log(a_{ij}^2)$$

Considering the previous example of a fully sequential repetitive process with $A \approx I$ diagonal matrix, one finds that since $H_r(A) \approx H_r(A^2)$, the resulting PIR is approximately zero. So in terms of considering the mutual information for one step prediction given the past since the process is nearly deterministic, knowing the past will determine both the next and the following steps, so there is little information passing from the present to the future when the past is known.

A simple example demonstrating the principal difference between IR and PIR is shown in Figure 2.5 In this example a five state probabilistic finite state machine is constructed with nearly deterministic (probability near one) for transitions each state i to state $i+1$, cyclically repeating from state 4 back to state 0, with negligible transition probabilities outside of the sequence, i.e. negligible probabilities of staying in a state or jumping to a non-consequential states. This generative model

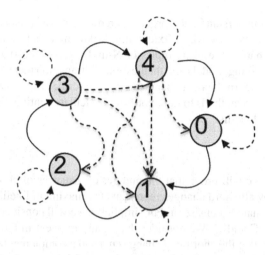

Figure 2.5 A simple example of a nearly repetitive sequence of five states represented as a Markov model of a probabilistic finite state machine. The nearly deterministic transitions are marked by continuous lines and the nearly zero probability transitions are marked by dashed line.

can be analyzed as Markov model of first order, with transition matrix $A = [a_{ij}]$ and stationary distribution π

$$A_{4\times4} = \begin{bmatrix} \varepsilon & 1-\varepsilon & \varepsilon & \varepsilon \\ \varepsilon & \varepsilon & 1-\varepsilon & \varepsilon \\ \varepsilon & \varepsilon & \varepsilon & 1-\varepsilon \\ 1-\varepsilon & \varepsilon & \varepsilon & \varepsilon \end{bmatrix} \qquad (2.10)$$

and the stationary distribution $\pi = [0.25, 0.25, 0.25, 0.25]$. For such border case we have $H(\pi) \approx \log_2(5)$, $H_r(A) \approx 0$ and $H_r(A^2) \approx 0$. Accordingly we have maximal IR $\approx log_2(5)$ and minimal PIR ≈ 0. This raises the question which measure best captures our interest in the sequence. According to IR, learning that the sequence is repetitive and using this knowledge to reduce our uncertainty about the future is maximally beneficial to the listener, while according to PIR, this sequence is not "interesting" since once the past outcome is known, very little information is passed between the next present and the next sample.

It is not clear which measure represents better the human sensation of surprise, as it seems that both make sense in different situations. If we consider the very predictable sequence as informative, then IR captures that, but one might as well say that such sequence is dull in terms of its music effect, and that the listener will favor music that carries a lot of local or immediate information, but without the past making it too redundant. In the following chapters we will consider yet another way of computing anticipation or average surprisal in the case of variable memory processes. In the Markov case, all the information about the future was contained in the previous state. Since music builds long motifs that continue, diverge, or recombine in unexpected ways, being able to understand such processes requires models that capture longer term relations in non-Markov ways. Extending Markov models to longer memories is computationally hard since using tuples or N-tuples grows the state space exponentially, and the resulting models and their estimated transition matrices are difficult to compute or estimate. In the next chapter we will describe string matching models and use of compression methods to find motifs and calculate continuations of phrases at different memory lengths.

2.6 EXERCISES

1. In this exercise, we will prove that the number of instances of chord change i to j (n_{ij}) divided by all chord changes represents the maximum likelihood estimate, and that this estimate is consistent. For simplicity, we will consider a song of two possible chords, C and G. We consider that at any moment in the song, there is some probability that the chord will change (p_c) and a complementary probability that the chord will not change ($1 - p_c$). We will model this as a binomial distribution (the distribution of n indepdendent Bernoulli random events with probability θ). The events can be either c (chord change) or nc (no chord change). So, the probability of a particular "song" is

$$P(S|p_c) = \binom{n_c + n_{nc}}{n_c} p_c^{n_c} (1 - p_c)^{n_{nc}}. \tag{2.11}$$

   Find the maximum likelihood estimator (MLE) of a song S; that is, find p_c to maximize the likelihood $P(S; p_c)$. We express this as

$$\hat{\theta} = \underset{\theta}{\operatorname{argmin}} P(S; \theta), \tag{2.12}$$

   where θ is parameter p_c. To do this, take the log of the probability function, and compute the derivative of this log. Setting this equal to 0, you can find the critical point which you can then verify to be a maximum. When n is large, what does this probability tend to?

2. In this exercise, we will compare the benefits of dictionary-based prediction versus fixed-order Markov models of prediction. For illustrative purposes, we will examine a poem by Langston Hughes, whose writing includes music-like patterns in motif, repetition, rhythm, and variation. Consider the opening of "Let America Be America Again":

   Let America be America again.
   Let it be the dream it used to be.
   Let it be the pioneer on the plain
   Seeking a home where he himself is free.

   (America never was America to me.)

Let's first consider modeling this poetry using an eighth order Markov model, and ignore case-sensitivity. How many rows (and columns) would need to exist in this probability table to represent all such 8-character sequences (including single space as a character)? This is the so-called "explosion" of the Markov model probability table.

We can see that on a character-by-character level, we find some repeating motifs, such as "Let", "America", "be", "it", etc. In fact, on an even more flexible level, all of these motivic sequences would be found in a (literal) dictionary of English words. To think about the potential computational savings afforded by a dictionary-based model, approximately how many "sequences" appear in an English dictionary?

Which model would you select to model poetry of similar structure? Where might this type of model fail? How does the incremental parsing method account for this failure case?

3. Assume a composer writes a melody by choosing for the first measure two notes from the 8 major scale notes spanning an octave, and for the second measure choosing the same two notes plus either the first or fifth scale degree. The purpose of the question is to consider how much information (bits) need to be sent if we already know something about how a sequence is generated, or how it may relate to another sequence (such as its own past).

   (a) If we treat the composer as an information source, and we know that they always use the above method for writing their melodies, how many bits are required to represent the first bar?
   Hint: Determine how many bits are required to represent initially the alphabet (the total number of possible notes in octave), which gives you # of bits per note without any prior information or compressions.

   (b) How many bits are required to represent the second bar?
   Hint: Consider the number of bits you need when you use the prior information from the first bar to encode the second bar.

   (c) If we represent the first bar as random variable X and the second bar as random variable Y, write the expressions for $H(X)$, $H(Y)$, and $H(Y|X)$.

   (d) What is the mutual information $I(X,Y)$ between the first and second bar?
   Hint: Think about how many bits of information are already contained in X in order to compose Y.

Additional questions and programming exercises are found in the **Probability** notebook at https://github.com/deep-and-shallow/notebooks.

3 Communicating Musical Information

"Music is the greatest communication in the world. Even if people don't understand the language that you're singing in, they still know good music when they hear it", said the great American record producer, singer, and composer Lou Rawls. What is missing from his quote is the definition of what "knowing good music" means, and why this knowledge amounts to communication. Evidently music is a signal that passes from the musician to their audience, so there is a sender-receiver structure to the way music operates. And there is an aspect of "knowing" inherent in the music listening process, which makes both the encoder/musician and the decoder/listener share some common understanding. In this chapter we will explore the basic premise of this book – that machine learning of music, production, and computer audition are all parts of a communication process.

3.1 MUSIC AS INFORMATION SOURCE

The basic one-directional model of communication assumes that the process of musical creation and listening comprises a series of activities that transmit information from a source/musician to a receiver/listener. Research on information theory of music is based on Shannon and Weavers (1949) communication model [33]. This basic communication model comprises an information source that is encoded into messages that are transmitted over a noisy channel, and a decoder that recovers the input data from the corrupted and/or compressed representation that was received at the output of the channel. The first step in this information-theoretical approach to modeling of music and musical style is accepting the idea that music can be treated as an information source. Accordingly, the process of music generation is based on the notion of information itself that essentially treats any specific message, and in our case any particular musical composition, as an instance of a larger set of possible messages that bare common statistical properties. As Claude Shannon, the father of information theory, expressed in his work *The Mathematical Theory of Communication* [33], the concept of information concerns the possibilities of a message rather than its content: "That is, information is a measure of ones freedom of choice when one selects a message". The measure of the amount of information contained in a source is done by means of entropy, sometimes also called "uncertainty", a concept covered in the previous chapter.

The initial interest in information came from communications: how a message can be transmitted over a communication channel in the best possible way. The relevant questions in that setting concerned compression and errors that happen during the encoding or transmission process. The model of information source is generative

DOI: 10.1201/9781003240198-3

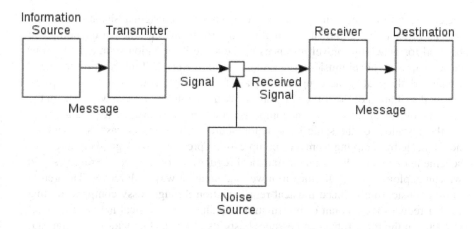

Figure 3.1   The basic model of a communication channel that includes encoder, decoder, and a noisy channel that establishes uncertain relations between the source messages and what appears in the output at the receiver's end. Since both the source and the channel errors are described probabilistically, information theory studies the terms under which the communication can be made more efficient. This includes methods for encoding or compression of the source in a lossless or lossy manner, and methods for coding that provide correction or more robustness to channel errors. In our work we mostly focus on compression aspects as a way for finding efficient representation of the source data, and investigating the tradeoff between compression and reconstruction error in the case of reduced representation modeled as lossy encoding.

in the sense that it assumes an existence of a probability distribution from which the messages are randomly drawn. The theory of information, as introduced by Shannon, encompassed three different domains of communication:

1. Lossless compression: any information source can be compressed to its entropy.
2. Error correction: all errors in communication can be corrected if the transmission is done at a rate that is less or equal to channel capacity. The concept of channel capacity is beyond the scope of this book, as we will be focusing our discussion on Theorems 1 and 3 and their relation to music generation.
3. Lossy compression: for any given level of reconstruction error or distortion, a minimal rate exists that will not exceed that error, and vise versa, for a given rate of transmission a coding scheme can be found that minimizes the distortion.

An example of a communications channel is shown in Figure 3.1.

Not all of the Shannon concepts are directly applicable to music generation, so we will limit ourselves to Theorems 1 and 3. The main concept that we borrow from Theorem 1 is that compression can be used as an efficient way to represent the structure of the information source. Music generation using compression methods uses the concepts from Theorem 1 in a reverse manner to the original Shannon design – instead of encoding a known information source, having an efficient encoding can be used for generating novel instances of the same information source, and in our case composing novel music in the same style. In the original information-theoretic framework the goal of encoding is to find an efficient representation to a known probability distribution of the source messages. We use compression as a way to learn the distribution, i.e. given an efficient compression scheme we can use it to produce more similar instances of the same information source, which in our case is generating novel music by sampling from a its compressed representation. A good compression scheme is one which has learned statistical regularities over a set of examples, and we can exploit these regularities in novel and creative ways. Moreover, Theorem 3 allows considering reduced musical representation through lossy compression that further reduces the amount of information contained in a musical message in order to focus on the more robust and essential aspects of musical structure. As such, statistical models derived from applying compression schemes to musical corpora in a particular style became also useful tool for *Stylometrics*, which is the study of structures and variations that are characteristic of musical materials that may be broadly defined as "style".

The initial work on using information theory for music started in the late 90's [34]. Today, the problem of generative modeling in music has become one of the formidable challenges facing the machine learning community and deep learning research in particular. Music is a complex, multidimensional temporal data that has long-term and short-term structures, and capturing such structure requires developing sophisticated statistical models. For historical as well as conceptual reasons, thinking about music in terms of a complex information source provides powerful insights to building novel machine learning methods. Using communication theory in music research not only puts music into a transmitter-receiver communication setting that takes into account both the composer and the listener, but it also captures the dynamics of music entertainment and creativity since co-evolution of musical knowledge that happens over time between the musician and the listener can be captured by methods of information theory, opening novel possibilities for man-machine co-creative interactions.

3.1.1 STYLE MODELING

Style modeling using information theory started with application of universal sequence models, specifically the well-known Lempel-Ziv (LZ) universal compression technique [35] to MIDI files [34]. The universality of LZ compression can be understood in terms of it not assuming any a-priori knowledge of the statistics of the information source, but rather having its asymptotic compression performance as good as any statistical model, such as Markov or finite state model. This is an empirical learning approach where a statistical model is induced through application of compression algorithms to existing compositions. Moreover, it captures statistics of musical sequences of different lengths, a situation that is typical to music improvisation that creates new musical materials at different time-levels, from short motifs or even instantaneous sonority, to melodies and complete thematic phrases. Specifically, the universal modeling allows application of the notion of entropy to compare sequences in terms of similarity between their statistical sources, as well as generation of novel musical sequences without explicit knowledge of their statistical model. One should note that "universality" in the universal modeling approach still operates under the assumption that musical sequences are realizations of some high-order Markovian sources. The information theoretical modeling method allows the following musical operations to be applied to musical data:

- stochastic generation of new sequences that have similar phrase structure as the training sequence, creating musical results in between improvisation and the original on the motivic or melodic level, and
- stochastic morphing or interpolation between musical styles, where generation of new sequences is done in a manner where new statistics are obtained by a mixing procedure that creates a "mutual source" between two or more training styles. The extent to which the new improvisation is close to one of the original sources can be controlled by the mixture parameters, providing a gradual transition between two styles which is correct in the statistical sense.

Early experiments with style morphing [36] used a joint source algorithm [37], later using more efficient dictionary and string matching methods [38] as will be explained below. In addition to generative applications, universal models are used for music information retrieval, such as performing hierarchical classification by repeatedly agglomerating closest sequences, or selecting most significant phrases from dictionary of parsed phrases in a MIDI sequence, selected according to the probability of their appearance.

3.1.2 STOCHASTIC MODELING, PREDICTION, COMPRESSION, AND ENTROPY

The underlying assumption in the information-theoretical approach to machine improvisation is that a given musical piece can be produced by an unknown stochastic source, and that all musical pieces in that style are generated by the same stochastic sources. The finite Markov-order assumptions do not allow capturing arbitrarily complex music structures, such as very long structure dependency due to musical form; nevertheless, by allowing for sufficiently long training sequences that capture dependence on the past, the universal model can capture much of the melodic structure of variable length in a musical piece.

This connection between compression and prediction is a consequence of the asymptotic equipartition property (AEP) [39], which is the information-theoretic analog to the law of large numbers in probability theory. The AEP tells us that if $x_1, x_2, \ldots$ are indepdent and identically distributed random variables distributed with probability $P(x)$, then

$$-\frac{1}{n} \log_2 P(x_1, x_2, \ldots) \to H(P) \qquad (3.1)$$

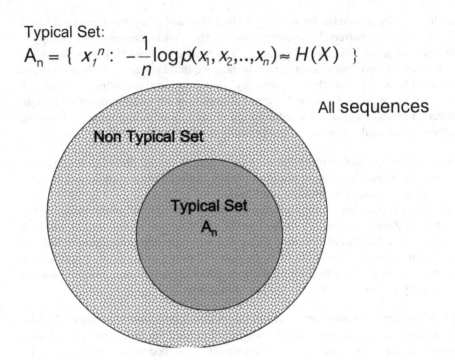

Typical Set:
$$A_n = \{\ x_1^n:\ -\frac{1}{n}\log p(x_1, x_2,..,x_n) \approx H(X)\ \}$$

All sequences

Non Typical Set

Typical Set
A_n

Figure 3.2   Asymptotic Equipartition Property of long sequences.

where $H(x)$ is the Shannon Entropy of the $x \sim P(x)$ (that is, $H(x) = -\sum_x P(x)\log_2 P(x)$, where the averaging is over all possible occurrences of the sequences x).

The AEP property is graphically represented in Figure 3.2. The outer circle represents all possible sequences of length n, which are combinatorial possibilities depending on the size of the alphabets. Shannon's theory proves that in view of the different probabilities of occurrence of each symbol (in the simplest case, these are unbalanced heads or tails, known as the Bernoulli distribution, with binary choice which takes the value 1 with probability p and the value 0 with probability $q = 1 - p$), the entropy of the probability can be used to define an effectively much smaller set of outcomes whose probability will tend to be one.

The Bernoulli Distribution

The Bernoulli distribution is a discrete probability distribution that represents the outcome of a single trial with two possible outcomes. The distribution is named after the Swiss mathematician Jacob Bernoulli, who introduced it in the late 1600s.

The probability distribution function of the Bernoulli distribution is

$$P(X = k) = p^k \cdot (1-p)^{1-k}, \qquad (3.2)$$

where $P(X = k)$ is the probability of getting the outcome k (either 0 or 1), and p is the probability of outcome 1 on a single trial, with $p \in [0,1]$.

The mean (expected value) and variance of the Bernoulli distribution are $E[X] = p$ and $Var[X] = p(1-p)$.

The Bernoulli distribution is often used as a building block for more complex distributions, such as the binomial distribution, which models the number of successes in a fixed number of independent Bernoulli trials.

This set of outcomes is called the "Typical Set" and is denoted here as A_n, where n is the number of elements in a sequence that needs to be sufficiently large. Moreover, all sequences of the typical set are equiprobable, or in other words, one can index these events in a way that assigns equal length codes to these events, and zero codes to any remaining events of the non typical set. This means that for long enough observations from a probability source, the possible outcomes split into two – sequences that deviate from the probability statistics, such as sequences that do not achieve the expected mean number of heads of tails in a Bernoulli probability, will never occur, while those that do occur, happen with equal probability. No further structure exists in the typical set, or otherwise additional compression could have be applied to exploit any remaining imbalance. In our case, for generative purposes, this means that one can generate new instances of a data source by accessing the strings from its typical set using a uniform random number generator. Conceptually it means that sampling from a typical set turns white noise into outcomes that have the desired statistical structure of that information source. For stationary ergodic processes, and in in particular, finite order Markov processes, the generalization of AEP is called the Shannon-McMillan-Breiman theorem [39]. The connection with compression is that for long x the lower limit on compressibility is $H(x)$ bits per symbol. Thus, if we can find a good algorithm that reaches the entropy, then the dictionary of phrases it creates can be used for generating new instances from that source. When the algorithm has compressed the phrase dictionary to the entropy, any excess compressible structures have been eliminated. This means that the dictionary is very efficient, so we can sample from the source by random selection from that dictionary.

3.1.3 GENERATIVE PROCEDURE

Dictionary-based prediction methods sample the data so that a few selected phrases represent most of the information. Below we described two dictionary based generative approaches: *incremental parsing* (IP) and *prediction suffix trees* (PST). IP is based on universal prediction, a method derived from information theory. PST is a learning technique that initially was developed to statistically model complex sequences, and has found applications also in linguistics and computational biology. Both the IP and PST methods belong to the general class of dictionary-based prediction methods. These methods operate by parsing an existing musical text into a lexicon of phrases or patterns, called **motifs**, and provide an inference rule for choosing the next musical object that best follows a current past context. The parsing scheme must satisfy two conflicting constraints: on the one hand, maximally increasing the dictionary helps to achieve a better prediction, but on the other, enough evidence must be gathered before introducing a new phrase to allow obtaining a reliable estimate of the conditional probability for generation of the next symbol. The "trick" of dictionary-based prediction (and compression) methods is that they cleverly sample the data so that only a few selected phrases reliably represent most of the information. In contrast to dictionary-based methods, fixed-order Markov models build potentially large probability tables for the appearance of a next symbol at every possible context entry. To avoid this pitfall, more advanced "selective prediction" methods build more complex variable memory Markov models. Although it may seem that the Markov and dictionary-based methods operate in a different manner, they both stem from similar statistical insights.

We use dictionary-based methods to model the musical (information) source in terms of a lexicon of motifs and their associated prediction probabilities. To generate new instances (messages), these models "stochastically browse" the prediction tree in the following manner:

- Given a current context, check if it appears as a motif in the tree. If found, choose the next symbol according to prediction probabilities.
- If the context is not found, shorten it by removing the oldest (leftmost) symbol and go back to the previous step.

These steps iterate indefinitely, producing a sequence of symbols that presumably corresponds to a new message originating from the same source. In some cases, this procedure might fail to find an appropriate continuation and end up with an empty context, or it might tend to repeat the same sequence over and over again in an infinite loop. The specific aspects of how the dictionary is created and how continuity is being maintained between the random draws will be discussed next.

3.2   LEMPEL-ZIV ALGORITHM AND MUSICAL STYLE

In *A universal algorithm for sequential data compression* [40], Lempel and Ziv take a series of symbols from a finite alphabet as input, and build a tree of observed continuations of combinations of the input symbols. This tree grows dynamically as the input is parsed using what is called the *incremental parsing* (IP) method. If the input is a sample of a stationary stochastic process, LZ asymptotically achieves an optimal description of the input in the sense that the resulting tree can be used to encode the input at the lowest possible bit rate (the entropy of the process). This implies that the coding tree somehow encodes the law of the process; for instance, if one uses the same tree (as it stands after a sufficiently large input) to encode another string, obeying a different law, the resulting bit rate is higher than the entropy.

3.2.1   INCREMENTAL PARSING

Here we introduce the incremental parsing (IP) algorithm [34] suggested by Lempel and Ziv [40]. IP builds a dictionary of distinct motifs by sequentially adding every new phrase that differs by a single next character from the longest match that already exists in the dictionary. LZ allows assigning conditional probability $p(x_{n+1}|x_1^n)$ of a symbol $x_n + 1$ given $x_1^n = \{x_1, x_2, ..., x_n\}$ as context according to the code lengths of the Lempel Ziv compression scheme [41]. Let $c(n)$ be the number of motifs in the parsing of an input n-sequence. Then, $\log(c(n))$ bits are needed to describe each prefix (a motif without its last character), and 1 bit to describe the last character (in case of a binary alphabet).

For instance, given a text $ababaa...$, IP parses it into $a, b, ab, aa, ...$ where motifs are separated by commas. The dictionary may be represented as a tree, where starting from a root representing an empty phrase, each new phrase that is found as a continuation of an existing phrase, is placed as a child branch labeled by the last continuation character, as shown in Figure 3.3. The LZ code for the above text example is sequence of pairs $(0, a), (0, b), (1, b), (1, a), ...$ where the first entry in each pair gives the position of the encoding for the prefix sequence in the list, with 0 referring to an empty motif at the start, and the second entry gives the next character that when placed as a continuation of the previous motif is comprising the new motif. One can verify that the original text $ababaa...$ can be recursively decoded from this sequence of pairs.

Ziv and Lempel have shown that the average code length $c(n)\log(c(n))/n$ converges asymptotically to the entropy of the sequence with increasing n. This proves that the coding is optimal. Since for optimal coding the code length is 1/probability, and since all code lengths are equal, we may say that, at least in the long limit, the IP motifs have equal probability. Thus, taking equal weight for nodes in the tree representation, $p(x_{n+1}|x_1^n)$ will be deduced as a ratio between the cardinality of the sub-trees (number of sub-nodes) following the node x_1^n. As the number of sub-nodes is also the node's share of the probability space (because one code-word is allocated to each node), we see that the amount of code space allocated to a node is proportional to the number of times it occurred.

3.2.2   GENERATIVE MODEL BASED ON LZ

In order to produce new sequences from an LZ tree, we create a generative model in two steps [34]:

1. First, the motif dictionary is transformed into a continuation dictionary, where each key will be a motif M from the previous dictionary, and the corresponding value will be a list of couples $(..., (k, P(k|W)), ...)$ for each possible continuation k in the sequence alphabet.
2. Second, a generation function that samples a new symbol from a continuation dictionary.

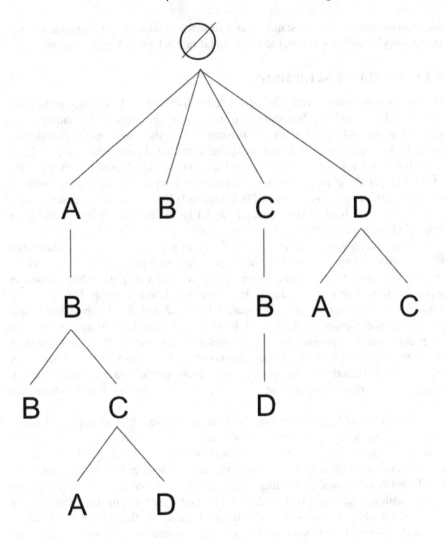

Figure 3.3 LZ based tree representation derived from incremental parsing algorithm of a sequence ababcabccbabbabcadabcddadc. See text for more detail.

The two steps of Incremental Parsing (IP) and Motif continuation are summarized in the following pseudocode. The *IPMotif* function computes a dictionary containing the IP motifs found in the text using a dictionary comprising of a set of pairs (key, value) where keys are the motifs and values are integer counters. We use the following notation conventions in the algorithm below – $value(dict, motif)$ gives the value associated with motif in dict, and $W!k$ denotes a new list resulting from appending character k to an existing list W

Algorithm 1 IPMotif

1: Parameter text
2: dict = *new dictionary*
3: motif = ()
4: **while** text *is not empty* **do**
5:     motif = motif *concat* text[0]
6:     text = text[1:]
7:     **if** motif *belongs to* dict **then**
8:         dict[motif] += 1
9:     **else** *add* motif *to* dict *with value* 1
10:        motif = ()
11:    **end if**
12: **end while**
13: **return** dict

Algorithm 2 IPContinuation

1: Parameter dict1
2: dict2 = *new dictionary*
3: **for** *each pair* (Wk, counter) *in* dict1 **do**
4:     W = Wk[:-1]
5:     k = Wk[-1]
6:     **if** W *belongs to* dict2 **then**
7:         *Add* (k, counter) *to* dict2[W]
8:     **else** dict2[W] = [(k, counter)]
9:     **end if**
10: **end for**
11: Normalize(dict2)
12: **return** dict

The *IPContinuation* function computes the continuation dictionary from the motif dictionary

The process can be demonstrated for a sequence example as follows:

$$Text = (ababcabccbabbabcadabcddadc) \tag{3.3}$$
$$IP = (a, b, ab, c, abc, cb, abb, abca, d, abcd, da, dc)$$
$$Motif\ dictionary = ((a)\ 6)((b)\ 1)((c)\ 3)((d)\ 3)((ab)\ 5)((abc)\ 3)((abb)\ 1)$$
$$((abcd)\ 1)...$$
$$((abca)\ 1)((cb)\ 2)((cbd)\ 1)((da)\ 1)((dc)\ 1)$$
$$Continuation\ dictionary = ((a)((b\ 1.0)))((ab)((c\ 0.75)(d\ 0.25)))((abc)$$
$$((d\ 0.5)(e\ 0.5)))...$$
$$((c)((b\ 1.0)))((cb)((d\ 1.0)))((d)((a\ 0.5)(c\ 0.5))$$

Suppose we have already generated a text $a_0a_1 \ldots a_{n-1}$. To predict the first value, first set a parameter L which is an upper limit on the size of the past we want to consider in order to choose the next object, and then initialize the current context length to the maximal length $l = L$; that is,

1. Current text is $a_0a_1 \ldots a_{n-1}$, context $= a_{n-p} \ldots a_{n-1}$.
2. Then, check if context is a motif in the continuation dictionary.
   - if context is empty (this happens when $p = 0$), sample from the root according to symbol probabilities and go back to step 1.
   - If non empty context is found, look up its associated dictionary value for the probability distribution of the continuation symbols. Sample this distribution and append the chosen object k to right of text. Increment $n = n + 1$, set p to max value $p = L$ and go back to step 2.
   - If context is non empty but its entry is not found in the dictionary key, shorten it by popping its leftmost object $p = p - 1$ and go back to step 1.

This procedure requires repeated search from the root of the tree, iteratively shortening the context each time the context is not found in the dictionary key entry, which is very inefficient. By inverting the sequences and accordingly changing the tree representation, the repeated search can be avoided and the algorithm becomes amenable to real time implementation, as described in [34]. The LZ algorithm has been implemented in OpenMusic [42] and Flow Machine [43] systems, and in view of its similarity to Markov generation, it has been often termed *Variable Memory Markov* (VMM), although from a strict mathematical point of view, the probability assignments are not estimated by n-gram approximations but rather rely on Feder's univeral prediction weighting scheme [41].

3.3 LOSSY PREDICTION USING PROBABILISTIC SUFFIX TREE

In 1996, Dana Ron et al. [44] developed the Prediction Suffix Tree (PST) algorithm, named after the data structure used to represent the learned statistical model. A PST represents a dictionary of distinct motifs, much like the one the IP algorithm generates. However, in contrast to the lossless coding scheme underlying the IP parsing, the PST algorithm builds a restricted dictionary of only those motifs that both appear a significant number of times throughout the complete source sequence and are meaningful for predicting the immediate future. The framework underlying this approach is efficient lossy compression. One variant of the PST algorithm uses a breadth-first search for all motifs that comply simultaneously with three requirements:

- the motif is no longer than some maximal length L,
- its empirical probability within the given data set exceeds a threshold P_{min}, and
- the conditional probability it induces over the next symbol differs by a multiplicative factor of at least r from that of the shorter contexts it subsumes, for at least one such next symbol.

The search collects only these motifs into a restricted dictionary. The empirical probability of a motif is assigned according to the number of its occurrences in the text divided by the number of times it could have occurred. For example, the empirical probability of the motif "aa" within the sequence "aabaaab" is $\frac{3}{6} = 0.5$. A conditional probability to observe a symbol after a given context is the number of times this symbol comes immediately after that context, divided by the total occurrences of the context in the text.

Thus, the conditional probability of seeing "b" after "aa" in the sequence "aabaaab" is $\frac{2}{3}$. Since the conditional probability of seeing "b" after "a" is $\frac{2}{5}$, the multiplicative difference between the conditional probability to observe "b" after "aa" and that after "a" is $\frac{2}{3}/\frac{2}{5} = \frac{5}{3}$. Written in terms of conditional probabilities, the multiplicative factor $p(b|aa)/p(b|a)$ is compared to a threshold r to decide if the longer motif should be retained.

The PST formulation incorporates the counts in a slightly different manner than in IP. Using the same notation as in the previous example, the probability for a next symbol extension x from a node labeled by string c is given by $P_c(x) = (1 - |\Sigma|g)P_c(x) + g$, where $|\Sigma|$ is the size of the alphabet and g is the smoothing factor, $0 < g < \frac{1}{|\Sigma|}$. Fractional probabilities are collected from all possible next-symbol extensions in proportion to their actual counts, then they are redistributed equally between all counts to achieve a minimal conditional probability for any continuation $P_c(x) \geq g > 0$.

PST Example

We provide an example of the PST analysis example for *abracadabra* with the following parameters: $L = 2$, $P_{min} = 0.15$, $r = 2$, and $g = 0$. For each node, the analysis associates the list of probabilities that the continuation may be, respectively, a, b, c, d, or r. Figure 3.4 shows the results of this analysis. Potential node "ba" failed the P_{min} criterion, while potential node "bra" passed that criterion but failed both the L and r criteria. Generation proceeds much like in the IP resulting tree. Now, however, $P(\text{generate "abrac"}) = P(a|\text{""})P(b|a)P(r|ab)P(a|abr)P(c|abra) = 5/11 \cdot 1/2 \cdot 1 \cdot 1 \cdot 1$.

3.4   IMPROVED SUFFIX SEARCH USING FACTOR ORACLE ALGORITHM

Historically, IP and its continuation methods quickly found their ways into novel music applications, opening a novel field of style learning which was enthusiastically showcased in a variety of interactive applications on stage, and as a new way of teaching music by playing music together with the machine in the classroom. One of the difficulties in building efficient music applications using previous methods is the asymptotic character of LZ parsing, requiring long sequences to achieve an efficient representation, or the "false notes" effect caused by the smoothing factor in

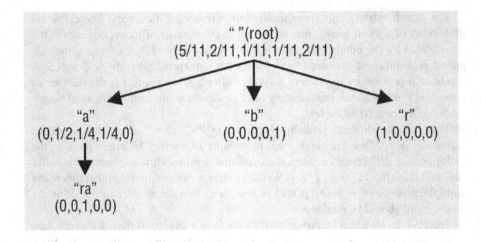

Figure 3.4 Prediction Suffix Tree example for *abracadabra*.

PST that accounts for dropping low probability sequences at the price of allowing an occasional generation of random notes. As both methods build tree structures during the learning stage that are then used for generation, an improvement to finding the best suffix was needed. Factor Oracle (FO) [45] makes the suffix search more efficient by taking into account partial repetitions that may occur between the parsing points of IP. It also replaced the tree representation by an automaton, that builds two sets of links, forward and backward suffix links, that point to related portions in the signal. In the original FO design, forward links were used to search for sub-strings, or factors, in the orignial data. In the process of FO construction, an auxiliary set of links $S(i) = j$ running backward are created, called *suffix links*. These links point to node j at the end of the longest repeating suffix (also called repeating factor) appearing before node i (i.e., longest suffix of prefix of i that appears at least twice in prefix of i). These suffix links are used for improvisation processes, by allowing jumps back to earlier instances of the data that share the same suffix when used in online fashion (adding states to FO while playing) or jumping back and forth if a complete musical sequence is available prior to improvisation.

FO automation provides the desired tool for efficiently generating new sequences of symbols based on the repetition structure of the reference example. Compared to IP and PST, FO is structurally closer to the reference suffix tree. Its efficiency is close to IP (linear, incremental). Moreover, it is an automaton, rather than a tree, which makes it easier to handle maximum suffixes in the generation process. This method also differs from Markov-chain-based style machines mentioned above in the extent of the signal history or context that it is able to capture. An oracle structure carries two kinds of links, forward link and suffix link. Suffix link is a backward pointer that

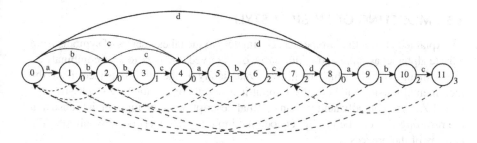

Figure 3.5 A *VMO* structure with symbolized signal $\{a,b,b,c,a,b,c,d,a,b,c\}$, upper (normal) arrows represent forward links with labels for each frame and lower (dashed) are suffix links. Values outside of each circle are the $\mathtt{lrs}$ value for each state.

links state t to k with $t > k$, without a label and is denoted by $\mathtt{sfx}[t] = k$.

$$\mathtt{sfx}[t] = k \iff \text{the longest repeated suffix of}$$
$$\{x_1, x_2, \ldots, x_t\} \text{ is recognized in } k.$$

Suffix links are used to find the longest repeated suffix in X. In order to track the longest repeated suffix at each time index t, the length of the longest repeated suffix at each state t is computed by the algorithm described in [46] and is denoted by $\mathtt{lrs}[t]$. $\mathtt{lrs}$ is essential to the on-line construction algorithm of an oracle structure [46] and its generalization for approximate matching by thershold search for model selection [47] for *VMO*.

Forward links are links with labels and are used to retrieve any of the factors from X. An oracle structure has two types of forward links; the first is an internal forward link which is a pointer from state $t - 1$ to t labeled by the symbol x_t, denoted as $\delta(t - 1, x_t) = t$. The other forward link is an external forward link which is a pointer from state t to $t + k$ labeled by x_{t+k} with $k > 1$. An external forward link $\delta(t, x_{t+k}) = t + k$ is created when

$$x_{t+1} \neq x_{t+k}$$
$$x_t = x_{t+k-1}$$
$$\delta(t, x_{t+k}) = \emptyset.$$

In other words, an external forward link is created between x_t and x_{t+k} when the sequence of symbols $\{x_{t+k-1}, x_{t+k}\}$ is first seen in X with x_t and x_{t+k-1} share the same label. The function of the forward links is to provide an efficient way to retrieve any of the factors of X, starting from the beginning of X and following the path formed by forward links. We exploited forward link's functionality by treating forward links as indications of possible transitions from state to state for our time series query-by-content tasks.

3.5 MODELING OF MUSICAL STYLE

As explained above, the Lempel-Ziv coding technique takes a series of symbols from a finite alphabet as input and builds a tree of observed continuations of combinations of the input symbols. This tree grows dynamically as the input is parsed using the incremental parsing method. If the input is a sample of a stationary stochastic process, LZ asymptotically achieves an optimal description of the input in the sense that the resulting tree can be used to encode the input at the lowest possible bit rate (the entropy of the process).

This fact can be used to test whether a new sample is likely to have arisen from the original process or not. Moreover, one can use the decoding algorithm on a totally random process of codeword selection; this produces samples of the process, or – in musical terms – it creates variations or improvisations on the same musical information source, at least in the sense that the re-encoding test will fail to distinguish it from a "genuine" sample. This information-theoretic approach to music gave rise to many investigations: first, the method has been evaluated on specific musical styles, using different choices of alphabet and approaches to polyphony. Second, although LZ is asymptotically optimal, many possible variants exist as well, such as some of the more recent results described in the section on music improvisation. Third, many researchers and teams are now applying these techniques for real-time improvisation and composition by computers.

3.5.1 MUSIC IMPROVISATION AS INFORMATION GENERATOR

Computer improvisation requires capturing the idiomatic style of a composer or a genre in attempt to provide the computer with creative human-like capabilities. An improvisation system consists of two main components: a learning algorithm that builds a model of music sequences in a specific style, and a generation algorithm that operates on the model and produces a new musical stream in the particular style, so that the next musical unit is selected in a manner that best corresponds as a continuation for the already generated sequence. In real-time applications, the system also must alternate between the learning / listening phase and the generating / improvising phase. This alternation can be seen as machine improvisation, where the machine reacts to other musician playing, after listening to and analyzing his performance.

As IP and PST build tree structures in the learning stage, finding the best suffix involves walking the tree from the root to the node bearing that suffix. We explored the use of Factor Oracle (FO) for the purpose of sequence generation in a particular style [48]. The use of FO for generation is shown in Figure 3.6. In order to use the automation for generation, a set of links $S(i) = j$ called Suffix Links running backward are used. These links point to node j at the end of the longest repeating suffix (also called *repeating factor*) appearing before node i (i.e., longest suffix of prefix of i that appears at least twice in prefix of i).

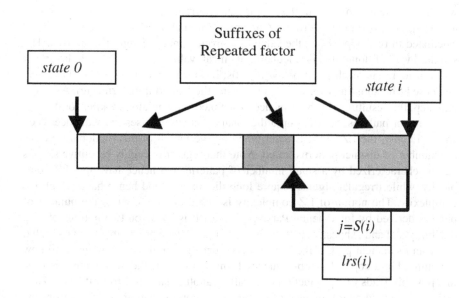

Figure 3.6 Machine improvisation using the FO structure as a way of generating variations by remixing existing segments is a recording that share common history, as pointed by the suffix links. The **lrs** indicates the length or repeated suffix, which can be used as a parameter to limit the "smoothness" versus amount of novelty happening during the improvisation process.

3.6 ESTIMATING MUSIC INFORMATION DYNAMICS USING LEMPEL-ZIV COMPLEXITY

Continuing our discussion of music information dynamics for various acoustic and musical models, we consider the evaluation of musical complexity as a measure of structure versus uncertainly unfolding in time. This complexity measure is expected also to reveal the effort that the listener puts into making sense of the sound stream through the process of such structural analysis, where the basic premise is that a memory process allows detection of repetitions, identification of motifs, and so on. Although it is hard, if not impossible, to relate mathematical complexity to perceptual or cognitive complexity, the first step is also to identify which musical aspect is being considered for musical comprehension. Researchers talk about six dimensions of musical complexity: melody, harmony, rhythm, timbre, structure, and acoustic properties. Each such aspect requires its own particular representation before a complexity measure can be applied. The idea of algorithmic composition that we introduced in the previous section naturally brings to mind the application of algorithmic information as a definition of complexity that could be applied to music. Measuring the amount of information contained in a sequence of numbers is known as *Kolmogorov complexity*. A popular way of thinking about Kolmogorov complexity, which is the length of the shortest computer program that reproduces a given pattern [49], is through considering LZ as proxy for such measure. LZ complexity is calculated in two steps. First, the value of a given signal of length is binarised. The standard way of doing this is calculating its mean value and turning each data point above it to 1s and each point below it to 0s; however, other possibilities have also been used (thresholding over the median, using the Hilbert transform, etc). As a second step, the resulting binary sequence is scanned sequentially, looking for distinct structures or patterns, building up a dictionary that summarises the sequences seen so far. Finally, the LZ index is determined by the length of this dictionary; i.e., is the number of distinct patterns found. Note that regular or highly repetitive signals can be characterized by a small number of patterns and hence have low LZ complexity, while irregular signals require long dictionaries and hence have a high LZ complexity. The notion of LZ complexity is based on the count of the number of phrases derived by Incremental Parsing phrases. It is based on two notions of producibility and and exhaustive history. A string is said to be producible from its prefix, i.e. from its ancient past, if the rest of the sequence from that past moment till now is nothing but a copy of a sub-sequence from that past. If the next symbol is new, this possibly leads to a production or recall of another subword from its past. Then history is defined as a sequence of consecutive, non-overlapping periods from the past. From all possible such partitions, an exhaustive history is considered as the one that has the longest possible partitions, which is exactly what the incremental parsing does (puts a comma or partition on the continuation symbol when no other identical subsequence can be found in the past). Finally, the number of components of this exhaustive history is called the *Lempel–Ziv complexity* of S. So for instance, the Lempel-Ziv complexity of $s = 101001010010111110$ is 8, because when scanned from left to right, different patterns observed in s are $1|0|10|01|010|0101|11|110|$. Using such simple counting process, LZ also provides a bridge between algorithmic and statistical or information complexity, as it is known to be an efficient estimator of the entropy rate of [50]. This link is based on representing the parsing as a tree of linked pointers for continuations and the interpretation of the relative weights of its branches as probabilities, as explained in the continuation algorithm. From this, one might derive the entropy rate of a sequence, which was defined in previous chapters as a Information Theory quantity which measures how predictable the sequence is overall from its past in terms of how many bits, or fraction of bits, are required on the average for each new data sample given its history [39]. The entropy rate can be also considered as an approximation to the probability of making an error with the best informed guess about the next sample [51]. Three last comments lead to motivations of the tools and theories developed in the subsequent chapters.

- The original binary formulation of the LZ-complexity can be applied to time series by binary quantization of the sample values relative to their mean value, assigning ones and zeros to samples whose values are above and below the mean, respectively. Such quantization can be generalized into more levels, resulting in an alphabet that is richer then binary. The immediate question that come up in such a case is what are the correct or optimal quantization levels for such **symbolization** of the time series, which can be also a multi-dimensional sequence of feature vectors. Methods of clustering by *Vector Quantization* (VQ) could be used to make such symbolization.

- LZ detects segments in the sequence's past in a non-overlapping fashion by partitioning the past into consecutive repeating events. It is not clear that such representation of sequence history is the most efficient way to capture the history of the sequence. Factor oracle finds repetitions that are overlapping, thus capturing the past history in more efficient manner.

- In the next section we will describe an extension of a Factor Oracle for time series, called *Audio Oracle* (AO), that combines FO's suffix search with quantization and compression steps. This allows AO to be used as a complexity measure to perform analysis of audio information dynamics, which in turn is used to find the optimal symbolization of feature vectors by taking into account the predictive properties of the quantized sequence instead of quantization based on values of the individual features. AO is used also as a generative method to create novel sequences of audio features for audio-based machine improvisation.

Symbolization and Vector Quantization

Symbolization is the process of data quantization or clustering of nearby data points into classes, which reduces the fidelity of the representation but creates a more compact set of symbols.

Vector quantization is one technique for symbolization, by which a large set of vectors is divided into smaller groups, often called clusters. The goal of vector quantization is to reduce the amount of data needed to represent a set of vectors by representing them using a smaller number of "code vectors" that closely approximate the original vectors. Each of the original vectors can be represented by the code vector that is closest to it in terms of some distance metric. With such a codebook created, it is possible to compress the data by transmitting only the index of the selected codeword.

A few examples of vector quantization pertaining to music and audio data include

- Pulse Code Modulation, widely used for audio compression. In PCM, the audio signal is quantized into discrete values represented using binary codewords. Adaptive Differential Pulse Code Modulation is an extension of PCM which uses a predictor to estimate the value of the next sample, then quantizes the difference between the predicted and actual sample.
- Wavelet-based Vector Quantization, which uses wavelet transforms [52] to decompose an audio signal into a set of sub-bands, each representing a different frequency range. These sub-bands can then be vector-quantized so that a compressed signal can be transmitted.

- Perceptual Vector Quantization, a method that quantizes based on the human auditory system's sensitivities. This results in high listening quality in the compressed audio since, in principle, some types of noise and distortion can be removed or reduced without significantly affecting the perceived signal.

3.6.1 THE ADVANTAGE OF BEING LOSSY

Introducing the concept of lossy representation and lossy compression is important for music for several reasons:

- It allows better generalization and more novelty during the generation process by ignoring partial or insignificant differences in the data.
- It allows finding repetitions in time series and continuously valued data, such as sequences of audio features, by reducing the fidelity of the representation through quantization or clustering of nearby data points into classes (symbolization).
- Reducing the amount of symbols or size of the alphabet is essential when dealing with complex symbolic data, such as multiple voices in MIDI representation. For example, to capture harmonic or chordal structure it is essential to ignore differences in voicing and possibly some passing or embellishing notes.
- It allows control of improvisation algorithms from partial specification, such as abstract scenarios.
- Creating a low dimensional representation allows mapping between different types of musical data that is needed for guiding improvisation from another musical input.
- Lossy compression can be used to extract features from music and can be used for representation learning.

The theory of lossy compression was formulated by Shannon in terms of Rate-Distortion. Rate distortion is measured in terms of mutual information $I(x, z)$ between a signal X and its compressed version Z, where a loss or distortion $d(x, z)$ occurs during the encoding process. This distortion allows transmission at rates that are lower then the lossless compression limit $H(x)$ of the signal entropy. It is intuitive that the two factors, information $I(x, z)$ and distortion $d(x, z)$ are at odds with each other. For example, a low resolution image or low sampling rate audio require less bits to encode than their full resolution version. What is interesting about the rate distortion theory is that it provides theoretical lower bounds for the rate of information transmission, given by $I(x, z)$, under the constraint that the distortion between the two signals $d(x, z)$ does not exceed a certain threshold.

An early example of applying lossy representation to sequence modeling is a VMM structure called Prediction Suffix Tree (PST) that was described earlier. The uderlying information theoretical framework in the PST approach is that of lossy compression, a topic which we will return to in the section on Rate-Distortion theory. It should be noted that both IP and PST build tree structures in the learning stage, where finding the best suffix consists of walking the tree from the root to the node labeled by that suffix. PST, which was originally designed for classification purposes, has the advantage of better collecting statistical information from shorter strings, with a tradeoff of deliberately throwing away some of the original sub-strings during the analysis process in order for it to maintain a compact representation. Another significant advantage of PST is aggregation of suffix statistics as a sliding window, thus obtaining more statistics for short sequences compared to incremental parsing approach that skips shorter sub-sequences in a previously recognized suffix. A possible disadvantage of PST is that partial retention of original data through lossy representation introduces more false notes into the generation procedure. Lartillot, Dubnov, et al. have carried experiments on using IP for music classification and music generation [53] [54] [55]. The pros and cons of these two approaches led to adoption of a different string matching approach, based on the Factor Oracle (FO) string searching algorithm, that will be described in the next section. FO effectively provided an indexing structure built on top of the original music sequence, pointing to its repetition points as a graph of suffix links. This allows an efficient re-combination of existing patterns for improvisation. From information theoretical perspective, this type of models belongs to family of lossless compression algorithms. The lossy version of the suffix links construction procedure, called Variable Markov Oracle (VMO), will be introduced in the next chapter. Finally, we will come back to the idea of lossy coding in the last chapter "Noisy thoughts...", when we discuss lossy encoding view of generative models using the so-called Evidence Lower Bound (ELBO) approximation. This approximate partial representation is linked to the broader music-theoretic idea of music analysis that finds a layer of background reduced representations, from which foreground music structure emerges. Such reduction step might be essential for revealing deeper musical structures and finding relations between voices on the abstract background layer.

3.6.1.1   Rate Distortion and Human Cognition

In psychology, ratedistortion theory was suggested as a principled mathematical framework for incorporating limits on the capabilities of the cognitive system. This entails reformulating the goal of perception from tasks related to storage, or reproduction of afferent signals, to task of minimizing some survival-related cost function [56]. The distinction of the rate distortion approach from other neural information processing theories, such as an efficient coding hypothesis [57] is that the costs and constraints are imposed not just by the constraints on the internal neural architecture but also by the goals of the organism and the structure of the external environment. For organisms it may be more important to be "good" than "efficient", where good means solving an important problem that exists in the environment. For example, rate distortion is used to explain the results of an absolute identification experiment where subjects are asked to respond with his or her best guess regarding the identity of the stimulus from a previously shown set of lines of varying length, or tones of varying frequency or loudness. The rate-distortion method showed that participants implicit goals in the experiment were not to identify each example precisely, but rather to select a broader response category that is as close as possible to the correct response. What is relevant in this approach for our purposes is that it shows that acts of exact memorization of musical materials (themes, phrases, or chords), without being able to group them into common categories, will not serve well the purposes of having a good music "behavior". For the purpose of music generation, lossy or partial representation of musical signal might be actually a desirable property, as it encourages creativity and allows producing different levels of music anticipation and surprise. By discarding irrelevant details of the musical surface, the intermediate latent encoding z becomes more susceptible to generating novel materials, while still maintaining some level of agreement with deeper or hidden aspects of the musical structure or style. Since music is in constant flux and variation, the development of music composition requires balancing between sense of coherence or structural unity and the sense of novelty and variety. Accordingly, viewing creativity as "useful novelty", the rate distortion framework offers a possible principled approach to such a problem.

It should be noted that in the latent space representation, the distortion is measured when the signal is decoded back into the same domain as the original observation. It should also be noted that the distortion, or error resulting from the encoding-bottleneck-decoding process does not have to be measured necessarily in terms of actual data errors, but rather as a statistical error of producing or decoding signals resembling the true statistics of the source data. Thus, choice of the distortion measure is important for finding a compressed representation that is right for the task at hand, shifting the burden from the problem of modeling and parameter estimation, to one of formulating the trade-off between representation complexity (encoding) and reconstruction error (decoding). In later sections we will be looking for the most compact representation of past musical data that results in the best prediction of its future. This generalization is motivated by the Bayesian brain theory that includes predictive coding as one of the goals of an organism trying to optimize its behavior. We mentioned these concepts earlier in the chapter about noise as the driving force in music. Moreover, the trade-off between complexity of representation and prediction error can be regarded as free energy minimization, an approach that brought broad inspiration to brain theories [58] that explain the learning process as an approximation of the world through generative models, which in the case of music can generalize existing musical styles or imagine novel possibilities for music creation. We will turn to these points in later sections on variational encoding.

3.7 EXERCISES

1. (a) For a biased coin with probability $P(head) = p$ and $P(tail) = 1 - p$, show that maximal entropy is achieved when the coin is fair.

    Hint: Write the expression of binary entropy as a function of p and find its maximum.

    (b) Plot $H(p)$ as a function of p, where p takes values from 0 to 1.

Figure 3.7   Excerpt for Exercise 2: LZ incremental parsing.

2. Consider the excerpt shown in Figure 3.7.
   (a) Ignoring rhythm, apply the Incremental Parsing algorithm by hand to the
       sequence of pitches to generate the motif dictionary. You may also ignore
       octave for this problem (e.g., G4 and G5 can both be given the same label
       "G").

   (b) Draw this motif dictionary as a tree.

Additional questions and programming exercises are found in the **Markov
Chain and LZify** notebook at `https://github.com/deep-and-shallow/`
`notebooks`.

4 Understanding and (Re)Creating Sound

Sound is produced by various physical phenomena, through human and animal vocalization, and later on in history, through man-made musical instruments, industrial machines, and most recently electronics. From the late nineteenth century, sound capturing devices, with the most well-known Thomas Edison's phonograph, began a new era of audio recording. This allowed inclusion of a novel set of sounds into the palette of musical materials. Electronic sound synthesis, sampling, and today generative neural methods of sound production offer a constantly expanding vocabulary of sonic possibilities. Understanding and creating sounds is one of the essential knowledge elements required for music. This chapter deals with the way audio signals are processed by a computer.

4.1 INTRODUCTION TO DIGITAL SIGNAL PROCESSING

In this section we describe the basic concepts of digital signals and system, focusing on the following concepts:

- The *sampling theorem*, which assures that a continuous physical signal can be fully represented by its digital version. This includes concepts of aliasing and conversion between analog and digital signals.
- *Linear filtering of signals*, which requires understanding of the concepts of *convolution* and *frequency response*.
- *Discrete Fourier Transform (DFT)* as a method of changing the representation from sampled time domain to a complex amplitude and phase vector. Understanding concepts of frequency resolution and what happens to frequencies that fall between the discrete frequencies of the DFT is important when doing frequency analysis of audio.
- Implementation of two basic types of filters as sum of forward delays and gains versus auto-regressive delay loops is presented in the context of phase cancellations and resonances.
- An extension of the DFT called *Z-transform* is presented as a way of representing forward and auto-regressive (AR) filters in the frequency or Z-domain. This allows understanding the filtering convolution operation as a multiplication in the Z-domain, and vice versa, that is, multiplication in time as convolution in Z-domain.
- The Z-transform will be further applied for modeling filters as fraction of polynomials (rational polynomials in Z-domain), a concept that will be essential for understanding all-pole filter models of vocal production as described in the linear prediction modeling.

DOI: 10.1201/9781003240198-4

4.1.1 SAMPLING

In this section we explain the important and fundamental Nyquist theorem that determines the conditions for sampling a continuous signal into a discrete time representation. This transition from analog to digital is essential for processing audio signals in the computer. Such transition is not evident since capturing only specific occurrences of the waveform in time assumes that in the in-between intervals the signals behave smoothly enough to be eventually recreated by some mathematical smoothing or interpolation method. What Nyquist did was to determine the conditions and the type of ideal interpolation that allow reconstruction of a continuous signal in time from its samples at discrete time intervals. Moreover, storing the samples in computer memory usually requires a certain precision of representing the value of the waveform at the sampling point. Since computers use finite precision, such amplitudes necessarily are represented only up to a certain fidelity. This process, known as quantization, is also important for quality of audio, but we will not discuss this in the book. There are variety of books on audio engineering that describe such phenomena and methods of reducing the artifacts of finite precision representation. We would like only to mention, as a reality-check example, that CDs are recorded at a 44,100 Hz sampling rate and 16-bit quantization. The 44,100 sampling affects the frequency contents, and the 16-bit quantization affects the dynamic range, or so-called quantization-to-signal noise. We will focus on the frequency content aspect since it is critical for understanding the spectral analysis methods that will be central to many of the following applications.

Nyquist Sampling Theorem

A bandlimited continuous-time signal can be sampled and perfectly reconstructed from its samples if the waveform is sampled over twice as fast as its highest frequency component.

The Nyquist Limit (f_{max}) defines the highest frequency component that can be accurately represented by samples collected at Nyquist frequency f_s:

$$f_{max} < \frac{f_s}{2}. \tag{4.1}$$

Conversely, the Nyquist Frequency can be thought of as the minimal requisite sampling rate to represent up to the Nyquist Limit:

$$f_s > 2f_{max}. \tag{4.2}$$

4.1.2 SPECTRAL ANALYSIS

Spectral analysis is a methods for translating a time signal into a different domain that we consider to be a frequency representation. The common method of doing this is the Fourier Transform, often implemented using a special algorithm called Fast Fourier Transform (FFT). The Fourier Transform transforms a signal from the time domain to the frequency domain.

$$x(t) \overset{\mathcal{F}}{\longleftrightarrow} X(f) \tag{4.3}$$

In the case of discrete-time signals (rather than continuous time), the Discrete Fourier Transform is employed to transform the signal to a frequency-bin representation.

$$x(n) \overset{\mathcal{DFT}}{\longleftrightarrow} X(k) \tag{4.4}$$

Moreover, due to randomness present in audio signals, the Fourier analysis might need to be carried over multiple adjacent frames and averaged, or applied to a signal's autocorrelation rather then the signal itself. Such averaging procedures better reveal the salient components in sound at the expense of losing the ability to precisely reconstruct the signal. Such statistical spectral analysis is known as *power spectrum*.

FFTs and the Power Spectrum are useful for measuring the frequency content of stationary signals (signals whose statistical properties do not change with time) or transient signals (signals of finite duration). FFTs reveal the frequency content of a signal over the entire time that the signal was acquired. Since in music the frequency contents change over time, you should either use FFTs for segments where you assume that the signal does not change (known as *stationary signal analysis*), or in cases where you need only the average energy at each frequency line, regardless of when that frequency appeared and disappeared.

When deciding whether to analyze a signal with FFT or Power Spectrum, the main difference between the two is that FFT captures the exact frequency details of a single frame or vector of sound samples, including the exact phases, while power spectrum averages over multiple frames to derive a stable estimate of the energy at different frequencies at the cost of losing phase information. Even though the FFT gives the exact phases, in many cases we choose to look at FFT amplitude only and disregard the phase. In such case special methods are required to recover the signal from amplitudes only, a topic that will be covered later in this chapter.

Most real-world frequency analysis instruments display only the positive half of the frequency spectrum because the spectrum of a real-world signal is symmetrical around DC[1]. This is demonstrated for a simple case of sinusoidal signal. In the complex Fourier representation, a cosine function can be recreated by combination of two complex phasors, one at a positive and one at a negative frequency with equal amplitude. We will explain about phasors more in detail below. For now it sufficed to think about it as an exponent with complex argument that is the frequency multiplied by time. This is written as

$$cos(\omega t) = \frac{e^{i\omega t} + e^{-i\omega t}}{2} \tag{4.5}$$

---

[1] You can think of DC as the zero point of the frequency x-axis.

In Fourier plot we would get two peaks, one at $+\omega$ and another at $-\omega$, respectively. For a sinusoidal waveform, the same math is repeated with phasor components shifted by $\frac{\pi}{2}$. So as long as we want to know what freqeuncies are present in the signal, and we do not care about the exact phase, knowing only the amplitudes of the frequency component on the positive axis is enough. If we need to reconstruct exactly the time signal from its frequencies, the phase of the positive and negative component are still required.

The frequency range and resolution on the x-axis of a spectrum plot of a discrete frequency analysis depend on the sampling rate and the number of points acquired; the Fourier transform can at most account for periods as large as the number of samples.

Here, we will talk through the technical basis for spectral analysis. Fourier proved that any periodic function can be decomposed into a sum of sine and cosine waves, which we call a Fourier series. We will begin from this understanding that Fourier Analysis is a means of decomposing a wave into such combinations. To simplify matters, let us first prove that any linear combination of sine and cosine waves can be expressed as a sine wave with a phase shift.

We seek to show that

$$A\cos t + B\sin t = C\sin t + \phi. \tag{4.6}$$

We can use the sine of a sum of angles expansion to re-write this equation as

$$A\cos t + B\sin t = C\sin\phi\cos t + C\cos\phi\sin t. \tag{4.7}$$

The coefficients for the $\cos t$ and $\sin t$ terms on right must match the coefficients on left; thus

$$A = C\sin\phi \tag{4.8}$$

and

$$B = C\cos\phi. \tag{4.9}$$

Accordingly,

$$C = \pm\sqrt{A^2 + B^2} \tag{4.10}$$

and

$$\phi = \arctan\frac{A}{B}. \tag{4.11}$$

So, for appropriate values of A and B, it is possible to generate sines of any phase, and any combination of signes and cosines and be reformulated as a sine with a phase shift.

As a means of maintaining information about both period and phase for any such wave, we next introduce the *complex phasor*:

$$e^{j\theta}, \tag{4.12}$$

and the associated identity

$$e^{j\theta} = \cos\theta + j\sin\theta, \tag{4.13}$$

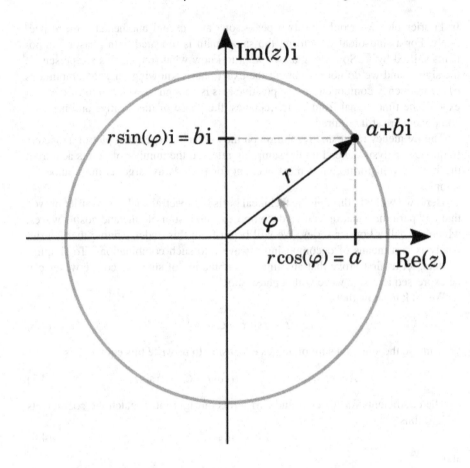

Figure 4.1 Visualization of a complex number $c = a + ib$. In the same way that we may use rectangular coordinates to reach a point in the Cartesian plane, we can parameterize a complex number using coefficients a and b. Analogous to polar notation, we can also parameterize this number with a modulus $|r|$ and angle ϕ. A phasor is a construct which represents any complex point constrained to the unit circle; as the value of ϕ increases, one can imagine such a vector rotating about the unit circle. The horizontal distance of the point represents the value $\cos \phi$, and the vertical distance gives the value of $\sin \phi$.

which can be readily noted by observing the Taylor Series expansion of sine, cosine, and the exponential function. You may recall that any complex number can be imagined as a point on the 2D plane defined by the real and complex axes, as shown in Figure 4.1; when these points are on the unit circle, their horizontal distance represents a cosine value, and their vertical distance represents a sine value for a corresponding angle drawn from the origin.

Because phasors are confined to the unit circle (fixed modulus of 1), their location at any moment can be parameterized by their angle, as shown in Figure 4.1. However, phasors are more effectively imagined as a spinning arrow, rotating about the unit circle at the rate of their frequency parameter.

Imagine we divide the unit circle into a fixed number of angular steps, N. For each step we take, we rotate an angle of $\frac{2\pi}{N}$ about the unit circle. For each of the N angular positions we reach, there is an associated sine value (on the imaginary axis) and an associated cosine value (on the real axis). We can represent these steps with powers of the phasor as:

$$W_N = e^{-j\frac{2\pi}{N}}. \tag{4.14}$$

With this concept in mind, we can formulate the Discrete Fourier Transform as a matrix of such phasors, where each row contains a phasor in motion at a different frequency, beginning at 0 and reaching a maximum of $\frac{(N-1)2\pi}{N}$ in evenly divided rate increases[2]. As an example, for $N = 8$, the first row represents a non-moving phasor (or, moving at a rate of $2\pi n$ rotations per time step, where n is any integer); the second row represents a phasor moving at $\frac{\pi}{8}$ cycles per time step; the third row represents a phasor moving at $\frac{2\pi}{8} = \frac{\pi}{4}$ cycles per time step; and so on, until the final row is moving almost as quickly as the first row (ironically, since the first row is "static") at a rate of $\frac{7\pi}{8}$ cycles per time step. This pattern is illustrated in Figure 4.2.

For this matrix, note also that each matrix entry can be written as

$$D_{N_{r,c}} = W_N^{(r-1)(c-1)}, \tag{4.15}$$

where r is the matrix row index and c is the matrix column index.

To recap, we have effectively created a matrix where each entry represents values of sine[3] and cosine at some point around the unit circle, following the specified pattern.

This matrix can be multiplied by a signal of length N to retrieve N complex values which represent the DFT of the signal.

To make sense of how such a matrix is able to extract a set of frequency components from the signal, consider that each row is in effect taking the cross-correlation of the input sequence with a complex phasor at the frequency specified by the row. Doing so creates the effect of a *matched filter* (essentially, a filter which searches for a match to a template signal) at that frequency. It is important to note that these frequency components are represented by N bins with overall resolution equal to the sample rate F_s divided by N; the size of the DFT matrix effectively limits how precisely the frequency components can be determined. Similarly, this transform results in $\frac{N}{2}$ possible amplitude and phase values.

---

[2]For an excellent video motivating the use of phasors and their application in the Fourier Transform, readers should visit Veritasium's YouTube video *The Remarkable Story Behind The Most Important Algorithm Of All Time*.

[3]Multiplied by i, that is, since each entry holds a complex number.

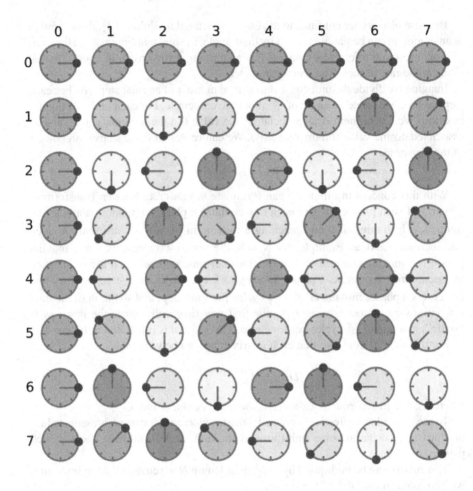

Figure 4.2 The rows of the DFT matrix represent the motion of a phasor at incrementally increasing frequencies, with each frequency $\frac{2\pi}{N}$ faster than the prior. Note that due to the formalism of representing the phasor with a negative frequency, each phasor is effectively spinning clockwise (the canonical "negative" direction).

To return from the frequency domain to the time domain, we can multiply the Fourier coefficients by the inverse of the DFT matrix.

Ideally reconstructing a signal with this method requires the amplitude and phase information (in other words, the complex values), because the phase tells us how each frequency component should align with the other frequency components, influencing where terms add or subtract in displacement. Yet, analysis often focuses only on magnitude components since these contain the information most relevant to the pitches we perceive (particularly helpful for understanding music). What we tend to lose when we neglect phase is information we use to perceive acoustic space, effects of multiple sound sources, and sound quality. Phase is certainly important, but not the driving component of many algorithms we will study. That said, we will examine ways that phase can be reconstructed when lost; these methods are not perfect, but suitable for restoring sound to an acceptable quality.

4.1.3 ANALOG-TO-DIGITAL CONVERSION AND ALIASING

Considering the transition from the analog waveform domain of continuous time and amplitude to the discrete representation in time, the sampling theorem provides the theoretical basis for doing such Analog-to-Digital conversion (ADC) and its reconstruction back to audio signal through Digital-to-Analog conversion (DAC). To understand how such conversion happens, we need to introduce notions of the continuous time Fourier Transform, which is not required for the rest of the book. Readers who are less concerned with the engineering aspects of analog signals might choose to skip this section. The important part for those using the digitized signal only is to note the aliasing effect that happens when the rules of sampling, namely the Nyquist sampling criteria, are violated. This is discussed toward the end of the section.

In one dimension, given a continuous signal $x_a(t)$, a sample can be considered to be a multiplication in time using a sequence of **delta functions** $\delta(t - n\tau)$ (that is, a delta function spaced every τ time units), to yield

$$x_s(t) = x_a(t)s(t), \tag{4.16}$$

where

$$s(t) = \sum_{n=-\infty}^{\infty} \delta(t - n\tau). \tag{4.17}$$

Delta Function

The delta function $\delta(x)$, also known as the Dirac delta, is an interesting function with frequent usage in signal processing. As described below, the delta function is an ideal sampling function; a signal's value at a particular time can be retrieved via multiplication with the delta function.

The delta function can be thought of as the limit of a narrow peak function that has unit area. To help imagine this, you can think of a square with area 1; imagine reducing the width of this square (well, now rectangle) and increasing the height accordingly such that the area of 1 is preserved. Of course, we must consider this function to be a "limit" since it is not possible to create area of 1 with 0 width or infinite height, but we can maintain this spike signal shape in a limit sense. This narrow peak is squeezed to be infinitesimally narrow; then, the multiplication operation with a narrow peak can be used to extract information from the continuous signal by accumulating (averaging) the energy of the signal over the short-time opening of the "extracting" period. We can describe this fundamental property with the equation:

$$\int_{-\infty}^{\infty} f(x)\delta(x-a)dx = f(a) \qquad (4.18)$$

We require an area of 1 to give the function meaning when used in integration, as the integral of a single "point" would be meaningless. This does, however, make it is hard to provide a clear graph describing the delta function. How does one draw a box approaching infinite height and near-zero width? We do our best in the figure below by using this arrow with height one, symbolic of the area contained under the unseeable curve.

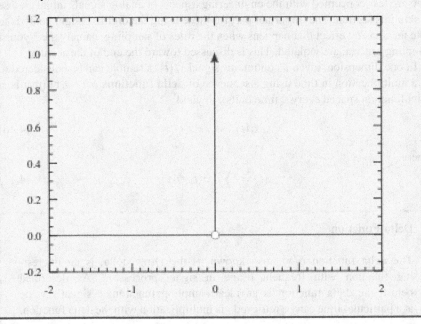

Using the Fourier transform we can obtain the frequency domain representation of these signals, thus

$$X_a(\omega) = \int_{-\infty}^{\infty} x_a(t)e^{-j\omega t}dt \qquad (4.19)$$

and

$$S(\omega) = \frac{2\pi}{T} \sum_{k=-\infty}^{\infty} \delta(\omega - k\omega_s), \qquad (4.20)$$

where $\omega_s = \frac{2\pi}{T}$ is the angular sampling frequency. We will next invoke the **convolution theorem** in continuous time that expresses a Fourier transform of a product of two time signals as a convolution of their respective Fourier transforms.

The Convolution Theorem

The convolution of two signals is itself a signal, defined as

$$(x * h)[n] = \sum_{m=-\infty}^{\infty} x[m]h[n-m].$$ (4.21)

The *convolution theorem* states that convolution in the time domain is equivalent to multiplication in the frequency domain, and vice versa. To provide a simple proof, let's assume that both the input x and the filter h are sequences of duration N, or vectors of size N. Then we can apply a DFT of size N to each vector as follows

$$\text{DFT}\{x * h\}[k] = \sum_{n=0}^{N-1} \left(\sum_{m=0}^{N-1} x[m] \cdot h[n-m] \right) e^{-i2\pi kn/N}$$

$$= \sum_{m=0}^{N-1} x[m] \left(\sum_{n=0}^{N-1} h[n-m] \cdot e^{-i2\pi kn/N} \right)$$

$$= \sum_{m=0}^{N-1} x[m] \cdot e^{-i2\pi km/N} \underbrace{\left(\sum_{n=0}^{N-1} h[n-m] \cdot e^{-i2\pi k(n-m)/N} \right)}_{\text{DFT}\{h\}[k] \quad \text{due to periodicity}}$$ (4.22)

$$= \underbrace{\left(\sum_{m=0}^{N-1} x[m] \cdot e^{-i2\pi km/N} \right)}_{\text{DFT}\{x\}[k]} (\text{DFT}\{h\}[k])$$

where the "due to periodicity" condition written below the brace on the third line implies that instead of a time limited vector $h[n]$ we use a periodic version where the filter coefficients are replicated periodically to the right and left of the interval 0 to N. This type of convolution is called "periodic convolution", which is required in order to deal with the fact that convolution operation between two sequences of size N results is a sequence of $2N - 1$ values. So in the case of DFT, the convolution theorem is valid for periodically extended versions of the original sequences. For Fourier Transform of infinitely long sequences or continuous signals the periodization trick is not required.

Similar relations can be shown to exist for a product of two sequences in time becoming convolution in frequency, which can be summarized as the following rules:

$$[x * h][n] \rightleftarrows X(f)H(f)$$ (4.23)

$$x[n]h[n] \rightleftarrows [X * H](f)$$ (4.24)

We need to be careful about the distinction between discrete and continuous time and frequency domains. For discrete time n, the DFT deals with frequencies f which are also discrete, but in the general case of Fourier Transform, f can be continuous and expressed via integral instead of a sum, and the length of x can be infinite.

$$\text{FT}\{x[n]\}[k] = X(f) = \sum_{n=-\infty}^{\infty} x[n] \cdot e^{-i2\pi f n}$$

(4.25)

$$x[n] = \int_0^1 X(f) \cdot e^{i2\pi f n} df$$

In this expression, we integrate from 0 to 1 because the frequency range is from negative Nyquist to Nyquist, or equivalently, from 0 to the sampling frequency (in this case, the summation of df from 0 to 1 implicitly representing this value).

Knowing these time-frequency convolution relationships is important for understanding of the aliasing effect. For example, it is important to consider that multiplication with delta functions in time results in replicates in frequency due to convolution in frequency domain, which we explore in the following box. Time-frequency convolution relationships will also come into play later in the chapter for source-filter modeling, where for instance in speech, the vocal tract filters amplify formant frequencies and shape the spectrum of a source sound originating from the vocal chords.

Covering continuous (integral Fourier relations between two continuous signals) and discrete time with continuous frequency transform relations is beyond the scope of this book. The readers are advised to consult some of the standard signal processing textbooks for detailed proofs[a]. In the book we focus on the Discrete Time and Discrete Frequency relations that are expressed via DFT and could most easily be understood as a change of basis in linear algebra. We find this interpretation especially useful since it carries with it a natural notion of basis functions, a concept we will elaborate on later when we talk about representation learning and dimensionality reduction.

---

[a]Interested readers are referred to the vast literature in signal processing, such as [59], [60], and [61].

Proof: A pulse train in frequency is a pulse train in time.

Sampling a signal can be thought of as multiplication by a pulse train at a given sample rate. This will, however, create replicates in the frequency domain since this multiplication in the time domain is equivalent to a convolution of the Fourier transformed signal with the Fourier transform of the pulse train, which is itself a pulse train (an idea we prove in this section).

Consider a function representing a pulse train

$$s(n) = \sum_{k=0}^{\infty} \delta(n - kT),\tag{4.26}$$

where T is the period of the pulse train (i.e., time in between spikes). For the purposes of our preliminary analysis, we consider a discrete length of the signal, stopping at an integer multiple of the period length (i.e., $\frac{L}{T} - 1$). Accordingly, our function can be written as a sum of complex exponentials as

$$s(n) = \frac{1}{T} \sum_{k=0}^{T-1} e^{\frac{j2\pi nk}{T}}.\tag{4.27}$$

To make clear the equivalence relationship between the Dirac delta form and the above complex exponential form, first consider values of n which are not at even spacings of period T (i.e., $n \neq kT$).
Re-writing the k as an outer exponent, we have

$$s(n) = \frac{1}{T} \sum_{k=0}^{T-1} e^{\frac{j2\pi n}{T}k},\tag{4.28}$$

and from the geometric series summation formula,

$$s(n) = \frac{1}{T} \frac{1 - e^{\frac{j2\pi n}{T}T}}{1 - e^{\frac{j2\pi n}{T}}}.\tag{4.29}$$

The numerator of this function reduces to $1 - 1 = 0$. So, the function is zero when off-period, and for the periodic values (i.e., $n = kT$), we have

$$s(n) = \frac{1}{T} \sum_{k=0}^{T-1} e^{\frac{j2\pi kT}{T}} = \frac{1}{T} \sum_{k=0}^{T-1} 1 = 1.\tag{4.30}$$

Thus, this sum of complex exponentials indeed represents a train of unit pulses.

Now, let's examine the Fourier transform of this function, without the above analysis. We assume the function can be written as a Fourier series, as

$$s(n) = \sum_{k=-\infty}^{\infty} c_k e^{\frac{j2\pi nk}{T}}, \tag{4.31}$$

and taking the Fourier transform of this gives

$$F(N) = \mathscr{F}\{\sum_{k=-\infty}^{\infty} c_k e^{\frac{j2\pi nk}{T}}\} = \sum_{k=-\infty}^{\infty} c_k \mathscr{F}\{e^{\frac{j2\pi nk}{T}}\} = 2\pi \sum_{k=-\infty}^{\infty} c_k \delta(N - kT). \tag{4.32}$$

In other words, the Fourier transform of a periodic signal is an impulse train, with ampliudes 2π times the Fourier coefficients of the signal.

In the exercises, you will show that the Fourier series coefficients for this pulse train are

$$c_k = \frac{1}{T}. \tag{4.33}$$

Thus, the Fourier transform of an impulse train is another impulse train.

Now, we will summarize the relationship between this mathematical artifact and the aliasing phenomenon. Sampling (multiplying a continuous-time signal with a train of Dirac delta functions in time domain) creates a discrete-time signal with a periodic spectrum. This periodic spectrum is a consequence of the convolution theorem, which states that multiplication in time domain corresponds to convolution in frequency domain. Specifically, the Fourier transform of a periodic train of Dirac delta functions is a periodic comb function in frequency domain. We see that this replication of the sampled signal's frequency spectrum will occur at multiples of the sampling frequency. This is the aliasing phenomenon.

When the sampling frequency is not high enough to capture the highest frequency component present in the signal, the replicas of the frequency spectrum in the frequency domain can overlap with the true original spectrum, and this is what results in an incorrect reconstruction of the signal (aliasing distortion).

We will talk about a discrete time convolution theorem later in the chapter when we talk about source-filter signal models. At this point we will simply invoke the theorem to give the following expression of the continuous sampled signal:

$$X_s(\omega) = \frac{1}{T} \sum_{k=-\infty}^{\infty} X_a(\omega - k\omega_s) \tag{4.34}$$

Figure 4.3 shows a graphical representation of the spectral effect of sampling and aliasing, by which the convolution theorem causes the spectrum of a sampled signal to be comprised of multiple replicated versions of the original signal's

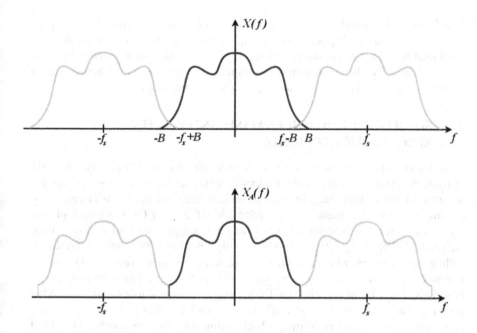

Figure 4.3 Demonstration of the aliasing effect. In the top panel in blue, we have $X(f)$ the continuous Fourier transform of some function. This function is sampled at some sample rate f_s. This results in the images shown in green, which overlap and add to the original transform in the discrete-time Fourier transform. However, consider that we may have had some other function, also sampled at f_s which has continuous Fourier transform $X_A(f)$ shown in blue in the lower panel. Both DTFTs are identical (when considering the sum action of the top panel), so we would refer to these DTFTs as *aliases*; that is, despite the original functions being distinct, the sampled sequences are identical. In effect, the audio of $x(t)$ and $x_A(t)$ would sound different, while the sampled versions of the audio taken at f_s would sound indistinguishable. The solution to avoid this aliasing is to increase f_s so that the green images no longer overlap with the blue portion of the transformed signal (in other words, satisfying the condition of Nyquist's sampling theorem and eliminating replica bleed-through into the originally band-limited region).

continuous-time spectrum. Nyquist's sampling theorem provides the conditions for sampling that would avoid aliasing – if a signal $x_a(t)$ is bandlimited with its spectrum $X_a(\omega) = 0$ for $|\omega| > \omega_a$, then there is no bleed-through of adjacent replicas of the spectrum of $x_a(t)$ into the original band-limited region. If this condition holds, then the original signal can be uniquely recovered by passing $x_s(t)$ through an ideal low-pass filter.

One should also note that aliasing might also occur when re-sampling a digital signal from one sampling rate to another. The easiest way to think about it is that the target re-sampling frequency should still withhold the Nyquist rule, so its analog signal equivalent should not have content that exceeds half of the new frequency. To assure that this indeed happens when changing sampling rate in the digital domain, the digital signal is low-passed prior to re-sampling. In most signal processing software packages, a dedicated resampling routine assures that low-pass filtering is done on the original signal prior to resampling to a lower sampling rate.

4.2 SHORT-TIME FOURIER ANALYSIS AND PERFECT RECONSTRUCTION (COLA)

Since the contents of audio signals change over time, we need to perform our DFT analysis on short segments where we can assume that the frequency contents are relatively stable or stationary. In order to do that, the usual approach in audio processing is to use a technique called overlap-add (OLA). For OLA, we multiply the signal with a window function $w(n)$, a function of length N defined as zero outside the window. *Windowing* effectively isolates only a portion of the whole audio signal, culling out the region where the window function is non-zero. Thus the windowing imposes the condition that any value outside length N is zero. There are multiple alternatives of how to cut out a portion from a long audio signal using a window. What matters for us is that when we sum all the windows back after processing the signal in frequency domain and converting it back to time, that the windows have so-called a "constant OLA property" or COLA:

$$\sum_{m=-\infty}^{\infty} w(n-mR) = 1. \qquad (4.35)$$

Equation 4.35 is the constant OLA equation, where R is called the step size. The reason we insist on COLA is that we want to make sure that cutting a long segment into shorter and usually overlapping segments is done in a way that does not lose or distort the signal, so if you sum those segments back, the effect of the window will be eliminated. The simplest way to satisfy COLA is simply to cut adjacent non-overlapping frames, which in signal processing language is called rectangular non-overlapping window. The problem with such analysis is that the rectangular window creates artifacts in the FFT output (an effect known as side-lobes of the windowing function). Without going into the theory of window function properties for Fourier analysis, we would only say that tempered windows that slowly fade-in and fade-out each segment are preferable for frequency analysis. In order for a sequence of such windows to satisfy COLA, one has to be careful about the selection of the windowing function and placement of subsequent windows so that a fade-out of previous segment sums with the fade-in of the next segment exactly to one. The Figure 4.4 demonstrates the effect of COLA for a windowing function.

If the COLA condition is not satisfied, the imperfect summation of sequence of windows is usually perceived as a buzz or modulation that happens at the window shift rate.

Applying Fourier Analysis to short-time windowed segments is the basis of so-called Short-Time Fourier Transform (STFT). Thus instead of running DFT on the

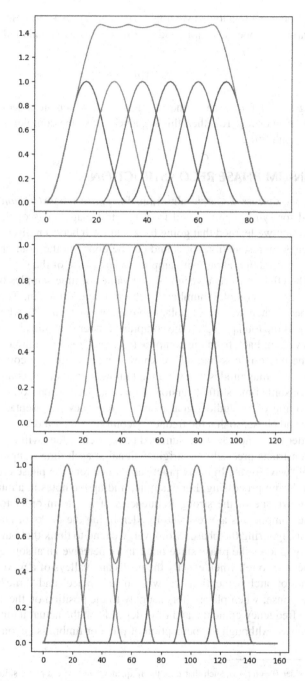

Figure 4.4   The constituent bell-shaped curves in the above plots represent Hann windows of length 33, taken at hop lengths of 11, 16, and 22 from top to bottom. The summation of these windows is provided in pink. Based on these figures, what percentage overlap of the Hann window satisfies COLA?

full signal $x(n)$, we use a windowed version $x_m(n) = w(n)x(n+mR)$. Because of the constant overlap-add property, simply adding the windowed signals will return the original signal

$$\sum_{m=-\infty}^{\infty} w(n-mR)x(n) = x(n). \qquad (4.36)$$

By applying the DFT to each of the M signals x_m, we create a sequence of M spectral domain signals X_m. Together, this sequence forms the complex spectrogram of the signal through time.

4.3 GRIFFIN-LIM PHASE RECONSTRUCTION

In this section we discuss a classic algorithm for *phase reconstruction*, a process that is required for synthesizing sound from spectral magnitudes of the STFT. In the previous section we learned that going back and forth between discrete time and discrete frequency representations of sound can be done via the Fourier transform, which contains information about both amplitude and phase of the signal frequency constituents. The DFT converts a vector of real values of time samples of the audio signal into a vector of complex numbers in the frequency domain. This vector of complex numbers, when written in polar representation as $Ae^{-j\theta}$, where A is the amplitude and θ is the total phase[4] of the complex number that allows reconstruction of the exact waveform back from the complex freqeuncy representation.

But when the phase is missing, all we know is what frequency components are present with specific magnitudes, but we do not know if each of the components is a sine, a cosine, or some time-shifted version of that oscillator or phasor. Accordingly, exact reconstruction of an audio signal from its frequency representation requires both amplitude and phase, so that the frequency components would be shifted in time correctly in order that when they are summed back, their values will be combine in a way that reconstructs precisely the original signal at each time sample, reproducing the original "waveform". In many practical applications the phase component is ignored or lost during processing. For example, finding the notes in a music recording requires knowledge of the strong frequencies of a note in order to determine its pitch. These components are revealed by identifying the peaks of amplitudes in Fourier Analysis, ignoring the phase. Moreover, we tend to think that our perception of sound largely ignores the phase since one cannot perceive an absolute phase of a waveform to be able to tell when exactly the peaks and valleys of a waveform occur in time. Theories of pitch perception deal with so call "place" and "time" theories of the cochlear response, when place refers roughly to the position on the cochlea that depends on the frequency contents, and time depends on the actual temporal details of the sound waves. Although the perception of pitch or timbre is beyond the scope

---

[4]We often consider $\theta = \omega t + \phi$, such that ω is the frequency and ϕ is the phase shift. This is why we call *theta* a total phase. Such notation is important when we talk about instantaneous phase at specific moment in time.

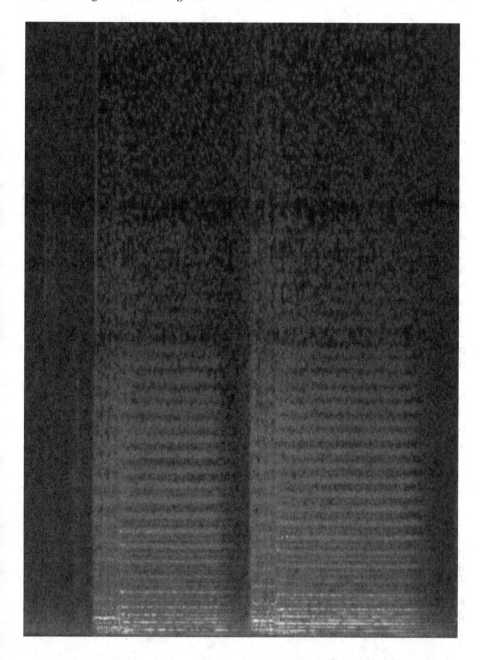

Figure 4.5 This is the resulting *spectrogram* from applying the STFT to the opening bars of Beethoven's fifth. The DFT is applied to short windowed segments of the audio, and the resulting frequency domain representations are concatenated. The x-axis represents time, and the y-axis represents frequency values present in the signal. Brighter color intensity indicates a stronger contribution of the associated frequency bin to the signal. Can you identify the well-known melodic and rhythmic patterns from the opening phrase?

of this book, we mention this to bring the awareness to the fact that the phase information is not totally lost during our perception – when a sound is transformed to firings of the inner ear hair, we "know" what hair cells fire (their place or frequency they detected), and the timing of the firing. So some perception of phase does comes through, such as in the case of various sound effects that affect the relative phases of the frequency components, such as phase coupling that occurs dues to non-linear aspects of sound production, or on the contrary, phase randomization that happens in reverberating environments, and more. So we do perceive phase effect in some indirect but possibly significant way, but for the purpose of our discussion here we consider practical applications where only the amplitude of frequency components is preserved and the waveform needs to be somehow reconstructed from partial information.

More specifically, considering STFT representation we maintain the magnitude-only part, denoted as STFTM. Inverting STFTM via the inverse Fourier transform operation is mathematically impossible, so we could in principle add random phases to STFTM to turn it into a complex STFT. Doing that will not work since the effect of inconsistent phases across adjacent STFT frames in time will result in reproducing sound frames with discontinuities that are perceived as clicks or noises. This effectively also creates spurious frequencies into the resulting sound waveform, so in this case the STFTM is not correctly preserved. The idea of trying to find a sequence of phase values that would sound smooth and preserve the desired STFTM is at the core of the Griffin-Lim Algorithm (GLA) [62].

GLA is a method for phase reconstruction that tries to create smooth waveforms by forcing a consistency across spectrogram windows or inter-bins dependency in time. This is done by iterating two projections, that upon convergence, recover a complex-valued spectrogram that is consistent in the sense that it maintains the given amplitude $\mathbf{A}$, and has a smooth phase transition across the bins in time. This is accomplished by the following alternative projection procedure, where $\mathbf{X}$ is a complex-valued spectrogram updated through the iteration:

$$\mathbf{X}^{[m+1]} = P_{\mathscr{C}}\left(P_{\mathscr{A}}\left(\mathbf{X}^{[m]}\right)\right) \tag{4.37}$$

In the above routine, $P_{\mathscr{C}}(\cdot) = \mathbf{STFT}(\mathbf{iSTFT}(\cdot))$ and $P_{\mathscr{A}}(\mathbf{X}) = \mathbf{A} \odot \mathbf{X} \oslash |\mathbf{X}|$ are projection operations achieved by using STFT and inverse STFT (iSTFT), and $\mathscr{A}$ is the set of spectrograms whose amplitude is the same as the given STFTM. $\odot$ and $\oslash$ are element-wise multiplication and division, respectively, and division by zero is replaced by zero. The reason we use the terms "set" and "projection" is that in the original paper the author prove the convergence of the method through a method called "projection onto convex sets".

Let us explain the math above:

What $P_{\mathscr{A}}(\mathbf{X})$ does is take an STFTM $\mathscr{A}$ and add to it a phase that is derived using an $\mathbf{X} \oslash |\mathbf{X}|$ operation. Dividing complex STFT values $\mathbf{X}$ element-wise by their magnitudes $|\mathbf{X}|$ gives a matrix of phase values. Then it is multiplied element-wise by $\mathscr{A}$ to make it into a possible STFT with desired STFTM. Mathematically, we can think of this as a projection of any $\mathbf{X}$ into a set of STFTs with amplitudes $\mathscr{A}$ and phases from $\mathbf{X}$. This STFT is converted to time using the iSTFT, and then back to frequency using a repeated STFT operation, as shown by $P_{\mathscr{C}}(\cdot)$. Because of signal discontinuities across bins, this operation will "throw us out" of the set of desired STFTM values. One should note that STFTM with amplitudes $\mathscr{A}$ is a convex set since any linear combination of such spectrograms will be still an STFTM with same amplitudes $\mathscr{A}$. Eventually GLA is shown to solve in iterative manner the following optimization problem:

$$\min_{\mathbf{X}} ||\mathbf{X} - P_{\mathscr{C}}(\mathbf{X})||^2_{\text{Fro}} \text{ s.t. } \mathbf{X} \in \mathscr{A}, \tag{4.38}$$

where $||||_{\text{Fro}}$ is the Frobenius norm. This equation minimizes the square error between spectrograms with the required STFTM and spectrograms undergoing the STFT and iSTFT opeartion sequence, i.e. resynthesis into time and spectral analysis. This is achieved by reducing the inconsistent frequency components under the constraint on amplitude which must be equal to the given STFTM.

We will not prove here the convergence of the method (for this, the reader is referred to the original paper), but for the mathematically inclined we will provide some intuition by saying the GLA is designed as as a method of alternate projections.

For each target STFTM frame at time mS and frequency ω, $Y(mS, \omega)$, there are multiple complex STFT values with different phases that match that magnitude, represented by the circle of a radius that matches the desired magnitude and circle showing all possible angles of the phase. The GLA method is designed so that the distance between the STFT $X(ms, \omega)$ and the target $Y(mS, \omega)$ is reduced at each iteration. So while the complex STFT at intermediate steps reside outside of the circle, the projection onto the circle in each step keeps the intermediate phase (represented by a line dropping from the complex STFT frame point to the origin), and then that point in the complex plane representing the intermediate STFT at the next step lands closer and closer to the circle, eventually stopping at some phase with the right magnitude.

GLA is widely utilized because of its simplicity, but it often involves many iterations until it converges to the desired STFTM spectrogram with high enough reconstruction quality. This can be improved if additional characteristics of the target signal are not taken into account in addition to the consistency requirement. Many of the neural synthesis methods actually try to exploit such additional characteristic to speed up or improve the quality of the resynthesis if GLA cannot be used within time or processing constraints of the synthesis (vocoding) application. The drawback of such neural methods is that the additional characteristics that are learned by neural networks have to be specific to the type of sound we want to resynthesize, such as speech or music played by single musical instrument. It is very hard to define or find strong characteristics for general sounds or complex multi-instrumental music. Finding neural resynthesis that can be general enough to vocode any sound is still an open problem.

4.3.1 MODEL-BASED AND NEURAL RESYNTHESIS FROM SPECTRAL INFORMATION

For the sake of completeness, we will mention briefly some of the current SOTA methods for spectrogram inversion using neural models. The simplest way to incorporate knowledge into spectrogram inversion is by assuming a certain model of sound production, such as the source-filter model of speech. We will discuss this in the next section since it provides deeper intuition into the process of sound production, specifically for the human voice. The drawback of such human engineering DSP sound synthesis it that often such models are over-simplified and produce synthetic or lower-quality voice. Much more complicated synthesis models can be learned using neural networks. We will not discuss the details and the theory of neural networks until later in the book, so the purpose of this survey is to provide the context and a larger picture of why neural networks might be useful for the same problem that GLA solves. Here the methods roughly divide into two: waveform synthesis methods that operate on the sound samples directly conditioned on STFTM, and spectral models where the STFTM is fed as an input to a network that is trained to reconstruct the sound waveform from spectral information. Let us summarize them briefly as follows:

- Waveform methods such as Wavenet [63] and sampleRNN [64] use autoregressive neural network structures that predict the next sample from the previous block of samples, often in a hierarchical or multi-resolution manner. These methods have produced SOTA results in text-to-speech synthesis, but less so for music. Unfortunately, their inference is slow and they are usually not suited for real-time applications.
- Spectral inversion models using neural networks are usually based on generative models such as VAE or GAN (the theory of such networks will be covered later in the book).

Other advances in synthesis deserving mention that will not be covered in the book include invertible transformations operating on audio, based on a method of Normalizing Flows such as WaveGlow [65], and diffusion method such as Wave-Grad [66] that gradually reconstruct the signal from a noise sample using multiple refinement steps. These method are much faster then Wavenet but require large memory and computing power. One should note the distinction between neural models for generating novel spectral data versus neural models for inversion from spectrum to waveform. Neural audio synthesis often comprises two steps:

1. generation of new spectrum, known as synthesis, and
2. spectrum to waveform inversion step, known as vocoding.

In some cases, such as SpecGAN [67], the neural networks are only used for generating new spectral information but do not invert the spectrogram itself, but rather rely on GLA to do the spectrum to waveform inversion.

4.4   FILTERS AND TRANSFORMS

The basic systems that we encounter in audio processing, such as audio equalizers, frequency filters or later on, models of human vocal tract production, exhibit the properties of linearity and shift invariance, referred to as linear time-invariant (LTI) systems. A shift-invariant system is one where a shift or delay in time of the input signal causes a corresponding shift in the output signal. So if the response of a system to an input $x[n]$ is $y[n]$, then the response to an input $x[n - \tau]$ is $y[n - \tau]$. We should note that we are dealing with discrete time, so the shift is an integer number.

A system is called *linear* if a weighted sum of two inputs results in the same weighted some of the outputs. More precisely, the system L is linear if for input-output pairs $y_0 = L(x_0), y_1 = L(x_1)$

- The response to $x_0[n] + x_1[n]$ is $y_0[n] + y_1[n]$ (additivity), and
- The response to scaling $x[n]$ by a is same scaling of the output $ay[n] = L(ax[n])$, where a is any complex constant.

An important concept in analysis of linear systems is the impulse response. If $x[n]$ is a unit impulse, $\delta[n]$, the impulse response $h[n]$ is the output sequence resulting from such unit impulse input. Acoustically, one might thing about measuring an impulse response of a room by clapping or shooting a cannon in a large hall. The echoes of such initial explosion, bouncing back and forth between the walls, comprises the impulse response. It can be shown that shift invariance and linearity properties of LTI systems lead to a mathematical definition of the filter operation as a convolution of the input $x[n]$ with its impulse response $h[n]$

$$y[n] = \sum_{k=-\infty}^{\infty} x[k]h[n - k] = \sum_{k=-\infty}^{\infty} x[n - k]h[k] \qquad (4.39)$$

which is also notated as $y[n] = x[n] * h[n]$.

In practice, a filter implementation of a convolution in time can be done in two manners. The direct way is by creating a set of delays and amplifications, so that a signal input delayed by k time steps will be multiplied with a factor $h[k]$, and all of the delayed and scaled replicas of the signal will be summed together to produce the output $y[n]$. This is exactly the process of bouncing echoes in our concert hall clapping experiment, but this time applied to any musical signal played in that hall.

The second implementation of linear filters is by producing a feedback effect. In such case, the delays and sums are fed from the output back to the input. Such feedback operation has a clear engineering implementation, but in terms of its impulse response, the decay can be infinitely long, or even oscillating. Such feedback systems are said to have infinite impulse response (IIR), as compared to the usual forward filters with finite convolution length known as finite impulse response (FIR).

In reality, both forward and feedback loops exist in linear filters, usually represented as two sets of coefficients. A diagram of a filter in Figure 4.6 shows the forward and backward components, with gains b_i and b_i matching to the delayed steps of i time steps of the input and the output feedback branches, respectively.

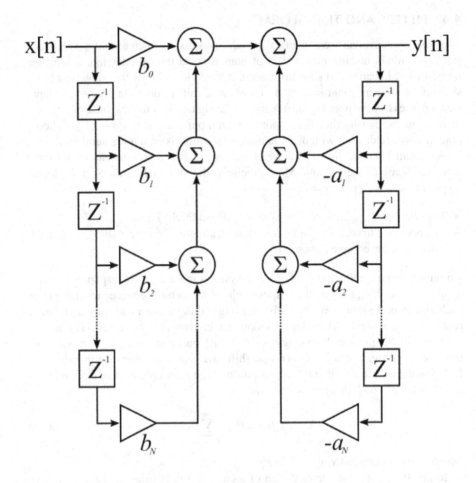

Figure 4.6 Direct representation of IIR. When only the forward branch is present, the filter becomes FIR.

4.4.1 FREQUENCY RESPONSE OF LINEAR FILTERS

To understand the effect of convolution on the frequency contents of the signal, one may perform DFT analysis of the input and output. It appears that by knowing the DFT properties of the impulse response, one can predict or calculate the frequency effect of the filtering operation directly in the frequency domain, without performing the convolution in time. Such relations, known as the convolution theorem, are also used sometimes to replace convolutions with frequency multiplications using efficient Fourier analysis algorithms such as the FFT. To the purpose of generality, and since such analysis is useful for later chapters when talking about speech formants in terms of filter poles and zeros, we will use a more general transformation than the DFT called the *Z-transform*. In its simplest form, one might think about the

Z-transform as a way to represent a sequence $\mathbf{a} = [a_0, a_1, ..., a_n]$ as a polynomial in the complex domain

$$Z(\mathbf{a}) = a_0 + a_1 z^{-1} + a_2 z^{-2} + .., + a_n z^{-n}. \tag{4.40}$$

One should note that if z is replaced with a complex exponent $e^{j2\pi\omega}$, we get an expression for the Fourier component at frequency ω. Thus, the Z-transform can be thought of as a generalization of the Fourier transform to points outside of the unit circle since the complex phasor points lie on a unit circle at an angle that corresponds to the frequency ω. Using the Z-Transform, and applying it to a forward and feedback linear system with coefficients $a[n]$ and $b[n]$ respectively, one gets the transfer function of a discrete-time linear system as

$$H(z) = \frac{a_0 + a_1 z^{-1} + a_2 z^{-2} + ... + a_M z^{-M}}{b_0 + b_1 z^{-1} + b_2 z^{-2} + ... + b_N z^{-N}} \tag{4.41}$$

Using the relation $x[n-k] \Longleftrightarrow z^{-k}X(z)$, this is the transfer function of a general filter written in terms of its forward and feedback coefficients as a linear difference equation, with $b_0 = 1$ and $y[n] = a_0 x[n] + a_1 x[n-1] + a_2 x[n-2] + ... + a_M x[n-M] - b_1 y[n-1] - b_2 y[n-2] - ... - b_N y[n-N]$, where one should note that the a_n coefficients multiply delayed versions of the input $x[n]$, and the b_n coefficients multiply the delayed version of the output $y[n]$, with the negative sign resulting from the convention of writing $y[n]$ part to the left side of the equal sign and the $x[n]$ part on the right. Moving the past of $y[n]$ to the right side makes the feedback coefficients negative.

Such analysis allows representation of the effect of filtering as an operation in the complex Z plane. The roots of the numerator are points in the Z-plane where the transfer function is zero, thus eliminating the signal at the output. Points where the denominator is zero are called poles, and these correspond to infinite or unstable filter output. Since in practice we are looking at the effect of the filter in terms of frequencies, one can evaluate the effect on the unit circle by comparing the distances to poles and zeros. Moreover, it is important that for linear *causal* systems that use past samples to predict the next step, the poles will need to reside inside the unit circle. We will not prove these relations in detail since that comprises a whole course in signal processing that is beyond the scope of the book.

4.4.2 POLE-ZERO PLOTS

If you liked thinking about filters as ratios of polynomials in the complex Z-plane, then the graphic representation of the top and bottom roots, the zeros and poles respectively, comes quite handy. Not only is this a graphical representation of the so-called rational transfer function[5], but it also provides some intuition as to the role of zeros and poles in forming the overall spectral shape or spectral response of the filter.

---

[5] rational from the word ratio, not rational as logical or reasonable.

The first observation is the angle to frequency mapping. Moving from angle zero to $/pi$ corresponds to scanning the whole frequency range from zero to Nyquist. The pole-zero plot is symmetric, and so is the shape emerging from moving past pi, basically tracing the similar amplitude (not phase though) in the negative frequencies or frequencies above Nyquist. Another immediate observation is what happens if we move the poles or zeros closer to the unit circle. Moving the poles creates a peak or resonance at the frequency corresponding to the angle of the pole. When the pole "hits" the unit circle, the resonance becomes infinite, and going outside the unit circle is forbidden (this makes the filter unstable). The same operation on zeros has the opposite effect: zeros cause dips in frequency, and when a pole falls on the unit circle, the dip becomes a notch (i.e., a dip that passes zero energy at that frequency). You can imagine now how the zero-pole plot can be useful for filter design. It is not a simple task to actually design the optimal filter just by adding or subtracting and moving around the poles and zeros, but it definitely gives a sense to their roles in shaping the spectrum. One must be also reminded that going back and forth between the filter coefficients and the roots is a known algebraic operation. For any polynomial we can represent it as a summation of powers or as a product of root expressions, such as the left and right sides of

$$x^2 - 3x + 2 = (x-1)(x-2) . \tag{4.42}$$

Packages such as scipy.signal have dedicated functions that help with going between pole-zero and filter coefficient representation.

An example of a pole-zero plot for a simple filter is shown in Figure 4.7.

4.5   VOICE AS A SOURCE-FILTER MODEL

In this section we will combine two important and basic notions that we introduced so far independently of each other. One is the filtering theory that we will use for modeling in terms of a "source-filter" acoustic model. The second is the idea of generative modeling that deals with production of novel signals by inputting random noise or some other excitation signal into a system.

The system, which in our case is a linear filter, operates as a function that maps input to output, but since we are dealing with time signals, the mapping is not instantaneous, but rather the filter uses delays and feedback loops to take into account multiple samples of the input signal and its own previous output to produce the next output sample.

When the input has no structure, or only a partial structure such as voiced or unvoiced signal of a vocal tract in the case of speech, the role of the system is to shape the input into a more meaningful output signal, such as sounds of different human vowels.

The application that we will consider here is vocal tract modeling that is applicable to speech and singing synthesis. Historically, an early speech synthesis system called Voder, invented by Homer Dudley, was considered as a curiosity that was presented by Bell Labs in the 1939 New York World Fair. The Voder comprised of ten band-pass filters and an excitation signal generated that had variable pitch or noise

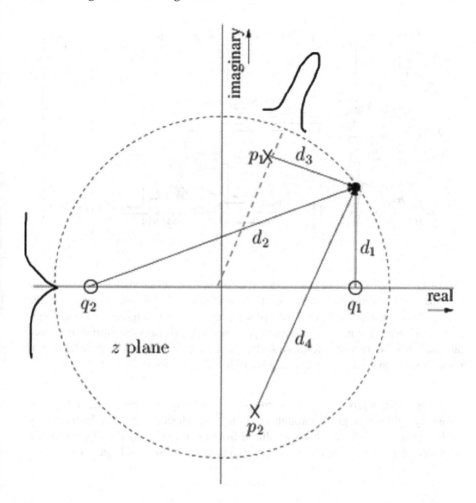

Figure 4.7 Pole-Zeros plot showing a simple example with two conjugate poles marked by crosses "x" and two zeros marked as "o". At any point on the unit circle, the amplitude response of the filter can be visually computed as a ratio of a nominator comprising of a product of distances to zeros, d_1 and d_2 in this case, divided by a denominator that is the product of the distances to zeros, d_3 and d_4, giving a responds of $\frac{d_1 d_2}{d_3 d_4}$ at the black point showing on the unit circle. Digital frequencies (points on the unit circle at appropriate angles) that are close to poles produce peaks and those close to zeros produce notches.

selection. The filters and the excitation were controlled by a human operator, a sort of a "typist" who controlled with their fingers the spectral keys and the pitch/noise excitation by pressing a foot pedal. A picture of the Voder is seen in Figure 4.8.

An alternative method for translating spectral information to sound was Haskins Laboratories' "Pattern Playback" machine. This early talking machine comprised of

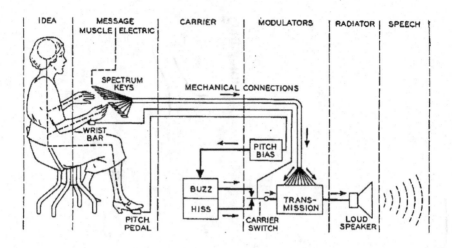

Figure 4.8 Schematic circuit of the voder. The system generates an original speech message in terms of a modified set of parameters. There is a transmission of control impulses by the "talker's" system, in the same way that a person's nervous system might move the appropriate vocal muscles. The muscles produce displacements of body parts formulating the speech information as a set of mechanical waves. These waves appear in the vocal tract in the case of normal speech, and in the fingers, wrist, and foot in the case of the voder.

a perforated paper tape with holes corresponding to frequency bands, and pitch controlled by light source going through a rotating tone wheel that created the frequency of the excitation. The sound was produced from the electric signal collected from a photocell. A picture of the Pattern Playback machine is shown in Figure 4.9.

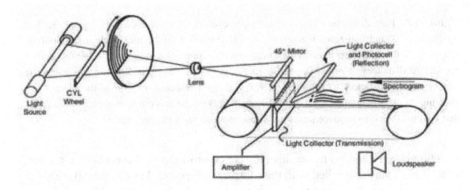

Figure 4.9 The pattern playback machine.

Same as in the early voice synthesizers, the main purpose of this section is to introduce the concepts of pitch, noise, and spectral envelope as a way of decomposing a signal into separate representations.

The next difficult and important question became automating the process of controlling the system parameters, namely finding the spectral keys and the excitation pitch or noise decision. Same as the Voder "typist" had to learn the patterns for different vowels, analysis-synthesis methods were developed to automatically extract the parameters from real voices in order to reconstruct that voice by the synthesis part. Reminding ourselves of previous chapters' discussion about audio representation and features, the analysis part could be considered as a feature extraction step, and the role of the synthesis part is reconstruction of the signal from the features.

Linear Predictive Coding (LPC) is one of the simplest and most straightforward approaches to perform such analysis-synthesis. More advanced spectral modeling techniques, including sinusoidal modeling and multi-band excitation, will be mentioned in the following discussion. Such models find their ways into hybrid neural and signal processing methods today, so their significance should not be underestimated, even if in their simple form these DSP methods have not achieved the parallel quality to today's deep learning speech models. Moreover, hybrid models, such as Differentiable DSP [68], Neural Source-Filter Models [69], and LPCNet [70] try to combine traditional signal processing parameter estimation methods [71] with neural networks.

4.5.1   PITCH, NOISE, AND FORMANTS

A source-filter model of human voice decomposes the vocal sound into two components: the sound production of the vocal chords, and the effect of the vocal tract on the vocal chord sound. In this model the source $e(n)$, which represents the signal produced by the vocal chords, is passing through a resonant filter $h(n)$ that models the vocal tract, resulting in a signal $x(n) = h(n) * e(n)$.

There are two possible signals for the source: an impulse train that represents the flapping of the vocal chords during so-called "voiced" regimes, and random white noise that happens when the vocal chords are relaxed, producing a noisy or whispering signal. In terms of phonetics, these signals model pitched vowels and plosive/fricatives respectively.

The effect of the vocal tract is to create resonances, or amplify certain frequency regions in the excitation sound. One important aspect of the source-filter modeling is that the source is assumed to be relatively flat in terms of its frequency content. When we say flat, we mean two things:

1. when the excitation is unvoiced, the noise is white, which means it has a flat frequency response with same amount of energy in all frequencies, and
2. when the excitation is voiced, the periodic signal is approximately a pulse train, which has equally spaced frequency lines (harmonics) at multiples of the fundamental frequency corresponding to the pitch, with all harmonics having equal amplitudes.

The "coloration", or creating an overall spectral envelope contour to the initially flat spectrum of the vocal tract excitation signal that is shaped in frequency as equally spaced and harmonic lines, or as a flat continuous spectrum of the noisy unvoiced excitation, is done by the resonances of the vocal tract. This shaping is shown in Figure 4.10 for a few typical formants corresponding to the vowels a-e-i-o-u. The

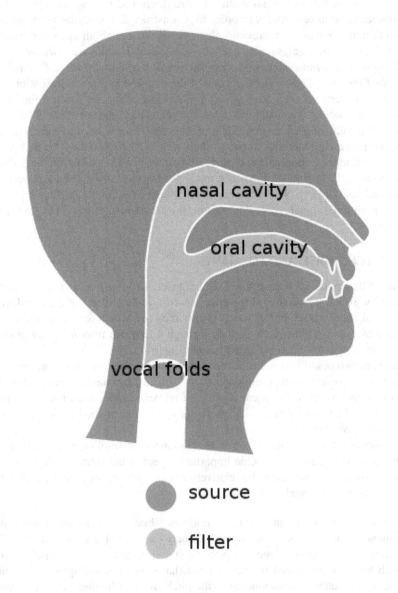

Figure 4.10 Vocal tract serving as a filter to Glottal pulses or noise signals serving as an input to a source-filter model of speech production.

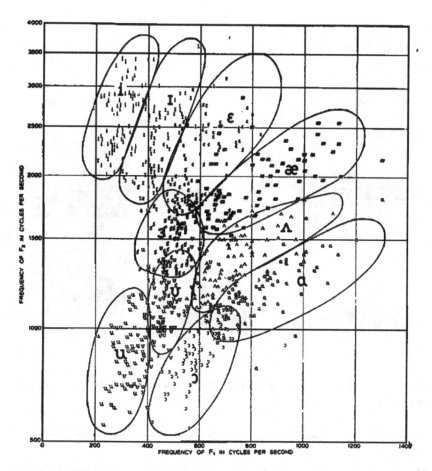

Figure 4.11 Vowels captured as points in the 2D space, plotting the relationship between the first and second formant frequency of the uttered vowel.

formants are defined as the center frequencies and bandwidths of the broad resonance areas that exist in the spectrum. One should thus distinguish between spectral lines, which are equally spaced sharp peaks due to pitch, and the broad "spectral envelope" shape due to the formant resonances.

To understand the perceptual significance of formants, we plot in Figure 4.11 the different vowel sounds in a space representation with axes showing the frequencies of the first two formants. This representation shows for each individual instance of a spoken sound the position of its two first resonances. The formants can also be identified in the image of magnitude of STFT as broad band amplification regions, as shown in Figure 4.12. As one can see, the vowels are distinctly positioned according to a trapeze-like shape following the a-e-i-o-u order. A list of a few formants and their bandwidths are provided in Table 4.1.

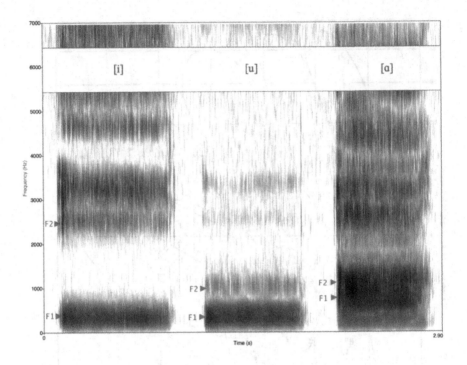

Figure 4.12 The location of the formants are visible as broad band amplification regions in a spectrogram.

Table 4.1

Table summarizing the three first formant freqeuncies and bandwidth for different vowels. This table can be used for synthesis of synthetic speech.

Vowel	Mean			Standard Deviation		
	F1	F2	F3	F1	F2	F3
/i/	328	2208	2885	27	80	575
/ɪ/	365	2108	2826	41	158	655
/e/	477	1975	2874	96	128	450
/ɪ/	627	1914	2850	73	101	406
/a/	735	1236	2489	84	119	294
/ʌ/	676	1266	2438	65	176	458
/ɐ/	650	1027	2445	72	84	387
/ɔ/	504	868	2654	62	108	299

4.5.2 ALL-POLE MODELING OF THE FORMANTS

In acoustics, resonances are achieved by creating a feedback of a sound that favors creation of oscillations or periodic waves of particular frequency range. In extreme cases of a plucked string or wind instrument pipe, these oscillations are perfect standing waves creating a periodic sound. In the case of formants, or broad resonances, the effect is less pronounced, and the role of the filter is to amplify a certain frequency region to shape the broad energy distribution of the sound energies, rather than produce sharp spectral lines of harmonics. Of course, a very narrow resonance filter can produce a sensation of pitch, but another aspect of formants is that they shape the spectrum around relatively high frequencies. If pitches or human voices or musical notes are in frequency ranges of few hundred Hz (recall the range of pitch sensation from Section 1.1), the resonances are in the hundreds to few thousands of Hz range.

The higher frequency of the resonances practically means that the feedback loop is relatively short, and the filter itself can be modeled only by few delays arranged in an auto-regressive manner. Referring to the prior section on FIR and IIR filters and their representation as delays in time or as a polynomial in Z-space, by applying the Z-transform, we can rewrite the relation between the input and output in the frequency domain as

$$X(z) = H(z)E(z) = \cfrac{1}{1 - \sum\limits_{k=1}^{p} a_k z^{-k}} E(z) \qquad (4.43)$$

so that the speech signal can be expressed in parallel as frequency or time filtering representation

$$X(z) = \sum_{k=1}^{p} a_k z^{-k} X(z) + E(Z) \qquad (4.44)$$

$$x(n) = \sum_{k=1}^{p} a_k x(n-k) + e(n). \qquad (4.45)$$

The LPC problem is to find the coefficients $a_k, k = 1...p$, while $e(n)$ can be one of the two types we mentioned earlier – pulse train with a certain pitch or noise. In our voice model, the pitch or voiced / unvoiced decision will be done separately from the filter estimation that represents the effect of the vocal tract.

The all-pole approach is also known as an auto-regressive (AR) model since finding the next value of a signal is "regressed" from its own past. What is interesting is that such autoregression acoustically corresponds to a resonant effect, as it uses feedback of past output values to construct the next sample. As such, it tends to favor repetitive phenomena resulting from such past feedback. We will derive the equations for the prediction filter next. The auto-regressive prediction can be written mathematically as a set of linear equations that link past samples to their next sample. Given p prediction steps with N samples, and assuming that $N >> p$, we get an over-determined system of equations. Using vector multiplication, these relations can be written in terms of a dot product between samples for frame number i, $\vec{\mathbf{f}_i} = [x(n-1+i), x(n-2+i), ..., x(n-p+i)]$ and the vector of coefficients $\vec{\mathbf{a}} = [a_1, a_2, ..., a_p]$, resulting in a prediction of the next sample for frame i, $x(n+i)$, with a residual error or noise $e(n+i)$

$$x(n) = \mathbf{f}_0 \cdot \mathbf{a} + e(n)$$
$$x(n+1) = \mathbf{f}_1 \cdot \mathbf{a} + e(n+1)$$
$$\vdots$$
$$x(n+N) = \mathbf{f}_N \cdot \mathbf{a} + e(n+N)$$

These coefficients are the parameters of the LP filter.

Rewriting this in a matrix form gives

$$
\begin{bmatrix} x(n) \\ x(n+1) \\ \vdots \\ x(N) \end{bmatrix}
=
\begin{bmatrix} x(n-1), ..., x(n-p) \\ x(n), ..., x(n-p+1) \\ \vdots \\ \vdots \\ x(n+N-1), ..., x(n+N-p) \end{bmatrix}
\begin{bmatrix} a_1 \\ a_2 \\ \vdots \\ a_p \end{bmatrix}
+
\begin{bmatrix} e(1) \\ e(2) \\ \vdots \\ \vdots \\ e(N) \end{bmatrix}
\tag{4.46}
$$

Denoting the data matrix in the equation above as $\mathbf{M}$ and the sound and noise vectors of length N as $\mathbf{x}$, and $\mathbf{e}$, respectively, we get

$$\mathbf{x} = \mathbf{M}\mathbf{a} + \mathbf{e} \tag{4.47}$$

Denoting the estimated audio vector $\hat{\mathbf{x}} = \mathbf{M}\mathbf{a}$ we get an expression for the error $\mathbf{e} = \mathbf{x} - \hat{\mathbf{x}}$ as the difference between predicted value and the true signal at each step. The resulting equation is a linear regression that tries to find a "good fit" for the next data point from its past p samples. A least square solution of the regression problem is given by the Moore-Penrose pseudoinverse M^+ given by $\mathbf{a} = M^+ \mathbf{x} = (M^T M)^{-1} M^T \mathbf{x}$.

Going back to the acoustical or siganl processing interpretation, the error signal e is the input into the AR filter. Ideally that input will be a small white noise. This is why, from the prediction perspective, the input signal is often called a "residual" – the remaining components of the output signal that is not created by the feedback loop, i.e the non-autogregressive part. In practice, the input signal to LP is either noise of a pulse train for pitched excitation. Estimating the period/pitch of the voiced excitation, as well as determination of voiced/unvoiced regimes, are beyond the scope of this chapter. Nethods such as zero-crossing, auto-correlation, cepstrum, and more, are used to find the pitch of the sound source. Moreover, for the pitched case one also needs to find the power of the source signal, which can be done by estimating the overall energy or variance of the residual $\mathbf{e}$. Lastly, we'd like to mention that in more advanced models, such as multi-band excitation, the input signal to the filter can be a mix of noise and spectral lines, each occupying different frequency bands.

4.5.3 CREATIVE USE OF LP

One of the interesting application of LP is the so-called "Cross-synthesis" or hybridization of sounds, where the excitation and the LPC filter come from separate sources. When the LPC comes from speech and the excitation from a musical instrument, this becomes a so-called "voice-box". In some DAWs this can be achieved by a process called "side-chaining" where a special voice-box filter that is placed on one audio track serving as the "carrier" can be fed a signal from another side-track that will control the spectral modifications (modulator). This routing method gives it the name "side-chaining".

The process of voice-box goes as follows: after running a voice through LPC, we are left with a different model of the filter, $h_m(n)$ at every time instance m. This filter controls the resonance or the utterance of the signal at that moment. Then we use a different source for the carrier, $e(n)$, and the filter of the speech (modulator $h_m(n)$) to create a hybrid output signal $y_m(n) = h_m(n) * e(n)$, thus cross-synthesis. The segments at different processing times m are then overlap-added to create a continuous and smooth transition between the vowels. An example of a voice box is included in the programming exercises of this book.

4.6 INFORMATION RATE IN SPECTRAL ANALYSIS

To understand the relation between information and spectral analysis, we explore in this section some of the more advanced statistical signal processing relations between spectrum and entropy. These theories allow us to estimate information rate from spectral analysis. Moreover, we will show that an exponent of the IR measure is equivalent to a well known measure of signal noisiness called *Spectral Flatness Measure* (SFM). Although the applicability of IR based SFM is limited to source-filter models driven by Gaussian noise, these relations are important for understanding the relation between noise and predictability, and will allow generalization of SFM to other more complicated cases.

We will discuss the ideas of information more in detail in future chapters when we deal with sequences of notes or symbolic representation of sound units. Here we focus on the relation between spectrum and entropy as a way to distinguish between periodic sounds and noise in the acoustic domain. To assess the amount of structure present in a signal in terms of its information content, we use the following relationships between signal spectrum and entropy. Entropy of a "white" Gaussian random variable x is proportional to the energy of the signal, or its variance σ_x^2, given by

$$H(X) = \ln\sqrt{2\pi e \sigma_x^2} \qquad (4.48)$$

The energy can be also calculated from the spectrum

$$\sigma_x^2 = \frac{1}{2\pi} \int S(\omega)d\omega \qquad (4.49)$$

thus giving the following estimate of entropy

$$H(X) = \frac{1}{2}\ln\left(\frac{1}{2\pi}\right)\int S(\omega)d\omega + \ln\sqrt{2\pi e} \tag{4.50}$$

When a noise is passed through a filter, the effect of summing delays and feedback loops create time dependencies that shape the spectrum. Thus, considering a source-filter model of an acoustic signal, we have a signal that is predictable to a certain extent. To account for this predictability, we measure instead of the entropy another measure introduced in the previous chapter: the *entropy rate*. Instead of looking at uncertainty of a single sample, entropy rate looks at a block of samples (a long sequence) and averages its entropy by the length of the block. Equivalently, entropy rate can be considered as the entropy of the last sample given the past.

$$H_r(X) = \lim_{N\to\infty}\frac{1}{N}H(x_1,..x_N) = \lim_{N\to\infty}H(x_N|x_1,..,x_{N-1}) \tag{4.51}$$

Entropy rate can be expressed in terms of the signal spectrum, know as the Kolmogorov-Sinai entropy

$$H_r(X) = \frac{1}{4\pi}\int \ln S(\omega)d\omega + \ln\sqrt{2\pi e}. \tag{4.52}$$

Although both expressions seem somewhat similar, there is an important difference in their results. While entropy integrates over the spectrum directly to obtain the energy of the signal, entropy rate integrates over log-Spectrum to find how predictable the signal is. Combining these two expressions gives a measure of that we call *Information Rate* (IR) that gives the difference between entropy of an individual sample $x = x_N$ and its past $\overleftarrow{x} = x_1,..,x_{N-1}$, also know as *mutual information* $I(x; \overleftarrow{x})$ between the present and the past of a signal

$$IR(x) = I(x; \overleftarrow{x}) = H(x) - H(x|\overleftarrow{x}). \tag{4.53}$$

Taking an exponent of IR gives us a new expression that is well known in audio feature literature, the *Spectral Flatness Measure* (SFM):

$$SFM(x) = e^{IR(x)} = \frac{exp(\int \ln S(\omega)d\omega)}{\frac{1}{2\pi}\int S(\omega)d\omega} \tag{4.54}$$

Rewriting this as a discrete sum in the case of a DFT with N frequency bins gives

$$SFM(x) = e^{IR(x)} = \frac{exp(\frac{1}{N}\sum_{i=1}^{N}\ln S(\omega_i))}{\frac{1}{N}\sum_{i=1}^{N}S(\omega_i)} = \frac{(\prod_{i=1}^{N}S(\omega_i))^{\frac{1}{N}}}{\frac{1}{N}\sum_{i=1}^{N}S(\omega_i)} \tag{4.55}$$

This provides a surprising and valuable insight into the significance of spectrum shape as a measure of noisiness in audio signals. SFM can be understood as a ratio of geometric mean and arithmetic mean of spectral amplitudes. When the spectrum is

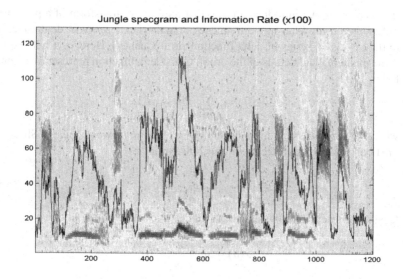

Figure 4.13 A recording of Jungle noises with calls and chirps seen as spectral lines and noise bands, respectively. The IR graph displayed on top of the spectral image shows that pitched portions have higher IR and noisy portions show less predictability manifested as drop in IR.

constant, $S(\omega_i) = c$ where c is some constant, one can easily check that the geometric and arithmetic means are equal and thus SFM equals one, but it is enough for a few of the spectral bins to be close to zero that geometric mean will become a very small number, while the arithmetic mean will be only slightly affected, resulting in SFM close to zero. This ability of SFM to measure the "flatness" of the spectrum made it into a common feature for characterizing how noisy versus periodic a signal is. Looking at this from an information theoretical perspective we get another insight into the meaning of noise – when a spectrum is flat, its IR is close to zero, which in other words means that almost no information is passed from the past of the signal to its present. If the spectrum shape has peaks, these resonant frequencies producing long periodic vibrations that induce a predictable temporal structure into the signal.

An example of IR analysis of audio signal based on SFM is shown in Figure 4.13.

4.7 EXERCISES

1. CDs use a sample rate of 44,100 Hz. What is the maximum frequency which can be reconstructed from this sample rate? What is the typical frequency range for human hearing? Is this an appropriate sample rate?

2. In this chapter, we introduce a proof that the Fourier transform of a pulse train in time is a comb filter in the frequency domain (i.e., a series of delta functions in time is also a series of delta functions in frequency). Here, you will explore some mathematical details of the proof. Consider a function representing a pulse train

$$s(t) = \sum_{n=-\inf}^{\inf} \delta(t - nT),   \tag{4.56}$$

where T is the period of the pulse train (i.e., time in between spikes). Show that the Fourier series coefficients for this pulse train are

$$c_n = \frac{1}{T}.   \tag{4.57}$$

3. Consider one cycle of the sinusoidal signal

$$x(n) = sin(\frac{2\pi n}{N} + \theta)   \tag{4.58}$$

stored in the memory of a digital signal processor, where $\theta = \frac{2\pi q}{N}$ and q and N are integers. This memory comes in the form of a wavetable, where N samples of the signal are stored, using n as an index and q as an offset. In this problem, we would like to create different frequencies and phases by reading from the table at different speeds or different initial offsets.

Can this memory table be used to obtain values of harmonically related sinusoids with the same phase? If so, how? Can it be used to obtain sinusoid signals with the same frequency but different phase? If so, how?

4. Consider the analog signal

$$x_a(t) = 3 \cos 100\pi t   \tag{4.59}$$

   a. What is the minimum sample rate to avoid aliasing?
   b. What discrete-time signal would be obtained after sampling at rate $F_s = 200$ Hz?
   c. What discrete-time signal would be obtained after sampling at rate $F_s = 75$ Hz? This undersampling violates the Nyquist criteria, which means there is a sinusoid signal with frequency less than $\frac{F_s}{2}$ which would yield identical samples.

   To show this, consider another analog signal with sinusoid frequency 25 Hz: $x_{a2}(t) = 3 \cos 50\pi t$. If sampling at 75 Hz, what discrete time signal is obtained? Using the identity $\cos \theta = \cos(2\pi - \theta)$, prove that these samples are in fact the same (in other words, the signals are *aliases* of each other when sampled at 75 Hz).

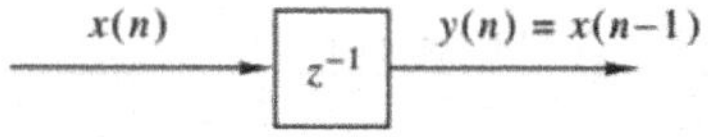

$$x(n) \xrightarrow{} \boxed{z^{-1}} \xrightarrow{} y(n) = x(n-1)$$

Figure 4.14 Graphical representation of a unit delay element. The unit delay is a special system that simply delays the signal passing through it by one sample. This basic building block requires memory.

5. Sketch a block diagram representing the discrete-time system described by input-output relation

$$y(n) = \frac{1}{4}y(n-1) + \frac{1}{2}x(n) + \frac{1}{2}x(n-1) \tag{4.60}$$

where $x(n)$ represents input and $y(n)$ represents output.
Note that there is a recursive (auto-regressive) relation here, because $y(n)$ is fed back to produce the current output. You may want to use the unit delay block illustrated in Figure 4.14.

6. Consider a rectangular signal which has value 1 for some finite duration $L > 1$, and value 0 everywhere else. First, compute by hand the convolution of two such rectangular signals. Then, write a Python function *convolve(x,h)* which computes the convolution of two signals of the same length (though not necessarily rectangular). Finally, graph the output of your function when passing two rectangular signals as input. Does it match the expectations of your original computation?

7. If $y(n) = x(n) * h(n)$, show that $\sum\limits_{n=-\infty}^{\infty} y(n) = (\sum\limits_{n=-\infty}^{\infty} x(n))(\sum\limits_{n=-\infty}^{\infty} h(n))$.

8. The equation for the discrete convolution of two signals is:

$$(x * h)[n] = \sum_{k=-\infty}^{\infty} x[k]h[n-k] \tag{4.61}$$

In the case of finite length signals, we assume both sides of the signal to be zero-padded.
Compute the convolution of the following signals. As a hint, you should expect your answer to be a vector written similarly to $x(n)$ and $h(n)$, with a length one less than the sum of the length of both inputs.
   a. $x(n) = [1,2,4]$, $h(n) = [1,1,1,1,1]$
   b. $x(n) = [1,2,-1]$, $h(n) = x(n)$

9. Compute and plot the convolutions $x(n) * h(n)$ and $h(n) * x(n)$ for $h(n) = h1(n)$ and $h(n) = h2(n)$ as shown in Figure 4.15.

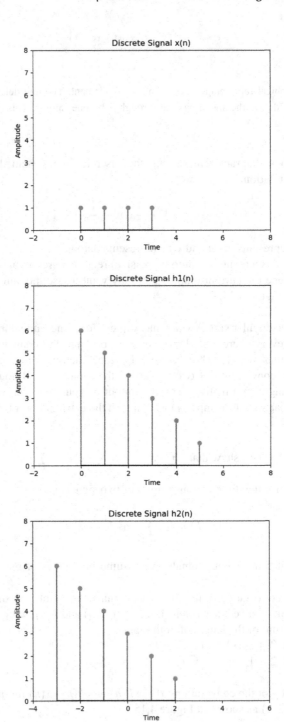

Figure 4.15 Signal pairs for Exercise 9.

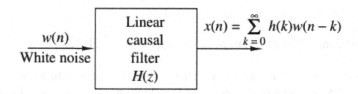

Figure 4.16   Filter for generating random process $x[n]$ from white noise.

10. Consider the filter shown in Figure 4.16, used to generate a random process $x[n]$ from noise w.

In general, the power spectral density function is given as

$$\Gamma_{xx}(z) = \text{z-transform}(cov(x)) = cov(H(z)w) = HH^*cov(w) \qquad (4.62)$$

When the power spectral density function of a random process can be expressed as a rational function,

$$\Gamma_{xx}(z) = \sigma_w^2 \frac{B(z)B(z^{-1})}{A(z)A(z^{-1})} \qquad (4.63)$$

then the linear filter $H(z)$ for generating the random process from a white noise sequence is also rational:

$$H(z) = \frac{B(z)}{A(z)} = \frac{\sum\limits_{k=0}^{q} b_k z^{-k}}{1 + \sum\limits_{k=1}^{p} a_k z^{-k}} \qquad (4.64)$$

for z within the radius of convergence. For such systems, the output is related to the input by the difference equation

$$x(n) + \sum_{k=1}^{p} a_k x(n-k) = \sum_{k=0}^{q} b_k w(n-k) \qquad (4.65)$$

For an autoregressive process, $b_0 = 1$ and $b_k = 0$ for $k > 0$.

For this problem, consider the power density spectrum of an autoregressive process $x(n)$ given as

$$\Gamma_{xx}(\omega) = \frac{\sigma_w^2}{|A(\omega)|^2} = \frac{25}{|1 - e^{-jw} + \frac{1}{2}e^{-2jw}|^2} \qquad (4.66)$$

where σ_w^2 is the variance of the input sequence. What is the difference equation for generating this AR sequence when the excitation is white noise?

Hint: observe that $H = \frac{1}{A(z)}$, *then find the delays and corresponding coefficients for each delay k.*

11. Compute the DFT of the four point sequence $x(n) = [0,1,2,3]$.

12. An N-point signal vector results after taking a DFT in N values, but in practice, for a real signal you only need to look at $\frac{N}{2}$ frequencies. From this idea, the first five points of an eight-point DFT of a real-valued sequence are $[0.25, 0.125 - j0.3018, 0, 0.125 - j0.0518, 0]$. Determine the remaining three points.

    Hint: Consider the symmetry properties of the DFT, and think about how many complex numbers need to be summed to represent one real number (in other words, to remove the complex part).

13. Consider the finite-duration signal $x(n) = [1,2,3,1]$. The inverse DFT formula

$$x(n) = \frac{1}{N} \sum_{k=0}^{N-1} X(k)e^{j2\pi kn/N}, \qquad n = 0, 1, ..., N-1 \qquad (4.67)$$

    can be used to calculate a signal from its DFT terms. In this problem, we will do the opposite: first, compute the signal's four-point DFT by solving explicitly the 4-by-4 system of linear equations defined by the above inverse DFT formula.

    A more direct approach to computing the DFT would use the DFT formula:

$$X(k) = \sum_{n=0}^{N-1} x(n)e^{-j2\pi kn/N}, \qquad k = 0, 1, ..., N-1 \qquad (4.68)$$

    Using this DFT formula, compute the four-point DFT and compare to your answer found using the inverse DFT formula.

    Additional questions and programming exercises are found in the **Discrete Fourier Transform, Spectrograms STFT and Griffin Lim**, and **Speech Formants & LPC** notebooks at https://github.com/deep-and-shallow/notebooks.

5 Generating and Listening to Audio Information

5.1 CONCATENATIVE AND RECOMBINANT AUDIO SYNTHESIS

Musical synthesizers are electronic musical instruments that generates audio signals. While traditional synthesizers used electronic oscillators to produce sounds, from the early days of computer music researchers were looking for algorithms that could produce digital waveforms that resemble sound waves of physical instruments. Sound programming languages comprise unit generators that could produce specific musical sounds such as sinuosids or other basic waveforms and noise. Such unit generators were then connected together into more complicated algorithms that eventually could produce enough timbres to resemble real instruments to be used for synthesis of music. One of the earliest digital sound synthesis systems, MUSIC I, was developed by Max V. Mathews[1] at Bell Labs in 1957. Since then many sophisticated algorithms were developed that allowed synthesis of music-like timbres from mathematical equations. Nonetheless, such synthetic sounds mostly lacked the detail of sound variations of a real musical instrument. This situation radically changed when actual recordings of musical sounds started being used for synthesis. A basic unit for sound generation became a pre-recorded waveform that could be played at different pitches by reading through the waveform at different speeds. Multiple notes were recorded across the range of sounds played by a musical instrument, capturing the changes in the timbre of the instrument at different registers (ranges of pitches) and dynamics. In a way, sample playback became a way to produce music by recalling and modifying sounds from a bank of recorded notes. While performing well for synthesis of musical pitches, sampling was not versatile enough to produce sounds that had more variability, such as speech or complex sound textures. Sampling of individual notes as sound units did not reproduce well details of note transitions or variations in expressive sounds. More realistic synthesized speech and music can be produced by concatenating sound units selected from a large database. The primary motivation for the use of large databases is that it should be possible to synthesize more natural-sounding sounds by finding and concatenating appropriate units of variable size with matching prosodic and timbral characteristics compared to what can be produced using only a small set of fixed sound units. In addition to speech concatenative synthesis, musical systems have been developed that play grains of sounds by search and retrieval of segments from a large corpus according to a desired sequence of descriptors. Such systems can be seen as a content-based extension of granular synthesis, which is a method of recombining grains of sounds to produce novel textures and complex sounds from prerecorded audio.

---

[1] https://120years.net/wordpress/music-n-max-mathews-usa-1957/

DOI: 10.1201/9781003240198-5

The most important issue to be solved to make a concatenative synthesis approach effective is the selection of appropriate units from the database, where multiple candidates might be labeled by same descriptors or assigned the same state label. The unit selection algorithm is a Viterbi path-search algorithm. Given a desired sequence of observations $O = (O_1, O_2, O_3, ..., O_N)$ we wish to determine the highest probable sound units or states sequence $S = (S_1, S_2, S_3, ..., S_N)$ that gives:

$$S^* = \arg\min(C(S|O)) \tag{5.1}$$

Where $C(S|O)$ is a total cost function of following states S given the observations O. To find the best S^* the Viterbi algorithm constructs a lattice of states and transitions, and looks for the optimal pass, or so-called "trellis", using dynamic programming techniques. Rather than exhaustively computing all the possibilities, the algorithm starts with the index of the final highest scoring hidden state and backtracks through the trellis structure beginning with that index, returning the accumulated list.

The Viterbi Algorithm

The Viterbi algorithm, widely used in applications related to speech, natural language processing, and other music or audio tasks, is a dynamic programming algorithm used to find the most likely sequence of hidden states in an HMM given a sequence of observed symbols.

The algorithm can be described by the following steps:

1. Initialization: Create an i by j table, where i is the number of hidden states and j is the sequence length. For each state i, set the entry $(i, 1)$ to the product of the initial state probability of i and the emission probability of i emitting the first observed symbol.
2. Recursion: For each observed symbol s_t from 2 to j, and for each state i, set the entry (i, j) to the product of the maximum probability of reaching state i at time $t - 1$ and the probability of transitioning from that state to s_t, multiplied by the probability of i emitting the observed symbol s_t.
3. Termination & Backtracking: the most likely path is the one that ends in the state with the highest probability in the last column of the generated table. Start from this state and follow the path that has the highest probabilities in each column.

Interested readers are encouraged to view a minimal worked example of the Viterbi algorithm by Roger Levy at https://github.com/deep-and-shallow/notebooks/blob/main/hmm_viterbi_mini_example.pdf.

Concatenative synthesis finds the globally optimal sequence of database units that best match the given target units using two cost functions:

1. a target cost that expresses the similarity of a target unit to the database units using a context around the target, and
2. the concatenation cost that predicts the quality of the join of two database units by join-point continuity of selected descriptors.

In real-time application a global Viterbi search is not possible, so that synthesis is limited to selection of the next unit that matches the next predicted descriptor to produce a continuity to the previously generated sound. In the next section we will describe a process of unit selection where the units themselves are discovered by clustering or so-called vector quantization (VQ) of sound features into a finite set of categories. We will explain the principles behind scalar and vector quantization in the next section. What is important here is that quantization is a technique to transform input sample values from a continuous range into output samples over a small or a finite set. This finite set of representative values is usually taken to be cluster centers of a data distribution. Then instead of transmitting or storing the actual data point, the closest cluster center is chosen and its index is retained instead of the actual sample value. In an encoder-decoder view, this set of representative signals or vectors comprises a code-book that is shared between the encoder and decoder. Encoding is done by sending the index of the closest code, and recovery of the signal value is performed by looking up the indexed values from the code book.

Then these codes, represented as symbolic sequences, are further analyzed for detection of repeated sequences in order to assure continuity with the next predicted symbol. This generative process of finding a symbolic representation of sound and generating continuation is the basis for machine improvisation on audio, known as "audio oracle" and implemented using the Variable Markov Oracle (VMO) method described in the following sections. Matching the improvisation to another musical signal in non-real time fashion can be done using the so-called query method. In this case, a variant of the Viterbi search is performed over possible unit combinations so as to best match another signal that is provided as a query. The musical use of such query method is to produce an accompaniment or a machine improvisation that matches another musical signal that is provided as a guide or constraint to the VMO generative method.

5.1.1 UNIT SELECTION AND VECTOR QUANTIZATION IN AUDIO

An essential step in recombinant concatenative synthesis is identifying the musical units that belong to distinct sound categories. Since one sound segment never exactly matches to another sound, construction of sound units requires a step of clustering or categorization of sounds into groups of similarity. Working with sound features, we need to find when two features are sufficiently similar or distinct to be considered as same or different sounds. Unlike traditional unit selection methods in speech where sounds are already annotated with known descriptors such as speech phonemes, the units in musical recordings are unknown a-priori and need to be discovered by some unsupervised learning method such as clustering.

> **Clustering** is the unsupervised learning problem of aggregating data into similarity groups.

The purpose of clustering is to consider the statistical distribution of sound features to identify regions in feature space were there is sufficient concentration of samples to be considered as a group, while at the same time being distinct or far enough from samples that are forming other groups. Automatic clustering of similar units for unit selection in speech is also done in the case where annotated audio is unavailable, such as in the case of working with a new language or if the audio contains many noises or non-speech sounds.

There are multiple techniques for clustering musical data. Among the common methods are Self Organizing Maps (SOM), k-Means, Gaussian Mixture Models (GMM) and a variety of so-called Vector-Quantization (VQ) techniques in general. SOMs are used in several musical applications, such as commercial plugins for DAWs that help visually arrange grain-sample-positions topographically by characteristics of their respective frequency spectra or other feature spaces. Such programs usually employ a GUI that combine clustering with dimensionality reduction to allow representation of the sound grains in a 2D-reduced feature space. The GUI then allows scanning and re-synthesizing sound from the samples by traversing through the different clusters. SOM are based on Neural Networks and bear close similarly to Autoencoders that will be mentioned later in the book. In this section we describe the k-Means algorithm which is the basic method for clustering based on iterative partitioning of points into regions that are then matched to their centroids and re-partitioned again, with the process repeating until convergence. GMM can be seen as a soft partitioning version of k-Means where instead of hard partitioning of points, a Gaussian probability function is used to give a measure of probability of belonging to a cluster. The probabilistic method is done by an iterative procedure called Expectation Maximization (EM), which bears close relation to a Variation method called Evidence Lower Bound (ELBO) that will be discussed in the advanced materials of the Neural Networks sections, in the context of Variational Autoencoders (VAE). Also from the mathematical modeling perspective, the idea of soft clustering in GMM blurs the boundary between clustering or hard labeling of data according to their cluster indexes and probabilistic modeling. Considering the clusters as latent random variables, the act of choice of the cluster according some prior probability turns GMM into a generative model. Finally, there is a growing trend in machine learning today to perform clustering "on-top" of probabilistic models (also known as probabilistic clustering). Models such as VQ-VAE show state of the art results in image and sound generation and are used in systems such as OpenAI Jukebox that uses transformers on top of VQ-VAE representation to learn and generate complete songs from lyrics input or from a short initial sound example. We mention these methods here in order to show how the more conventional "shallow" machine learning methods can be used to build the intuition for later deep learning models where more complex mathematical models and neural networks capture more subtle relations between music data.

5.1.1.1   Scalar and Vector Quantization

As we mentioned above, a common term in signal processing that refers to clustering of feature vectors into a set of discrete labels is Vector Quantization (VQ). The term quantization itself is very broad and applied to any action that makes a discrete approximation to a real valued sample (scalar) or feature vector by limiting the number of outcomes to a set of particular instances or representative cases. Quantization could happen in very many situations, so the particular meaning or use of the terms has to be carefully understood in the context of the system where it is applied. As such, the quantization we are going to be discussing should not be confused with quantization that happens in physical acoustics, sampling or in score representation. In acoustics, quantization can be a result of the boundary condition in a physical system, in signal processing it is a finite precision representation of signal samples, and in MIDI as correction of timing deviations in music performance.

For example, the vibration modes of a classical string with two fixed ends are quantized (e.g., the string in a violin) to make sound waves which are the superposition of harmonics that are integer multiples of the base frequency, while any other modes of vibration dissipate and quickly disappear. Another quantization happens when discrete time samples of audio signals are stored in a finite computer memory. In such case, not only the time is discretized (see that sampling theory chapter) but also the magnitude values of the samples have to be represented using a limited number of bits. This limits the precision of the actual signal value to a set of possible numbers of finite precision. For instance, CD audio quality represents the amplitude with 16 bits, which limits the range of amplitude levels to a staircase of 2^{16} steps, pushing the intermediate values to the closest step. This adds so-called "quantization noise" to the signal, which is often perceived in very soft signals. Another music quantization is common in MIDI file representation where slight timing deviation due to imperfect timing of a performance are "pushed" to the closest integer grid matching a fraction of a bar so as to fit the minimal allowed note duration, such as sixteenth notes. Anything in the note duration that is deviating from a multiple of sixteenth note then will be disallowed so as not to over-complicate the rendering of the MIDI file to music notation. In this section we will discuss VQ, which is yet another aspect of quantization that is broadly used in lossy-data compression, pattern recognition, probability density estimation, and clustering.

The simplest case of so-called scalar quantization takes into account the one-dimensional probability distribution of the sample values. Given a particular quantization level (i.e., the number of partitions or clusters), the distribution is divided into segments of equal probability. This makes wide regions for low probability portions and narrower segments for high probability regions. This differs from equal partition that happens in the case of a simply representing the signal values by a finite precision number. In such case, the levels of the signal are equally divided between maximal and minimal signal values, while in the case of scalar quantization these regions are adaptive to the distribution of the signal values.

In k-means clustering, we are given a set of n data points in d-dimensional space and an integer k. The task is to determine a set of k points in d-dimensional space that can be put at the center of regions that minimize the mean squared distance between the data points to its nearest center. A popular heuristic for k-means clustering is Lloyd's (1982) algorithm. This Lloyd-Max scalar quantizer can be seen as a special case of a vector quantizer (VQ) that finds regions of equal entropy, and it is implemented by the Linde Buzo Gray (LBG) algorithm.

An example of probability adaptive quantization and its use for finite bit number representation is shown in Figure 5.1; at the algorithm's termination, the one-bit representation is divided at 0, while the two-bit representation thresholds are located at 0 and ± 0.981, and the three-bit representation thresholds are located at 0, ± 0.500, ± 1.050, and ± 1.748.

The Lloyd algorithm functions as follows:

1. Given a probability density function of signal x, $x \sim f(x)$, choose an initial set of reconstruction codes $\{c_j^0\}_{j=1}^N$. Set iteration number $k = 0$, distortion $D^0 = 0$ and set threshold ε.

2. Find decision boundaries $b_j^k = \frac{y_{j+1}^k + y_j^k}{2}$, for $\{j = 1, 2, .., N - 1\}$

3. Compute the distortion $D^K = \sum\limits_{i=1}^{N} \int_{b_{i-1}^k}^{b_i^k} (x - c_i)^2 f(x) dx$

4. if $D^k - D^{k-1} < \varepsilon$, stop; otherwise, continue

5. Compute new code values

$$c_j^k = \frac{\int_{b_{i-1}^k}^{b_i^k} x f(x) dx}{\int_{b_{i-1}^k}^{b_i^k} f(x) dx} \tag{5.2}$$

6. Set $k = k + 1$. Go to Step 2.

The essential steps in Lloyd's algorithm are the boundary selection that divides the range of signal values into quantization segments, and the choice of mean values of each segment as the code value. This approach is generalized to the vector case by replacing the boundaries with multi-dimensional Voronoi regions and means with centroids. One other point that is important to mention is that practical implementations of quantization (scalar and vector) do not use the full probability distribution function but rather calculate the quantization parameters from a set of representative samples. This makes the Lloyd method essentially equivalent to k-means. Various works propose initialization methods for the algorithm, with a more popular one being the so-called *splitting technique* that begins the quantization from a single point (codebook of size one), and progressively doubling the number of codes by splitting the quantization regions by adding a perturbation to the previously found codes.

Vector Quantzation (VQ) essentially generalizes the LBG algorithm to the case of multi-dimensional signals such as feature vectors extracted from audio. The algorithm basically partitions a multi-dimensional space into regions that optimally partition the distribution of the vector values in such a way that each region can be effectively summarized into a single vector which is the centroid of that region or cluster. The regions are often referred to as "clusters" so the VQ method is also

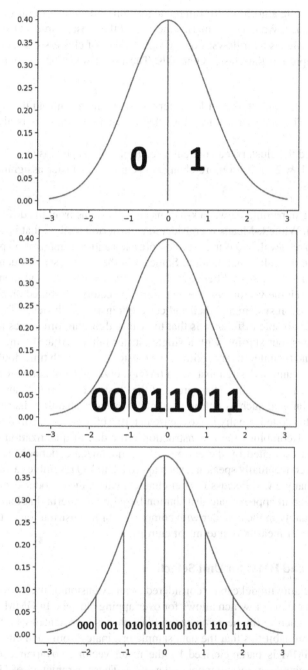

Figure 5.1 This figure shows the thresholds found by the Lloyd-Max algorithm for one, two, and three bit quantization adaptive to a zero-mean unit-variance Gaussian distribution. The thresholds represent optimal boundaries such that the squared error of the samples is minimized. Optimal reconstruction values are also found via the Lloyd-Max algorithm, providing a codebook for reconstruction of signals with minimal distortion.

known as a clustering algorithm. To run the algorithm, the number of clusters has to be known in advance. We may summarize the step of the most simple VQ algorithm, also known as k-Means as follows: For a given number of clusters k select initial k data points to represent the cluster centroids. The initial selection is often done in random.

1. Assign each data point to one of k-clusters by selecting a centroid that is nearest to that point. The boundaries of regions that deliniate the clusters is also called Voronoi-regions.
2. Having created the clusters, calculate new centroids for each cluster.
3. Repeat steps 1 & 2 until no more changes occur in the cluster assignments and their centroids.

The difference in naming between k-Means and VQ stems from the different uses of this algorithm. While k-Means is considered a clustering method that is useful for data analysis and retrieval, VQ is used for compression and communication purposes, similar to the use of scalar quantization. Same as in the case of scalar quantization, the quantization level are shared between the encoder and decoder and their indices are transmitted, so it the vector case the quantization vectors are shared on both ends of the communication system and their indices are transmitted, instead of the actual samples. Another notable difference is that the LBG algorithm often uses a process similar to k-Means, but starting with a single cluster initialized at the mean of the complete data, and then iteratively splitting the cluster center, each time doubling the number of clusters until a desired distortion (error) between the quantization and the data points is reached. To control the spread of the clusters a constraint can be added to the optimization goal such as entropy penalty over the probability distribution of the VQ codes. This added penalty makes sense in terms of the overall communication goals of VQ as it combines the reconstruction error due to quantization with the transmission cost estimated by the entropy of the quantized codebook. It is worth pointing out that conceptually speaking, such approach to VQ resembles a variational modeling idea that we will discuss in later chapters where the encoder-decoder pair are designed using an approximate distribution based on a criteria that balances the reconstruction quality in the decoder with complexity of the distribution of the latent states in the encoder measured in terms of entropy.

5.1.1.2 GMM and HMM for Unit Selection

The Gaussian mixture model can be considered as an extension of the vector quantization model, an extension which allows for overlapping clusters. In GMM a feature vector is not assigned to the nearest cluster, but rather is represented as a weighted combination of probabilities that the data sample originates from each cluster. Representation in GMM is parameterized by the mean vectors, covariance matrices, and mixture weights from all component densities. These parameters of GMM are

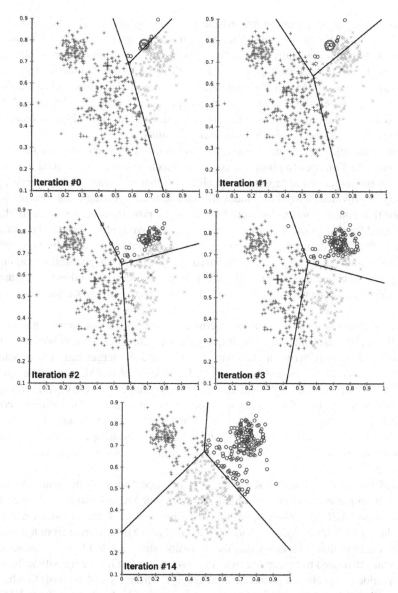

Figure 5.2 Showing a set of iterations in the k-means clustering operation: starting from the point distribution with random initial centroid assignment (Iteration #0), the boundary lines separate the points into the three Voronoi regions. In Step 2, the centroid estimates are updated according to these regions. In Step 3, a new boundary is created according to the centroids found in previous step, and in Steps 4 and 5 the centroids are updated and their boundary is calculated, leading to the next iteration state (Iteration #1). We show two additional repetitions, so that the shift of the estimated centroids (shown as a large red plus, yellow x, and blue o) can be observed. In the last step (Iteration #14), the shift of the centroids is negligible compared to their position in the previous step, so the process is terminated.

estimated using the expectation maximization (EM) algorithm[2]. The difference between VQ and GMM can be considered in terms of the application of each method. Vector quantization is usually viewed as a process of data compression in which a small set of feature vectors is produced from the large set of feature vectors of a particular speaker. GMM, on the contrary, is commonly viewed as a classification method since it gives a likelihood of a new sample given a GMM model. Since both methods do not take time into consideration, an additional modeling layer is required to capture the transition probabilities between the units.

Markov models can be used to maximize probabilities over sequences of features, while unit selection tries to minimize costs for selection of each individual unit relative to some target sound or outside specification that is often called a "query". If no query is provided, a Markov model still can be used to create a randomized sequnence that concatenates units according to the Markov transition probability that was learned for that sound. In such case the concatenative synthesis method operates as a texture synthesis method that creates free variations on a sound by randomly selecting the units according to the unit-based Markov transition probability and outputting a concatenation of short sound snippets that correspond to these units, usually performing a fast cross-fade between adjacent clips to assure a smooth sounding output.

It is important to make a distinction between the two modes of operation of concatenative synthesis: with and without query. In the case when a target sound query is provided, the costs between each database unit and the target can be computed from its distance to the closest code in VQ. In the case of GMM, multiple models are trained to represent the different units, and the probability of the GMM with the highest likelihood, also called "emission probability", is selected. An additional cost of concatenation that has to be taken into account is the sum of transition probabilities when following such sequence of units. Thus the resulting concatenation cost comprise two factors – the matching cost per unit, and concatenation cost of the transitions.

HMM provides a powerful set of method for modeling both the emission and the transition parameters for a given sound. A hidden Markov model is defined as a triplet $\lambda = (A, B, \pi)$ with A being the transition matrix, B the emission matrix, and π the initial probability distribution. What makes HMM different from a normal Markov chain is that it assumes that the transition states are hidden (i.e., these are latent states that need to be derived from the observations). Given a transition matrix A, each hidden state also emits an observable symbol from a set of symbols that have a probability distribution captured by the emission matrix B. The details of HMM training are beyond the scope of this book, and an interested reader is referred to an excellent Rabiner tutorial [72]. It is important to mention the three different functions that HMM performs:

---

[2]The general EM algorithm is not covered in this book, but is a common topic in statistical learning; readers may be interested in *The Elements of Statistical Learning* by Hastie, Tibshirani, and Friedman.

1. Recognition – Given an input (observable sequence) HMM gives the probability that this sequence was generated by the HMM. This is useful where multiple HMMs are trained to model different types of sounds (often used for speaker or speech modeling), and the task is to recognize the category (pick the model that gives the highest probability) of the input sound.
2. Segmentation – Given an observable sequence, segment the sequence into hidden states. This is useful for identifying the temporal structure of the input, such as decoding a sound into syllables when the hidden states represent the different vowels or other vocalizations. Such segmentation is also important for the purpose of alignment between musical score and a recording in score following applications.
3. Learning – Given a model with its parameters $\lambda = (A, B, \pi)$ and an observable sequence for training, the parameters of the model are adjusted so as to maximise the probability of this training data.

HMM is trained using a EM method specifically derived for this type of model. The decoding problem is solved using the Viterbi algorithm. The details of these algorithms are provided in detail in Rabiner's tutorial [72].

In the following we will describe a quantization method that has been used for machine improvisation on audio signals called Audio Oracle (AO). This model finds a variable Markov model over a set of quantized audio representations. In the AO application the discrete codes are used to find motifs and create re-combinations using continuations found by a string matching algorithm generalizing the Factor Oracle (FO) that was described in the previous chapter so as to deal with audio signals. The algorithm behind AO, and its later extension called Variable Markov Oracle (VMO), apply string matching methods to sequence of feature vectors or learned embeddings. The temporal modeling of the AO provides an alternative to Markov models, allowing prediction to be made based on past segments (factors) of variable length. Unlike HMM, AO is finding codes that optimize the predictive properties of the discrete sequence, thus taking into account the information dynamics of the musical signal. The number of clusters in AO is determined by an exhaustive search over different quantization levels, which makes the number of codes adaptive to signal information dynamics. Same as other concatenative methods, AO and VMO can be used for sound generation in a free or query-based manner. The query-based generation in VMO, to be described later in this chapter, uses a variant of the Viterbi algorithm to find a best path through a database of units that resembles another audio signal. This allows producing an accompaniment to a given solo, or vice versa, produce a solo for a given recording of a band that gives the harmonic progression structure for the machine improvised solo.

5.2 AUDIO ORACLE

Audio Oracle (AO) is an analysis method and a representation of musical structure that extends the Factor Oracle algorithms to audio signals. AO accepts a continuous (audio) signal stream as input, transforms it into a sequence of feature vectors and

---

Algorithm 3 On-line construction of Audio Oracle
___

Require: Audio stream as $S = \sigma_1 \sigma_2 \cdots \sigma_N$
 1: Create an oracle P with one single state 0
 2: $S_P(0) \leftarrow -1$
 3: **for** $i = 0$ to N **do**
 4:      $Oracle(P = p_1 \cdots p_i) \leftarrow$ Add-Frame $(Oracle(P = p_1 \cdots p_{i-1}), \sigma_i)$
 5: **end for**
 6: **return** Oracle $(P = p_1 \cdots p_N)$

---

submits these vectors to pattern analysis that tries to detect repeating sub-sequences or factors in the audio stream. Mathematically speaking, the AO generalizes the FO to allow for partial or imperfect matching that operates over metric spaces instead of exact matches in the symbolic domain. One of the main challenges in producing an AO analysis is determining the level of similarity needed for detecting approximate repetition. As we will discuss below, this is done using information theoretic considerations about the structure of the resulting AO. In other words, the "listening mechanism" of the AO tunes itself to the differences in the acoustic signal so as to produce a optimal representation that is the most informative in terms of its prediction properties. Like the FO, AO outputs an automaton that contains pointers to different locations in the audio data that satisfy certain similarity criteria, as found by the algorithm. The resulting automaton is passed later to an oracle compression module that is used for estimation of Information Dynamics, as will be described in the following section.

Algorithms 3 and 4 demonstrate psuedo-codes for Audio Oracle construction. During the online construction, the algorithm accepts audio frame descriptors (user-defined audio features) as vectors σ_i for each time-frame i and updates the audio oracle in an incremental manner. Algorithm 3 shows the main online audio oracle construction algorithm.

Algorithm 3 calls the function Add-Frame – described in Algorithm 4 – which updates the audio oracle structure using the latest received frame descriptions. This function works very similar to Factor Oracle except that (1) it accepts *continuous* data flow rather than symbolic data, (2) does not assign symbols to transitions (instead each state has a one-to-one correspondence with frames in audio buffer), and (3) it uses a distance function along with a threshold θ to asses the degree of similarity between frame descriptions. The set of links in Audio Oracle are forward transitions $\delta(i, \sigma)$ and suffix links $S_p(k)$.

Similar to the Factor Oracle algorithm, forward transitions correspond to states that can produce *similar patterns* with alternative continuations by continuing forward, and suffix links correspond to states that share the *largest similar sub-clip* in their past when going backward.

Algorithm 4 Add-Frame function: Incremental update of Audio Oracle

---

Require: Oracle $P = p_1 \cdots p_m$ and Audio Frame descriptor vector σ
 1: Create a new state $m+1$
 2: Create a new transition from m to $m+1$, $\delta m, \sigma = m+1$
 3: $k \leftarrow S_P(m)$
 4: **while** $k > -1$ **do**
 5:     Calculate distances between σ and S
 6:     Find indexes of frames in S whose distances from σ are less than θ
 7:     **if** There are indexes found **then**
 8:         Create a transition from state k to $m+1$, $\delta(k,\sigma) = m+1$
 9:         $k \leftarrow S_P(k)$
10:     **end if**
11: **end while**
12: **if** $k = -1$ (no suffix exists) **then**
13:     $s \leftarrow 0$
14: **else**
15:     $s \leftarrow$ where leads the *best* transition (min. distance) from k
16: **end if**
17: $S_{p\sigma} \leftarrow s$
18: **return** Oracle $P = p_1 \cdots p_m \sigma$

5.3 AUDIO SYMBOLIZATION USING MUSIC INFORMATION DYNAMICS

In previous chapters we introduced a measure of Information Rate (IR) as a practical tool for analysis of Musical Information Dynamics (MID) that characterizes the reduction in uncertainty of a signal when a predictor is applied to the signal in order to reduce the uncertainty about its next instance. It is formally defined as mutual information between past $x_{past} = \{x_1, x_2, ..., x_{n-1}\}$ and the present x_n of a signal x

$$IR(x_{past}, x_n) \quad = \quad H(x_n) - H(x_n | x_{past}) \tag{5.3}$$

with $H(x) = - \int P(x) \log_2 P(x) dx$ and $H(x|y) = - \int P(x,y) \log_2 P(x|y) dx dy$ being the Shannon entropy and conditional entropy respectively, of variable x distributed according to probability $P(x)$. In [47] an alternative formulation of IR using AO was developed

$$IR_{AO}(x_{past}, x_n) \quad = \quad C(x_n) - C(x_n | x_{past}) \tag{5.4}$$

with $C(\cdot)$ being the coding length obtained by a compression algorithm, and measured in terms of the number of bits required to represent each element x_n [48].

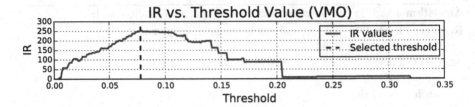

Figure 5.3 *IR* values are shown on vertical axis while θ are on horizontal axis. The solid curve in blue color shows the relations between the two quantities and the dashed black line indicates the chosen θ by locating the maximal *IR* value. Empirically the *IR* curves possess quasi-concave function shapes, thus a global maximum could be located.

In order to estimate the compression, the length of a longest repeated suffix is calculated. This is obtained through a quantity called *LRS* that recursively increments the length of the common suffix between two positions in the signal – the immediate past of the current frame and immediate past at a location pointed to by the suffix link. When a new frame $(i+1)$ is added, the suffix link and *LRS* for this frame are computed. In [73], a lossless compression algorithm, Compror, based on FO is provided that uses the LRS for construction of efficient codes. Compror was shown to have similar or better compression performance to *gzip* and *bzip2* algorithms. Further detail about how Compror, AO, and IR are combined is provided in [47]. In the context of time series pattern and structure discovery with AO and VMO, higher IR values indicate the presence of longer repeating subsequences (ex. patterns, motifs, themes, gestures, etc.) resembling the current music materials, compared to music instances having lower IR value that have less or no prior occurrences of partially similar music material.

In the process of AO analysis, the system is estimating IR for a range of different quantization thresholds θ, where for each threshold the AO constructs a FO with a different suffix structure. The way suffixes are used to derive different symbolization of the time series is shown in Figure 5.4. The forward links from state zero are indicative of the instances where new symbol is introduced. Accordingly, the size of the alphabet for a given quantization (threshold) level can be readily obtained by counting the number of forward links from state zero. Alternatively, Compror is applied to the FO for a given threshold level to find sub-sequences that allow efficient representation by pointer to its past. A simple example of such encoding is provided in the next section. As shown in Figure 5.4, at very low quantization threshold, all instances of the time series are assigned a different state, resulting in an Oracle structure that has no repetitions and forward links being only the direct links from each state to the next one and the indirect forward links from state zero. In the case of a very high threshold, all time series values are considered similar, resulting in an Oracle structure that has a single state that always repeats, as indicated by the chain of suffix links pointing from every state to its immediate previous state. To select the symbolization level that has most informative structures, IR is used as the

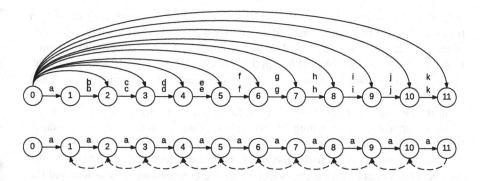

Figure 5.4 Two oracle structures with extreme values of θ. The characters near each forward links represent the assigned labels. (Top) The oracle structure with $\theta = 0$ or extremely low. (Bottom) The oracle structure with a very high θ value. It is obvious that in both cases the oracles are not able to capture any structures of the time series.

criterion for model selection. AO compares between different structures generated by different θ values [74] [47] in terms of their compression properties relative to the size of the quantization alphabet. This way IR measures the relative reduction of uncertainty of the next sample in a time series when past samples are known.

5.3.1 A SIMPLE EXAMPLE

As a simple example of using compression for estimation of IR in the symbolic case, the word *aabbabbabbab* will be encoded as follows: if a suffix link to a previous location in the sequence is found and the length of the repeating suffix is smaller then the number of steps passed since the last encoding event then the whole preceding segment is encoded as a pair (length of string to be recopied, position to start recopying from). Accordingly, in our string example, the first letter will be encoded using the letter *a* using 1 bit over an alphabet $\{a,b\}$. The next occurrence of *a* can be encoded as a pair $(1,1)$, but since encoding it will take more bits then encoding *a* individually, we will use the shorter encoding. We will proceed to encode the next *b* individually and then deciding between representing the following *b* as a pair $(3,1)$ or as a single letter, choosing the latter option. So far we have encoded the four first characters as $a(1,1)b(1,3)$, with little code length savings. The compression advantage appears for the remaining portion of the string. According to the encoding method this segment can be recopied recursively from the second position for 8 characters, which is encoded as a pair $(8,2)$, resulting in the encoding of the complete sequence as $a(1,1)b(1,3)(8,2)$. The reconstruction proceeds as follows: the initial reconstruction is simple recopying. As we reach the later sequence since we have already encoded *aabb*, we start recopying the remaining part from position 2, initially generating continuation *abb*, which results in a sequence *aabbabb*, which by further recopying will keep adding symbols until we exploit all 8 steps to create the full *aabbabbabbab* sequence. If we assume that we use 3 bits to encode each element in the encoding pair that can assume values up to 8, or $(log_2(8))$ bits, then the encoding of the last 8 characters as $(8, 2)$ will use 6 bits, compared to encoding of the 8 characters individually using 8 bits. Although this example is very schematic and artificial, one can see how long recopying can save bits compared to encoding of individual elements.

In the AO case, the symbols are replaced by feature vectors, and repetitions are found by approximate matching between those features up to a certain similarity threshold. From the resulting AO structure we can find the points where the compression occurs according to the method described above. For every frame that occurs between the encoding events we compute the compression gain in terms of the number of bits required to represent the pair $(length, position)$, divided by the length of the encoded segment. Since each AO for a specific threshold value can exhibit a different structure, the IR measurement can be used to select the optimal AO by selecting the one having the highest total IR.

The music analyzed here is a recording of the fourth movement of Sergei Prokofiev's "Visions Fugitives" [75]. We generated a good AO representation using a distance threshold of 0.21, analysis frames of 16384 samples (approximately 372 milliseconds) and using Mel-Cepstrum Coefficients (MFCCs) as our audio feature. A graph showing the IR analysis of this piece is shown below in Figure 5.5.

The reading of the code reveals the basic properties of the AO representation and the grouping done by the compror method. Each entry represents a pair of (number of frames in a sound clip to be recopied, recopying position). When a new frame arrives that can not be recopied, we mark it as zero in the first number of the pair. In such case the second number represents the location of a new sound instance in the original file. As we do not actually use this method for compression, the pairs should be regarded as ways to "understand" the musical structure. More discussion of this follows below.

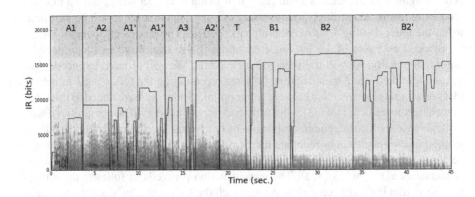

Figure 5.5 Formal structure of Prokofiev's "Visions Fugitives Mvt. 4", with information rate plotted against the signal spectrogram.

Returning to our sequence, we see that the first sound frame is new, and is then followed by three repetitions. The fifth, sixth, and seventh frames are also new. The eighth is a recopy of the sixth. Following the same syntax, we see longer recopied blocks in the middle of the piece, some of which are immediate repetitions of a new sound, others of which are repetitions from earlier in the piece. It is also worth noticing that the tendency to recopy longer blocks increases in time, but toward the end of the recording three new instances occur, which many times can be due to public applause or even a reverberation tail that was not heard before.

5.3.2 MUSIC EXPERIENCE OF EXPECTATION AND EXPLANATION

In *Atoms of EVE': A Bayesian Basis for esthetic analysis of style in sketching* [76], Burns proposes an interesting interpretation of aesthetic experience that elaborates the anticipation approach of Huron by adding a posterior step of explanation that the listener goes through in order to consolidate his experience in the case of expectation violation. This theory, called EVE', is based on three basic aesthetic components: expectations (E), violations (V), and explanations (E'). Burns compares the relations between the IR approach, in its information theoretic formulation, and the Bayesian view of EVE'. It is beyond the scope of this book to survey the relations between the two models, but for our purposes it would be sufficient to say that the ability to explain an object or make sense of a musical stream seem to be natural elements in our enjoyment of music. In Burn's approach, explanation is the discrepancy between models that occurs before and after we have seen the object or listened to music. It is closely related to Baldi and Itti's model of Surprisal that considers an event to be surprising if the explanations (i.e., the underlying models, sometime also called latent parameters) change significantly before and after observing new data [77]. Moreover, Huron includes an a-posteriori aspect in his Imaginative-Tension-Predictive-Reactive-Appraisal (ITPRA) theory of anticipation. According to Huron, the first two steps in forming expectations occur prior to the onset of a stimulus, while the three remaining steps are post-outcome and are related to fast unconscious and slower reactive responses that require learning and appraisal of the reactive reflex. Finally, maybe the best justification for explanation E' can be found in Aristotle's *reversal-recognition* idea, where he writes: "A whole is that which has a beginning, a middle and an end". In between these three parts are two paths – complication (beginning-middle) and unraveling (middle-end). Aristotle explains that "an effect is best produced when the events come on us by surprise; and the effect is heightened when, at the same time, they follow as cause and effect". This is why deus ex machina ("god from the machine") are considered poor plot devices as they provide interventions to a seemingly unsolvable problem in ways that deny explanation or cause-and-effect[3]. However, one should be careful in employing or giving too much significance to

---

[3]The name deus ex machina comes from a crane (mekhane) that was used to lower actors playing gods onto the stage to resolve the plot. Such arbitrary resolution "from above" denies the audience the ability to find their own explanation or understanding of the plot outcome.

Algorithm 5 Incremental IR from AO compression code

Require: A sequence of codeword pairs ($L = length, location$) and total signal
　　length N
1: Create counters H_0 and H_1
2: **for** $i = 1$ to N **do**
3: 　　$H_0 \leftarrow \log_2$(number of new states ($L == 0$) up to i)
4: 　　$H_1 \leftarrow \dfrac{\log_2 (\text{number of all codewords up to } i)}{\text{length L of a block to which state } i \text{ belongs}}$
5: **end for**
6: **return** $IR = H_0 - H_1$

---

the names we use to denote the different phases of aesthetic perception, as our language seems to be poorly fitted to distinguish between the fine details of the different modeling approaches. For the purpose of the current discussion, we will consider expectations as a zero Markov order entropy, or in other words, the effort required to encode a sequence of musical events when no memory is employed to find repeating structures (beyond instantaneous recognition of a sound object as belonging or new to some set of sounds heard before). The explanation aspect in our model will be considered as an ability to recognize a segment of music and link it to a prior occurrence of a similar segment. We can draw a fairly straightforward mapping between the encoding methods presented in the previous section and EVE'. Since V is considered in Burn's theory as negative E, and is omitted from actual calculations, we will be using E and E' as follows:

- Expectation (E) will be measured in terms of the growth in the size of the alphabet (i.e., the number of new sounds) that occur over time during a listening process.
- Explanation (E') will be measured in terms of the saving in coding length when links to earlier occurrences of sound were found, as represented by the AO compression pairs.

The total experience of pleasure, fun, or flow F (these terms are used interchangeably in [76]) is a weighted sum of E and E', written as F = G*E + G'*E', where weights G and G' are set using various heuristic considerations. In our case we will measure E as entropy H_0 and E' as H_1 and the flow is equated to IR as $IR = H_0 - H_1$. The pseudo-code for estimating H_0, H_1 and IR, (or E, E' and F, respectively) is provided in Algorithm 5.

This algorithm counts the size of the alphabet up to moment i both with and without using information about similar blocks in the past. Whenever a new and distinct sound frame is encountered ($L = 0$), the alphabet increases by one more element. The number of bits needed to encode an alphabet of size Q is $\log_2(Q)$. This is also the upper limit to the entropy of encoding a sequence of drawn from a set of Q possible outcomes. Accordingly, as time passes, more and more new states (frames) are encountered, and the size of the alphabet increases. In our interpretation, this is the upper limit to the entropy of the signal up to moment i, which represents the "Expectation" part of the Fun equation. The "Explanation" part is considered in

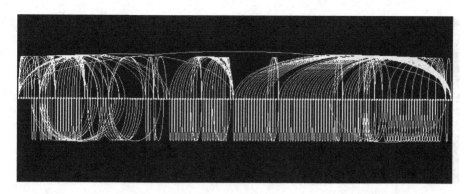

Figure 5.6 Optimal Audio Oracle structure built on the fourth movement of Sergei Prokofiev's "Visions Fugitives".

terms of the ability to trace links to the past (explaining the present via the past) and is measured as the coding length using the AO compression scheme. In this case, a new codeword appears with every encoded block, but the advantage in terms of coding length is that a long block of sound frames is captured by a single compror pair. Accordingly, the number of bits required to encode any individual frame is the number of bits needed to encode the codeword divided by the length of the block.

For a more intuitive understanding of IR and how it relates to the AO structure, consider Figures 5.6–5.8. These figures demonstrate the difference between an oracle constructed using a well-chosen distance threshold and one constructed where the threshold is too low or too high. The first, shown in Figure 5.6, is considered the

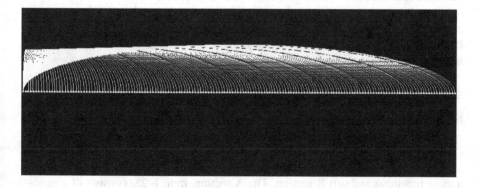

Figure 5.7 Audio Oracle structure built on Prokofiev work – distance threshold was chosen to be 0.000001, and total IR was 0.

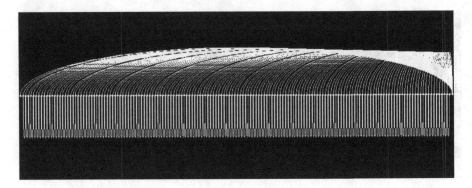

Figure 5.8   Audio Oracle structure built on the Prokofiev work. The distance threshold was chosen to be 0.9, and the total IR was 0.

optimal oracle. Through an iterative process, we compare the total IR of each of a range of possible distance thresholds, and select the particular threshold which maximizes total IR. Figure 5.3 shows the total IR as a function of the distance threshold. The peak of this function yields the optimal AO, though it is often worth studying oracles formed using secondary peaks as well. In the case of the Prokofiev work, the optimal distance threshold was found to be 0.21, which yielded a total IR of 1592.7. Figure 5.7 shows an oracle where the distance threshold was too small. In this case, no similarity between any sound frames was found, and all frames were considered to be new. Each frame has only a link from state 0, indicating that this is its first appearance in the sequence. AO has determined the input to be a "random" sequence, where all frames are unrelated and no repetitions or patterns occur. Conversely, Figure 5.8 shows an oracle where the distance threshold was set too high, lumping disparate frames together, and producing an oracle where all frames were considered to be repetitions of the first. Each frame has a suffix link to the previous frame, indicating this repetition. Note that in these diagrams, suffix links to the 0th frame, present when a new frame is detected, are omitted for visual clarity.

5.3.3   ANALYZING "VISIONS FUGITIVES"

In order to experiment with IR measure we analyzed a solo piano work by the composer Sergei Prokofiev. We chose the fourth movement of the "Visions Fugitives" (1917) because of its short duration and clear form. The piece is in a simple binary form, with a highly active and dynamically varied A section contrasting with a more repetitive and soft B section. The A section, mm. 1–28, consists of a series of short thematic materials, and has a periodic four bar phrase length throughout. Section A is subdivided into 6 subphrases, built using three main materials. The first two phrases, in mm. 1–4 and mm. 5–8, present materials A1 (shown in Figure 5.9) and A2 (Figure 5.10). A1 is characterized by a descending pattern built around a half

Figure 5.9   *A1* material from Prokofiev work.

Figure 5.10   *A2* material from Prokofiev work.

Figure 5.11   *A3* material from Prokofiev work.

step. A2 builds on this half-step idea, but with an emphasis on harmony. The introductory material, A1, returns in modified form as A1' in mm. 9–12 and A1" in mm.
13–16. New material, based on a descending melodic pattern played over descending arpeggiated major seventh chords, is introduced in m. 17. This material, labeled
A3 (Figure 5.11), continues until m. 21, where a modified version of A2 is played.
This A2' combines the harmonic and rhythmic character of A2 with the descending
melodic pattern of A3. Four bars of transitional material, labeled T, follow from mm.
25–28, and connect the half-step motion of section A with the ostinati built on thirds
of section B. The B section, from mm. 29–49, consists of three longer sub-phrases

Figure 5.12 *B2'* material from Prokofiev work.

of uneven duration. The first, running from mm. 29–33, is labeled B1. This phrase establishes the harmonic context of the section, and combines the half-step patterns from before with a minor third ostinato. B2 and B2', mm. 34–39 and 40–49, respectively (Figure 5.12), embellish this material with a simple half-step melody. The piece ends with a single, sustained low G. The clear form of the piece allows for better appreciation of the role of expectation and explanation in forming the musical structure. Figure 5.5 shows our analysis of the work in terms of sectionality and related phrases. It is important to note that there is a "semantic gap" between the signal features used in IR analysis and our subjective musical analysis. We do not claim that IR measures or recognizes concepts like harmony, melodic contour, or rhythmic motives, but it seems apparent that low-level signal features relate to these concepts in some way. Both our sectional analysis and the IR measure are shown on top of the signal spectrogram. The audio features used for analysis were 38 cepstral coefficients estimated over signal frames of 8,192 samples (approximately 186 milliseconds) in duration. Of particular note is the way in which the IR measure corresponds with our subjective musical analysis of the work. IR shows an overall pattern of growth over the piece, as the ability to explain new materials as repetitions of past ones increases. As new materials are introduced, IR momentarily drops, and many of the significant drops in IR correspond to section or phrase boundaries. As an example, consider sections A1, A1', and A1". A1 is the first material of the piece, so its IR is low. As the phrase passes, it becomes possible to explain the new sound frames as being repetitions of past frames. Each successive variation on A1 exhibits higher IR than the previous, and it is particularly revealing to examine the IR contour of A1' and A1". These variations share a similar shape, with the IR of A1" slightly higher than that of A1'. As we reach the second half of the piece, the B section, IR blocks become longer in length, and moments of low IR become shorter. This is due to two factors: first, the material during the second section is more repetitive than that in the first, and second, an overall larger number of frames can be explained by the past.

The Audio Oracle used to perform this IR analysis is the same as that pictured in Figure 5.6. It is possible to observe aspects of the musical structure directly from the AO graph. For example, the dynamic and constantly changing section A corresponds to the many forward links from the first sound frame. Each of these forward links corresponds to the appearance of a new frame. In contrast, section B consists of

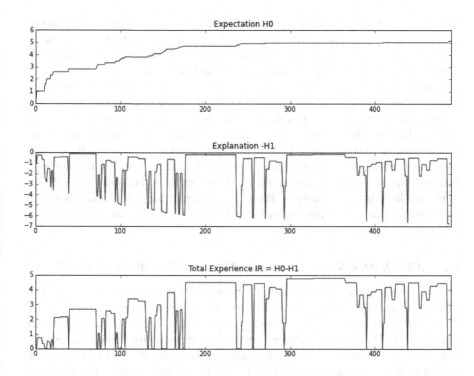

Figure 5.13 Expectation, explanation, and total experience of Prokofiev's "Visions Fugi-tives", as calculated from entropies of encoding the MFCC features without and with consid-ering the repetition structure as found by the Audio Oracle.

repetitions of a few sound frames in varying patterns. This is in agreement with our structural analysis of the work as well.

The graph in Figure 5.13 shows the three elements H_0, H_1 and IR over time for a recording of the Prokofiev. The top graph shows the increase in the coding length as more new frames appear over the time course of the composition. This graph follows the general shape of a logarithmic curve, with flat segments corresponding to regions where the existing alphabet is used to represent the musical events, and vertical jumps occurring every time a new and yet unheard frame is added to the musical materials. The second frame represents the Explanation part, captured by negative entropy computed using the AO compression method. Starting from high Explanation during the first appearance of the A1 theme (first materials are encoded / explained as repetition of a single first event), the Explanation drops as more new sounds appear that can not be traced back to previously heard materials. As time passes, more repetitions are detected and thus longer segments in the song can be "explained" in terms of recopying of earlier sounds. As seen in the final graph and

Figure 5.5, drops in explanation are often related to transitions between sections of the song. The overall experience is considered as a sum of expectation and explanation, which in our case is taken with equal weights. The question of weighting the expectation and explanation components is left for future research.

It should be also noted that our analysis depends on the similarity threshold that is used by AO to detect the repetitions. High thresholds tend to capture longer repetitions, but they adversely affect the expectation graph since fewer new states are detected. Low thresholds tend to favor higher expectation (more new materials are detected) but this adversely affects the ability to find repeating segments, thus lowering the explanation graph. In the graphs shown in Figure 5.13, we used a difference threshold that was found by taking the maximal total IR value (area under the IR graph) resulting from our analysis. For an evaluation of the AO-IR analysis with a more detailed analysis of Beethoven Piano Sonata No. 1 in F minor, the reader is referred to [47].

5.4   ACCOMPANIMENT USING QUERY-BASED IMPROVISATION

Let R be the query observation indexed by n, denoted as $R = r_1, r_2, \ldots, r_N$. The matching algorithm provided in Algorithm 6 takes R as input and matches it to the target VMO, $Oracle(S = s_1, s_2, \ldots, s_T, X = x_1, x_2, \ldots, x_T)$, constructed by a target time series, X. The algorithm returns a cost and a corresponding recombination path. The cost is the reconstruction error between the query and the best match from X given a metric on a frame-by-frame basis. The recombination path corresponds to the sequence of indices that will reconstruct a new sequence from X that best resembles the query.

The query-matching algorithm tracks the progress of traversing the oracle using forward and backward links, finding the optimal path via a dynamic programming algorithm. We separate the algorithm into two steps, initialization and decoding. In Algorithm 6, the initialization is in line 1 to line 6. During initialization, the size of the alphabet, M, is obtained from the cardinality of Σ. Then for the mth list, the frame within the mth list that is closest to the first query frame, R_1, is found and stored. After the initialization step, the decoding step (line $7-13$ in Algorithm 6) iterates over the rest of the query frames from 2 to N to find M paths, with each path beginning with the state found corresponding to the respective label in the initialization step. It could be observed that the proposed query-matching algorithm is similar to the Viterbi decoding algorithm for HMM and max-sum inference algorithm for graphical models [78] in the sense that each update in the decoding step depends only on its neighboring findings, thus making it efficient to compute and of no need to search over the whole state space. A visualization of Algorithm 6 from initialization to decoding for one path among the M paths is shown in Figure 5.14.

5.5   COMPUTATIONAL AESTHETICS

Eighty years ago, the physicist and mathematician Birkhoff formalized the notion of aesthetics in terms of the relations between order and complexity [79]. This idea

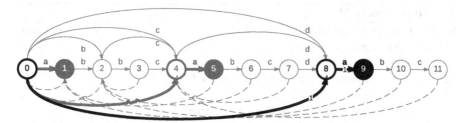

(a) At $t = 1$ (Initialization for label **a**); –**a**, 9″, the pair of label initialized and frame matched. At initialization, for label **a** the choices for the first frame are stored in the list, $\{1,5,9\}$ from Σ. Assuming the closest frame in X to r_1 with label **a** is X_9, then the first frame for path beginning with label **a** will be 9. With the help of keeping track of Σ, the calculation between r_1 and $\{x_1, x_5, x_9\}$ is straight forward.

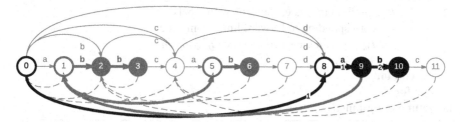

(b) At $t = 2$ (Decoding); –**b**, 10″, the pair of label identified and frame matched. At $t = 2$, the only possible label following label **a** from $t = 1$ is **b**, thus making frames in $\{2,3,6,10\}$ the possible candidates. Let s_10 be the closest frame from the candidates to r_2

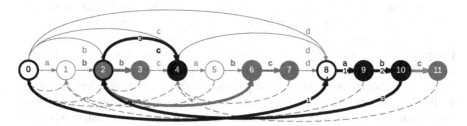

(c) At $t = 3$ (Decoding): –**c**, 4″, the pair of label identified and frame matched. At $t = 3$, the possible labels following label **b** from $t = 2$ is **b** and **c** by examining the forward links from state 10. The possible frames are now the union of labels **b** and **c**, $\{2,3,4,6,7,10,11\}$. Let the closest frame from the candidates to r_3 be x_4, the result path beginning at label **a** is $\{9,10,4\}$. The steps from (a) to (c) are done for all other 3 possible paths as well

Figure 5.14   Decoding steps: Consider the target time series represented as the *VMO* shown above, the same from Figure 3.5. The light gray parts of each subplot are the same from Figure 3.5. In each subplot, parts marked by black with thick arrows indicate the path for the chosen state, dark gray ones with thick arrows represent possible paths and filled circle represents the candidate states. Numbers on the thick black arrows are step numbers. In this example, the query R, is assumed to have 3 frames and the subplots demonstrate hypothetic steps for the path started with frames in X in cluster labeled by **a** (among 4 possible paths started via **a**, **b**, **c**, or **d**). Here the visualization of the query time series is omitted and the path is chose generically to demonstrate Algorithm 6.

Algorithm 6 Query-Matching

Require: Target signal in *VMO*, $Oracle(S = s_1, s_2, \ldots, s_T, X = x_1, x_2, \ldots, x_T)$ and query time series $R = r_1, r_2, \ldots, r_N$
 1: Get the number of clusters, $M \leftarrow |\Sigma|$
 2: Initialize cost vector $C \in \mathbb{R}^M$ and path matrix $P \in \mathbb{R}^{M \times N}$.
 3: **for** $m = 1 : M$ **do**
 4:    $P_{m,1} \leftarrow$ Find the state, t, in the mth list from Σ
              with the least distance, $d_{m,1}$, to r_1
 5:    $C_m \leftarrow d_{m,1}$
 6: **end for**
 7: **for** $n = 2 : N$ **do**
 8:    **for** $m = 1 : M$ **do**
 9:       $P_{m,n} \leftarrow$ Find the state, t, in lists with labels
                 corresponding to forward links from state
                 $P_{m,n-1}$ with the least distance, $d_{m,n}$ to $R[n]$
10:       $C_m \mathrel{+}= d_{m,n}$
11:    **end for**
12: **end for**
13: **return** $P[\arg\min(C)], \min(C)$

---

was later reformulated in terms of information theory by Bense, who suggested that "complexity" is measured in terms of entropy, and that "order" is the difference between uncompressed and compressed representations of the data [80]. In the case of music, past musical events can be used for compression. Our method of modeling musical anticipation resembles the computational aesthetics approach, as it provides a graph of order (where order = uncompressed complexity − compressed complexity). This serves as motivation to develop methods for estimating these "local aesthetics" − measures for explaining the pleasure or fun the audience derives during the listening process. Moreover, an algorithmic composer should be equipped with similar sensibilities in order to guide them through the choice of materials, either autonomously or according to user input in our meta-composition design approach.

5.5.1 THEORY OF REWARD IN AESTHETICS

Historically, the leading tradition in psychological research on aesthetics has been Daniel Berlyne's psychobiological model, as represented by the "new experimental aesthetics" movement of the 1970s. That theory mostly emphasized the arousal-modifying "collative properties" of art by identifying factors such as complexity, novelty and uncertainty. More recently, appraisal theories have provided new perspectives on emotional responses to art, bringing to the forefront of research aspects of interest and enjoyment, and also informing other theories (e.g., prototypicality models, fluency, and so on). Emotions are grouped according to their appraisal structures. In this approach, rather than attributing features like complexity, novelty, etc., to the stimulus object itself, the viewer appraises the stimulus as having these features. Interest is a central contributing emotion when considering aesthetic interest, and consists of two components. The first is a novelty check, and the second is a coping-potential check. Increasing coping-potential by giving foreknowledge was shown to increase interest (Silvia, 2005).

Leder, Belke, Oeberst, and Augustin propose a model of aesthetic experience involving perceptual analyses, implicit memory integration, explicit classification, cognitive mastering, and evaluation [81]. This model results in aesthetic judgment, which is evaluation of the cognitive mastering stage, and aesthetic emotion, which is a byproduct of the earlier stages. It is argued that aesthetic experience is largely depending on aesthetic attitude, which determines "information processing of aesthetic stimuli". This attitude is defined by pre-existing context, although it is also possible for aesthetic experiences to influence the attitude itself.

- **Perceptual analyses**: Previous work has shown that small amounts of contrast along a single dimension can affect aesthetic judgment; that visual complexity is important relative to arousal potential, with preference for a moderate level; that symmetry is detected early and preferred over non-symmetry; and that grouping and "order" variables are preferred.
- **Implicit memory integration**: Familiarity and repetition have been generally shown to be important in aesthetic preferences, although this effect is reduced or eliminated by novelty and complexity in a previously familiar stimulus; prototypicality is preferred; and there is a peak-shift effect in which perceivers respond more strongly to objects that exaggerate characteristic qualities of familiar objects ("art as a search for essential features").
- **Explicit classification**: Conscious and deliberate analyses are made in regard to content and style; there is processing of stylistic information and the pleasure of generalization; there is recognition of alienation into a novel style.
- **Cognitive mastering**: This stage involves semantic associations and episodic memory; knowledge of styles and conscious understanding of distinctive features; and other top-down knowledge such as expertise and integration of external information ("elaborate titles", etc.).

After evaluation and integration of all of these stages, artwork may generate a perceptually pleasure-based or cognitive-based reception. Since aesthetic experience may involve either or both, this complicates empirical work that tests aesthetic processing theories. This is closely related to functions of rewards that are based primarily on their effects on behavior and are less directly governed by the structure of the input events as in sensory systems. Therefore, the investigation of mechanisms underlying reward functions requires behavioral theories that can conceptualize the different effects of rewards on behavior. The investigation of such processes is done by drawing upon animal learning and economic utility theories. This approach offers a theoretical framework that can help to elucidate the computational correlates for reward functions related to aesthetics features that are derived from computational models and information theoretic analysis of musical data.

5.5.2   RELATION TO FOLLOWING MATERIALS

The desire to generate credible musical materials using artificial means has been advancing since the early days of computer music from problems of sound synthesis,
trying to imitate individual notes of musical instruments, to problem of generating
longer musical elements by capturing statistics of sequences of sound units. Moreover, so far we have separated our discussion into sequence modeling and sound
analysis-synthesis, also in view of the different technical tools required for dealing
with signal versus symbolic domains. Using concatenative methdos with unit selection, both problems can be merged into a problem of recombinant synthesis with
sequence statistics learned from hidden states, such as cluster centers derived by various VQ methods.

Recently, VQ methods were applied to generative neural methods as part of a
neural representation learning. By considering latent-space vectors derived from a
compbined VQ and Variational Autoencoder (VAE) process, novel method of discrete neural representations, also know as VQ-VAE, gained in popularity. Since going into the details of VQ-VAE requires introducing VAE first, the details of this
methods are deferred to later chapter *Noise Revisited: Brains that Imagine*. Nonetheless, we would like to point here that VQ-VAE is special in that it combines both
steps of learning the latent embedding and quantization in one setting. In a sense,
not only the cluster centers are sought from existing representations, but during the
learning phase the latent representation itself that VQ tries to cluster is changed so
as to optimize the trade-off between the size of the discrete space and the quality
of representation. To accomplish this, the process is done through separate iterative
steps where the latent vectors are updated using back-propagation according to reconstruction loss using fixed VQ codes, and then the codes (i.e., cluster centers in
VQ) are updated for the newly learned latent vectors.

5.6   EXERCISES

1. The EM algorithm seeks to maximize the likelihood function for a particular
   model. For a Gaussian mixture model, the parameters to be estimated are the
   means and covariances of the components, as well as the mixing coefficients
   which describe the contribution of each Gaussian to the mixture. These coefficients can be thought of as the prior probability of picking the k-th component of
   the mixture. If we consider the posterior probability of picking the k-th compo-
   nent, that is, $p(k|x)$, this is referred to as the *responsibility*.

   The EM algorithm begins with an initialization of means, covariances, and mixing
   coefficients. These are used to calculate the initial value of the log likelihood:

$$\ln p(X|\mu, \Sigma, \pi) = \sum_{n=1}^{N} \ln \sum_{k=1}^{K} \pi_k \mathcal{N}(x_n|\mu_k, \Sigma_k) \qquad (5.5)$$

Next, in the E step, the responsibility is evaluated using the current parameter values:

$$\gamma(z_{nk}) = P(z_{nk} = 1|X) = \frac{\pi_k \mathcal{N}(x_n|\mu_k, \Sigma_k)}{\sum\limits_{j=1}^{K} \pi_j \mathcal{N}(x_n|\mu_j, \Sigma_j)} \tag{5.6}$$

In the M step, the parameters are re-estimated using the calculated responsibilities. Prove that the values of the new parameter estimates are:

$$\mu_k^{new} = \frac{1}{N_k} \sum_{n=1}^{N} \gamma(z_{nk}) x_n \tag{5.7}$$

$$\Sigma_k^{new} = \frac{1}{N_k} \sum_{n=1}^{N} \gamma(z_{nk})(x_n - \mu_k^{new})(x_n - \mu_k^{new})^T \tag{5.8}$$

$$\pi_k^{new} = \frac{N_k}{N} \tag{5.9}$$

where

$$N_k = \sum_{n=1}^{N} \gamma(z_{nk}) \tag{5.10}$$

Hint: begin with the expression for log likelihood $\ln P(X|\theta)$, and differentiate to maximize the expression.

Additional questions and programming exercises are found in the **VMO Audio Oracle** notebook at `https://github.com/deep-and-shallow/notebooks`.

6 Artificial Musical Brains

6.1 NEURAL NETWORK MODELS OF MUSIC

In this chapter, we will describe musical applications of machine learning with neural networks, with emphasis on representation learning or feature learning (methods by which a system automatically discovers representations needed for feature detection or classification from the original data).

Musical neural networks are not a new research direction; a 1991 book by Peter M. Todd and Gareth Loy, Music & Connectionism, explores the topic. At the time, *connectionism* referred to the movement in cognitive science that explained intellectual abilities using artificial neural networks. Now, we see neural networks, especially deep learning techniques, applied widespread among many domains of interest. Naturally, this has renewed interested in musical applications, with research in other domains spilling over to music as well, providing interesting and important results. With the technical advances of algorithm optimization, computing power, and widespread data, it is possible for many to enjoy creating and experimenting with their own musical neural networks.

Before visiting these applications, we will begin with a preliminary tour of the vocabulary, algorithms, and structures associated with neural networks.

6.1.1 NEURAL NETWORKS

Consider a simplified model of the brain as a network of interconnected neurons. The structure of the linked neurons allows information (in the form of electrical and chemical impulses) to propagate through the brain. Organizing a series of mathematical operations and instructions as a **neural network** allows the computer to function analogously to a brain in certain tasks.

In a standard circuit, we may expect an electronic signal to be passed forward, either as-is or in an amplified or reduced form. In a neuron, this message passes through an additional barrier; if its excitement passes a particular threshold, it will emit an action potential, or "fire", and otherwise, the signal will not move forward. In this simplified model, we can imagine a collection of these neurons to act like a collection of interconnected light switches; if the right sequence are left "on", the signals may pass through in a combination such that a correct destination "bulb" may light.

DOI: 10.1201/9781003240198-6

6.1.2 TRAINING NEURAL NETWORKS

> **Preliminary Vocabulary**
> A neural network is composed of a collection of scalar values which are used in mathematical operations to achieve a desired output. These scalar values are referred to as network **weights** or **parameters**. We can measure the network's performance on a task using a function which returns a value called the **loss**.

The goal of training a neural network is to modify the network weights such that forward passes of data through the network lead to minimal loss. We achieve this through combining the processes known as backpropagation [82] (used to calculate gradients of weights in the neural network) and optimization (methods by which the weights are modified to reduce the loss). Some popular optimization methods include gradient descent (and its stochastic and mini-batch variants) and Adaptive Moment Estimation (Adam) [83].

6.1.2.1 Loss Functions: Quantifying Mistakes

Imagine multiple pedagogical environments in which a person might learn to play the piano. In one classroom, this person may have an excellent teacher who explains a technique in such great, concrete, retainable detail that the person is immediately able to execute the performance technique after the lesson. In another classroom, this teacher may briefly instruct the student on the intended technique, then ask the student to perform. The student gives a suboptimal performance, and the teacher points out the student's mistakes. From these corrections (repeated as often as necessary), the student then (eventually) learns the proper performance technique.

When it comes to neural networks, the learning process is much like that of our second piano student. The teacher (in this case, the expected labels or *ground truth* associated with our data) must be cleverly turned into a quantifiable metric which can be used by the learning algorithm to adjust the network parameters. We call such a metric a **loss function**.

Utilized loss functions will vary from problem to problem. Two notably recurring loss functions are Mean Squared Error (MSE) and Categorical Cross-Entropy.

- Mean Squared Error is typically used when performing regression tasks (that is, the possible output exists on a continuum, like the real numbers). For a given vector of legnth N, MSE generally follows the formula

$$MSE = \frac{1}{N} \sum_{n=1}^{N} (Y_{output_n} - Y_{truth_n})^2. \tag{6.1}$$

- Categorical Cross-Entropy is typically used when performing classification tasks (that is, assignment of input to one of C possible classes). Cross-Entropy generally follows the formula

$$CCE = -\sum_{c=1}^{C} \mathbb{1}(c = y_{truth}) \log P(c), \qquad (6.2)$$

where $\mathbb{1}(c = y_{truth})$ is an indicator function with value 1 when c is equal to the true class, and 0 otherwise. Because classification problems expect as output a vector of class probabilities, this function essentially leverages the properties of the logarithm function to create strong values when the model fails to predict the known class (that is, a log value approaching negative infinity, inverted by the negative sign in front of the equation) and weak, near-zero values when the model correctly (or near correctly) predicts the known class since $\log(1) = 0$.

6.1.2.2 Gradient Descent

After quantizing the value of loss in the form of a loss function, we next desire to modify the weights of our neural network such that the loss is reduced. A common method to achieve this is gradient descent:

$$W_{\text{new}} = W - \alpha \nabla L(W) \qquad (6.3)$$

For a fixed input x, the value of the loss function varies only with respect to the weights W. We can compute a gradient by considering the derivative of the loss function with respect to each weight w_i in W. This gradient describes the direction and magnitude of steepest ascent toward the maximum value of loss; therefore, the negative of the gradient points in the steepest direction toward the minimum, with magnitude proportional to the rate of change of loss in the associated direction. Therefore, the gradient descent equation adjusts the weights in a direction toward the minimal loss for the input, scaled by the hyperparameter α, also referred to as the learning rate.

6.1.2.2.1 Chain Rule for MLP

In a feedforward neural network, input is passed through an initial layer where it interacts with network weights, and in the case of a multi-layer network, these resulting values (often referred to as features) are passed to a next layer, and so on. Mathematically, a *multilayer perceptron* (our classic feedforward network) is essentially a composite of functions. To compute the gradient, we make use of the chain rule. Consider the basic example network shown in Figure 6.1, consisting of a single perceptron unit.

For some loss function L, we desire to compute the components of the gradient $\frac{\partial L}{\partial w_i}$ for each weight w_i. However, in a multi-layer perceptron, each weight is effectively buried under a composition of functions which eventually lead to the network output (and loss). The chain rule allows us to compute the desired gradient:

$$\frac{\partial L}{\partial w_i} = \frac{\partial L}{\partial y_j} \frac{\partial y_j}{\partial w_i},$$

where y_j is an output in a preceding layer directly used in computing the loss.

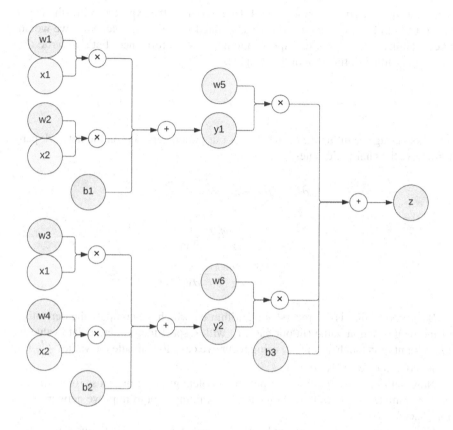

Figure 6.1 An example multi-layer perceptron, consisting of input (yellow), network parameters (green for weights, blue for bias), intermediate nodes (orange), and output (red).

This rule can be iterated over $\frac{\partial y_j}{\partial w_i}$ using the preceding nodes, until the input layer of the network is reached.

As an example, consider the network shown in Figure 6.1. We provide to this network some training sample $\vec{x} = \{x_1 = 1, x_2 = 2\}$, associated with expected training output $z_{truth} = 5$. Assume that network parameters have been initialized such that all $w_i = 1$ and $b_i = 1$.

When the network weights are applied to the input, we reach

$$z = w_5 y_1 + w_6 y_2 + b_3$$
$$= w_5 (w_1 x_1 + w_2 x_2 + b_1) + w_6 (w_3 x_1 + w_4 x_2 + b_2) + b_3$$
$$= 1 * (1 * 1 + 1 * 2 + 1) + 1 * (1 * 1 + 1 * 2 + 1) + 1 = 9$$

Using squared-error as a measure of deviation from the expected value, there is a loss (our term for this deviation) of 16 associated with this sample. Now, we would like to adjust our weights to improve the network performance. Let's re-write the loss expression as a function of the weights.

$$L = (z - z_{truth})^2 = (w_5 y_1 + w_6 y_2 + b_3 - z_{truth})^2$$

Considering the influence of just one of our parameters, w_1, on the network performance, the chain rule states:

$$\begin{aligned}
\frac{\partial L}{\partial w_1} &= \frac{\partial (z - z_{truth})^2}{\partial w_1} \\
&= \frac{\partial (z - z_{truth})^2}{\partial z} \frac{\partial z}{\partial w_1} \\
&= \frac{\partial (z - z_{truth})^2}{\partial z} \frac{\partial z}{\partial y_1} \frac{\partial y_1}{\partial w_1}
\end{aligned} \quad (6.4)$$

Backpropagation is the recursive algorithm by which we compute the derivative of the final function value (in our case, L) with respect to an intermediate value in the computation (such as any w_i) using recursive calls to compute the values $\frac{\partial L}{\partial w_j}$ for all w_j computed directly from w.

Now with the possibility to compute a complete gradient over loss for each network parameter w and b, how do we use the training data to improve network performance?

Consider our first training sample. The loss value associated with this sample is:

$$L = (9 - 5)^2 = 16$$

We will compute an exact value for our gradient term $\frac{\partial L}{\partial w_1}$:

$$\begin{aligned}
\frac{\partial L}{\partial w_1} &= \frac{\partial (z - z_{truth})^2}{\partial z} \frac{\partial z}{\partial y_1} \frac{\partial y_1}{\partial w_1} \\
&= 2(z - z_{truth}) w_5 x_1 \\
&= 2(9 - 5)(1)(1) = 8
\end{aligned} \quad (6.5)$$

Determining formulas for the remaining gradient components is left as an exercise at the end of the chapter; values of these components for this particular training sample are given here:

$$\frac{\partial L}{\partial w_2} = 16$$

$$\frac{\partial L}{\partial w_3} = 8$$

$$\frac{\partial L}{\partial w_4} = 16$$

$$\frac{\partial L}{\partial w_5} = 32$$

$$\frac{\partial L}{\partial w_6} = 32 \tag{6.6}$$

$$\frac{\partial L}{\partial b_1} = 8$$

$$\frac{\partial L}{\partial b_2} = 8$$

$$\frac{\partial L}{\partial b_3} = 8$$

If we write these as a complete gradient, we have

$$\nabla L = \begin{bmatrix} \frac{\partial L}{\partial w_1} \\ \frac{\partial L}{\partial w_2} \\ \vdots \\ \frac{\partial L}{\partial w_6} \\ \frac{\partial L}{\partial b_1} \\ \frac{\partial L}{\partial b_2} \\ \frac{\partial L}{\partial b_3} \end{bmatrix} = \begin{bmatrix} 8 \\ 16 \\ 8 \\ 16 \\ 32 \\ 32 \\ 8 \\ 8 \\ 8 \end{bmatrix} \tag{6.7}$$

This is where gradient descent comes into play. We adjust the weights according to the formula given in Equation 6.3, employing a learning rate of 0.1 for our example:

$$W_{\text{new}} = \begin{bmatrix} 1 \\ 1 \\ 1 \\ 1 \\ 1 \\ 1 \\ 1 \\ 1 \\ 1 \end{bmatrix} - 0.1 \begin{bmatrix} 8 \\ 16 \\ 8 \\ 16 \\ 32 \\ 32 \\ 8 \\ 8 \\ 8 \end{bmatrix} = \begin{bmatrix} 0.2 \\ -0.6 \\ 0.2 \\ -0.6 \\ -2.2 \\ -2.2 \\ 0.2 \\ 0.2 \\ 0.2 \end{bmatrix} \tag{6.8}$$

Now, let's see if our network has "learned" to improve its performance:

$$z = w_5 y_1 + w_6 y_2 + b_3$$
$$= w_5(w_1 x_1 + w_2 x_2 + b_1) + w_6(w_3 x_1 + w_4 x_2 + b_2) + b_3$$
$$= -2.2 * (0.2 * 1 + -0.6 * 2 + 0.2) + -2.2 * (0.2 * 1 + 0.2 * 2 + 0.2) + 0.2 = 3.72$$
$$\text{(6.9)}$$

Our loss now drops from 16 to

$$L = (3.72 - 5)^2 = 1.6384,$$

exactly like we wanted! We could continue our descent until we approximately reach a local minimum (or reach suitable performance for our particular problem).

While this example illustrates a method for calculating the useful gradient, note that these gradients are computed in efficient, vectorized fashion in deep learning software.

6.1.2.3   A Note on Initialization

Before we can begin training, the network weights must be initialized to some value so that a gradient can eventually be computed. We saw that our "set all weights to 1" approach in the previous example may not have been too effective, especially since both halves of the network effectively learned symmetrically, making them redundant. A better option is to initialize weights randomly. This is a very important step, because if network weights are too small, the corresponding nodes will never be activated by the data, and the weights may be too small for the loss gradient to enact meaningful changes to the weights. Similarly, if network weights begin too large, the values may "explode", creating too strong of a response from the corresponding nodes, and consume all of the gradient descent effects to prevent learning on other network weights (especially when values exceed the limits of your programming language's numeric representations and become NaN or infinite).

Xavier Glorot and Yoshua Bengio show that using an initialization randomly sampled from a uniform distribution bounded by

$$\pm \frac{\sqrt{6}}{\sqrt{n_{\text{in}} + n_{\text{out}}}}, \qquad \text{(6.10)}$$

now popularly termed "Xavier initialization", maintains near identical variances of weight gradients across network layers during backpropagation [84]. In this equation, n_{in} is the number of edges into the layer, and n_{out} is the number of edges out of the layer.

6.1.2.4   Modeling Non-Linearity

Our simplified network example is missing one major component which mimics the "firing" behavior we seek from our neurons. This ability to propagate a signal when

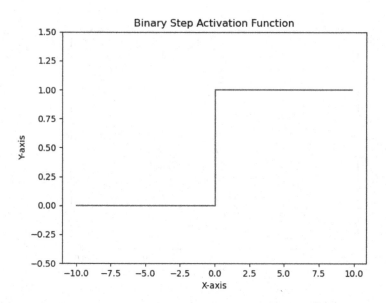

Figure 6.2   Binary activation function.

a certain threshold is passed is a *non-linear* behavior, as opposed to the structure in our simplified example, which can effectively be reduced to a series of linear equations (matrix multiplications). **Activation functions** are applied after such standard multiplication layers to introduce thresholding. Importantly, activation functions are (mostly[1]) differentiable, which allows us to continue to use backpropagation to learn network parameters. This is exactly why the binary activation function shown in Figure 6.2 cannot serve as our activation function; given input 0, the it is unclear whether the weights should face no change from the associated derivative, or *infinite* change.

However, there exist plenty of other functions which share an ability to operate as a thresholding function while still maintaining near differentiability. Some common activation functions include:

- Sigmoid (or Logistic) Function: described in Equation 6.11, this function tends to 0 on the left and 1 on the right, just like the binary step. Critically, it is smooth and differentiable between these limits. It is shown in Figure 6.3.

$$s(x) = \frac{1}{1 + e^{-x}} \qquad (6.11)$$

---

[1] Some activation functions have points of non-differentiability; in practice, these points are assigned the derivative associated with the nearest point. As an example, ReLU (rectified linear unit) is not differentiable at 0, so a value of 0 (left derivative) or 1 (right derivative) may be assigned at this point.

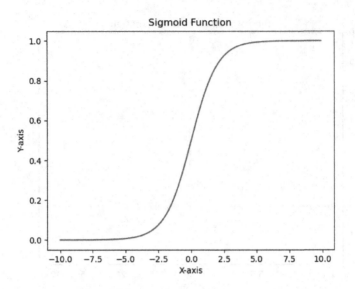

Figure 6.3 Sigmoid activation function.

- Hyperbolic Tangent: the function tanh x is very similar to the sigmoid function in shape, but its larger range allows for a wider range of output values to propagate forward in the network. It is shown in Figure 6.4.

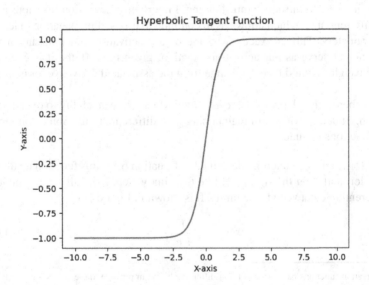

Figure 6.4 Hyperbolic tangent activation function.

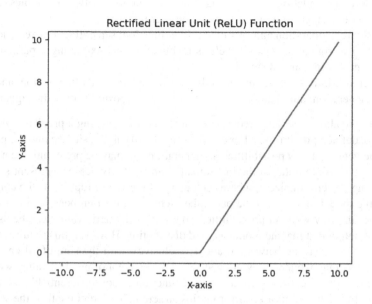

Figure 6.5   Rectified Linear Unit (ReLU) activation function.

- Rectified Linear Unit (ReLU): described in Equation 6.12, this function deviates from the former by introducing an unbounded right side; the benefit of this is that there is an unlimited range of values which can move forward in the network, while still maintaining a "cutoff" behavior for values that do not meet the threshold. It is shown in Figure 6.5.

$$\text{ReLU}(x) = \begin{cases} 0 & \text{if } x < 0 \\ x & \text{if } x \geq 0 \end{cases} \tag{6.12}$$

With these tools in place, it is now possible to construct neural network architectures which model real-world phenomenon (that is, patterns which are not necessarily linear) through connections of matrix-multiplication-like layers (often fully-connected tapestries of nodes) followed by activation functions, with successive layers repeated, modified, and tailored to the content of the task at hand.

6.2   VIEWING NEURAL NETWORKS IN A MUSICAL FRAME

One application of neural networks for music is the field of music information retrieval. Information retrieval deals with the ability to search and find content by some query. A few examples of problems in music information retrieval include

1. Music Classification: sorting music based on properties such as genre, style, mood, etc.,

2. Music Recommendation: determining musical similarity between samples and corresponding suggestion of music based on user history,
3. Music Source Separation and Instrument Identification: separating a mixed audio signal to its original signals, as well as recognizing and extracting a particular instrument within a mixed signal,
4. Music Transcription: converting an audio recording to a symbolic notation, and
5. Music Generation: automatic creation of musical compositions or audio signals.

Many of the above problems require an output used for making a prediction over multiple predefined possibilities. For example, in classifying music, we may be predicting one genre out of n possibilities. In generation, we may be predicting the next note, given n possible notes in the instrument's range. We typically represent such outputs using a vector of size n, where each entry of the vector represents the confidence of the model in selecting the particular element. It is often beneficial to treat these values the way we treat probabilities, so that their numeric values can be used to generate output that matches some learned distribution. However, this requires the values in the vector to be between 0 and 1 (inclusive), with the sum of all entries equal to 1. You may wonder, why not just select the element of greatest value, without normalizing the vector? Such an *argmax* function is non-differentiable, so the network will lose the ability to learn from this structure. To overcome this, the **soft-max** function is used, notable for its normalization property, its ability to preserve numeric ranking among entries, and its differentiability.

Softmax Learning
The **softmax** equation is

$$\text{softmax}(v)_i = \frac{\exp v_i}{\sum_{j=0}^{n-1} \exp v_j}. \tag{6.13}$$

Note that the output of softmax is another vector of length n.

Recall that the vector output by softmax can be imagined as a probability distribution over the classes.

Sometimes, we want the distribution to be very sharp, with nearly all probability associated with one particular value, indicating a strong confidence for a particular class. Other times, particularly with generating so-called creative output, we may want a softer distribution, where values still preserve order but may introduce some ambiguity and lack of confidence (quantified by the magnitude of the probability). Put differently: there is a tradeoff between distribution flatness and novelty of repeated sampling. If we repeatedly sample a uniform distribution to predict the next note of a sequence, we

---

will have a very random (aleotoric) sequence. By contrast, if we repeatedly sample a distribution with probability 1 for note G and 0 for all other notes, our piece will certainly not contain the variance we come to expect in music.

The mathematical mechanism we can use to influence these distributions is referred to as **temperature**. Temperature is reflected in coefficient T, using which we rewrite softmax with temperature:

$$\text{softmax}_T(v)_i = \frac{\exp \frac{v_i}{T}}{\sum\limits_{j=0}^{n-1} \exp \frac{v_j}{T}}. \tag{6.14}$$

You can think of T as a scaling factor which increases (or decreases) distance between the points of v on the number line; the concavity of the exponential function then amplifies these differences, meaning that points pushed further apart on the number line have even greater relative values to their neighbors, and points pushed inward have less strength. Accordingly, $0 < T < 1$ will create a sharper distribution, while $1 < T < \infty$ creates a softer distribution. In the exercises at the end of the chapter, you will show that the distribution approaches uniformity when T approaches infinity.

Consider again our equation for categorical cross-entropy for classification:

$$CCE = -\sum_{c=1}^{C} \mathbb{1}(c = y_{truth}) \log P(c). \tag{6.15}$$

Using the properties of logarithms, we can reformulate this as:

$$CCE = -\log \prod_{c=1}^{C} P(c)^{\mathbb{1}(c=y_{truth})}. \tag{6.16}$$

(You will prove this as an exercise at the end of the chapter.)

In the spirit of temperature, we can reformulate this expression for cases when the goal is not to learn a single-probability result, but rather a distribution over outcomes. We replace the indicator function $\mathbb{1}(c = y_{truth})$ with target probability for class c, t_c:

$$CCE = -\sum_{c=1}^{C} t_c \log P(c). \tag{6.17}$$

Using the properties of logarithms, we can reformulate this as:

$$CCE = -\log \prod_{c=1}^{C} P(c)^{t_c}. \tag{6.18}$$

(You will prove this as an exercise at the end of the chapter.)

The term inside the logarithm is in fact the *likelihood function* of the network parameters θ given observation $X = (x, y_{truth})$. This is stylized as $\mathscr{L}(\theta|X)$, and it is equal to $P(X|\theta)$.

Our measure of error depends on these output probabilities $P(c)$, which we will refer to as output vector y. It is also clear that these probabilities depend on the input provided to the softmax layer (the values that become "scaled" into probabilities). Let's refer to these inputs as vector z. A natural question arises in order to backpropagate: how does the error change with respect to z? In other words, what is the gradient $\frac{\partial L}{\partial z}$?

For any component,

$$\frac{\partial L}{\partial z_i} = -\sum_{j=1}^{C} \frac{\partial t_c \log y_i}{\partial z_j}$$

$$= -\sum_{j=1}^{C} t_c \frac{\partial \log y_i}{\partial z_j} \tag{6.19}$$

$$= -\sum_{j=1}^{C} t_c \frac{1}{y_j} \frac{\partial y_i}{\partial z_j}$$

In the exercises, you will show that

$$\frac{\partial y_i}{\partial z_j} = y_i(1 - y_i) \tag{6.20}$$

when $i = j$, and

$$\frac{\partial y_i}{\partial z_j} = -y_i y_j \tag{6.21}$$

when $i \neq j$. We will use this result in our gradient computation:

$$\frac{\partial L}{\partial z_i} = -\frac{t_c}{y_i}\frac{\partial y_i}{\partial z_i} - \sum_{j \neq i}^{C}\frac{t_c}{y_j}\frac{\partial y_j}{\partial z_i}$$

$$= -\frac{t_c}{y_i}y_i(1-y_i) - \sum_{j \neq i}^{C}\frac{t_c}{y_j}(-y_j y_i)$$

$$= -t_i + t_i y_i + \sum_{j \neq i}^{C}t_j y_i \qquad (6.22)$$

$$= -t_i + \sum_{j=1}^{C}t_j y_i$$

$$= -t_i + y_i\sum_{j=1}^{C}t_j$$

$$= y_i - t_i$$

With this gradient available, our network can learn a distribution associated with a sample using the softmax function.

Now that we have shown a way to learn by tuning weights, let's think through some immediate architectural ideas and consequences. We will begin by considering two dimensions of contraction or expansion of our network. We can grow vertically (that is, adding or subtracting neurons to a particular layer) or horizontally (adding additional layers to the network).

- What happens when we shrink vertically? In this case, we may *underparameterize* our model; that is, we are trying to represent a complex problem or pattern with too few variables. When we do so, the model may succeed in generalizing and perform well in the most typical cases, but may fail for the nuanced, less frequent cases.
- What happens when we grow vertically? In this case, we may *overparameterize* our model; we have created so many variables that each sample in our data may be fit to its own subset of the variables. The model may fail to generalize to the underlying pattern in the data, so while it may perform perfectly in training, it will be unlikely to perform on unseen data.
- What happens when we shrink horizontally (i.e., make the network more "shallow")? In this case, the model will lose its ability to combine preceding pieces of information, a process we refer to as generating higher-level features. In this type of abstract reasoning, we may begin to observe a musical piece and reason about its individual notes at early layers (for example, hearing an F#, then another F#, then a G...). In a middle layer, we might combine some of these notes together to form an idea of a small motif (like a scale ascending a minor third). At even

deeper layers, motifs may be combined to form a phrase (a scale ascending a minor third, then descending a perfect fifth...ah, perhaps this is the Ode to Joy!). Our model's ability to combine features and learn on these combinations is limited by the depth of the network.

- We might think that a solution to this shallow learning challenge is to make the network even deeper. But, what happens when a network is made too deep? This leads to what is commonly referred to as the **vanishing gradient problem**.

Vanishing Gradient Problem

Consider a very simple neural network which is actually shaped like a chain. A single input is fed into a node, which is then thresholded with a sigmoid activation function. We repeat this chainlink 3 times (that is, three weights w_1, w_2, w_3, each separated by a sigmoid function), then apply final weight w_n to provide the output.

Let's refer to the intermediate states between nodes as h_n; that is, $h_1 = \text{sigmoid}(w_1 x)$, $h_2 = \text{sigmoid}(w_2 h_1)$, and so on, ending with output $h_n = w_n(\text{sigmoid}(w_3 h_3))$. We will refer to the sigmoid function as $S(x)$.

We will consider a common regression problem which makes use of an MSE loss function $(y - h_n)^2$, and will compute our gradient as before:

$$\frac{\partial L}{\partial w_n} = h_n \tag{6.23}$$

$$\frac{\partial L}{\partial w_3} = \frac{\partial L}{\partial h_n} \frac{\partial h_n}{\partial w_3} \tag{6.24}$$

In the exercises, you will show that the derivative of $S(x)$ is $S(x)(1 - S(x))$; we will use this result here:

$$\frac{\partial L}{\partial w_3} = \frac{\partial L}{\partial h_n} \frac{\partial h_n}{\partial w_3}$$
$$= 2(y - h_n) S(w_3 h_3)(1 - S(w_3 h_3)) h_3 \tag{6.25}$$

Remember that h_n is the result of $S(w_3 h3)$, so its derivative with respect to w_3 requires application of the chain rule, giving the h_3 found at the end of the above equation, and the w_3 we see below.

Let's continue finding our components, next considering $\frac{\partial L}{\partial w_2}$:

$$\frac{\partial L}{\partial w_2} = \frac{\partial L}{\partial h_n}\frac{\partial h_n}{\partial h_3}\frac{\partial h_3}{\partial w_2}$$

$$= 2(y-h_n)S(w_3 h_3)(1-S(w_3 h_3))w_3 S(w_2 h_2)(1-S(w_2 h_2))h_2 \qquad (6.26)$$

One thing we immediately notice is that we now have two $S(x)(1-S(x))$ terms in the "deeper" gradient value. Likewise, when computing $\frac{\partial L}{\partial w_1}$, we would find a third term. Why is this important?

Recall the shape of $S(x)$. The function is bounded by -1 and 1. If $S(x)=1$, $1-S(x)=0$ and the product is 0 (no gradient – no learning!). What is the maximum value this product can take on? $S(x)(1-S(x)) = S(x)-S(x)^2$, with derivative $1-2S(x)$. Setting equal to zero, we have $S(x)=\frac{1}{2}$; thus, product $S(x)(1-S(x))$ has maximum value $\frac{1}{4}$. This means that each time the term appears in the gradient, at best we are reducing the gradient value by $\frac{1}{4}$. As the depth of the network n increases, the gradient decays faster than (or equal to) $\frac{1}{4^n}$! As an example, at just 10 layers, this would be multiplication by 0.00000009 – hence, the term "vanishing gradient".

Beyond information retrieval, an additional strength of neural networks is their ability to find efficient representations of the information available in the musical data. There is an important question across multiple applications of machine learning which asks us to consider the effectiveness and efficiency of human-engineered features or mathematical transforms to extract useful information for a task while preparing the data, versus letting the network build its own internal structures to capture things that may not have been considered or captured in a manual approach. This *representation learning* is a specific field within machine learning, and specifically to music, this task is important because rather than looking for representations of predefined specific elements that exist within the theory of the domain (for example, words, phonemes, and lexicons in natural language processing, where rules of grammar and syntax are known), the rules of musical structure and musical meaning are comparatively hard to define. Some examples may be the emotional content of music, which by comparison to the "good" or "bad" sentiment of a word would be much more ambiguous in definition and classification. Some areas in which music theorists have conducted discourse on musical meaning include self-referential repetition and management of expectations and anticipations [85] (related to information dynamics). In general, these terms are vague, so to have a musical representation via neural network (whether the internal structure is understood or not) can be a useful tool in approaching musical problems.

The other problem in representation learning is that music has a great amount of variability between genres, cultures, style, etc. This makes it difficult to theorize in a general sense to define meaningful units for analysis common to a full range of musical examples. Networks that create representation of musical patterns can learn to improvise beyond rigid, specific rules, and possibly in a variety of styles.

An example of learning a lower dimensional representation of music comes from the Piano Genie project by Chris Donahue[2] [86]. The Piano Genie is controlled by an 8-button controller, but is able to play phrases along the entire span of the piano. The system makes use of an internal bottleneck which compresses the knowledge in some specific way, so that it can be represented by just 8 keys. This model is generative; new musical examples can be created by triggering the internal representation in either totally random or, in this case, less random ways (i.e., 8 button controller), by which Piano Genie can decode and reconstruct the structure. We've looked at encoding/decoding in information theory, and the terminology has a reference to the idea that we find some encoding in the data and then decode it. Of course, this is a lossy representation, by nature of the bottleneck and dimension reduction. For Piano Genie, Donahue trained a sequence-to-sequence RNN, meaning a sequence of notes goes in, passes through internal network structure mapping to lower dimensional outputs, and then the network learns to decode this output to reconstruct the original sequence. In this way, Piano Genie acts similar to an autoencoder, explored in the next chapter, because it seeks to reconstruct the original information (though made complex by the sequential aspect of musical reconstruction).

Encoders create some new representation of the data, while **decoders** return the data from the new representation back to the original. We refer to this new representation as the **latent state**.

As we will see common to the neural networks we explore, it is very difficult to interpret the latent state in a meaningful way (i.e., translate the latent state to its corresponding input or output).

6.3 LEARNING AUDIO REPRESENTATIONS

In previous chapters we have considered extraction of features capture essential aspects of music or audio data. These features are then used in downstream tasks, such as classification, processing and generation of new music. When the features are extracted from the data in ways that are adaptive to the specific properties of the training data, we consider this process as representation learning. An important notion is that despite the fact that representations are meant to be operated on by other algorithms, they are extracted using statistical considerations applied to the data itself without specifying the particular computational end goal. In such case, the learning task is unsupervised, or in other words, it the representation is learned without knowing the

---

[2]This project was originally created with Google's Magenta team. Magenta is an open source research project exploring the role of machine learning as a tool in the creative process; you can read more about Magenta in the Appendix.

target application. Some of the most widely used unsupervised learning techniques and the sorts of representations they produce include:

- Clustering methods that map data points to a discrete set of data points that are representative of groups or clusters of points. In such a case the representation is a set of integer or indices, pointing to a code book that holds the representative instances.
- Linear dimensionality reduction algorithms like PCA and factor analysis that map data points to a low-dimensional space where Euclidean distance, linear combination, and dot products can be used to perform further deductions.
- Nonlinear dimensionality reduction algorithms, such as multidimensional scaling, ior Isomap, that map data points to a low-dimensional space where Euclidean distance is meaningful.
- Neural network representation learning using methods such as Auto Encoders (AE) and other generative models that use hidden or latent representations to encode the data, which can be later "decoded" back into the original data space in ways that preserve some quality criteria.

In this section we will discuss PCA and related linear factorization methods, which will serve as a preparation to introducing neural AE methods.

6.3.1 PRELIMINARIES: PRINCIPAL COMPONENT ANALYSIS AND KARHUNEN-LOEVE TRANSFORM

Imagine all of the quantitative properties you might use to describe a musical sound for the purpose of classifying between different sounds [87]. As suggested by Peeters et al. in [88], depending on the types of sounds you are analzying, you could extract properties such as log-attack time, harmonic spectral centroid and spread, harmonic spectral variation over time, harmonic spectral deviation from the global envelope, and temporal centroid. Of course, there are plenty of other such features you can define and extra from the sound data, but not all of these may be equally useful in differentiating between sounds. From whatever set of features you have imagined, you can create a vector representation of the sound. However, because there is no shortage of possible descriptors we can create to define each sound, we pose this problem: is there some minimal combination of these features that can represent the sounds, such that this representation preserves the characteristic variance between different sounds? We can see immediately that the naive approach to this problem will fail; if we pick any one feature to preserve, such as log-attack time (i.e., reduce the data dimensionality to 1), we will quickly find that all pieces with similar attack times are grouped together, even if other features vary wildly; in other words, we lose our information to distinguish between pieces which share a similar attack. Is there a better way to choose this reduced basis?

Principal Component Analysis (PCA) is a technique for creating a reduced-dimension dataset which transforms the data to a basis which maximizes the information preserved from the original data. Of course, since we are losing information when reducing dimension, the accuracy of the data will be degraded; the tradeoff is between data simplicity and accuracy. PCA projections are chosen so that the maximum variability of the data is represented using the smallest number of dimensions.

The first step in PCA is standardization; to standardize, we subtract the mean and divide by the standard deviation of values for each feature. Standardization is important so that features which have a greater range of values do not dominate the transformation.

The second step of PCA is computation of the covariance matrix. The covariance matrix is a square matrix with height and width equal to the initial data dimensionality. Collectively, the entries describe the covariance between all pairs of the initial variables. When data is highly correlated, redundancy of information can be reflected in the covariance matrix. Some facts about the covariance matrix:

- The diagonal describes the covariance of each variable with itself (i.e., the variance of the variable).
- Covariance is commutative, so matrix entries are symmetric with respect to the diagonal.
- When a covariance is positive, the variables are positively correlated, so the values should increase or decrease together. When a covariance is negative, the variables are negatively correlated, so the values should increase or decrease in oppositie. When a covariance is zero, the variables are not correlated, so knowing information about one variable does not provide information about the other.

The third step of PCA is the computation of covariance matrix eigenvectors and eigenvalues. During this step, we will define the principal components, which are linear combinations of the initial variables. These components define axes which explain a maximal amount of variance among the data. Maximizing variance of data points along this axis means that the data points have greatest dispersion along this axis, thus, measurements along this axis are most useful in distinguishing between data points. In this way, we say the data (when projected along this axis) has the most possible information. This is where the eigenvectors come into play; the eigenvectors of the covariance matrix are the directions of the axes with maximal variance, and the eigenvalues describe the amount of variance associated with the corresponding axis. When sorted in descending variance order, these principal components have three important properties: the nth component contains maximal information, more information is explained by the nth component than the $n + 1$th component, and all components are uncorrelated. Because of these properties, later principal components can be discarded as a means of reducing data dimensionality while preserving most information. It is worth noting that though the dimension is reduced, because the data is now represented by a linear combination of features, the interpretability of the features themselves becomes obfuscated. But in fact, sometimes this feature obfuscation helps us to reveal and interpret patterns in the data; if we reduce to 1, 2, or 3 dimensions, it becomes possible to plot and view relationships between data which would otherwise be too highly dimensional to visualize.

6.4 AUDIO-BASIS USING PCA AND MATRIX FACTORIZATION

A particularly helpful view of PCA is as form of matrix factorization. Matrix Factorization "breaks up" the original matrix into a product of other matrices, where the goal of such decomposition is to find a representation that is more amenable to analysis or that allows some sort of data reduction or noise robustness. In the case of PCA, the factorization method so-called *Singular Value Decomposition* (SVD), accomplishes the same results but using a different method. We will not cover the details of SVD here, but would like only to mention that while PCA operates on a square correlation matrix, SVD generalizes the eigenvector decomposition to data matrix of any shape, operating on the data matrix directly. Other matrix decomposition methods used for audio include *Non-Negative Matrix Factorization* (NMF), *Independent Component Analysis* (ICA), and more. To be applicable to audio one needs to determine the data matrix first – are these the audio samples, spectral vectors or other features extracted from audio? In the next section we will discuss a decomposition for audio samples, called *Karhunen-Loeve Transform* (KLT) that uses matrix decomposition to find an alternative transform to DFT or other basis function. Such operation is important for better representation, compression and noise removal from the audio data samples themselves when the goal is to recover the audio directly. In many other application we are interested in factorization of some partial representation, such as magnitude spectrum or matrix comprising of some other feature vectors. In such a case the downstream application is information retrieval or some form of data analysis, rather then signal reconstruction per se. An example of matrix factorization applied to audio spectrogram is shown in Figure 6.6. The bottom right large matrix represents a magnitude spectrogram of a sound that visibly can be inspected to contain some note or percussive onsets, viewed as high vertical lines occupying the whole frequency range, with some differences in the details of the spectral shape, including some slightly visible spectral lines in some of these notes. Applying matrix factorization to this DFT magnitude matrix ends up with basis vectors or templates, shown to the left, and their activation over time shown on top. In this example, three audio basis were extracted and their three activation function indicate the amount of presence of each of the basis functions in the DFT magnitude matrix at every moment. One can think about it as creating a variable mix of the basis functions at every instance in time so that it best approximate the complete DFT amplitude data. It is as if the matrix factorization finds the notes or instruments that contributed most to the final sound, comprising the Audio Basis, and the activation functions find the way these Audio Basis templates are played in time. In future chapters we will show methods of using such decomposition using neural networks for the purpose of audio source separation. The ability of Neural Networks to find efficient representations of audio samples or of audio spectra greatly surpasses the previously known linear methods of matrix factorization. Nevertheless, the mathematical clarity and intuition of the linear methods is important both for understanding the later neural network "black box" models, and as a rigorous tool for pre-processing and analyzing audio data without having to go through a process of training large models and collecting big amounts of data.

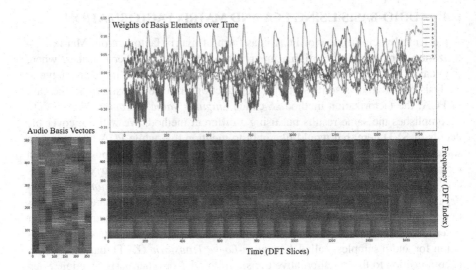

Figure 6.6 An example of matrix factorization applied to sound spectrogram to maintain an Audio Basis and its activation functions. Please see the text for more explanations.

6.4.1   A HEURISTIC DERIVATION OF THE KARHUNEN – LOÉVE TRANSFORM

We consider Karhunen–Loéve Transform (KLT) as a way to connect deterministic transforms such as the DFT to the case of probabilistic signals, where the "usefulness" of the resulting change in signal representation is judged in terms of finding salient features or efficiency of the signal representation in the transform domain. Accordingly, we shift our view of signal representation from physically or mathematically motivated coordinate change into a statistical view that is judges transform efficiency in terms of its lossy compression or denoising performance.

In the DFT section we showed how a periodic signal can be expanded into a basis of orthonormal functions, namely sines and cosines, or their complex numbers equivalent. The KLT transform is considering $x(n)$ as a random signal, with the goal of expanding this onto a set of orthonormal functions that is taking into account the statistics of the signal (also called stochastic process). A general two-dimensional unitary (orthogonal) transform is of the form $Y = AX$ and $X = A^T Y$ where X is the source data matrix, Y is the matrix of transform coefficients, and A is the unitary matrix of eigenvectors. When choosing the A matrix to be used for purposes of compression or noise removal, some selection criterion must be used. One criterion selects a transform matrix that places as much energy as possible into a fixed number of the transform coefficients. If such a transform matrix is selected using an optimal MSE fit, the Karhunen-Loeve transform (KLT) results. For the KLT the A matrix is built from the eigenvectors of the data covariance matrix.

In statistical terms, the goal of KLT is to extract features that are optimally uncorrelated, while capturing most of the data variation, a goal that is sometimes termed as highest energy compaction. The correlation matrices of y and x, R_y and R_x respectively, are related through A matrix multiplication

$$R_Y = \mathbb{E}[YY^T] = \mathbb{E}[A^T X X^T A] = A^T R_X A .$$

Choosing A as matrix whose columns are the eigenvectors of R_x with with eigenvalues $\Lambda = Diag(\lambda_i)$ we get

$$R_Y = A^T R_X A = \Lambda ,$$

since the correlation matrix is symmetric, the eigenvectors of R_x, which comprise the columsn of A, a_i are orthonormal.[3]

KLT can show similarity to a matrix eigendecomposition. In the case of a continuous signal in time instead of a matrix, the autocorrelation function is used to determine the type of continuous deterministic eigenfunctions $\phi(t)_i$ weighted by random components X_i. Retaining only the strongest components effectively achieves optimal lossy compression of the signal that is adaptive to its statistical properties. The theory of continuous stochastic signals is beyond the scope of this chapter. For a discussion of the continuous case see section 7.11 in [89]. This architecture is similar to a matched filter receiver, where the orthogonal eigenfunctions serve as a "detector" of a specific type of information, and anything in the signal that is not encoded into a combination of these filters is basically eliminated from the output.

6.4.2 PRE-TRAINING WITH AUTOENCODER

The autoencoder can be considered as a nonlinear generalization of PCA, comprising of two neural networks – an "encoder" that transforms the high-dimensional input into a low-dimensional code, and a "decoder" that approximately and optimally reconstructs the original data from the code. The two networks can be trained together by gradient descent to minimize some discrepancy function between the original data and its reconstruction. In the case of multiple layers, using the backpropagation chain rule becomes difficult. If the initial random weights are large, autoencoders tend to be stuck in local minima, and if the initial weights are small, the network is very slow to train since the gradients are small. The solution to this problem is doing sequentially a separate training for each layer as a shallow autoencoder, using the results of an earlier layer to train the next one. In such a scheme the distribution of inputs and outputs needed for training the next layer are obtained from the results of training the layer preceding it. It was shown that such a method brings the initial weights close to a good solution, which then can be fine tuned end-to-end with all layers unfolded into a deep (stacked) autoencoder. The deep AE can be fine-tuned in unsupervised way, or can be turned into a multi-layer deep classifier by adding a last fully connected layer trained in a supervised manner for some other target data.

A supervised training of a deep network using pre-training is divided into a sequence of steps:

---

[3]The orthonormality is achieved because eigenvectors of symmetric matrix are orthogonal, and we can normalize them at will to achieve orthonormality.

- Unsupervised Deep Pre-Training: Train a sequence of shallow autoencoders one layer at a time in unsupervised manner using the input data,
- Last Layer Supervised Training: Add a fully connected layer after the last encoder layer and train it in a supervised manner using the output target, and finally
- End-to-End Fine-Tuning: Unfold the entire network and use back-propagation to fine-tune it using input and target data in supervised manner.

The great success that unsupervised pre-training brought to supervised tasks, such as MNIST classification[4], lead researchers to realize the importance of representation learning for machine learning. Having a single layer of features is insufficient to model the structure of a variety of images. After learning one layer of feature detectors, deep networks can treat their activations as data for learning a second layer of features. Then the first layer of feature detectors become the visible units for learning the second layer, and this process can be repeated layer after layer multiple times. Interesting analogies were found between convolutional neural network and simple and complex cells of our visual system, where progressively deeper layers learned higher level concepts going from edges to patterns to complete parts of images.

As introduced in the previous section, in past decades, neural nets used activation functions such as $\tanh(z)$ or $\frac{1}{1+e^{-z}}$, which were relatively smooth and led to slower learning rates. At present, the most popular non-linear function is the rectified linear unit (ReLU). ReLU activation typically learns much faster in networks with many layers, allowing training of a deep supervised network without unsupervised pre-training. Regardless of this fact, understanding the importance of good initialization and the separate roles of each layer in a deep network is important for designing DL solutions.

Understanding in full what deep neural networks learn is still an open and very important problem, usually known as Explainable AI. Moreover, due to the complexity of features learned by modern Deep NN, they are also susceptible to malign manipulation. Adversarial attacks of NN have shown that small perturbations, often nearly invisible to the human eye, can lead to huge misclassification.

Representation Learning is closely related to the desire to capture and possibly visualize the structure of data in a way that is both intuitive, meaningful, and compact. As such, methods of dimensionality reduction are natural candidates for accomplishing the representation learning task. Another important aspect of learning representation is that the problem is often defined in an "unsupervised" manner. Although one could ask the question of what is a "useful", or compact or meaningful representation of your data for a supervised task, or in other words, find ways to efficiently parse or cluster the data of source X when a target Y is provided, in many data science tasks the amount of labelled data is small or the cost of labeling is prohibitively high. Moreover, in some cases the labeling itself is problematic because the categories are ill-defined. If the task is simply compression, visualization, or data exploration, then

---

[4]MNIST stands for Modified National Institute of Standards and Technology; this is a laboratory in the US Department of Commerce, and one of their datasets of handwritten digits has been used extensively as a base challenge for image classification models.

no labeling is available. In such situations we might want to find a transformation of the data into a another representation that has some optimal properties. For this purpose, representation learning deals with finding a set of basis functions that are fitted by solving some optimization task. After learning is accomplished, these pre-existing basis functions can be further used to transform new data into the new target coordinates. The basis function later can be used to fit another regression model or initialize a neural network, and only train for a short-time. In fact, unsupervised "pre-training" was one of the genius solutions that led to the revival, and today's explosion, in deep learning.

6.5 REPRESENTATION LEARNING WITH AUTO-ENCODER

We build on the notion of the Auto-Encoder (AE) as a way to define the representation learning task. AE's task is to find a representation of feature vectors without any labels that can be later used to reconstruct the original data. Moreover, AE is defined as a two-step mapping or function from data to features and from features back to data. As such, one common way to denote the two-step nature is by calling the first part of going from data to features as "encoder" and then back to data as "decoder". This immediately suggests a relation to information transmission, where the tasks of the encoding is to find a compact representation. It should be noted of course that compression is not the only viable criteria for AE, but the common idea is that there is some sort of a bottleneck that forces the data to get rid of its irrelevant aspects, leaving only the essential aspects that are needed for later reconstruction. The encoder function can be viewed as transformation of the original data into another space, where the values of the feature vector found at the output of the encoder are considered as weights of the basis function of that space. Formally this can be implemented as matrix transformation, neural network, and more.

For the purpose of this chapter, it would be useful to consider matrix transformation as a particular case of a neural network without activation functions. Accordingly, we will use the term "neural network" in these notes in a broad sense of a mapping that can be optimized in iterative way by fine-tuning its parameters by some sort of back-propagation mechanism. Later on we will also show how the same problem can be solved as a closed-form inverse matrix problem in the case where the neurons are linear (or in other words, when there is no non-linear activation function present in mapping the weighted inputs to outputs).

An AE is a vector-valued function that is trained to approximately return its input $\mathbf{x} \sim \mathbf{F}(\mathbf{x})$. In the most simple case we set up a transformation matrix T to define our mapping as $\mathbf{F}(\mathbf{x}) = T\mathbf{x}$, where we also may find the trivial solution with $T = \mathscr{I}$ as identity mapping. Accordingly, some constraints are required to find an interesting representation, such as reducing the dimension of some internal step.

6.5.1 DIMENSIONALITY REDUCTION

One possible constraint is to form a bottleneck by the use of a neural network with input of dimension N and hidden layer of K units where $K \ll N$.

$$\mathbf{h} = g(V\mathbf{x} + \mathbf{b}^{(1)}) \tag{6.27}$$

$$\mathbf{f} = g(W\mathbf{h} + \mathbf{b}^{(2)}), \tag{6.28}$$

where V is a $K \times N$ weight matrix, W is a $N \times K$ weight matrix, and the g's are element-wise non-linear activation functions. The function pair $\mathbf{h}, \mathbf{f}$ can be considered as encoder and decoder for a lossy compressor. The network compresses an input vector of N values down into smaller set of K numbers, and then decodes them again back into the original dimension, approximately reconstructing the original input. This creates effectively a mapping $\mathbf{F}(\mathbf{x}) = \mathbf{f}(\mathbf{h}(\mathbf{x})) \approx \mathbf{x}$, where the quality of approximation or the reconstruction error needs yet to be defined.

We consider PCA as a linear autoencoder where activation function is an identity function $g(a) = a$.

$$\mathbf{h} = V\mathbf{x} \tag{6.29}$$

$$\mathbf{f} = W\mathbf{h} \tag{6.30}$$

where, without loss of generality, we may assume that the mean of our data x is zero, which can be shown to allow removing the bias terms $\mathbf{b}^{(1)}$ and $\mathbf{b}^{(2)}$. The goal of our minimization problem now becomes minimizing an error function between the network output $\mathbf{F}(\mathbf{x}) = WV\mathbf{x}$ and the desired output $\mathbf{y}$, which in the autoencoding case is $\mathbf{x}$ itself. Without loss of generality, let us write the error for any target $\mathbf{y}$, parameterized by V and W, as

$$E(V,W) = \|\mathbf{y} - WV\mathbf{x}\|^2 = (\mathbf{y} - WV\mathbf{x})^T (\mathbf{y} - WV\mathbf{x}) \tag{6.31}$$

The goal of our neural network is to learn the parameters of the matrices V and W to minimize the error E, which eventually will lead to saddle or extreme point where $\frac{\partial E}{\partial v_{ij}} = 0$ and $\frac{\partial E}{\partial w_{ij}} = 0$, where v_{ij} and w_{ij} are elements of the matrices V and W, respectively.

Let us denote the output of the first step of the transformation as $\mathbf{z}$, i.e. $\mathbf{z} = \mathbf{h}(\mathbf{x})$. This vector is indeed the compact representation or the latent or hidden layer in the encoder-decoder network, also sometimes referred to as "features". At this point we have not yet specified what are the constraints on the behavior of $\mathbf{z}$ apart from requiring it to be of a lower dimension $K < N$. During the course of the book we will revisit this same formulation by adding other constraints on the desired features.

Our task is to show that a neural network that learns through the process of iterative parameter optimization, such as backpropagation, indeed arrives (for the autoencoding case) to the classical solution of PCA, which is finding the eigenvectors of the data correlation matrix Σ_{xx} and using the first K eigenvectors with the largest eigenvalues as the columns of the matrix V or, equivalently, rows of W. For those not familiar or needing refreshing of PCA, the PCA algorithm can be summarized by the following Python code:

```
# Find top K principal directions:
# Input data X contains multiple rows of samples x, each of
# dimension N
L,V = np.linalg.eig(np.cov(X.T))
iL = np.argsort(L)
V = V[:, iL[:K]] # reduction of N to K
x_bar = np.mean(X, 0)
# Reduce X to K dimensions
Z = np.dot(X - x_bar, V)  # (K,N)
# Transform back to N dimensions:
W = V.T
X_proj = np.dot(Z, W) + x_bar  # (N,K)
```

Feel free to try this code on your own data and add plots of the feature Z for K=2 to see it in 2D.

The goal of this section is to show that a neural network with linear neurons achieves the same solution. This can be also viewed as an alternative proof of the PCA principle, i.e. that matrices V and W that PCA finds are a solution of the optimization problem and thus they are the best representation in terms of mean square error (MSE) for a data reduction to a lower dimensional space.

Let us assume first that we have a fixed decoding matrix W. Finding the least error E for such a case amounts to finding the best set of features $\mathbf{z}$, so that $E(\mathbf{z}) = \|\mathbf{y} - W\mathbf{z}\|^2 = \|\mathbf{y}\|^2 - 2\mathbf{y}^T W\mathbf{z} + \mathbf{z}^T W^T W\mathbf{z}$ is minimized. Taking the derivative, one finds the solution $\mathbf{z} = (W^T W)^{-1} W^T \mathbf{y}$.

This expression is known as the pseudo-inverse of W. In other words, if we have a transformation that reduces the dimension of $\mathbf{y}$ into K dimensional vector $\mathbf{z}$ by the relation $\mathbf{y} \approx W\mathbf{z}$, the best $\mathbf{z}$ for a fixed W is $\mathbf{z} = pInv(W)\mathbf{y} = (W^T W)^{-1} W^T \mathbf{y}$. The total transformation of the input $\mathbf{x}$ to output $\mathbf{y}$ can be written now as $\mathbf{y} = WV\mathbf{x}$.

Going back to the autoencoding case $\mathbf{y} = \mathbf{x}$, we see that that best features to represent x are $\mathbf{z} = V\mathbf{x} = (W^T W)^{-1} W^T \mathbf{x}$, so the encoding matrix V should be the $pInv$ of W. The total transformation of $\mathbf{x}$ through the network becomes $WV\mathbf{x} = W(W^T W)^{-1} W^T \mathbf{x} = P_W \mathbf{x}$, where P_W is known as a projection matrix $P_W = W(W^T W)^{-1} W^T$ that projects any vector of dimension N into a lower dimensional space K spanned by the columns of the matrix W (in our notation W is (N,K)).

Returning to our error function, we can write now for the average error for an auto-encoding case

$$\langle E(V,W) \rangle = \langle \|\mathbf{x}\|^2 - 2\mathbf{x}^T P_W \mathbf{x} + \mathbf{x}^T P_W^2 \mathbf{x} \rangle$$
$$= \langle \|\mathbf{x}\|^2 \rangle - \langle \mathbf{x}^T P_W \mathbf{x} \rangle = tr(\Sigma_{XX}) - tr(P_W \Sigma_{XX}), \tag{6.32}$$

where we used the relation $P_W^2 = P_W$ (projecting the results of a projection on more time does not change it), the multiplication property of a trace of a matrix $tr(A^T B) = tr(BA^T)$, and the notation Σ_{XX} to denote a correlation matrix of X that can be written as $\Sigma_{XX} = \frac{1}{M} X^T X$, where M is the number of samples (with a slight abuse of notation since we introduced here averaging of multiple samples of $\mathbf{x}$ arranged into a matrix X as approximation to statistical mean, which allowed us to consider now the average error as a function of the correlation matrix).

This gives us the following insight into how to choose the K basis vectors

$$E(V,W) = tr(\Sigma_{XX}) - tr(P_W \Sigma_{XX}) = \sum_{i=1}^{N} \lambda_i - \sum_{i \in I} \lambda_i \qquad (6.33)$$

or in other words, the error becomes the sum of the residual eigenvalues for the eigenvectors we did not choose to go into our projection.

We are almost done here, so before proceeding to the last PCA step, let us discuss the expression above. What we see is that the optimal encoding and decoding over a large set of data points can be achieved by finding an encoding matrix W so that the difference between the trace of the data correlation matrix and the trace of the correlation matrix projected into a lower dimensional space spanned by the encoder is minimized. We are ready now to use a couple more neat mathematical properties of correlation matrices to complete our proof of optimality of PCA.

First, we want to explore the eigenvectors of Σ_{XX}. Let us denote by U a matrix of its eigenvectors (N vectors of N dimensions), and by Λ the diagonal matrix of its eigenvalues. The expression for eigenvector relations is by definition $\Sigma_{XX} U = U\Lambda$. Because Σ_{XX} is a real symmetric matrix, its eigenvectors are a complete orthnormal set, i.e. the vectors u_i, u_j for any member of the set of eigenvectors $U = [u_1, u_2, .., u_N]$ are orthonormal, i.e. $u_i^T u_j = \delta_{i,j}$, or zero when $i \neq j$ and one when $i = j$.

Second, let us choose encoding matrix W to be a subset of K vectors from U. The only remaining task would be to decide which K vectors to choose. Let us denote this subset by index I, so $W = U_I$. Going back to the expression of the error $E(V,W)$, we can write $P_W = U_I (U_I^T U)^{-1} U_I^T = U_I U_I^T$ where we eliminated the middle inverse part since $U_I^T U_I = \mathscr{I}$ because of its orthonormality.

We leave this as a proof for the reader (and an exercise at the end of this chapter) to show that for any other matrix that is not aligned with the eigenvectors U_I, the trace of $P_W \Sigma_{XX}$ will be smaller then $\sum_{i \in I} \lambda_i$. Intuitively, this can be seen as generalization of a projection in the one dimensional case. It is clear that if we want to project a given vector on some basis function, the largest projection will be in the direction of the vector. In other words, if we can rotate the projection vector, the projection will be zero for orthogonal vector and then proportional to cosine of the angle, which will be maximal when the angle is zero.

This brings us to Q.E.D, i.e. we demonstrated that choosing K eigenvectors of Σ_{XX} that have the largest eigenvalues gives the best encoding of the data X into a lower K-dimensional space, with the remaining error being the sum of the eigenvalues of the "missed" dimensions.

In practice, this situation is not guaranteed in neural network types of optimization. The process of finding the encoding matrix parameters can be stuck in local extrema (despite the fact that the problem is convex and has a single global minimum).

The advantages of finding a closed form solution of PCA instead of using an autoencoder with gradient methods are:

- There are efficient solvers for finding eigenvectors that might be faster than gradient search,
- With enough data and a sufficiently good estimate of the data covarience, we know that this is an optimal solution, and
- We have better intuition into the meaning of the latent representation (features) while a neural network remains a black box.

On the other hand, there is a big deficiency with PCA compared to neural network autoencoders. By allowing a non-linear function $g()$ to process the encoding and decoding vectors, we can successively apply autoencoding in multiple steps, each one gradually reducing the dimensionality and the amount of information extracted from the data. Such a gradual approach is not possible in the linear case (no activation function) since any product of matrices can be represented as a single final matrix, so gradual reduction of dimensions from N to $K_1 < N$ to $K_2 < K_1$ is equivalent to reducing it straight to K_2.

6.5.2 DENOISING AUTOENCODER

When the units of an autoencoder are linear with an architecture that has a bottleneck shape (i.e., the dimension of hidden units is smaller then the dimension of the data), and the loss is a mean squared error, the representation it finds is similar to that of PCA. One way to think about it is that minimization of the error during learning drives the AE to seek the best representation, which consequently forces the connection matrix to reside in a subspace that is spanned by the principal components of the data.

Autoencoders with nonlinear activation of its neurons are able to learn much more powerful representations. One can think about it as a nonlinear generalization of PCA. Moreover, the non-linearity allows gradual reduction of representation complexity through multiple layers, allowing for very complex function mapping from input to the hidden units and to the output. Unfortunately, such powerful mapping may result in autoencoders that learn to memorize the training set, mapping input to output without extracting useful information about its distribution. There are several ways to try avoid this over-fitting problem. One of them is the **Variational Autoencoder** that will be discussed in later chapters. Before going into such modeling, it makes sense to think about this problem through a regularization approach. In regularization, rather than limiting the model capacity by keeping the encoder and decoder shallow and the hidden state dimension small, the solution is to add an additional component to the loss function that forces the model to have some smooth or constrained hidden layer properties that will avoid copying input to output.

Another solution to the exact recopying is even more ingenious – instead of feeding the same data in the input and output and the expecting the AE to learn the best possible reconstruction, the denoising-AE feeds a corrupted version of the data in the input, and clean data at the output. The denoising autoencoder (DAE) is trained to predict the original uncorrupted data point as its output.

Such prediction can be thought of as a map from corrupted data $\hat{x}$ that is distributed accordingly probability $\hat{x} \sim C(\hat{x}|x)$, pointing it back to the original data point x. If we assume that x resides on a smooth lower-dimensional surface (manifold), adding noise most likely will throw the data in directions that are orthogonal to the manifold. Of course we do not know what the manifold is, but we assume that it has a lower dimension than the data itself. So for large dimensional data residing in a low dimensional space, adding noise will locally effect only a few dimensions, while the majority of the noise will happen in other dimensions. When the denoising autoencoder is trained to minimize the average of squared errors $||\mathbf{g}(\mathbf{f}(\hat{x})) - x||^2$, with $\mathbf{f}$ and $\mathbf{g}$ denoting the encoder and decoder, respectively, it can be shown that the reconstruction $\mathbf{g}(\mathbf{f}(\hat{x}))$ estimates $\mathbb{E}_{x,\hat{x} \sim p_{data}(x)} C(\hat{x}|x)[x|\hat{x}]$, which is the center of mass of the clean points x that could have resulted in samples $\hat{x}$ after application of the corruption. The difference vector $g(f(\hat{x})) \sim \hat{x}$ does an approximate projection on the clean signal manifold.

6.5.3 PROBABILISTIC PCA

In preparation for the idea of generative models, we would like to switch our point of view from representation of the data to representation of its distribution. This Bayesian idea, though not new in ML, turned out to be very powerful for neural networks as it led to a whole new generation of machine learning algorithms that first used sampling methods to establish the learning processes, and later used variational methods, where some of the units in the network became stochastic units that, strictly speaking, are non-differentiable. Thus, a statistical approach to neural networks comes from the network fitting parameters of a probability distribution, rather then fitting the data. As a way to introduce such methods, we consider a Gaussian model for a probabilistic version of PCA where we assume that our low-dimensional feature vectors lie on a low-dimensional subspace where they are distributed as a zero mean and uncorrelated Gaussian (spherical distribution). The model assumes that the observed data was generated by a K-dimensional Gaussian variable $v \sim \mathcal{N}(0, \mathbb{I}_K)$ that was then transformed up into N-dimensions, $\mathbf{x} = Wv + \mu$, where W is a $N \times K$ matrix. This transforms our initial zero mean and unit variance variable v into a new variable $\mathbf{x} \sim \mathcal{N}(\mu, WW^\top)$. So effectively our low-dimensional randomness is "spread out" over many more dimensions (from K to N), but if we look at the covariance matrix of the data, it is low rank because it has only K independent rows or columns. We are in a very similar situation to deterministic PCA where all vectors $\mathbf{x}$ generated from this model lie on a linear subspace of K dimensions.

Since real data of N dimensions rarely lies exactly on a lower-dimensional subspace, the full Gaussian model actually loads an extra diagonal matrix to the WW^T matrix, $\mathbf{x} \sim \mathcal{N}(\mu, WW^T + \sigma^2 \mathbb{I})$. In other words, we added uncorrelated noise to all dimensions to account for spread of the data over the whole N-dimensional space.

The importance of Probabilistic PCA (PPCA) is not so much in the model itself but in the conceptual shift of how it estimates the model. Instead of fitting the data, the model actually tries to estimate a probability function that is a multi-variate Gaussian of K dimensions (how to know what is K is a separate question), so that the likelihood of the data in that probability will be maximized. This introduces a *maximum-likelihood* way of thinking about fitting generative models to data.

Given a data set $X = \{x_n\}$ of observed data points, its log likelihood function is given by

$$\ln p(X|\mu, W, \sigma^2) = \sum_{n=1}^{N} \ln p(x_n|\mu, W, \sigma^2) \tag{6.34}$$

$$= \frac{NK}{2} \ln(2\pi) - \frac{N}{2} \ln|C| - \frac{1}{2} \Sigma_{n=1}^{N} (x_n - \mu)^T C^{-1} (x_n - \mu) \tag{6.35}$$

where $C = WW^T + \sigma^2 \mathbb{I}$. The features or latent variables in PPCA are the vectors v that are estimated using Bayes rule

$$v \sim p(v|x) = \mathcal{N}((WW^T + \sigma^2 \mathbb{I})^{-1} W^T (x - \mu), (WW^T + \sigma^2 \mathbb{I})^{-1} \sigma^2) \tag{6.36}$$

It should be noted that for $\sigma^2 \rightarrow 0$, the mean parameter is a pseudo-inverse matrix multiplication of the data vector x with zero-mean (i.e., with mean vector subtracted from the data). Moreover, Tipping and Bishop [90] showed that the maximum of the likelihood function is obtained for a matrix $W_{ML} = U_K(\Lambda_K - \sigma^2 \mathbb{I})^{1/2}$, up to an arbitrary rotation (omitted here), with U_K being a matrix comprised of K eigenvectors with the largest K eigenvalues, and Λ_K is the diagonal matrix containing these eigenvalues.

Intuitively speaking, for $\sigma^2 \rightarrow 0$ the matrix that projects data into the latent space is exactly the same as in the deterministic PCA case, with the vectors scaled by a root of their respective eigenvalues. This scaling is needed since unlike the PCA case, where different dimensions appear with different scales, here we project everything into a spherical latent variable with unit variance, so each dimension needs to be re-scaled according to its variance.

6.6   EXERCISES

1. Derive formulas for the remaining loss gradient components in Figure 6.1.

2. Show that as softmax temperature parameter T approaches infinity, a categorical output distribution approaches a uniform distribution.

3. Considering the definition of categorical cross-entropy and using the properties of logarithms, show that

$$- \sum_{c=1}^{C} \mathbb{1}(c = y_{truth}) \log P(c) = -\log \prod_{c=1}^{C} P(c)^{\mathbb{1}(c=y_{truth})}. \tag{6.37}$$

4. Considering the definition of categorical cross-entropy with temperature and using the property of logarithms, show that

$$- \sum_{c=1}^{C} t_c \log P(c) = -\log \prod_{c=1}^{C} P(c)^{t_c}. \tag{6.38}$$

5. Considering the softmax function output y and input z, show that

$$\frac{\partial y_i}{\partial z_j} = y_i(1 - y_i) \qquad (6.39)$$

when $i = j$, and

$$\frac{\partial y_i}{\partial z_j} = -y_i y_j \qquad (6.40)$$

when $i \neq j$.

6. Consider some matrix A, and the matrix U_I composed of the subset of the eigen-vectors of A with the K greatest eigenvalues. Let P_W be the projection defined by $U_I U_I^T$. Show that any other projection matrix P_{W_0} not aligned with these eigen-vectors, when multiplied by A as $P_{W_0} A$, will have a trace which is smaller than the sum of the K greatest eigenvalues of A.

7. Apply the code presented in this chapter for dimensionality reduction using PCA to a dataset of your choice (for example, you may want to draw your data from a collection of multivariate Gaussian distributions). Reduce the data to $K = 2$ dimensions, and plot this reduced 2D feature Z. Do you notice a relationship be-tween Z and the underlying distribution of the full-dimensional data?

8. In binary classification, we seek to associate an input x_n with its appropriate target value: $t_n = 0$ for class C_0, and $t_n = 1$ for class C_1. The cross-entropy error function is of the form

$$E(w) = -\sum_{n=1}^{N} \{t_n \ln y_n + (1 - t_n) \ln(1 - y_n)\} \qquad (6.41)$$

Assuming a neural network with output units which use the logistic sigmoid acti-vation function,

$$y_n = \sigma(a) = \frac{1}{1 + e^{-a}} \qquad (6.42)$$

show the derivative of the above error function satisfies

$$\frac{\partial E}{\partial a_k} = y_k - t_k \qquad (6.43)$$

Hint: show that $\frac{d\sigma}{da} = \sigma(1 - \sigma)$. Use this relation to simplify the expressions for the derivatives of $\ln(y)$ and $\ln(1 - y)$.

9. In probabilistic PCA, the observations are assumed to be generated from latent variable z with added noise ε according to

$$x = Wz + \mu + \varepsilon \qquad (6.44)$$

(a) Using expressions for the mean and covariance of x, prove that

$$E[x] = \mu \tag{6.45}$$

and

$$cov[x] = WW^T + \sigma^2 \tag{6.46}$$

In your explanation, use the assumption that

$$z \sim N(\vec{0}, I) \tag{6.47}$$

Explain where you use this assumption.

(b) It can be shown that

$$p(z|x) = \mathcal{N}(z|M^{-1}W^T(x - \mu), M^{-1}\sigma^{-2}) \tag{6.48}$$

where M is defined as

$$M = W^T W + \sigma^2 I \tag{6.49}$$

Show that as $\sigma \to 0$, the posterior mean for z given x becomes

$$E(z|x) = (W^T W)^{-1} W^T (x - \mu) \tag{6.50}$$

(c) In non-probabilistic (regular) PCA, the goal is to approximate a vector x that has D dimensions by combination from a smaller set of basis vectors $w_1, w_2, ... w_M$ with $M < D$. Arranging the basis vectors as columns of a matrix W, consider $\hat{x} = Wz$ to be a low dimensional approximation to x. Explain why z is M-dimensional, and show that for a fixed W, the optimal z is found by the pseudo-inverse of W given by

$$(W^T W)^{-1} W^T \tag{6.51}$$

Compare this to the maximum likelihood result for probabilistic PCA, and describe your observation.

Hint: to find a pseudo-inverse, write $x = Wz + error$. Then, write an expression for MSE and minimize with respect to z, showing that optimal z is given by $(W^T W)^{-1} W^T x$.

Additional questions and programming exercises are found in the **PCA with Linear Autoencoder** notebook at https://github.com/deep-and-shallow/notebooks.

7 Representing Voices in Pitch and Time

Music and Audio Artificial Intelligence is an interdisciplinary field between computer science and music. In comparison to more established AI fields such as natural language processing (NLP) and computer vision (CV), it is still in its infancy and contains a greater number of unexplored topics. As a result of this, deep learning models from natural language processing and computer vision are frequently applied to music and audio processing tasks. Take neural network architectures as an example. Convolutional neural networks (CNNs) have been extensively used in audio classification, separation, and melody extraction tasks, whereas recurrent neural networks (RNNs) and transformer models are widely used in music generation and recommendation tasks. We have seen various models of RNN, CNN, and transformer gradually outperform traditional methods to achieve new state-of-the-arts in recent years.

In this chapter we introduce two basic basic neural network architectures that are used to learn musical structures in time and pitch or time and frequency, namely the Recurrent Neural Network (RNN) and Convolutional Neural Network (CNN). However, the extent to which these architectures are capable of handling music and audio tasks remains debatable. In this chapter, we illustrate the similarities of music and audio problems with NLP and CV tasks by comparing music generation with text generation, and music melody extraction with image semantic segmentation. This provides an overview of how RNN, CNN, and transformer architectures can be applied to these problems. Then, we examine the uniqueness of music and audio problems in comparison to tasks in other fields. Previous research has demonstrated that certain designs for these architectures, both in terms of representation and multitaskstructure, can result in improved performance in music and audio tasks.

The RNN caught the attention of music research as early as 1990s, after opening up the field of neural networks to modeling language and sequences. In [91], Peter Todd describes a connectionist approach to algorithmic composition based on Elman and Jordan networks[1]. The early approaches were mostly monophonic and were difficulty to train. With the advent of long short-term memory networks (LSTMs) and the success of modern RNNs in Natural Language Processing, these tools because the first go-to neural architecture for modeling the sequential structure in music. Inspired by the success of CNNs in computer vision, and thinking about music as a time-frequency 2D structure, CNNs were also applied to music. The big difference between the two architectures is in their treatment of relations between frequencies and times. In RNN the model is purely sequential; all the temporal relations

---

[1]Elman network, which became the modern RNN, uses feedback connections from the hidden units, rather than from the output in the Jordan design.

are summarized into the tokens that are used to represent either single or multiple voices. Thus, tokenization will be our first topic of study. In CNN, the convolutional filters are applied both in time and across notes (in MIDI pianoroll representation) or frequencies (in audio spectral representation). The main difficulty in using CNNs for music is the limited span or "receptive field" of the convolutional kernel (filter). While RNN has a decaying memory that is arbitrarily long, CNNs field of view is limited to the size of the filter. Using dilated CNNs (kernels that skip samples) and hierarchical structures, such as WaveNet, became possible ways to overcome the limitation of the short-time scope of the filter response. Some hybrid variants were proposed as well, including biaxial-RNNs that apply RNNs both to the time and the frequency/notes axis, or combinations of CNN-RNN that try to combine the local feature extraction aspect of CNNs with long term memory aspect of RNNs.

7.1 TOKENIZATION

How do we pass musical input to a neural network[2]? This is the question addressed by tokenization, the process of converting musical information into smaller units called tokens.

Tokenization is used widely in Natural Language Processing. To illustrate the variety of tokenization approaches, consider the two possible tokenizations of Einstein's sentence, "If I were not a physicist, I would probably be a musician." In one such letter-based tokenization, we create a representation for each token {I,f,w,e,r,n,o,t,a,p,h,y,s,c,u,l,d,b,m}. In a different word-based tokenization, we create a representation for each token {If, I, were, not, a, physicist, would, probably, be, musician}. What are the possible benefits of the different tokenization methods? If we have a model with which we would like to learn how to spell or construct words, the letter-based tokenization will be much more useful. On the other hand, if we would like to learn the relationship between words in a sentence for proper grammatical and semantic usage, the word-based tokenization is more appropriate. Similarly, the way we tokenize musical data has a direct impact on what our models can efficiently learn from the data, and the types of output they can produce.

Now thinking in terms of input and output, if we want to learn end-to-end a complete MIDI file, why is MIDI not the best representation? The network would need to learn the formatting specifications of the MIDI encoding, which are not related to the musical information itself. So, we can tokenize the musical information itself to help our network learn musical patterns – in essence, we extract and translate the musical building blocks from the MIDI data.

MidiTok [92] is a Python package which implements multiple popular MIDI tokenization schemes:

1. MIDI-Like [93]: This scheme contains 413 tokens, including 128 note-on and note-off events (one per MIDI pitch), 125 time-shift events (increments of 8ms to

---

[2]Thanks to Ke Chen for his contributions to this section.

1 second), and 32 velocity events. MidiTok added additional quantization parameters in their implementation to allow for different numbers of tokens to accommodate different memory constraints or precision goals.

2. Revamped MIDI-Derived Events (REMI) [94]: REMI maintains the note-on and note velocity events from MIDI-like. Note-off events are instead replaced with Note Duration events; a single note is therefore represented by three consecutive tokens (note-on, note velocity, and note duration). The authors propose this to be advantageous in modeling rhythm since the note durations are more immediately informative to rhythm than placing a series of time-shift events between a note-on and note-off in MIDI-like. Additionally, the problem of a "dangling" note-on event is resolved, should the model fail to learn that note-on and note-off events must (naturally) appear in pairs.

3. Structured [95]: Unlike MIDI-Like, with Structured tokenization, tokens are provided in standardized order of pitch, velocity, duration, time shift. This encoding cannot accommodate rests or chords, so it is only suitable for modeling particular musical examples.

4. Compound Word [96]: At this point, you may have considered an odd artifact of MIDI encoding. Oftentimes, there are events which are intended to be simultaneous, but due to the one-instruction-at-a-time nature of MIDI, they are provided as a sequence. For example, a combination of a note-on instruction and its associated note velocity would be provided as a sequence of two sequential instructions in MIDI, but these instructions are intended to describe the same event. This idiosyncrasy is corrected in Compound Word. These compound words are supertokens – that is, combinations of tokens for pitch (vocabulary size 86), duration (17), velocity (24), chord (133), position (17), tempo (58), track (2), and family (4). Including "ignore" tokens for each category, there are a total of 338 vocabulary items to form a Compound Word supertoken. The "family" token allows for distinction between track events, note events, metric events, and end-of-sequence events. Similar encodings include Octuple [97] and MuMidi [98].

MidiTok uses four parameters to tokenize for each of the implemented schemes:

1. Pitch Range: minimum and maximum pitch values (integers in MIDI).
2. Number of Velocities: how many MIDI velocity levels (range 0 to 127) to quantize to.
3. Beat Resolution: the sample rate per beat, and the beat ranges for which the sample rate should be applied. Specifying a high resolution for notes with a short number of beats can improve the precision of time shifts and note durations.
4. Additional Tokens: opportunity to specify additional tokens to be included in addition to the standard set. This includes:
   a. Chord: a token which indicates a chord is being played at the particular timestep.
   b. Rest: explicit definition of a time-shift event. It is helpful to insert a tokenized rest for understanding input/output, as opposed to simply placing the next note at a later timestep since rests are an important, notated feature of most music.

c. Tempo: a token to represent the current tempo; a range of possible tempos and the number of tempos to quantize within this range should be provided to MidiTok.

7.1.1   MUSIC GENERATION VS. TEXT GENERATION

So what is the relation between Music Generation versus Text? Music generation's objective is to create musical content from input data or machine representations. The music content can be in the form of symbolic m usic notes or audio clips. Typically, the input data serves as the generative condition, such as the previous musical context, motivation, or other musical information (e.g., chord progression, structure indication, etc.). Text generation's objective is to generate natural language in response to a condition. This condition could be a couple of initial words, the conclusion of a sentence, or a change in mode (e.g., professional, neutral, creative, etc.). By and large, music and text generation have a similar conditional probability of decomposing formats:

$$\mathbf{y} = y(y_1, y_2, ..., y_T) \tag{7.1}$$

$$p(\mathbf{y}|\mathbf{c}) = \prod_t p(y_t|\mathbf{y}_{1:t-1}, \mathbf{c}) \tag{7.2}$$

where y denotes the token in different sequential tasks, and c denotes different conditions as we discussed above. In symbolic music generation, this token can be a single musical note or a latent embedding of a measure/phrase of music. In text generation, this token can be a single character, a word embedding, or even a sentence embedding with prompt learning.

Music and text generation both follow a similar probability model. As a result, successful RNN and transformer models for text generation can be easily transferred to music generation tasks. Earlier models of music generation, such as MidiNet [99] and Performance-RNN, directly applied RNN-family architectures (LSTM, GRU) to the melody generation task.

7.1.2   REPRESENTATION DESIGN OF MUSIC DATA

While text and music generation share a time sequential model, music generation is distinguished by two characteristics: (1) the spatiality of musical content; and (2) the hierarchy of musical conditions.

The musicalnote is the fundamental element of music. To begin, as illustrated in Figure 7.1, music sequences contain information beyond the temporal dimension – the vertical or spatial relationship of notes. Each time step in a text sequence contains a single word or letter; in a music sequence, each time step contains multiple notes. Whereas the piano piece depicted in the figure is a relatively straightforward form of music composition, multi-track compositions (e.g., symphony, concerto, polyphony) contain more vertical relationships between notes and even different instruments.

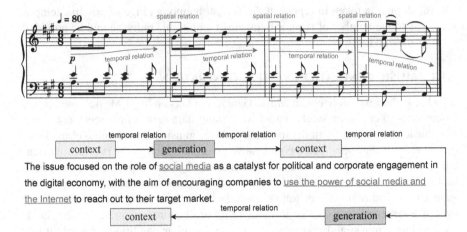

Figure 7.1 The music score of Mozart Sonata K331, first variation (top), and text data from the internet (bottom). The black part is the given context and the red one is the text generation.

This data violates one of the fundamental assumptions of RNN and transformer architectures (based on positional encoding) – that the sequence naturally contains sequential temporal information for each step of the input. Simply encoding the music data results in many steps of the input containing the same temporal information. As a result, the architecture introduces erroneous conditional dependencies on various music notes mathematically.

Second, as illustrated in Figure 7.2, music has a more complex structure than text. Apiano piece is composed of paragraphs, phrases, sub-phrases, harmonic functions,

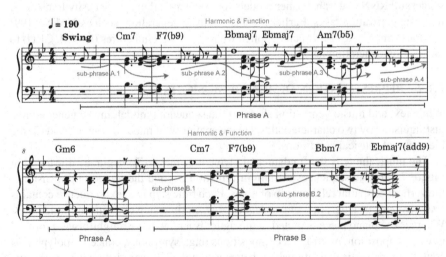

Figure 7.2 The music structure analysis of a jazz composition – Autumn Leaves, by Bill Evans.

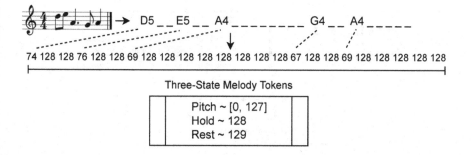

Figure 7.3 The three-state melody tokens of music data.

melodies, and textures. It becomes even more complex when the expressiveness structure is added (volume changes, rhythmic changes). While such a structure may exist in a typical novel's text generation (prologue, scenes, characters, paragraphs, and content), it is frequently absent from a large number of text generation samples. More importantly, music's structure is dynamic as well as hierarchical in nature. As illustrated in Figure 7.2, melody and texture change with each beat; harmonic functions change with certain intervals; phrases and sub-phrasesundergo even greater changes. A significant flaw in the current music generation model is the absence of long-term structure in the generated samples (e.g., repetition and variation of musical motives). In the following sections, we will discuss some of the designs ofmusic data representations and discuss how they affect the performance of music generation models.

7.1.2.1 Three-state Melody Tokens

The basic representation of music data is shown in Figure 7.3. It encodes the music into three types of tokens:

1. Pitch, the musical pitch of the note, range from [A0, C8].
2. Hold, the duration of the note, to maintain the last pitch tone.
3. Rest, the rest note.

MidiNet [100], Performance-RNN [101], and Folk-RNNgenerated music directly from tokenized representation. Consequently, MusicVAE [102], Music InpaintNet [103], EC2-VAE [104], and Music SketchNet [105] combined it with variational autoencoder (VAE) to generate latent variables to handle a piece of music as the basic generation unit. This is an intuitive representation of music that retains the essential musical information. The model's inputs and outputs are directly the representation itself, eliminating the need for additional structures to decode. The disadvantage of this representation is also self-evident: it cannot describe polyphonic music (i.e., multiple notes played simultaneously), but only monophonic melodies, because its temporal information has already been bound to the sequence's position, as is the case with text generation.

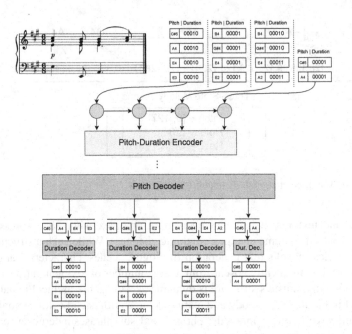

Figure 7.4 The simultaneous note group encoding of music data, by Pianotree-VAE [106].

7.1.2.2 Simultaneous Note Group

To encode polyphonic music as input, we must consider overlapping notes structure. To address this issue, Pianotree-VAE [106] proposes a vertical representation – simultaneous note group. As illustrated in Figure 7.4, it groups the simultaneous notes. by grouping multiple note events that share the same onset, where each note has several attributes such as pitch and duration. The model's input is further encoded using RNN with simultaneous group as the fundamental unit, which is further transformed into hidden states by GRU in the Pitch-Duration Encoder; in the decoder, the model is expanded with another GRU layer for predicting the pitches of each group and an final fully connected layer for predicting the duration of each note. This results in final latent z vector representation, that captures the structure of music for every 2 bars without overlap. The paper compares midi-event tokens, simultaneous note structure and latent z for a downstream music generative applications. showing that the simultaneous notes and latent vector representation are subperior to midi-event encoding.

7.1.2.3 MIDI Message

Although the above three representations have their own ways to process the music data, they miss a crucial part of encoding other music information besides the notes. MIDI message encoding, from Music Transformer [107], breaks this limitation by introducing more music content information to music generation task. As shown in

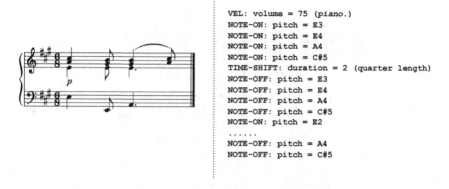

```
VEL: volume = 75 (piano.)
NOTE-ON: pitch = E3
NOTE-ON: pitch = E4
NOTE-ON: pitch = A4
NOTE-ON: pitch = C#5
TIME-SHIFT: duration = 2 (quarter length)
NOTE-OFF: pitch = E3
NOTE-OFF: pitch = E4
NOTE-OFF: pitch = A4
NOTE-OFF: pitch = C#5
NOTE-ON: pitch = E2
......
NOTE-OFF: pitch = A4
NOTE-OFF: pitch = C#5
```

Figure 7.5   The MIDI message encoding of music data.

Figure 7.5, the MIDI message is a 4-state token:

1. NOTE-ON (128 pitch classes): the starting signal of one note.
2. NOTE-OFF (128 pitch classes): the ending signal of one note.
3. TIME-SHIFT (32 interval classes): the duration mark to move the timeline.
4. VEL (128 volume classes): the velocity changes.

In REMI [108], the MIDI message is expanded into six states, including note onset, tempo, bar line, phrase, time, and volume. With this representation, the model is able to acquire additional musical data and discover new patterns, resulting better well-structured and varied musical compositions.

7.1.2.4   Music Compound Word

Music Compound Word [109] proposes a new structural design for MIDI messages, complete with an improved input and output network module. As illustrated in Figure 7.6, the state of the music input in a compound word transformer is comparable to that of a MIDI message, but the input and output mechanisms are entirely different.

Music compound word can be adapted into different scenarios of music generation by changing the types of states along with the decoding layers. Figure 7.7 shows three types of music compound words for (1) music generation with performance labels, (2) multi-track music generations with multiple instruments, and (3) music generation with structural labels. Besides that, because the music compound word contains the position state (e.g., beat, bar, etc.), the transformer architecture can be used without any positional encoding. This begins to differentiate the music generation task from the text generation task when the same architecture is used.

7.1.2.5   Discussion: Signal Embedding versus Symbolic Embedding

In the previous chapter we saw an embedding of an audio signal that can be used to obtain salient audio components, such as audio basis, compression, or noise removal.

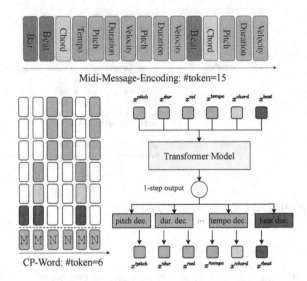

Figure 7.6 The compound word encoding of music data, compared with MIDI-message encoding.

We used the analogy between PCA and linear AE to get an intuition that embedding is a subspace where the meaningful part of the signal resides. In particular, we showed for the sinusoid+noise example that this embedding is very similar to signal transformation using Fourier methods. Projection to a lower dimensional space of sinusoids not only allows discarding noise, but can also be used as a representation

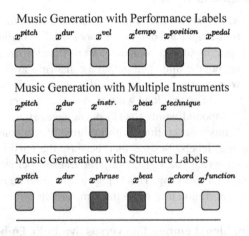

Figure 7.7 The compound word encoding of three music generation scenarios.

of the "meaningful" part of the signal. Representation in the latent space found by the AE and representation found by Fourier transform share similar basic vectors.

But can such embedding also be applied to MIDI? Autoencoding of categorical variables is a poorly defined problem – after all, the neural network embeddings assume that similar concepts are placed nearby in the embedding space. These proximities can be used to understand music concepts based on cluster categories. Then, they can also serve as an input to a machine learning model for a supervised task and for visualization of concepts and relations between categories.

It is natural to represent categorical variables as one-hot vectors. The operation of one-hot encoding categorical variables is actually a simple embedding where each category is mapped to a different vector. This process takes discrete entities and maps each observation to a vector of 0s and a single 1 signaling the specific category. The one-hot encoding technique has two main drawbacks:

- For high-cardinality variables – those with many unique categories – the dimensionality of the transformed vector becomes unmanageable.
- The mapping is completely uninformed: "similar" categories are not placed closer to each other in embedding space.

So embeddings could be obtained using either a manually designed representation, or could try to obtain it from the data. This type of contextual embedding is what we commonly refer to as "representation learning". In the case of temporal sequences, we might want to obtain a representation of a complete sequence. In many musical applications, RNN (the topic of our next section) is used to pre-process the sequences before the representation learning happens.

7.2   RECURRENT NEURAL NETWORK FOR MUSIC

7.2.1   SEQUENCE MODELING WITH RNNS

RNNs are a way to model time sequences, an early neural network application. They are used to represent a function where the output depends on the input as well as previous output. In other words, the model must have memory for what has happened before, maintaining some representation of internal state.

We can imagine the RNN to be learning the probability of a sequence of tokens, $P(w_1, w_2, ..., w_n)$, from a collection of example sequences used in training.

Once this language model is learned, we can solve the problem of predicting the next token of a sequence (that is, computing $P(w_n|w_1, w_2, ..., w_n)$).

This can be framed as a supervised learning problem, in which the sequence $(w_1, w_2, ..., w_{n-1})$ acts as input which corresponds to output w_n.

Essentially, an RNN is two neural networks: one which acts on the input, and one which acts on the hidden state.

$$h_t = f(h_{t-1}, x_t) \quad \text{(general form)} \tag{7.3}$$

$$h_t = tanh(W_{hh}h_{t-1} + W_{xh}X_t) \quad \text{(NN with activation)} \tag{7.4}$$

$$o_t = W_{hy}h_t \quad \text{(output)} \tag{7.5}$$

In these equations, h represents the hidden state and x represents the input.

Hello World from an RNN

To introduce RNN architecture, we will build an example which learns to say "Hello World". More accurately, this model will learn to output a sequence of letters that match the sequences it has been trained on (in this case, "Hello World"). Given a starting letter (or set of letters), the model generates the next character of output. We will continue building this example through the section as we cover the foundations of RNNs.

First, how shall we represent input to this network? Because the mathematical operations in the neural network must operate on numbers, we must convert our letter data ("h","e","l","l","o") into numerical data.

For simplicity, we will work in a hypothetical world with a reduced alphabet: E-D-H-L-O-R-W.

One scheme for encoding the letter "h" would be to replace the letter with its positional index in the alphabet (2, in the case of our reduced alphabet [and using 0-indexing]). However, this introduces an issue as the value of different numbers will carry different apparent weights; mathematically, we recognize 5 to be a larger number than 2, but we would not say that the letter R has a different implicit significance than the letter H.

The solution for this is to use the previously introduced one-hot encoding. In this schema, the letters are treated as categorical (rather than quantitative) variables, so any one letter is replaced by a 7-vector of zeros – with the exception of the index associated with the letter we represent, where we find a one. In this way, every letter has an equal magnitude in the representation, while information distinguishing between letters is preserved.

It is important to note that this method fails for large (or expanding) vocabulary sizes. To overcome these particular challenges (or simply to reduce the input dimensionality), the technique of embedding can be used, a concept recurring through our discussion in prior and following chapters.

But even though we've learned to encode single letters to vectors, the input is still not ready for the RNN. RNNs are meant to operate on *sequences* rather than singular input. So, the input *length* may actually vary depending on use cases. In our Hello World example, we will use an input length of 3 (so, a 3 by 7 matrix when considering the encoding for each sequence element), but in other problems this length can grow to 1000s of values. We will explore the challenges associated with large input sequence lengths in

---

this chapter.

What about the output? Like other classification problems, our network will output a fixed-length probability vector, representing the probability that the next token is a particular word from a predefined vocabulary set. Think about how the dimensionality of this vector may change between domains; for forming English words, we have 26 letters, but for forming English language, there are over 171,000 words in the dictionary alone (excluding all sorts of proper nouns). For Western music, we have 12 chroma, but for a single instrument, the vocabulary may span the entire playable range, and for some instruments (such as the piano), our vocabulary grows exponentially with the number of possible simultaneous notes possible in a chord.

So, let's start our RNN example by preparing the one-hot encoding scheme. First, we will import necessary packages:

```
import numpy as np
import tensorflow as tf
from tensorflow import keras
from tensorflow.keras import layers
import keras.backend as K
```

Next, we will define our letter encoding:

```
def letter_to_encoding(letter):
    letters = ['e','d','h','l','o','r','w']
    vec = np.zeros((7),dtype="float32")
    vec[letters.index(letter)] = 1
    return vec
```

We can see the effects of this encoding with this sample:

```
for letter in "hello":
    print(letter_to_encoding(letter))
```

which gives output

```
[0. 0. 1. 0. 0. 0. 0.]
[1. 0. 0. 0. 0. 0. 0.]
[0. 0. 0. 1. 0. 0. 0.]
[0. 0. 0. 1. 0. 0. 0.]
[0. 0. 0. 0. 1. 0. 0.]
```

For our example, we will use a single-layer RNN. The network will take an input with shape 3x7xN, where 3 represents the input sequence length, 7 represents the size of the data vector associated with each input, and N is the number of samples in a training batch.

The RNN layer is a Keras SimpleRNN; each of the 3 nodes of this RNN will create a 7-dimensional output (again used to represent the likelihood associated with a single character in our alphabet). Though each length-3 input will map to a length-3 output, we take only the third (final) output to represent the predicted "next character" of our phrase. Had we left off the "return_sequences" parameter, the network would output only this final character (but for sake of example, it will be interesting to see the entire predicted sequence). To normalize the raw output into a probability-like representation, we apply a softmax activation function prior to output.

Here is the model definition:

```
model = keras.Sequential()
model.add(keras.Input(shape=(3,7,)))
model.add(layers.SimpleRNN(7, activation="softmax",
                           return_sequences=True))
model.summary()
```

The exercises at the end of the chapter asks you to think about why this network has 105 trainable parameters. As a hint, recall that the input to the RNN node is made up of the input vector, plus the hidden state, plus a bias term, and that these inputs are fully connected to the generated output.
In the below code, we create our training data. In our hypothetical world, the only phrase that exists is "helloworld", so we train the network on fragments of this phrase. For those following along by running the code, you can see in the below example that for each three-letter portion, the output matches the next predicted letter following each letter of the input.

```
train_text = "helloworld"*30
def generate_train_set(train_text, as_words=False):
    x_train = []
    y_train = []
    for i in range(len(train_text)-4):
        if as_words:
            x_train += [[train_text[i:i+3]]]
            y_train += [[train_text[i+1:i+4]]]

        else:
            x_train += [[letter_to_encoding(letter)
                        for letter in train_text[i:i+3]]]
```

```
                y_train += [[letter_to_encoding(letter)
                            for letter in train_text[i+1:i+4]]]

    if as_words:
        print(x_train[0][:5])
        print(y_train[0][:5])
    else:
        print(np.array(x_train)[0,:5])
        print(np.array(x_train).shape)

    return np.array(x_train), np.array(y_train)

generate_train_set(train_text, True)
x_train, y_train = generate_train_set(train_text)
```

So what happens when we generate an output phrase using the untrained network?

```
letters = ['e','d','h','l','o','r','w']

seed = "hel"
result = "hel"
input_data = np.array([[letter_to_encoding(letter)
                        for letter in seed]])
model.get_weights()

for i in range(7):

    out = model(input_data)
    print_output = K.eval(out)
    for row in print_output[0]:
        next_letter = letters[np.argmax(row)]
    result += next_letter
    print(result)
    input_data = np.array([[letter_to_encoding(letter)
                            for letter in result[-3:]]])
```

After running the above code, we reach something like this:

```
hele
helee
heleee
heleeee
heleeeee
```

```
heleeeeee
heleeeeeee
```

The model weights are not yet optimized; we train with the following lines:

```
model.compile(optimizer=keras.optimizers.Adam(
            learning_rate=0.01),
            loss=tf.keras.losses.CategoricalCrossentropy())
model.fit(x_train, y_train, batch_size=24,
            epochs=300, verbose=0)
```

And, after training, we try again to produce output:

```
input_data = np.array([[letter_to_encoding(letter)
                        for letter in seed]])
model.get_weights()
result = "hel"
for i in range(7):
    out = model(input_data)
    print_output = K.eval(out)
    for row in print_output[0]:
        next_letter = letters[np.argmax(row)]
    result += next_letter
    print(result)
    input_data = np.array([[letter_to_encoding(letter)
                        for letter in result[-3:]]])
```

Giving us the following output from our simple RNN:

```
hell
hello
hellow
hellowo
hellowor
helloworl
helloworld
```

Is a recurrent neural model of music appropriate for generating music that "sounds like" other music by a particular composer or within a genre? An ideal statistical model would learn from all possible sequence inputs to create the an expected musical output, but the size of possible inputs is v^n, where v is vocabulary size and n is input sequence length. Even considering just 88 piano keys and 10 notes in a sequence creates 2.785^{19} combinations!

To overcome this, think back to the Markov assumption introduced in Chapter 2. If we approximate that a prediction depends only on a small number of preceding tokens, the problem becomes much more tractable to model. But, in doing so, we lose the ability to model long-range effects of earlier tokens.

So, how do neural models maintain long-range effects?

A first attempt to solve this problem could consider combining the sequence of input tokens into one mega-token, for which a corresponding prediction can be made. A neural network can be applied over this input matrix, with dimensions of vocabulary size or embedding vector length by number of elements in input sequence. Note that we have a built-in limitation with such a model: tokens further away than the number of elements in the input sequence cannot influence the model output.

Recurrent neural networks overcome this constraint; that is, recurrent neural networks can learn extensive long-range influences despite limited-length input sequences. It does so by encoding the sequential history into a hidden state, which we will refer to at time t by h_t in this discussion (you can imagine "h" to stand for "history"). This state h_t is updated with input x_t, then used in predicting output y_t. Encasing this history state in a black box, the RNN appears to receive a sequence of vectors $x_0, x_1, ..., x_T$ as input, and produces a sequence of vectors $o_0, o_1, ..., o_T$ as output. Internally, we can imagine the process to begin with the computation of the history state:

$$h_t = F(h_{t-1}, x_t), \tag{7.6}$$

then prediction of output using the updated history:

$$o_t = G(h_t). \tag{7.7}$$

The relationships between the inputs, multi-dimensional hidden history state, and outputs can be learned with neural network training procedures, as studied in previous chapters. These relationships are represented by functions F and G, which may be composed as:

$$F(h,x) = A_1(W_{hh} * h + W_{xh} * x) \tag{7.8}$$

and

$$G(h) = A_2(W_{ho} * h). \tag{7.9}$$

In this notation, A_i stands for an activation function, and W_{IO} stands for a matrix of learnable weights which map from the dimensionality of the matrix's input vector class to the matrix's output vector class. W_{xh} describes the influence of the input on the next state, W_{hh} describes the influence of the current state on the next state, and W_{ho} describes the influence of the next state on the next output. An illustration of the relationships between input, hidden state, and output are shown in Figure 7.8.

If we ignore the intermediate outputs $o_1, ..., o_{N-1}$, this is really just a feedforward network, with initial inputs h_0 and x_1, and with additional inputs concatenated to the outputs of particular intermediate layers. However, in a traditional feedforward network, the weights between layers are uniquely learned. In the case of an RNN, these weights are *shared*; that is, the same weights will act on the input x_t regardless

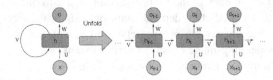

Figure 7.8 In its compact form (left), and RNN consists of a learned hidden state h, which is driven by both the current input and past values, and itself drives the output o, as described in the RNN equations. To make explicit the development of state h over time and its relationship to input and output, we can imagine the RNN in its "unfolded" form (right).

of time, and the same weights will act on one state h_t to create the next state (or to create output) regardless of time.

How do we learn in this shared-weight scenario? In our previous backpropagation example, the derivative of loss with respect to a particular weight could be calculated, and the weights adjusted accordingly. Now, for the same weight, we have multiple possible derivatives since there are multiple inputs influenced by that parameter!

Without diving too deep into theory, let's consider an approach by which we take the average of these gradient contributions. That is, for any of the N instances of w_i in the network, which we can call w_{i_n}, we can compute $\frac{\partial L}{\partial w_{i_n}}$. Then, when deciding how to modify shared parameter w_i, we use

$$\frac{\partial L}{\partial w_i} = \frac{1}{N} \sum_{n=1}^{N} \frac{\partial L}{\partial w_{i_n}}. \tag{7.10}$$

In principle, the average should move us closer toward an optimal solution since the largest amount of "mistake" explained by the weight applied at a particular layer will have the largest amount of influence on this averaged gradient component.

There is one critical issue with this approach (and in fact, with any networks sufficiently deep), referred to as the **vanishing gradient problem**, as discussed in Chapter 6. This problem is particularly notable for modeling sequential data since it effectively limits how far back in time a model can learn to "reach" to influence its output; while the RNN is capable of representing long sequences of data, it loses the ability to learn at length.

Methods to mitigate the problem of long-range influence have been developed, including the Gated Recurrent Unit (GRU) and Long Short-Term Memory (LSTM) network.

Gated Architectures: Long Short-Term Memory Network and Gated Recurrent Unit

A Long Short-Term Memory network, or LSTM, is an RNN architecture designed to deal with the vanishing gradient problem that plagues traditional

RNNs, causing difficulty in learning long-term dependencies commonly found in music and audio.

The LSTM architecture introduces a new type of unit called the *memory cell* that can store information for long periods of time. This represents the "long" component of the LSTM. The memory cell is controlled by three gates:

1. the input gate,
2. the forget gate, and
3. the output gate.

Each gate is typically activated using a sigmoid function which determines how much of the input should be let through to the memory cell, how much of the memory cell's contents should be forgotten, and how much of the memory cell's contents should be output.

The "short-term" component of the LSTM is accounted for by the addition of a hidden state at each time t, similar to an RNN. The hidden state is updated based on the current input, previous hidden state, and (a key distinction) memory cell output. This state can help to carry time forward from each step of the input sequence as well as call upon long-term information.

All three gates of the memory cell receive the current input and the previous hidden state to inform their evaluation. By using memory cells and gates to control the flow of information, LSTMs are better able to learn long-term dependencies in the input sequence.

Like the classic RNN and LSTM, a Gated Recurrent Unit architecture, or GRU, processes input one sequence element at a time and maintains a hidden state updated by a combination of both current input and previous hidden state. What differentiates GRUs is the addition of new types of gating mechanisms to control the flow of information through the network. GRUs use two types of gates:

1. an update gate, to decide how much information from the previous state should be retained and incorporated into the new hidden state, and
2. a reset gate, to decide how much of the previous hidden state should be discarded.

The benefit of the GRU is its simpler architecture, with fewer parameters than a comparable LSTM. This helps to avoid overfitting on small datasets, a common problem to overparameterized models. Both LSTMs and GRUs offer a gated mechanism for modeling long-term dependencies, and the choice between the architectures ultimately falls to considerations related to the task at hand, such as dataset size, expected time dependencies, and computational constraints.

7.2.2　SEQUENCE-TO-SEQUENCE MODELING WITH RNNS

Sometimes we seek not to learn only an estimated distribution for a sequential pattern, but a mapping from one sequence to another. For example, pretend you are a jazz saxophonist, and you attend a friend's classical piano recital. A striking melody from one of their pieces catches your attention, and you'd like to improvise on it when you practice later that day. In this case, you are taking an input sequence of the melody in a classical context, and translating it to a jazz melody (which may have different styles of ornamentation). Such a problem is solved using sequence-to-sequence (often abbreviated seq2seq) modeling.

Formally, we can describe such problems this way: Given vocabularies V_z and V_x and training data pairs (z_n, x_n) independently and identically distributed from some distribution p, can we estimate the distribution $p(x|z)$?

Framing the above problem in this notation, V_z are the possible notes from the piano, and V_x are the possible notes from the saxophone. We can collect samples of the same melody played once by the classical pianist (z_n) and again by the jazz saxophonist (x_n), and use these to learn a distribution of what we expect the jazz saxophone to sound like (x) for a given piano melody (z). There are numerous other problems we can frame as seq2seq, including the problem of transcription (given an audio sequence, returning the same represented music in symbolic notation).

7.2.3　PERFORMANCE RNN

Now, we extend our RNN exploration to a musical example. Performance RNN [101] is a network which generates performance-quality MIDI piano output [3]. In fact, Performance RNN was the project which introduced the MIDI-Like tokenization scheme introduced in the previous section. To understand Performance RNN, let's examine its components:

- Data: Performance RNN is trained on the Yamaha e-Piano Competition dataset (introduced in Appendix D). This is a collection of approximately 1,400 MIDI files, generated by recording the keypresses of highly skilled classical pianists. Accordingly, the music is expressive in both timing (rubato) and velocity (dynamics).
- Tokenization: MIDI-Like tokenization is employed. At each step, the input to the RNN is a single one-hot 413-dimensional vector representing the 413 possible note-on, note-off, velocity, and time-shift events.
- Model Architecture: Three hidden layers of LSTMs with 512 cells.
- Training and Loss: The model is trained using the RNN technique of *teacher forcing*.

---

[3]Performance RNN is a product of Google Magenta, introduced in Appendix A. You can learn more about Performance RNN on the authors' blog (https://magenta.tensorflow.org/performance-rnn), and run the code yourself with instructions available in their GitHub Repository (https://github.com/magenta/magenta/tree/main/magenta/models/performance_rnn).

> **Teacher forcing** helps models reach stable convergence during training by providing the correct (rather than predicted) output as input to each sequential step. For example, imagine a model meant to learn a C-major scale (C-D-E-F-G-A-B-C). In a non-forced training, if the model is given input C to the first cell, and incorrectly predicts an output of E, the E would propagate as input to the second sequential cell. In teacher forcing, the input to the second sequential is forced to D to match the ground truth. While this is beneficial to efficiently learn the given pattern, it should be noted that this reduces the model's ability to learn from variations on the pattern which may not be represented in the training data (but may exist otherwise). For generative models which seek to perform and innovate (rather than replicate), this could be detrimental in some cases.

Log loss (i.e. categorical cross-entropy) is the loss function used to drive training backpropagation.

- Output Generation: beam search.

> **Beam Search**
>
> Beam search is a heuristic search algorithm used to find the most likely sequence of output given an input sequence. It is a variant of the *breadth-first search* algorithm, which attempts to balance exploration and exploitation, a problem common to search algorithms as well as the AI subfield of reinforcement learning[a].
>
> The basic idea behind beam search is to generate multiple possible outputs at each step, but keep only the top-K most probable candidates. This value K is referred to as the *beam width*. The algorithm then proceeds to the next step, generating a new set of candidate outputs for each of the previous K candidates, continuing until a stopping criterion is met.
>
> In theory, the beam search algorithm eliminates low-probability candidates early on to speed up and improve the quality of the output sequence search. However, beam search can also suffer from the problem of getting stuck in local optima, where the most likely candidates at each step do not necessarily lead to the overall most likely output sequence or reflect desired long-term behavior.
>
> As an example, consider a diatonic melody which starts on C, and will choose the next note from the C major scale. The predictive model may output probabilities for each of these notes: (C, 0.1), (D, 0.1), (E, 0.1), (F, 0.2), (G, 0.3), (A, 0.15), (B, 0.05). If we use a beam width of 3, we select

the top 3 most likely possible sequences, CF, CG, CA, and associate these with respective probabilities 0.2, 0.3, 0.15.

Now, the next three sets of next sequence options are generated, conditioned on *each* of these selections; this may be something like

- CF: (C, 0.05), (D, 0.025), (E, 0.25), (F, 0.3), (G, 0.3), (A, 0.05), (B, 0.025)
- CG: (C, 0.3), (D, 0.025), (E, 0.25), (F, 0.05), (G, 0.3), (A, 0.05), (B, 0.025)
- CA: (C, 0.2), (D, 0.025), (E, 0.2), (F, 0.3), (G, 0.2), (A, 0.05), (B, 0.025)

The score for each of the resulting possibilities is the probability of the prior sequence times the probability of the next token. For example, considering the first row above, we would have as possibilities (CFC, 0.01), (CFD, 0.005), (CFE, 0.05), (CFF, 0.06), (CFG, 0.06), (CFA, 0.01), (CFB, 0.005). We repeat this for all three beams, and from the resulting scores, select again the top 3 candidate sequences – these are the only sequences which will continue propagating forward. Once the desired sequence length is reached, the beam search is concluded and the available sequence assigned the most probability can be selected.

---

[a]While reinforcement learning is outside the scope of this book, readers are encouraged to consider that generation in a creative or imaginative sense requires this same consideration of exploring new ideas versus utilizing known patterns.

7.2.4 SAMPLERNN

In the introduction of *SampleRNN: An Unconditional End-to-End Neural Audio Generation Model* [64], Mehri et al. highlight primary challenges associated with audio generation:

1. A large discrepancy between the dimensionality of the audio signal and the semantically meaningful unit (e.g., 1 word is, on average, around 6,000 samples at a 16 kHz sample rate).
2. Structure occurs at various scales (correlations between neighboring samples as well as samples thousands of units apart).
3. Compression of raw audio to meaningful spectral (or other handcrafted) features.
4. Necessary correction of audio after decompression (for example, consider the complexity of Griffin-Lim for reconstructing phase).

SampleRNN seeks to reduce this complicated, engineering-heavy pipeline by allowing a neural network to learn these compression and reconstruction processes as well as relationships between the many samples comprising meaningful audio signals.

SampleRNN approaches this task using a hierarchical framework, where lower-level modules operate on individual samples, but higher-level modules operate at a larger timescale and lower temporal resolution. This is one example approach toward learning audio (or musical) trends which operate at different scales to overcome limitations of a rudimentary sample-by-sample RNN framework.

How are the model outputs of SampleRNN evaluated (and, in general, how can we evaluate the performance of generative audio models)? In this case, **AB Testing** with human rates is employed. Pairwise combinations of SampleRNN with other comparative models (including WaveNet) are presented to human raters, who then express preference for "A" over "B" (or vice versa). Then, one can compute a number of statistics, the most common being the percentage of times that samples from the model in question were preferred over the alternative. The subjectivity of evaluating artistic or preference-based generative models creates difficulties in presenting conclusive metrics, but AB preference testing is one such approach that is generally accepted and useful.

7.3 CONVOLUTIONAL NEURAL NETWORKS FOR MUSIC AND AUDIO

In this section we will introduce Convolutional Neural Networks (CNN) for 2D representation of music and audio. CNNs are popular for image processing and use an implementation of a local filtering approach over neighboring pixels. The idea of CNN, in a way similar to the adaptive filtering approaches we encountered in the DSP part of the book is that data is used to estimate or train the filter parameters to perform some desired task. Thinking about CNN as a filter, we must note that

- CNNs implement multiple local filters,
- They are often trained for feature extraction and inference, i.e. some classification tasks and not as an audio filter, and
- The local properties (finite impulse response) of CNNs are often implemented in 2D, which in our case will span both time and frequency, or time and voices in spectral or piano-roll representations, respectively.

One must note that one of the big advantages of CNNs in the visual domain is that many of the features in images are local and translation invariant. In other words, we want to detect lines, corners, or part of faces and so on, regardless of the exact position where these visual elements appear in the picture. In music, local relations might exist between notes or frequency elements in time, and also across frequencies or notes, such as in the case of harmonic or polyphonic (multi-voice) relations. The big difficulty is that such relations are usually much longer or distant in time then what a normal visual patch would be. We will talk about capturing long term relation when we discuss attention in RNN and transformers in a later chapter. Regardless of the limitations, CNNs have been found to be very useful tools for analysis of time-frequency structures, or in other words, representing voices in time.

7.3.1 WHAT IS A CNN?

CNNs are defined by the presence of *convolutional* layers. Many signal processing textbooks explain the mathematical details of convolution, and here we present the material in a conceptual manner. Convolution is the result of iterating through and operating upon portions of a signal using another signal (referred to as a convolutional filter or kernel); the nature of this interaction is typically a sum of elementwise multiplications. An example is shown in Figure 7.9. During convolution, the filter is applied to every sub-region of the signal that it passes over, generating a scalar value for each position it assumes. The pseudo-image created from the mosaic of these scalar values is called a *feature map*. When defining the convolution operation, it is possible to vary the spatial pacing of the filter as it passes through the image

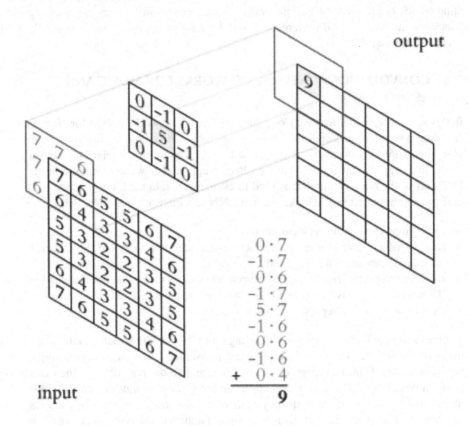

Figure 7.9 The 2D convolution operation. A kernal (middle) is applied to the input image (left) in a dot-product operation where each grid cell of the kernel is multiplied by its corresponding cell in the input image, then added to a running sum for a given kernel position. This sum becomes the output value in the feature map (right). The kernel then slides across the image to the next position, until every position of the image has been covered.

(referred to as *stride*) as well as the extent to which the filter is used at the edges of the signal (commonly addressed via *padding*). Stride, filter size, and number of filters are sufficient to define a convolutional layer within a CNN architecture.

These filters become a powerful tool for extracting meaningful information from a signal. Readers who have studied signal processing are likely familiar with a basic ensemble of filters (low-pass, high-pass, bandpass, etc.) which allow certain frequency components to be extracted from a composite signal. When it comes to 2D convolution, filters can be used for many informational and transformational purposes; as two examples of the many possibilities, some filters can extract meaningful qualities such as edges (locations in the image with intense transitions from dark to light or vice versa), and others can transform an image by taking local averages (referred to as image smoothing or blurring).

In the above cases, the image filter is strictly defined, then applied to the image. For example, a Laplacian operator, which acts as a great detector of strong intensity changes by approximating a local second derivative, always features a strong, positive value at the central location, surrounded by a ring of weaker, negative values. Other times, it may be useful to use filters which adapt to the problem you intend to solve. Such is the case with object template matching, where a filter is designed by selecting values that exhibit a strong value when convolved with the template object, and weak values elsewhere. We will reserve details about implementation and theory of such filters for a digital image processing textbook, but the driving principle should be remembered: filters can be tuned to highlight particular types of information from an image. Selecting or handcrafting these filters often leads to two situations:

- The selected theoretical filter is so general that it can only find particular low-level features (e.g., local intensity changes in a particular direction).
- The handcrafted filter is so specific that it can only find exact matches to particular high-level entities (e.g., a very specific pattern in a spectrogram from a violinist playing a phrase, which would not have the same strength of response if a different violinist played the same phrase).

This is where *convolutional neural networks* come into play. Instead of selecting or crafting convolutional filters, each filter's parameters are *learned* during training. Each convolutional layer consists of a bank of n filters, defined by their height and width. These filters are eventually optimized for the task at hand through the usual methods of backpropagation and gradient descent. Convolutional layers are stacked (creating *deep* neural networks), and through this stacking mechanism, features are extracted and combined at low, mid, and high levels of abstraction (e.g., edges combine to become geometric shapes, which combine to become recognizable object patterns).

7.3.1.1 Pooling

Consider the effect of a bank of 10 3x3 filters acting on a 20x20 pixel single-channel image. This layer would require 90 parameters. After this convolutional layer (and assuming appropriate padding), the output feature map would maintain a spatial dimension of 20x20, but with a depth of 10 features. If this convolutional layer is comprised of an additional 10 filters, each filter would now need 3x3x10 parameters, requiring 900 parameters for the layer.

Following this trend, we can see that the requisite parameters quickly explodes the deeper the data propagates through the network. As a means to reduce this issue, we can use the technique of *pooling*. Pooling provides a means of reducing the spatial dimensionality of a feature map, operating on the assumption that the reduced feature map will still exhibit the useful, informative patterns available at full scale.

In a pooling scheme, a square region of an image is replaced by a single value intended to represent the region. Example selected values may be the region's maximum (*maxpooling*) or average (*averagepooling*).

As convolutional and pooling layers progress (with padding reduced), eventually we reach a spatial dimension of 1 with a deep set of features; from this point, the network is typically concluded with a series of fully connected layers.

7.3.2 CNN AUDIO EXAMPLE: WAVENET

Slightly contrary to our above discussion, we will begin our examples of CNNs with WaveNet, a model which actually does not act on image-like 2D representations (piano roll, spectrogram, etc.); WaveNet is a deep generative model used to process raw audio waveforms.

WaveNet has been shown to generate speech mimicking the human voice[4] and synthesize musical audio signals. WaveNet directly models the raw audio waveform sample-by-sample, in direct contrast to historical methods of speech synthesis where phonemes from a bank can be concatenated to create words, or vocoders can produce synthetic sound fragments. This allows for improved realism and flexibility in the model, but why has this approach been a long-standing challenge?

The large issue at play is the rate of prediction necessary to support sample-level modeling; while phonemes may change on the scale of milliseconds, audio files change value at a rate of 16,000 samples (or more!) per second. To make matters worse, we have seen from our earlier discussion on deep neural networks that long-term patterns become increasingly hard to model the further back they exist in time (relative to the current predictive position); when we are moving at 16,000 samples per second, there is a huge gap between our current position and information we may need to effectively model the sound!

Researchers at Google DeepMind had a solid basis for taking the leap of faith to model massive sequential lengths; previously, the research team developed Pixel-CNN and PixelRNN. These neural networks acted on images, but there are themes drawn from this work that translate to the audio domain:

---

[4]Examples are available from DeepMind at https://www.deepmind.com/blog/wavenet-a-generative-model-for-raw-audio

- Recurrent Layers, as we studied in the previous section, parameterize series of conditional distributions.
- Residual Connections are used to share information between different network depths.
- Generated samples are crisp, varied, and globally coherent, three properties which are of equal concern when generating audio.

After seeing promising results that an image could be generated pixel-by-pixel (that is, row-wise sequentially, as opposed to a more expansive upsampling method), similar techniques were applied to audio data, which is naturally sequential.

The dilation of the WaveNet architecture varies at each layer; this allows WaveNet to maintain an enormous *receptive field*, referring to the range of time from the original signal subtended by the network to generate its next output. This WaveNet architecture has become a standard tool to other works in audio processing. Considering the original goals of the authors, it proved effective in modeling realistic voices for text-to-speech translation, and even showed promise in learning patterns across different speaking voices. The authors additionally trained WaveNet on classical piano recordings, and the results are unique piano recordings which sound realistic, with minute amounts of noise seemingly an artifact of a phantom recording process rather than spurious musical decisions.

7.3.3 CNN AUDIO EXAMPLE: UNET FOR SOURCE SEPARATION

We earlier introduced the problem of *source separation*, the isolation of individual sounds (or sources) in an audio mixture[5]. Techniques such as active source estimation can help to solve for the mixture of source energies between spectral frames of the audio signal, and can even be extended with information from an audio-aligned written score for enhanced estimation [111]. As we will see in the following paragraph, CNNs have also become a popular approach toward this task, as their convolution and transpose (reverse) convolution operations can be used to generate masks to filter spectral representations of audio into individual sources.

Such a *mask* layer can be overlaid on the original spectrogram (or mathematically speaking, element-wise multiplied) to allow only the information associated with a particular source to pass through. From this masked spectrogram, the sound of a single source can be approximately reconstructed. To do this, the size of the output of the CNN must match the size of the input (that is, the mask must be the same size as the spectrogram so that it perfectly covers). This naturally requires an encoder-decoder structure to the network, so that the learned parameters can be structured in a way that rebuilds the downsampled input to its original size. The UNet architecture [112] is a popular architecture for such problems due to its symmetric U-shape, use

---

[5]A fantastic resource to learn about this problem and its applications comes from a tutorial by Ethan Manilow, Prem Seetharaman, and Justin Salamon at the 2020 International Society for Music Information Retrieval conference [110].

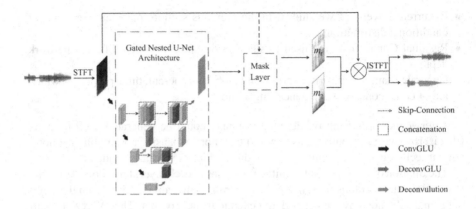

Figure 7.10 Geng et al.'s illustration of the Gated Nested UNet [113]; in this use case, the network generates a mask which can be elementwise multiplied with the original audio to separate the sources.

of residual "skip connections" to pass information between spatial resolutions, and inclusion of layers of parameters at the decoding side to assist in reconstruction.

Two examples (of many) which use this technique can be found in works by Geng et al. [113] and Kong et al. [114]. Geng et al. use a UNet variant called "gated nested" UNet (GNUnet), where there are nested series of layers "filling in" the center of the U. The original U "backbone" has gating units applied, a mechanism originally proposed for RNNs which control the information flow throughout the network to allow for modeling more sophisticated interactions. The outputs of GNUNet are used to create a time-frequency spectral mask to generate two masks: one for singing, one for accompaniment. The two masks can be multiplied by the magnitude and phase spectra of the mixture, then transformed back into time-domain signals simultaneously, as opposed to networks which isolate and extract only one source. Also using a UNet architecture, Kong et al. additionally estimate complex ideal ratio masks (that is, decoupling the masks into a mask for magnitude and a mask for phase) to decrease reconstruction error. The result is a system effective at separating vocal tracks, bass, drums, and more.

7.4 PRETRAINED AUDIO NEURAL NETWORKS

Within the realm of computer vision (where CNNs have been enjoying great success), it is very common to see the same network architecture repurposed for a new problem. For example, we might imagine a network used to classify instruments from an image could be a structural twin of a network used to identify whether a person is holding or actively playing an instrument; to make an explicit example, we can pretend both use the popular ResNet architecture. For both problems, it is a reasonable approach to train the network from scratch; that is, randomize the weights, and use the training data to begin learning. However, from our understanding of the problem space, it's also known that some basic, mid-level patterns should appear in both models, such as recognizing keys or mouthpieces of an instrument, or even a learned template of the full instrument. Even though the ending layers may be doing something different with the information between use cases, the same patterns should be learned. For this reason, *pretraining* a network is often very useful, especially when annotated data for one problem may be less abundant. Pretraining allows a network to start learning from some base amount of knowledge, typically in the form of low or mid-level features. Even when we don't have data from such a similar task, it's still often beneficial to pretrain with some real-world image data, such as ImageNet; even though you might not expect to see a car or a cat in your dataset, you will certainly share meaningful low-level features such as edges and standard geometries.

The authors of "PANNs: Large-Scale Pretrained Audio Neural Networks for Audio Pattern Recognition" propose this same idea of network pretraining for a variety of use cases within audio machine learning, such as

- Audio Tagging: predicting metadata tags associating with an audio clip.
- Acoustic Scene Classification: a specific form of audio tagging which typically categorizes audio into ambient classes, such as "train station", "park", "shopping mall", etc.
- Music Classification: another style of audio tagging, but this time within musical categories (examples include genre, artist, instrumentation, etc.).
- Music and Speech Emotion Classification: beyond the ambiguities and complexities of emotion, this is a challenging process due to technical differences in emotion labeling and comparative features. Koh and Dubnov [115] show that state-of-the-art pre-trained deep audio embedding methods which efficiently capture high dimensional features in compact representation can be used in Music Emotion Recognition (MER) tasks. Two such deep audio embedding methods (L3-Net and VGGish) are discussed later in this section.
- Sound Event Detection: recognizing sound events and their respective temporal start and end time in audio. Sound events often occur in noisy environments with multiple events occurring, making this a challenging problem.

When it comes to pretraining methods, what is the analogous audio dataset to ImageNet? This would be AudioSet, a dataset from Google containing 632 audio event classes and a collection of 2,084,320 human-labeled 10-second sound clips drawn from YouTube.

As opposed to WaveNet and other one-dimensional time-domain CNN systems, the authors constructed two-dimensional CNN systems named Wavegram-CNN and Wavegram-Logmel-CNN. These systems have frequency information available so that sound events associated with pitch shifts can be better captured. The Wavegram component of the system refers to a learned image similar to a log mel spectrogram, with a horizontal axis meant to represent time, and a vertical axis analogous to frequency – however, this vertical axis is a *learned* (instead of defined) transform.

These pretrained networks have been proven effective at audio tagging on multiple datasets across domains, and may be useful for additional tasks in audio ML.

7.4.1 EXISTING ARCHITECTURES

There are several existing deep audio embedding methods that use CNNs. L^3-Net and VGGish, which are state-of-the-art audio representations pre-trained on 60M AudioSet [116] and Youtube-8M data [117]. AudioSet and Youtube-8M are large labeled training datasets that are widely used in audio and video learning with deep neural networks.

7.4.1.1 Look, Listen, and Learn Network (L^3-Net)

L^3-Net is an audio embedding method [118] motivated by the original work of Look, Listen, and Learn (L^3) [119] that processes the Audio-Visual Correspondence learning task in computer vision research. The key differences between the original L^3 (by Arandjelovi and Zisserman) and L^3-Net (by Cramer et al.) are (1) input data format (video vs. audio), (2) final embedding dimensionality, and (3) training sample size.

The L^3-Net audio embedding method consists of 2D convolutional layers and 2D max-pooling layers, and each convolution layer is followed by batch normalization and a ReLU nonlinearity (see Figure 7.11). For the last layer, a max-pooling layer

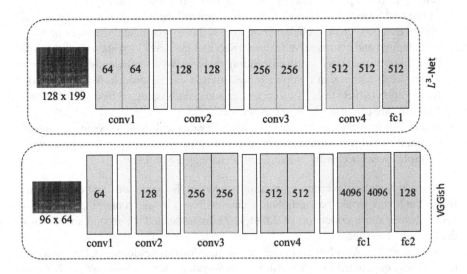

Figure 7.11 Network Architecture of L^3-Net and VGGish. The input spectrogram representations are 128x199 for L^3-Net and 96x64 for VGGish. Blue boxes, yellow boxes, and green boxes denote the 2D convolutional layers, max-pooling layers, and fully connected layers, respectively. The number inside of the blue box is the size of filters and the number inside of the green box is the number of neurons.

is performed to produce a single 512 dimension feature vector (L^3-Net allows for multiple options of output embedding size). The L^3-Net method is pre-trained on the previously mentioned Google AudioSet 60M training samples containing mostly musical performances[6] [116].

7.4.1.2 VGGish

Another deep audio embedding model is VGGish [120]. VGGish is a 128-dimensional audio embedding method, motivated by VGGNet [120], and pre-trained on the large YouTube-8M dataset [117]. The original VGGNet targeted large scale image classification tasks, and VGGish is targets extracting acoustic features from audio waveforms. The VGGish audio embedding method consists of 2D convolutional layers and 2D max-pooling layers to produce a single 128 dimension feature vector (see Figure 7.11). VGGish has an open-source implementation available at https://github.com/tensorflow/models/tree/master/research/audioset/vggish.

7.5 EXERCISES

1. Consider the vocabulary of an input space to an RNN designed to model music from a standard piano keyboard of 88 keys.
    a. If we are encoding a monophonic sequence of uniform rhythm, how many elements exist in the vocabulary space?
    b. If we now wish to allow our model to include the possibility of two pitches sounding at the same time, how many elements exist in the vocabulary space?
2. In the Hello World RNN example, the network has 105 trainable parameters. Why are there 105 parameters in this case?
3. What is the dangling note problem associated with MIDI-like (and resolved by REMI) representation?
4. Tokenize (insert measure image here) using (recommend tokenization scheme here).
5. Continue the beam search example introduced in the RNN section. Which three three-note sequences would propagate forward to the next iteration of the search? Repeat the example using a beam of two.

Additional questions and programming exercises are found in the **Generating Music with RNN** and **Parallel CNN - RNN** notebooks at https://github.com/deep-and-shallow/notebooks.

---

[6]The OpenL3 open-source implementation and library is available at https://openl3.readthedocs.io/en/latest/index.html.

PROJECTS

1. **Tokenization** MidiTok welcomes contributions to their package; they have defined the following open problems:
   a. Time Signature Representation
   b. Allowance for switching between beat and second time units
   c. Automatic data augmentation
   Choose one of these possible enhancements (or one of your own design), and propose, implement, and demonstrate a method for tokenization.
2. **Deep Learning to Isolate Vocals from Stereo Music**. Audio Source Separation is the problem of recovering or reconstructing one or more source signals that, through some linear or convolutive process, have been mixed with other signals. The field has many practical applications including speech denoising and enhancement, music remixing, spatial audio, and remastering. In the context of music production, it is sometimes referred to as unmixing or demixing. For this project, you will implement a convolutional neural network which isolates a vocal track from accompaniment using a spectrogram image of the track.
   Suggested reading:
   - Audio AI: isolating vocals from stereo music using Convolutional Neural Networks[7]
   - Open Resources for Music Source Separation[8]
3. **Chord Estimation from Audio using HMM**. Automatic chord detection has been a MIREX task since 2008 with submissions in 2012 surpassing 72 percent accuracy. Hidden Markov Models have been used as a successful modeling strategy using beat synchronous chroma vectors (Pitch Class Profiles) as the feature vectors. The goal of this project is explore combinations of NN/HMM models for acoustic modeling for the task of chord recognition, as well as use of pre-trained audio embeddings such as Vggish or L3net.
   Suggested reading:
   - MIREX Tasks[9]
   - An End-to-End Machine Learning System for Harmonic Analysis of Music [121]
   - Chord Segmentation and Recognition using EM-Trained Hidden Markov Models [122]
   - Understanding How Deep Belief Networks Perform Acoustic Modelling [123]
   - OpenL3 Library[10]
   - VGGish[11]

---

[7]https://towardsdatascience.com/audio-ai-isolating-vocals-from-stereo-music-using-convolutional-neural-networks-210532383785

[8]https://sigsep.github.io/

[9]https://www.music-ir.org/mirex/wiki/2020:Main_Page

[10]https://openl3.readthedocs.io/en/latest/index.html

[11]https://github.com/tensorflow/models/tree/master/research/audioset/vggish

4. **Music Classification or Clustering**. There are many ways we may want to organize music; perhaps by key, by composer/artist, by instrumentation, by genre, by tempo, etc. Can you create a model which accurately classifies musical data (audio, MIDI, or some other form) into your desired groupings?

Alternatively, you can perform the task in an unsupervised manner as a clustering problem. If you are trying to group pieces by one composer, what audio features would you extract to help in your identification? Is it possible to learn clusters that capture the underlying similarity? Clustering by composer, as a possible example, may prove difficult, as a Beethoven Symphony may be more similar to a Mozart Symphony on certain features than a Beethoven String Quartet.

Suggested reading:

- Inception Time[12]
- Calculating Audio Song Similarity Using Siamese Neural Networks[13]
- Building a Song Recommendation System using Cosine Similarity and Euclidian Distance[14]
- Algorithmic clustering of music [124]
- A Survey of Prospects and Problems in Hindustani Classical Raga Identification Using Machine Learning Techniques [125]

---

[12]https://github.com/hfawaz/InceptionTime

[13]https://towardsdatascience.com/calculating-audio-song-similarity-using-siamese-neural-networks-62730e8f3e3d

[14]https://medium.com/@mark.rethana/building-a-song-recommendation-system-using-cosine-similarity-and-euclidian-distance-748fdfc832fd

8 Noise Revisited: Brains that Imagine

Art, as any creative endeavor, including scientific inquiry, requires imagining situations that go beyond experiences that the system previously had, producing fantasies of possible reality the go beyond evidence that was already collected. In Neural Networks, the ability to make inferences on unseen data is referred to as "generalization". The main impediment to generalization is over-training, i.e. when the network simply memorizes the data. In such case, the system cannot see "beyond" the evidence, or find underlying regularities or structures that capture the essential aspects of data rather than simply storing it. A different approach to modeling data is treating it as inherently a random or stochastic phenomenon. In such case, rather than making inference by learning a mapping of the data into some meaningful set of attributes, the inference is done probabilistically using Bayes rule.

Learning probability distribution of the data instead of mapping, categorizing, or labeling data allows drawing new samples from that distribution. "To recognize shapes, first learn to generate images" is a title of a famous 2007 paper by G. Hinton [126] where he advocated for learning feature detectors without supervision by alternating the steps of recognition that convert sensory input into an internal representation, and a reverse generative process that converts hidden causes into sensory data. Such two-step learning, called "wake-sleep" process, was an early precursor to the variational Bayesian methods. These early methods, implemented using Helmholtz and Restricted Boltzman Machines (RBM), will not be covered in the book. What is important for our discussion of network imagination is the idea of wake-sleep algorithm where "the network generates fantasies by starting with a pattern of activation of the top-level units ... These fantasies provide an unbiased sample of the networks generative model of the world. Having produced a fantasy, we then adjust the recognition weights to maximize the log probability of recovering the hidden activities that actually caused the fantasy" [127].

Bayesian inference uses a stochastic model that generates "fantasies" about new data by sampling from a distribution of hidden states. The causality between hidden state and the observations is probabilistic since each instance of a cause Z alters the likelihood of observations according to $p(x|z)$. Accordingly, relation between observations and causes is formulated in terms of the joint probability $p(x,z)$ of observations X and the worlds hidden causes Z. We assume that there is some prior distribution of hidden states $p(z)$, known regardless of any observations. The inference process consist of finding the posterior probability $p(z|x)$, which denotes the systemss updated knowledge about possible world states given the observations. The log-probability of observing the data itself, $\log(p(x))$, is called *evidence*, and its

DOI: 10.1201/9781003240198-8

negative version is sometimes called called *surpirsal.*

$$p(x)p(z|x) = p(x|z)p(z) \tag{8.1}$$

$$p(x) = \sum_z p(x,z) = \sum_z p(x|z)p(z) \tag{8.2}$$

The prior and likelihood together comprise the generative model. Knowing the two probabilities $p(z)$ and $p(x|z)$ is sufficient to compute the evidence $\log(p(x))$ and infer the state of the world (its hidden causes) given the observations as $p(z|x)$. Since the true distribution of the data and latent states is unknown, the learning task is formulated as finding an approximation to $p(x,z)$ through another probability $q(x,z)$ that is estimated from encoding and decoding the training data. In VAE this problem is formulated as optimization with two goals: reconstruction of the data distribution that approximates the true evidence, and inference of the latent states that approximates the prior. This approximate probability learning, called *Variational Bayes Inference*, is learned by an autoencoder neural network that maps input X to stochastic latent states Z using $Q(Z|x)$ as the encoder, and then decoding it back into the data. The two optimization goals are optimizing the quality of the reconstruction by computing an error between the input and the decoding output, and at the same time also requiring that the encoded latent states, which are the variational inference estimates, be as close as possible to the assumed prior $p(z)$.

This approach makes explicit two goals of music machine learning: modeling the music data, and inference of its hidden structure. In our effort to use machines to learn music, we proceeded in these two directions: being able to generate novel examples by composing or improvising and being creative with computers, while also finding good representation that reveals meaningful structure in music. Ideally, we would like to have both aspects present in our machine learning models of music – we want the computer to find good representation so that the interaction between human and a machine will be done along meaningful dimensions, while at the same time being also useful for generation of new music.

To dive deeper into the question of generative models, we will define and identify the differences between classification and generation tasks. Moreover, when we discuss the underlying modeling approaches for each of these tasks, we will need to clarify the differences between generative (probabilistic) and deterministic latent models. In fact, a large part of our discussion will be around the paradox that powerful generative models might not allow finding simple explanations, and vice versa, models that can capture and reveal (and thus explain) essential aspect of data often have difficulty generating quality novel data. This difficulty will be addressed later in the chapter when we talk about the Variational Auto Encoder (VAE) and the Generative Adversarial Network (GAN). Both approaches follow a common idea – they both take noise as input and shape it into music. The difference between GAN and VAE is that VAE operates in a encoder/decoder fashion, while GAN operates as a decoder-only generator. One can think of the encoding part in VAE as something analogous to listening or inference act – VAE tries to find a representation that is both compact and meaningful, capturing the hidden structure in the data before generating it back. GAN on the other hand learns not by trying to reconstruct the data from a latent representation, but rather trying to fool a critic or discriminator that constantly compares the synthetic data generated by the GAN generator to other true instances drawn from the same data corpus. By framing the learning task in such adversarial (generator versus discriminator) manner, the generator will actually learn superior ways of faking the data since the critic starts paying attention to more and more fine details in order to "catch" the fake synthetic instances. This often makes GAN results more realistic, as it captures minute detail that VAE omits during the inference step. Both methods have difficulty in controlling the generative process – having both VAE and GANs learn probability distribution of musical data, we want to be able to control the generative process by specifying some desired aspects of the hidden "causes" so as to drive the generative model by navigating the latent variable space toward a desired output.

In order to understand deeper the distinction between generative and latent representation aspect of our models, the VAE model will be also discussed from information theoretical perspective. This view allows us to focus on the information dynamic aspects of music encoding/decoding, or listening/composition duality. Communication between human and a machine is much more readily seen in this perspective, as we try to consider reduced or lossy ways of encoding musical information as a way of actually improving the communication between human and a machine. This understanding is essential for design of human-computer creative interfaces since reduced and lossy representation is essential in order to establish meaningful, albeit ambiguous communication between musician and their artificial musical companion.

In the GAN section, we will explain how the adversarial setting of the generator/discriminator achieves its "deep fake" abilities, but without much control over what fakes or novel compositions will be generated. We will talk about the mode collapse problem in GAN where the lack of control over the latent space leads deep fakes to replicate only a narrow subset from the great variety of the training data. This again points to the difficulty in controlling the generator or making it produce novel examples to our desire. The solution to this problem is learning conditional GANs, such as a setting of so-called pix2pix translation, where the goal of the generator is mapping partial representation of input data into a complete instance, such as coloring images or rendering photorealistic images from sketches, or in the musical case, improvising on a sequence of chords or reduced music representation such as chroma vectors. Finally, we conclude this chapter with a broader discussion of how music information dynamics analysis is affected by using reduced representations in latent spaces.

8.1   WHY STUDY GENERATIVE MODELING?

At the time of this writing, models like GPT-3 and DALL-E have received mass public attention for their ability to generate (sometimes uncanny) human-like creations, including chatbot discussions and images from text. Recent generative models can even turn text or image into audio [128] [129] [130] [131], an interesting complexity beyond the predict-next-token sequential models we observed in the last chapter.

Beyond the novelty of its musical output, what training capabilities and insights into our data can generative modeling provide? For one, generative models can provide insight into an architecture's ability to represent the high-dimensional probability distributions that underlie data. When a model is able to create in a way that is reminiscent but not identical to input, we can take this as evidence that the model has learned underlying patterns rather than overfitting to training samples. Generative models are also able to help "fill in the gaps" in training data, particularly in cases when there is a large amount of labeled data, but the model would benefit from further samples from a pool of generated data, where the label can be implied. In this way, the generative model can be used to enable a semi-supervised learning process for the task at hand.

In general, this chapter will introduce statistical generative models, which (in a mathematical sense) refer to probabilistic latent representations that turn structure to noise, then back into structure. This broad topic includes a variety of ideas found in the next sections (Variational Autoencoder, Generative Adversarial Networks, etc.) and extends to more recent methods beyond the scope of this book (flow, diffusion, etc.). As a brief comparative summary,

- GANs use adversarial training to learn a latent representation,
- VAEs maximize a variational lower bound on the log-likelihood of the data, known as the evidence lower bound (ELBO),
- Flow-based models learn an invertible transform of distributions from a standard probability distribution (such as Gaussian) to the target distribution, and
- Diffusion models gradually add Gaussian noise, resulting in a sequence of points approaching the target distribution.

Previously discussed methods of RNNs and CNNs provide a means to learn mappings between complex types of data, especially in the case of temporal sequences like music (hence, their description as "representing voices in time"). An additional recent development in this lineage is the Transformer model, introduced in the next chapter. DALL-E and related models combine these two ideas (statistical generative models and models which learn mapping between complex data), using architectures like the UNet-style CNN and Transformers to first map the musical and textual data into joint latent representations, and then to process the latent representations from noise to structure.

8.2 MATHEMATICAL DEFINITIONS

To derive mathematically the equations for variation function approximation, we need to introduce some statistical notions:

- Kullback-Leibler divergence (or Kullback-Leibler distance), which is a measure of discrepancy between two distributions
- Entropy H of a distribution and its conditional version for the case of two variables

Kullback-Leibler Divergence

Kullback-Leibler Divergence (often shortened to KL-divergence) is a measure of how different one probability distribution is from another. It can also be conceptualized as the information lost when using one distribution to represent another. The KL-divergence is defined as

$$D_{KL}(p||q) = \sum_{i=1}^{N} p(x_i) \cdot (\log p(x_i) - \log q(x_i)) \qquad (8.3)$$

Notice that this shares a similarity with our definition of *expectation* because we are multiplying by p_{x_i}. So what is it we are taking the expectation over? In this case, it is the log difference between the probability of data in the first and second distributions. Recall the definition of entropy,

$$H = -\sum_{i=1}^{N} p(x_i) \cdot \log p(x_i), \qquad (8.4)$$

which tells us the number of bits needed to represent a distribution. In the same way, our KL-divergence definition tells us the number of bits of information we expect to lose when representing one distribution with another. Using the definition of expectation and the properties of logs, we can write KL-divergence in two additional ways that may be useful in later discussion:

$$D_{KL}(p||q) = E_p[\log p(x) - \log q(x)] \qquad (8.5)$$

and

$$D_{KL}(p||q) = \sum_{i=1}^{N} p(x_i) \cdot \log \frac{p(x_i)}{q(x_i)}. \qquad (8.6)$$

Here we make a few notes about definitions and notations. The sums in the above expressions are computed over all possible realizations of the outcomes of the random variables $\mathbf{x}$ and $\mathbf{y}$. This should not be confused with summing over samples of data points collected from the world or training corpus. With sufficient amount of samples, mean can be approximated by an average, but as far as the definitions themselves go, the elements in the summation are log-probabilities, i.e. the weights in the summations $p(x_i)$ or $p(x_i, y_j)$ are probabilities and the sums are over the possible values of the variables x and y.

Another comment in place is about the ambiguity or duality in notation and meaning of these expressions as functions of probability of the random variable. In many respects, the approximation process is context dependent. Writing $H(\mathbf{x})$ or $H(p)$ where $\mathbf{x} \sim p(\mathbf{x})$ is equivalent. A confusion in terminology might occur when we think about encoder and decoder as complex functions that map data to representation, or as $q(\mathbf{z}|\mathbf{x})$ and $p(\mathbf{x}|\mathbf{z})$, respectively, which are probabilities. In statistical terms, encoder and decoder are two different distributions, each one linking the latent variable

x and **z** through a joint probability $p(\mathbf{x}, \mathbf{z})$ and $q(\mathbf{x}, \mathbf{z})$. The function that implement the encoder and decoder can be pretty complex, and the mapping of input x into internal latent z can go through many steps or nodes, each having its own intermediate variables. The Markov properties of such models is useful here; conditioning on the so-called "Markov blanket" of a given node renders the node independent of all other variables. A Markov blanket defines the boundaries of a system (e.g., a cell or a multi-cellular organism) in a statistical sense. It is a statistical partitioning of a system into internal states and external states, where the blanket itself consists of the intermediate states that separates them. As we mentioned above, q is a *variational* approximation of p, where the neural network serves as Markov blanket between the outside "real world" of data observations and the internal "mental world" of the internal model variables.

8.3   VARIATIONAL METHODS: AUTOENCODER, EVIDENCE LOWER BOUND

In our learning of generative models we are seeking to optimize the parameters of a probabilistic model to find a distribution where the true data samples will be highly likely. In other words, if we have a choice of multiple possible models, our best choice would be the one with highest evidence $\log(p(x))$. Of course if we knew what this model was, we would not need to learn it, but in practice we will construct some neural network or another computationally tractable representation of possible probability distribution of the data, and fine tune its parameters so that it will give the highest evidence.

This approach to machine learning is a very different from optimization that is done in signal modeling or signal representation in a feature extraction setting. Instead of applying some optimal transformation to the data itself, the goal of probabilistic modeling is to find an approximation to distribution of data in the real world. So not only the randomness is assigned to some noise that is considered irrelevant to the data, but the data itself is stochastic. A probabilistic model allows estimate of likelihood of the data in that model. For example, in the case of a language model, we hope that a good model will assign high probability to real sentences, and low probability to badly structured or meaningless text. In fact, we want to be able to judge what events are probable and what are improbable in the world.

In this setting, encoding of data **x** into a latent representation **z** is done by a probabilistic model that estimates the posterior probability of the latent states given the data $p(\mathbf{z}|\mathbf{x})$. The whole process of modeling becomes a process of probability approximation, done by searching for the best probability function by optimizing its parameters. In the case of Variational Autoencoder (VAE), these parameters are the learned by a neural network.

Before going directly into the mathematics of VAE, it helps to consider the problem of statistical approximation known as variational inference on a somewhat higher level and almost conceptual setting. To understand the learning aspects of generative models, it helps to think about the role imagination plays in the relations between the organism and the world it exists in. Such an organism, be it our brain or a machine learning system, tries to adopt to the environment though a process of observing and making sense of the evidence that the system collects through its sensory modalities. The easiest way to think about whether incoming data "makes sense" is checking if what the system imagines as a possible outcome actually matches the reality happening in the world. In musical terms, if the world is a corpus of music in a particular style, then the ability to generate continuations or assign high likelihood to real music can serve as an indicator of the adaptive quality of the system. The process of music learning then becomes a way for the system to adapt to a particular style in order to maintain some optimal functioning or interaction with the other musicians operating in the same domain. This approach to learning resembles something that is known in biological systems as homeostasis, where learning is meant to update the model parameters maintained by an organism so as to maximize its ability to function in the world.

Since the early days of Deep Learning it was common to express the joint probability of (data, latent states) by an overall Energy of the system, as

$$p(\mathbf{x}, \mathbf{z}) = \frac{e^{-Energy(\mathbf{x}, \mathbf{z})}}{Z} \tag{8.7}$$

where Energy, which is a positive value, appears as negative in the exponent, and Z is a normalization constant called a partition function, which is a summation of the numerator over all internal system states $\mathbf{z}$ and external conditions $\mathbf{x}$, that makes it into a probability

$$Z = \sum_{z,x} e^{(-Energy(\mathbf{x}, \mathbf{z}))} . \tag{8.8}$$

In this formulation, minimizing energy leads to more probable system configurations. Explanation for data x becomes a configuration of a system z that is distributed according to marginal probability $p(z)$. The energy or cost of explanation z for data x is the average of the system energy over its configurations z [132].

$$Energy(p(z)) = \mathbb{E}_{p(z)}[\log p(\mathbf{x}, \mathbf{z})] \tag{8.9}$$

This brings us to a central concept in generative models: given $p(x,z)$ as the true probability of world events and their hidden causes, the leaning method tries to find a system that behaves according to an approximate probability $q(x,z)$ to match or replicate the world behavior. Then, by sampling a random z according to $q(z)$, the system can "dream" about data x according to $q(x|z)$, or when the system is awake, it can take in data x and infer it (find an explanation) in terms of z distributed according to $q(z|x)$. Writing such learning goal can be done by minimizing the discrepancy in terms of KL distance

$$KL(q(z)|p(x,z)) = \mathbb{E}_{q(z)} \log \frac{p(x,z)}{q(z)}$$
$$= \mathbb{E}_{q(z)}[-\log(p(x,z)) - H(q(z))]$$
$$= Energy(q(z)) - Entropy(q(z)) \triangleq \mathscr{F}(q)$$

Here the Energy is coming from the true world and is averaged according to the distribution of the system parameters, or in other words, the energy is the true evidence (world probability) of both the data and its true hidden states, averaged over the hidden states that the system can infer or imagine. The entropy of the system is the distribution of its states, which should be as unassuming as possible or evenly distributed. The KL expression thus will be minimized both by finding $q(z)$ that minimizes the energy, while at the same time maximizing its entropy.

Due to resemblance to principles of thermodynamics, such minimization goal is often called *Free Energy*, denoted as $\mathscr{F}(q)$, which is a principle that claims that systems in interaction with their environment not only try to minimize their energy but also maximize their internal entropy or the extent of spread of the system's states. In thermodynamics there is often a multiplicative weighting parameter added to entropy that is proportional to temperature. In such case systems at zero temperature are governed by energy, while systems at higher temperature are governed by entropy. We will encounter a somewhat similar parameter later when we deal with considerations of balancing the representation precision versus complexity in context of latent information dynamics.

Another intuition about the minimization criteria in variational modeling can be derived by relating the learning goals of our system to the overall evidence of data, independently of the learning system. Writing $\log p(x)$ as a marginal probability over observations and hidden states gives rise to the following inequality based on properties of convex functions, also known as Jensen inequality:

$$\log p(x) = \log \sum_z p(x,z) \frac{q(z)}{q(z)} \tag{8.10}$$

$$= \log \mathbb{E}_{q(z)}\left[\frac{p(x,z)}{q(z)}\right] \tag{8.11}$$

$$\geq \mathbb{E}_{q(z)}\left[\log \frac{p(x,z)}{q(z)}\right] \tag{8.12}$$

$$= -\mathscr{F}(q) . \tag{8.13}$$

8.3.1 COMPUTING THE EVIDENCE LOWER BOUND (ELBO)

We have arrived now at the following problem setting: given a set of data distributed in the real world according to some unknown probability $p(\mathbf{x})$, and assuming that there is a latent cause that governs the appearance of this data, we want to use a learning system to infer the latent causes and also be able to generate the data from these causes. Think about data as notes and causes as chords. Chords or harmoinic anlaysis is often "hidden" from the musician, of course unless the music is written as a lead sheet with chords instead of notes. But let's assume we do not know the harmonic analysis ahead of time, but we assume that the notes were generated by those chords, or at least that we can infer the "belonging" of a note to a chord. This uncertainly bout relation between notes and chords is expressed as $p(\mathbf{x},\mathbf{z})$, and in order to learn these relations, we propose another more tractable distribution $q(\mathbf{x},\mathbf{z})$

that can be effectively estimated by a learning algorithm that operates through statistical optimization. In the next section we will see how this can be implemented using a Neural Network.

Using the definition of KL and the definition of conditional probability $p(z|x) = \frac{p(x,z)}{p(x)}$, we can see that

$$KL(q(\mathbf{z}|\mathbf{x}), p(\mathbf{z}|\mathbf{x})) = \int q(\mathbf{z}|\mathbf{x}) \log \frac{q(z|x)p(x)}{p(x,z)} dz \qquad (8.14)$$
$$= KL(q(\mathbf{z}|\mathbf{x}), p(\mathbf{x}, \mathbf{z})) + \log p(\mathbf{x}) ,$$

where the averaging over z does not affect the data evidence $\log(p(x))$, thus leaving it outside the integral. The term on the left of the equality sign expresses the statistical difference between the inference of the latent states by the encoder $q(z|x)$ and the true data posterior $p(z|x)$ when data x is entered into the system. The first term on the right of the equal sign is our Free Energy, only that this time it is expressed in terms of conditional probability $q(z|x)$ rather then $q(z)$. Both ways of writing Free Energy with $q(z)$ or $q(z|x)$ are common, but this duality often causes some confusion. See the insert box for more explanations.

For the sake of completeness, let us write this optimization criteria here in terms of a lower bound on the data evidence, or ELBO, denoted by $\mathscr{L}(q)$, using the relations established in Equation 8.15

$$\log p(x) = KL(q(z|x), p(z|x)) + \mathscr{L}(q) \qquad (8.15)$$
$$\mathscr{L}(q) \triangleq -KL(q(z|x), p(x,z)) = -\mathscr{F}(q) \qquad (8.16)$$

The above expressions bring up an important relation between data evidence and free energy. The negative free energy, which is the evidence lower bound (ELBO), will be the function expressing our learning goals. Minimizing Free Energy or maximizing ELBO $\mathscr{L}(q, \theta)$ is a way to find the best model by altering the model parameters θ so that it closely approximates the true statistics of the data as they appear in the world. This idea is summarized in Figure 8.1.

A very similar expression to Free Energy in Equation 8.10 can also derived using $q(z|x)$ instead of $q(z)$. It is written as

$$\mathscr{F}(q) = KL(q(\mathbf{z}|\mathbf{x}), p(\mathbf{x}, \mathbf{z})) = \int q(z|x) \log \frac{q(z|x)}{p(x|z)p(z)}$$
$$= KL(q(\mathbf{z}|\mathbf{x}), p(\mathbf{z})) - \mathbb{E}_{q(\mathbf{z}|\mathbf{x})}[\log p(\mathbf{x}|\mathbf{z})]$$

where we abuse the notation for $\mathscr{F}(q)$ to denote both cases, depending on the way the problem is formulated. This manner of writing Free Energy is used whenever one needs to emphasize the dependence of z on x, such as in the case when z is derived from x by a process of encoding. We will encounter

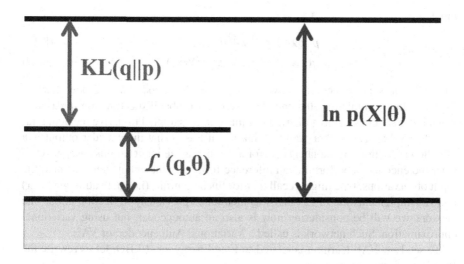

Figure 8.1 Evidence lower bound approximates the data evidence up to a gap that comprises the KL difference between the approximate and true distribution. See more detail in the text.

these expressions in the next section when we talk about neural implementation of VAE where a neural network is trained to make inference of latent z from x as the input.

Another important notation aspect is that ELBO is negative of Free Energy,

$$\mathcal{F}(q) = -\mathcal{L}(q, \theta) \tag{8.17}$$

where the parameters of the approximation function q are made explicit through notating them by θ. In physical terms the goal of the system is to minimize the Free Energy, which is the same as a machine learning goal to maximize ELBO.

8.3.2 ENCODER-DECODER NEURAL APPROXIMATION

So how does one create a probabilistic model with a neural network? The idea is to use an encoder and decoder network, but instead of using the encoder to find a latent state that is a lower dimensional projection of the data, the encoder is used to find estimates of the mean and variance of a multivariate Gaussian, from which the latent variable is sampled. Then, this variable is passed to the decoder to reconstruct the input as

$$p(\mathbf{x}|\mathbf{z}) = g(W\mathbf{z} + \mu) \tag{8.18}$$

$$q(\mathbf{z}|\mathbf{x}) = \mathcal{N}(g(V_\mu \mathbf{x}), g(V_\Sigma \mathbf{x})), \tag{8.19}$$

where W and V are the neural network weights of the encoder and decoder, respectively. In this formulation, the encoder itself is a probabilistic function $q(z|x)$ that maps input samples x into a distribution that can be sampled to derive the actual latent state values z. Another way to think about this is that the encoder output is a likelihood function for the latents z's for a given x as the input. In this case, we consider the encoder as performing an inference from of z, the latent states, from x, the input observations. One might recall that for linear neurons (i.e., activation $g(x) = x$) this AE implements the PPCA that was mentioned previously in Section 6.5.3. The network we will be considering now is also an autoencoder, but using variational approximation. Such network is called a Variational Autoencoder, or VAE.

To see how VAE learning is related to Free Energy, or -ELBO, let us rewrite the Free Energy once more in terms of

$$\begin{aligned}\mathscr{F}(q) &= KL(q(\mathbf{z}|\mathbf{x}), p(\mathbf{x}, \mathbf{z})) \tag{8.20}\\ &= KL(q(\mathbf{z}|\mathbf{x}), p(\mathbf{z})) - \mathbb{E}_{q(\mathbf{z}|\mathbf{x})}[\log p(\mathbf{x}|\mathbf{z})]\end{aligned}$$

This expression allows us to relate the encoder inference of z, $q(z|x)$, to a prior distribution of the latent variables $p(\mathbf{z})$. This is where our assumption about the nature of the world comes in, expressed in terms of a prior $p(\mathbf{z})$. As we mentioned earlier, one cannot observe $p(\mathbf{z}|\mathbf{x})$, but we can guess or assume that the latent or "hidden" causes in the real world that are responsible for generating the observations $\mathbf{x}$ behave in a certain way. This is a very strong assumption, and in most VAE applications it is limited to a multi-variate, zero-mean and uncorrelated Gaussian distribution, which allows us to derive some powerful learning rules, as we will soon see. One should also note that we have no way of experimentally observing the true $\mathbf{z}$, so this is a theoretical equality which has an important meaning. Mathematically this relation between evidence and Free energy adding together to be equal to the KL distance between true and estimated posterior is well defined and will be used in subsequent discussion..

So let's now discuss more in detail what we have here. This amounts to two separate goals, or parts of the loss function or tasks for the network to learn:

1. find a model that maximizes the likelihood of the generated data by the network, $\mathbb{E}_{q(\mathbf{z}|\mathbf{x})}[\log p(\mathbf{x}|\mathbf{z})]$
2. minimize the KL distance between the inference (latent states that our encoder finds) and the prior $KL(q(\mathbf{z}|\mathbf{x}), p(\mathbf{z}))$ (prior is an assumed distribution of the latent state in the real world $p(\mathbf{z})$. Reminder – this prior distribution is our modeling assumption)

So we have a cross-entropy criteria applied to the output of VAE, and a KL criteria applied for estimating the stochastic part of the encoder. This way of deriving an

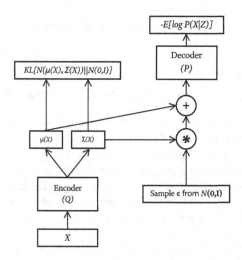

Figure 8.2   Encoder-Decoder with reparameterization for neural training that allows back-propagating the errors to estimate the mean and variance estimation networks.

objective learning function is known as the *variational principle* of estimating generative models. Also, because ELBO can be written as free energy, it is also known as the *variational free energy*. This big success of the VAE model is that the above mathematical relations could be re-written (reparameterized) into sampling process of a random variable ε of zero mean and unit variance Gaussian distribution, and then adding and multiplying it by numbers that shift it to a random variable with prescribed mean and variance. The reparameterization process is shown in Figure 8.2. We have seen this expression earlier when we introduced the concepts of Free Energy and ELBO[1].

It is worth mentioning that there is a whole branch of Deep Learning that is inspired by statistical physics that considers Deep Learning models as thermodynamic systems. One such recent advance is diffusion models governed by dynamics very similar to physical diffusion processes. Similar consideration are applied to biological systems that live in balance with the environment. In such a case the sensory, or even more basic chemical reactions between the world and the organism are interpreted as a data processing problem that leads to a homeostasis or finding a balance between the adaptive system states and the world that these systems see or experience. Applied to Neurosience, this approach led to emergence of a research field called "Free Energy of the Brain", that led to several psychology and even philosophical interpretations of what comprises human experience.

---

[1] As a reminder, the difference between the original Free Energy definition and the equations presented for VAE is that we replace the prior $q(z)$ with an encoding probability $q(z|x)$ as our learning goal.

Summing these relations once more, we have the following expression for log-likelihood.

$$\log p(\mathbf{x}) = KL(q(\mathbf{z}|\mathbf{x}), p(\mathbf{z}|\mathbf{x})) - KL(q(\mathbf{z}|\mathbf{x}), p(\mathbf{z})) + \mathbb{E}_{q(\mathbf{z}|\mathbf{x})}[\log p(\mathbf{x}|\mathbf{z})]$$
$$= KL(q(\mathbf{z}|\mathbf{x}), p(\mathbf{z}|\mathbf{x})) - \mathbb{E}_{q(\mathbf{z}|\mathbf{x})}[\log p(\mathbf{x}, \mathbf{z})] + H_{q(\mathbf{z}|\mathbf{x})}(q(\mathbf{z}|\mathbf{x}))$$

We do not know how to compute the first component in the above log-likelihood expression since $KL(q(\mathbf{z}|\mathbf{x}), p(\mathbf{z}|\mathbf{x}))$ requires knowledge of a true posterior $p(\mathbf{z}|\mathbf{x})$ that is not available to us. During the process of VAE modeling, as explained above, we assume a prior distribution for $p(\mathbf{z})$, but not the posterior. The solution to this problem is discarding the first component. Since KL is greater or equal to zero, this equation is replaced with an upper bound, removing the $KL(q(\mathbf{z}|\mathbf{x}), p(\mathbf{z}|\mathbf{x}))$ part

$$\log p(\mathbf{x}) \geq \mathbb{E}_{q(\mathbf{z}|\mathbf{x})}[\log p(\mathbf{x}|\mathbf{z})] - KL(q(\mathbf{z}|\mathbf{x}), p(\mathbf{z})) \qquad (8.21)$$

and the right hand side is often called Evidence Lower Bound (ELBO). The nice property of ELBO is that it can be computed using various approximation methods, and VAE is one of them (another method called Expectation Maximization (EM) does it in iterative manner, but we won't cover such methods right now).

8.3.3 NEURAL NETWORK IMPLEMENTATION OF VAE

The implementation of VAE is done through the so-called "reparameterization" trick, which led to the modern VAE popularity. Instead of estimating the encoder by sampling methods, the normal distribution of the latent prior $\mathbf{z}$ is distributed with a mean μ and variance σ^2. This is written as a transformation of a zero mean and unit variance Gaussian variable $\varepsilon \sim \mathcal{N}(0, \sigma^2)$ as $x = \sigma^2 \varepsilon + \mu$. This can be effectively implemented by drawing a random variable ε and then multiplying its value by variance and adding the mean.

This expression can be generalized for multivariate Gaussians with a vector mean and covariance matrix. The parameters of the prior distribution are estimated by minimizing the KL distance between the encoding and prior. The KL objective can be explicitly written as KL between the zero mean and unit variance Gaussian that we assume to be the prior of $\mathbf{z}$ and the estimated posterior through the decoder $q(\mathbf{z}|\mathbf{x})$

$$KL(\mathcal{N}(\mu, \sigma) \parallel \mathcal{N}(0, 1)) = \sum_{x \in X} \left(\frac{\sigma^2 + \mu^2}{2} - \log \sigma - \frac{1}{2} \right) \qquad (8.22)$$

which is a particular case of a general KL distance between two Gaussian distributions

$$KL(p,q) = -\int p(x) \log q(x) dx + \int p(x) \log p(x) dx \qquad (8.23)$$

$$= \frac{1}{2}\log(2\pi\sigma_2^2) + \frac{\sigma_1^2 + (\mu_1 - \mu_2)^2}{2\sigma_2^2} - \frac{1}{2}(1 + \log 2\pi\sigma_1^2)$$

$$= \log\frac{\sigma_2}{\sigma_1} + \frac{\sigma_1^2 + (\mu_1 - \mu_2)^2}{2\sigma_2^2} - \frac{1}{2}$$

The implementation of VAE uses two neural networks as function approximations for estimators of the mean and variance parameters, where the *KL* expression serves as the loss function for the back-propagation procedure. One note of caution needs to be said about what precedes these networks. The input data is encoded by a neural network that maps $\mathbf{x}$ to $\mathbf{z}$, and then the mean and variance are obtained by two linear fully connected networks that implement the reparametrization trick. The kind of encoding from $\mathbf{x}$ to $\mathbf{z}$ depends on the type of data, and it can be as simple as a single dense layer or have multiple layers in a complex deep convolutional network. Moreover, since $P(\mathbf{x}|\mathbf{z})$ at the output of the network is Gaussian, the cross entropy at the output can be approximated by averaging the Euclidean distance between the decoded and true data values, an expression that appears in the exponent of the Gaussian probability function. Since $p(\mathbf{x}|\mathbf{z}) \sim \mathcal{N}(\mu, \sigma^2 \mathscr{I})$, we may estimate the mean parameter by averaging over the data reconstructed by the decoder $\hat{\mu} = \mathscr{E}_{q(\mathbf{z}|\mathbf{x})}[\hat{\mathbf{x}}]$. Accordingly, in order to estimate $\mathscr{E}_{q(\mathbf{z}|\mathbf{x})}[\log p(\mathbf{x}|\mathbf{z})]$ we take an approximate mean by averaging over multiple encoding-decoding reconstruction samples $\hat{\mathbf{x}}$.

$$\log p(\mathbf{x}|\mathbf{z}) \sim \log\exp(-(\mathbf{x} - \hat{\mu})^2) \sim -\Sigma(\mathbf{x} - \hat{\mathbf{x}})^2 \qquad (8.24)$$

where the sum is over a batch of data training examples $\mathbf{x}$ that are passed through VAE[2] to reconstruct $\hat{\mathbf{x}}$.

Figure 8.2 summarizes the steps of variational approximation with the reparameterization steps for a neural network implementation. The Encoder and Decoder are not specified and may comprise a variety of neural network architectures such as multi-layer perceptron, convolutional network, or RNNs. The mean and variance encoders are linear networks that further split the output of the encoder into estimators of the latent Gaussian probability parameters.

8.4 GENERATING MUSIC AND SOUND WITH VARIATIONAL AUTOENCODER

Variational methods create an approximation of the data statistics by learning a simpler tractable approximation, such as a multi-variate Gaussian. Sampling from this

---

[2]For more rigorous detail about the specific implementation, see Appendix C.2 in the original Kingma's VAE paper [133] where he talks about Gaussian MLP as encoder-decoder.

distribution creates latent vectors that are decoded back into the data space via the decoder. Generating music using VAE can be done in few different manners. The simplest way is sampling from the approximate Q distribution, which is done in practice by randomly sampling from a simple zero mean, unit variance Gaussian and then multiplying it by the variance and adding the mean using the reparameterization trick. Another way of working with VAE is by encoding and decoding where the inputs are taken from a slightly different, but not too distant, distribution. When done carefully, such methods create a sort of style transfer since the pre-trained encoder-decoder will render a signal into space that has the style of the training data. Another powerful application is so-called inpainting that we describe next.

8.4.1   HIERARCHICAL VAE FOR MONOPHONIC SYMBOLIC MUSIC

To introduce some applications and extensions of Variational Autoencoders in musical settings, we begin by examining the research of Pati et al., "Learning to Traverse Latent Spaces for Musical Score Inpainting". Many works [102, 103, 134, 135] explore the encoding method of monophonic music that contains one note at a time. In this section, we explore a hierarchical VAE model [103, 136] for the encoding and decoding of monophonic music.

Inpainting is the name given to reconstruction of missing (or degraded) information. The term can be applied across different media; a painter might restore a damaged painting, a tailor might patch a pair of designer pants, and a sculptor might fix a chipped statue. We can picture situations where inpainting may be necessary in a musical context; perhaps we find another unfinished work by Schubert, and need to fill in some gaps, or find a record in a family member's attic with some damage to part of the track. But, these same tools can also be used for musical creation, such as generating new musical ideas within a defined style, bridging gaps between musical styles, or making variations and extensions to sections of a score. Inpainting differs from our past-studied "predict-next" style of generation, because in this problem setting, we assume some knowledge of past *and* future musical context.

VAE is a convenient model for inpainting since it allows making up of missing data by interpolation between the latent vectors on its boundaries. Such interpolation is impossible to perform on the MIDI or audio data directly, and the hope is that VAE representation actually captures meaningful aspect of the data in a lower dimensional manifold that has some local linear structure, so that moving in straight lines in that space actually creates a correct filler for missing data segments after decoding it through the VAE decoder. More sophisticated inpainting methods were later suggested using the transformer, by actually learning to complete a musical piece after masking or removing segments of data from it. We will cover transformers in later chapters of the book.

We have perviously discussed encoders as a means of transforming data from a high-dimensional to low-dimensional representation; for the inpainting case, Pati et al. consider a high-dimensional space of all possible one-bar melodies. These melodies are encoded using the method introduced by Hadjeres et al. in "Deep-Bach: a Steerable Model for Bach Chorales Generation", [137] very similar to the previously-discussed *three-state tokens*. In DeepBach, the sixteenth note was used as the finest resolution (which is fair for representing Bach chorales). As typical for researching new applications, Pati et al. expand the tokenization scheme relative to their musical application space by including encoding options for triplets. So, in the end, 24 tokens comprise each 4/4 measure, and with each token able to take on all possible pitches within the instrument space (plus rest and hold), we have a 24-dimensional input space with (in the case of an 88 key keyboard) 90^{24} possible configurations per measure.

As shown in Figure 8.3, this method consists of pre-processing a series of musical notes into a token sequence, with three types of tokens:

- Pitch: encoding what pitch onset (from C0 to G10) this time step has.
- Hold: encoding that indicates if this time step continues with the last pitch.
- Rest: encoding that indicates if this time step is a rest (silence).

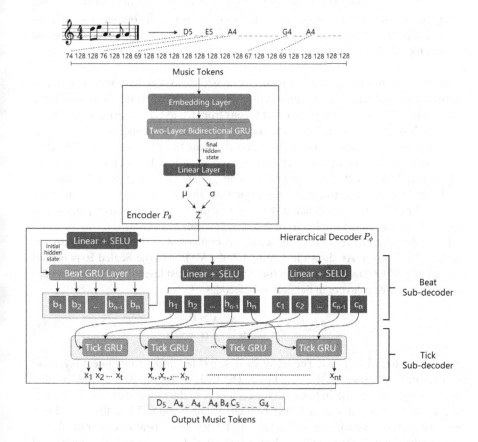

Figure 8.3 The network architecture of monophonic music variational autoencoder.

Next the tokenized data is fed into a VAE model. The encoder is composed of an embedding layer, two bidirectional-GRU recurrent layers, and a linear layer for constructing the mean and the logarithmic standard deviation of the latent distribution parameters, in accordance to the common training paradigm of VAEs. The decoder has a hierarchical structure with two sub-decoders. The first is a beat sub-decoder that extracts the latent variable from the encoder into a short hidden state sequence. Every hidden state is analogous to single beat in music. The second tick sub-decoder then disassembles each beat's hidden state into tick sequence in time, which consists of the pitch, hold, and rest tokens. Both sub-decoders comprise GRU layers and several linear layers. This hierarchical decoder is considered to be a representation of the structural prior in the VAE model, where the beat sub-decoder first outputs some large note groups, and the tick sub-decoder further outputs each note by decoding these groups. By training the model, the parameters of the neural networks are tuned so as to optimize the efficiency and accuracy of the decoding. The output of the tick sub-decoder is regarded as the final output, with the reconstruction loss function being the multi-cross entropy between the input tokens and the output predictive tokens. Finally, the complete VAE training loss function consists of the reconstruction loss and the KL divergence loss between the latent state distribution and the assumed prior.

As depicted in Figure 8.3, a sequence of music melody (e.g., one or two music measures) is tokenized into a sequence of integers. In the example of Figure 8.3, the numbers 0-127 represent the pitch onset tokens from C0 to G10. The number 128 denotes the hold token, and 129 (nonexistent in the Figure 8.3) denotes the rest token. Then, this melodic sequence is sent into an embedding layer by converting 129 numbers into latent embeddings. This embedding sequence is fed into two bidirectional-GRU layers and outputs the final hidden state vector. The last part of the encoder is a linear layer (or two linear layers) to map the final hidden state vector into the mean and the logarithmic standard deviation of the latent distribution parameters. The latent variable z is sampled from this distribution.

In the decoder, the first beat sub-decoder is composed of three linear layers and one Beat GRU layer. As shown in Figure 8.3, the VAE uses the Scaled Exponential Linear Unit (SELU) as the activation function after the first linear layer in the decoder and two entry linear layers in the beat sub-decoder:

$$SELU(x) = \begin{cases} \lambda x, x > 0 \\ \lambda \alpha e^x - \lambda \alpha, x \leq 0 \end{cases} \quad (8.25)$$

where $\alpha \approx 1.673, \lambda \approx 1.051$. The latent variable z is fed into the first linear layer and taken as the initial value of the Beat GRU. The Beat GRU outputs each hidden state vector $b_1, b_2, ..., b_n$ as the initial state for each beat in the music measure. Each beat state is further mapped into two types of hidden state h and c. Then, the second tick sub-decoder utilizes each pair of (h, c) in a Tick GRU. Each beat state pair (h, c) generates t tokens within the timeline, where h is the initial value and c is the conditional value of the Tick GRU in each beat state. The final output x is a discrete symbol in each time state, obtained by a fully connected layer to map the output of Tick GRU

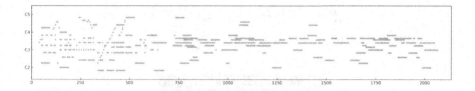

Figure 8.4 An example of pianoroll. The x-axis is the timeline and the y-axis is the pitch. Orange pieces denote the notes appearing within the timeline.

into a probability vector and taking the argmax[3] of it. The cross-entropy loss is computed between the original ground truth (one-hot vector) and the probability vector to train the VAE model.

8.4.2   VAE FOR GENERAL POLYPHONIC MUSIC

Finding a principled latent representation of polyphonic music is an open problem in music research, with several works proposing multi-track music encoding, decoding and a combined toolbox [106, 138, 139]. Here we describe a simple extension of a piano-roll format to construct a vanilla VAE model for encoding and decoding polyphonic music. The piano-roll format was discussed earlier as a basic representation of polyphonic music consisting of a matrix where the x-axis (row) corresponds to time step and the y-axis (column) is the pitch map, with a binary value for each pitch class denoting presence or lack of note activation at that time instance:

$$Pianoroll(t, p) = c \in \{0, 1\} \tag{8.26}$$

Figure 8.4 shows a piano-roll example of polyphonic music.

Since pianoroll uses slices of time to capture active notes, it is impossible to know in an individual slice if the notes are newly played (triggered at this moment) or they are continuations of previously played note. In order to capture the difference between note onsets and continuing notes, each slice in the piano roll is extended with a copy or one hot vectors that indicate only the newly triggered notes. This extended piano-roll matrix is next flattened into a sequence of length $T \times 2 * P$ (T is the total number of time steps, and P is the total number of pitches). Each $2 * P$-step group is a concatenation of P multi-hot vector for active notes and P vectors for new onsets for each time step.

As shown in Figure 8.5, the simplest polyphonic music VAE encoder consists of two linear layers. A linear layer is used to map the input sequence to an integrated latent vector. This vector is similar to the final state output of the GRU layer in the monophonic VAE architecture. Then, we implement another linear layer to map the

---

[3]This is the name for the function which finds the index whose value contains the maximum probability value, introduced in Chapter 6.

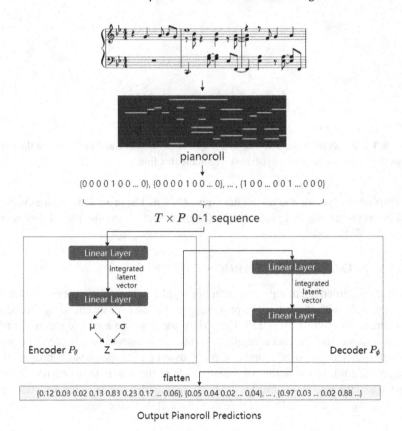

Figure 8.5   The network architecture of polyphonic music variational autoencoder.

integrated latent vector into the mean and the standard deviation of the latent VAE distribution. Similarly, the decoder comprises two linear layers that map the latent variable back into an output piano-roll matrix. The reconstruction loss function is the binary-cross entropy loss between the input matrix and the output matrix. Following the standard VAE method, the total training loss constitutes of the piano-roll reconstruction loss and a KL divergence loss between the latent distribution and a Gaussian prior.

There are two reasons for the use of linear layer to process the pianoroll instead of recurrent layers or convolutional layers. First, different from monophonic music, polyphonic music possibly contains more than one note in many time steps. This requires predicting the probability of every note in every time step. In the monophonic VAE, the recurrent layers only process sequences of length T, while in the polyphonic VAE, the sequence length for RNN is increased to $T \times P$, making the training difficult and requiring high GPU memory. As for the CNN, it is hard for convolutions to process a long sequence since the filters only contain a limited perceptive field to capture each segment of the sequence. A final step in the VAE model is processing the multi-hot pianoroll vectors back into pianoroll. Since the final output of each time step of the decoder is also a multi-hot vector, another step is required to determine how many notes are actually playing in each time step. This adds more parameters to the model and is often implemented as a simple heuristic, such as fixing a probability threshold on the multi-hot vector not to exceed a certain maximal number of simultaneous active notes. The polyphonic VAE is an easy-to-implement method that allows implementation of polyphonic models that are similar in terms of computing resource requirements to the monophonic VAE.

8.4.3 VAE FOR AUDIO

The use of VAE for audio signal is challenging because of the large amount of samples that are required to represent even very short audio segments, or the large matrices of features vectors. One should note that transformations, such as STFT, result in spectral matrices that contain as many or often more data points then the original audio signal since the analysis is done in overlapping fashion. Even after removing the phase, with 50 percent overlap, the spectrograms have the same number of points as the signal[4]. Several works have utilized VAE models for exploring audio representations, including VAE models for finding disentangled audio representations [140] and VAE for modeling audio containing speech [141]. Apart from VAE, convolutional models are used in different music tasks such as music recommendation [142] and source separation [143]. We provide below an example of a simple convolutional VAE that maps short-time Fourier transform (STFT) representation of audio into a lower dimensional latent representation.

The encoder and decoder of such audio VAE have a symmetrical structure consisting of convolutional layers and linear layers. One such example is provided in Figure 8.6.

The encoder is constructed of five 2D convolution layers with max pooling layers located after the third convolution layer, and after the last convolution layer. The final layer is flattened and processed through two linear layers to obtain a mean and a logarithmic variance. From the mean and logarithmic variance, the latent variable is sampled from a normal distribution. The decoder nearly mirrors the encoder architecture. The latent variable is first passed through a linear layer to obtain the correct shape when unflattened. Following are five 2D transpose convolution layers and two upsampling layers to restore the shape of the spectrogram.

The reconstruction loss function is the mean-squared error between the input and output spectrogram, and the whole VAE training loss constitutes ofthe reconstruction loss and the KL divergence loss. Since mean-squared error does not accurately

---

[4]Such situation might be avoided using so-called critical sampled filter banks or special representations, such as wavelets or Gabor filters.

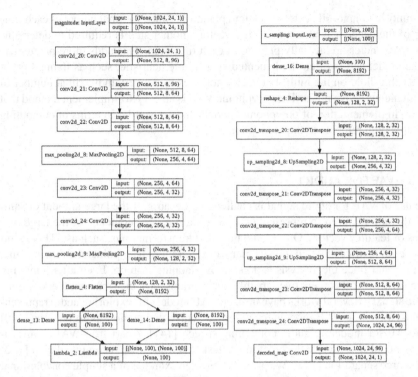

Figure 8.6 Audio VAE encoder (left) and decoder (right). The encoder consists of five 2D convolutional layers and two max pooling layers. Two linear layers generate the mean and logarithmic variance used to sample the output of the encoder. The decoder also consists of five transpose convolution layers and two upsampling layers to restore the output to the original shape of the input.

portray perceptive audio reconstruction quality, the reconstruction quality of audio is evaluated using log spectral distortion between the two power spectrograms S and $\hat{S}$:

$$LSD = \frac{1}{T} \sum_{t=1}^{T} \sqrt{\frac{1}{N} \sum_{i=1}^{N} (S_{ti} - \hat{S}_{ti})^2} \tag{8.27}$$

8.4.4 MUSIC APPLICATIONS OF VAE

These and other version of music VAE representation learning are the first step toward more complete music applications. The most immediate use of VAE is a sort of style transfer using the encoding/decoding aspect of the model. By training VAE on a particular style and then using music of different style as an input, the encoding is extracting the salient features of the input while reconstructing the output with the details of the style it was trained on. One such example is the piece "In Fleeting Visions" that used a series of short pieces of Prokofiev by the same name as an input to a VAE trained on a different piece of same composer of a different period and style [144].

Other applications of VAE include generation by random sampling from the prior distribution, interpolation between existing sequences and manipulation of existing sequences via latent vectors. In [102] MusicVAE learns a latent space of musical MIDI files for short sequences (e.g., 2-bar "loops"), by using a bidirectional LSTM encoder and LSTM decoder and applying the VAE latent modeling on the final hidden state of the LSTM. For longer sequences the authors use hierarchical LSTM decoder, which helps the model learn longer-term structures.

Music inpainting deals with completing musical materials given past and future musical contexts. One can think of it as a musical "repair" task where part of a musical piece is removed from the score, and the Neural Network is required to complete the missing section in away that is not only musically smooth but also following the dynamic evolution of the musical piece that is being learned specifically for such a task. Linear interpolation is often insufficient for the inpainting task since one needs to find more complex paths through VAE latent space to make a completion that forms a coherent musical sequence. In [103], a LatentRNN model was trained to model the sequential dynamics of latent vector sequences from an input vector that comprised of concatenation of latent vectors of the initial and final measures VAE encodings. Finally the same measure VAE decoder was used to render the sequences of latent vectors back to music.

Applying VAE to polyphonic representation can be done in several ways. A straightforward way of dealing with polyphony by encoding groups of notes from pianoroll was described above in Section 8.4.2. In Pianotree [106], a latent z representation using a combination of GRU and VAE is proposed as a way to represent the structure of music for every 2 bars without overlap. This representation can be further used for other generative applications, as mentioned earlier in the context of simultaneous note representation in Section 7.1.2.2. A combination of Convolutional, Variational, and Recurrent Neural Network is proposed in [145]. To generate sequential data, the model uses an encoder-decoder architecture with latent probabilistic connections to capture the hidden structure of music. Using the sequence-to-sequence model, the generative model exploits samples from a prior distribution and is shown to be able to generate a longer sequence of music with approximately repeating polyphonic patterns that better resemble the statistics of the training corpus.

Controllable and personalized VAE methods were explored [99, 146]. There are many musical features that could be imposed on music generation. For example, the popular aspects related to note density, pitch range, rhythmic complexity and more, can be used to control asepcts of VAE. Attribute-Regularized VAE (AR-VAE) uses a additional regularization loss that forces each specific attribute of interest to align with a specific latent dimension. This is done by comparing the pairwise distances between attributes of the samples generated by the VAE to distances between their latent variable along the desired dimension, and using the error as a regularization loss. This forces that specific attribute to behave in a manner that is proportional or monotonically related to the latent dimension along which one wants to encode the attribute.

Personalizing the generation of VAE is done in [99] where the idea is to train a smaller VAE on MusicVAEs latent space so as to summarize the essential musical feature of a particular melody. This personalization is done in two steps. First, by passing a user provided musical MIDI sample through a pre-trained VAE, a subspace of all latent features that bears most resemblance to the user provided example is found. Second, this subset is further summarize in to a smaller subset of four super-sliders that allow the user further intuitive manipulation of the model to achieve desired results.

These works are part of a larger problem of controlling generative models by leveraging prior knowledge encoded in musical features and relating that to latent structure of the embedding space. The common idea is that constraints can be enforced either during training, or post-hoc on pre-trained unsupervised generative models. Allowing VAE to be modified or fine-tuned on a new small set of curated subset of musical examples that has some desired properties, or retraining it with conditioning variables that can be then used to control it, is required for many creative applications.

Another approach to learning to control latent spaces involves training an actor/critic model using conditional GAN (cGAN) techniques, which are beyond the scope of this chapter. This procedure is computationally inexpensive relative to training a generative model from scratch, thus providing an attractive opportunity for use of pre-trained models in interactive creative settings where the model has to quickly and realistically respond to yet unheard music or adapt to novel idiomatic style of a musician.

8.5 DISCRETE NEURAL REPRESENTATION WITH VECTOR-QUANTIZED VAE

In our journey of deep and shallow music and audio modeling, the problem of music understanding and generation was divided between representation and prediction, or in other words, short-time versus sequential aspects of music and sound structure. As we have seen already in the chapter on VMO, capturing long terms structure in music requires limiting the sensibility to slight variation in audio features or otherwise we will not be able to capture repetitions in the signal or its feature since real numbers or continuous values of features describing the signal will be always slightly different even when repeating very similar sounds. Moreover, string matching and language models that are very powerful in finding temporal structures require a finite alphabet. Converting continuous representations into discrete set of codes was done in VMO by search over all possible thresholds of quantization. Thus modeling of long term, language-like aspects of music using neural networks would also benefit from a discretization step since it will allow combining representation learning with predictive (autoregressive) or temporal masking models of Transformers that we will discuss in a later "Paying Musical Attention" Chapter 9.

Vector quantizing variational autoencoders (VQ-VAE) and later vector quantizing GANs (VQ-GAN) try to derive discrete representation through encoder-decoder neural networks that employ forward approximation and backward optimization steps that can be solved via gradient descent. The quantization step in VQ-VAE is achieved by modifying the loss function in the variational method so that the entire function is written as a combination of three factors:

- Reconstruction loss, which optimizes both the encoder and decoder, same as in the usual VAE.
- Quantization loss between the VAE latent embeddings Z and their codes c_j for $j = 1...K$, where the number of possible codes is set a-priori. This part updates the codes.
- Commitment loss, a function for updating the encoder for a given set of codes. The relative rates of updates to the codes and updates to the encoder are controlled via a weight factor β. The purpose of this function is to measure the degree to which the encoder is committed to driving its latent output toward the frozen codebook entries.

The combined loss is given by

$$L = \log p(x|z) + ||sg(z) - c||^2 + \beta ||z - sg(c)||^2 \tag{8.28}$$

where sg stands for *stop-gradient* operation that stops the learning updates from being performed for that variable. These loss terms are further explained in the following discussion.

Strictly speaking, VQ-VAE is not a traditional variational method since it does not assume (or require) a fixed prior distribution of the latent space $p(z)$ to which an approximate encoding distribution $q(z|x)$ is being matched during the learning process. In other words, and as a reminder of the variational theory explained in section 8.3, if the latent states z are viewed as features that summarize some essential aspects of the data x, then in the traditional variational approach the training of the encoder-decoder model serves to create a match between $q(z|x)$ to $p(z|x)$, i.e. finding an approximate inference of the features that matches their true distribution in the real world. This is achieved by using the ELBO approximation that breaks up this goal into separate reconstruction loss $E_{q(z|x)}[\log p(x|z)]$ and a KL regularization between the inference $q(z|x)$ and a prior $p(z)$, $KL(q(z|x), p(z))$. In VQ-VAE we maintain the reconstruction loss $\mathbb{E}_{q(z|x)}[\log p(x|z)]$ by using a decoder that receives the approximate latent states from an the encoder $q(z|x)$ and evaluating their quality by the decoder using $\log p(x|z)$ as the reconstruction loss. What is different in VQ-VAE case is the latent approximation loss. Distribution of the codes which represent cluster centers of the VQ changes during the learning process can not be assumed a-priori since the codes themselves change when the encoder is updated. Accordingly, minimization of the error between the encoding and its quantized representation $||z - c||^2$ comprises two factors: changes to the choice of which cluster center (code) to use in decoding, and also changes to the encoder that as a result causes changes to the codes themselves. Learning the best codes is accomplished by updating the probability distribution over the codebook indexes for a fixed encoding, which is done by stopping the gradient (sg) of the encoding to minimize $||sg(z) - c||^2$, a term called *codebook-loss*. Changing the latent representation z is done by updating the encoder for fixed codes, which is expressed as minimization of $||z - sg(c)||^2$, a term called *commitment-loss*. Since these updates are performed in different domains, the size of the gradient update can be different in each case. The total loss is written as a combination of $Loss_{VQ-VAE} = reconstruction\text{-}loss + codebook\text{-}loss + \beta commitment\text{-}loss$, with β controlling the relative rate of updates between the changes in the codebook choices and updates of the encodings. During the learning phase the decoder optimizes the reconstruction loss only, the encoder optimises both reconstruction and commitment losses, and the embeddings are optimized by the middle codebook-loss term.

8.5.1 MUSICAL USES OF VQ-VAE

Due to the advantages of working with symbolic representation and at the same time learning that representation from data, the VQ-VAE became a popular tool in music processing. The symbolic aspect allows using novel powerful sequence modeling tools, such as transformers, to capture the long term structure in audio better the RNNs. We will briefly mention some of such systems since we will discuss them more at length in Chapter 9 on attention. In audio, VQ-VAE was applied both the waveform and spectrum information. In OpenAI jukebox, VQ-VAE was used in a hierarchical fashion with symbolization done at different temporal resolutions. In an inpainiting and audio editing system NOTONO, a similar hierarchical VQ-VAE model was used for spectral information, specifically the Mel-IF representation of GANSynth that will be discussed later. In the MIDI domain, the FIGARO system uses the VQ-VAE method to encodes bar-long music segments into a set of discrete codes.

An interesting application of VQ-VAE in waveform generation and modification is descriptor-based synthesis [147]. The acoustic properties of musical timbre, such as centroid, bandwidth, or fundamental frequency are mapped to synthesis of new timbre by selection of the best matching latent features to human explainable descriptors. This also allows specifying novel musical ideas through abstract descriptors that can be extracted from another sound, such as a vocal sketch of musical idea. This generalizes the concept of timbre transfer to larger musical expressions. As an example, [147] use VQ-VAE by modeling the raw waveform of a source instrument through an encoder, which learns associated features from a codebook associated with a target instrument. Using neural subtractive synthesis, an encoding of the original waveform is combined with the codebook values to create a timbre resembling the target instrument.

It is interesting to note the growing use of combining signal processing techniques with neural modeling. A sinusoids plus stochastic decomposition is used in the Neural Source Filter (NSF) [69]. The sinusoidal portion of the decomposition can be thought of as the "ideal" representation of a sound's spectral content; since real-world sounds often contain additional noise or randomness that cannot be fully captured by a set of pure tones, the model also accounts for a stochastic noise-like residual component. Differentiable Digital Signal Processing (DDSP) [68] model uses an additive synthesizer for the harmonic components for a given pitch parameter, combined with a subtractive noise synthesizer. The Universal Music Translation Network [148] generalizes this by using a multi-domain shared encoder paired with domain-specific decoders. In the VQ-VAE timbre model the encoder translates each sound segment into a continuous latent vector which is then matched to a vector from a discrete embedding of another instrument. Then the decoder predicts coefficients for a filter (subtractive synthesis) to modify the timbre of the input to match the desired target. In order to disentangle loudness from the latent timbre embedding, the encoder predicts an additional scalar gain g_t. In view of the simplicity of the subtractive approach compared to the more powerful sinusoidal models, the quality of synthesis is secondary to the versatility that the VQ approach offers for mapping the timbre latent vectors to other acoustic descriptors for the descriptor-based synthesis and composition.

8.6 GENERATIVE ADVERSARIAL NETWORKS

8.6.1 WHAT IS A GENERATIVE ADVERSARIAL NETWORK?

In the orchestra or similar ensemble, the group will create musical output, and the conductor will make a judgment and provide feedback, such that the next instance of sound (whether the next note or the next performance) will be better than the last. There are two elements of this relationship that we will analogize here:

- The relationship is **generative**; the orchestra will create complete musical output.
- The relationship is **adversarial**; when the orchestra creates better music, the conductor's job as adjudicator becomes more difficult. When the conductor is most critical, the orchestra's performance is held to the most challenging standard.

Though this adversarial framing may have negative effects for human performers, in the case of artificial intelligence, this relationship helps to create models which are highly effective at imitation. Such networks are named **generative adversarial networks**, or GANs for short, and they pose two neural network components at odds: a generator (G) and a discriminator (D).

Before we discuss the roles of the generator and discriminator, we will first consider what it means to create a generative model. We hope to find some collection of parameters θ which can be used to represent the distribution of data we are trying to model, such that we can sample this distribution to generate "new" data which still has properties similar to the collected (real) data.

If we consider the set of all possible values of the parameters of θ, we can formalize our goal in training such a model. We seek to find θ^*, such that:

$$\theta^* = \underset{\theta}{\operatorname{argmax}} \prod_{i=1}^{m} p(x^i | \theta) \tag{8.29}$$

In other words, we seek to select parameters which maximize the likelihood of the data we have observed (since the likelihood of all data is the product of the probability of each sample). In the exercises, you will show how this can be expressed as a sum instead of a product.

In section 8.1, we introduce KL-divergence; a dual way to imagine the process of training is to find a model which minimizes the KL-divergence between the model distribution and the (ideal) data distribution. Because we often do not know the inherent underlying distribution of our data source, we use an empirical estimate obtained by collecting data samples, as usual for all of our machine learning methods.

With this in mind, we will formally define our orchestra-conductor relationship in mathematical terms: We have a generator G, comprised of parameters θ_G, which takes some latent representation z as input and outputs observed variable x. We have a discriminator D, comprised of parameters θ_D, which takes observed variable x as input and outputs judgment (real or fake).

The loss function is a combination of discriminator loss and generator loss, each (by necessity) reliant on parameters and output of both model components. We first look at the discriminator's loss:

$$L_D(\theta_G, \theta_D) = -\frac{1}{2}\mathbb{E}_x \log D(x) - \frac{1}{2}\mathbb{E}_z \log(1 - D(G(z))) \qquad (8.30)$$

Remember, the discrimintator's goal is to output 1 when it detects a real sample, and 0 when it detects a fake sample. So, the first expectation is taken over all x sampled from the real data, and in an ideal case we would be repeatedly taking the log of 1 ($= 0$). As the probability decreases, the loss from this term will increase. The second expectation is taken over the discriminator's guesses on the generator's output (induced on latent variable z). At best, we expect these guesses to be 0 (determined "fake"), so subtracting this output from 1 before taking the log maintains that perfect performance (creates 0 loss), while increases in discriminator probability that a "fake" sample is "real" will increase the loss.

Next we consider the generator's loss. Goodfellow [149] showed that KL-divergence can be minimized using loss function

$$L_G(\theta_G, \theta_D) = -\frac{1}{2}\mathbb{E}_z e^{\sigma^{-1}(D(G(z)))}, \qquad (8.31)$$

where σ is the logistic sigmoid function introduced in Chapter 6 and D is assumed to be an optimal discriminator. We will discuss the formulation for this later in the section.

In his GAN tutorial, Goodfellow provides an analogy for the training of generative models under the principle of maximum likelihood. Training samples are shown as points sampled along some axis, and the sample likelihood relates to some probability distribution that we seek to learn. If we estimate the distribution of the data using these samples, a perfect estimate would have probability spikes at each sample point, and 0 elsewhere, but this presents two immediate problems: first, we know this is highly unlikely to be the actual distribution (this would be overfit to our training data), and second, this is too complex a relationship to be modeled by the Gaussian distribution we have adopted (defined by only mean and variance). But, if we instead imagine some unit force generated per sample which is applied to some flat line, we can imagine that these forces will apply some shape to the line, creating a curve that is smooth *and* resembles the distribution we seek to model. In this way, the estimated distribution is shaped strongly by the density of sample values, in accordance with the principle of maximimum likelihood (fitting a model that best explains the data).

While we most of our learning has been framed as optimization problems throughout the book, GANs can actually be dually imagined as a game between two players. Like most games, the GAN performance depends on the state of both players' pieces (that is, the model parameters of both the generator and discriminator), and neither can control the other's parameters. Just like we seek a minimum for an optimization problem, we seek a *Nash equilibrium* as a solution to a game. This local differential Nash equilibrium is a tuple (θ_D, θ_G) which is a local minimum of L_D with respect to parameters θ_D and a local minimum of L_G with respect to parameters θ_G.

How is such an equilibrium found in training? We employ a variant of stochastic gradient descent, where we sample two minibatches: one from the "real" data X and one from the latent variable distribution Z. These minibatches are used to adjust θ_D and θ_G to reduce L_D and L_G respectively[5].

In an ideal setting, GANs play a *zero-sum game*, where the total loss between players each turn is zero (that is, improvement for one player creates equal and opposite detriment for the other player). We can express this as an equation:

$$L_D + L_G = 0. \tag{8.32}$$

Since knowing one of L_D and L_G completely defines the other, we can express the game's value using just one; we name this value $V(\theta_D, \theta_G)$. Solving the game is done using the *minimax algorithm*:

$$\theta_G^* = \underset{\theta_G}{\text{argmin}} \, \underset{\theta_D}{\max} \, V(\theta_D, \theta_G) \tag{8.33}$$

Goodfellow shows this loss to be helpful to understand GANs as a theoretical game, but there are some practical challenges due to the non-convexity of deep neural network parameter space discussed in [149].

For any generator θ_G, the performance of the model can be described by criterion $\max_{\theta_D} V(\theta_D, \theta_G)$. For optimal discriminator $D = D_G^*$ for a fixed generator G, this criterion is equal to $-\frac{1}{2}\mathbb{E}_x \log D_G^*(x) - \frac{1}{2}\mathbb{E}_z \log(1 - D_G^*(G(z)))$.

$G(z)$ can be considered a space similar to the actual data distribution x $p(x)$, which we will call x_G $p_G(x)$. So, we re-write the above as $-\frac{1}{2}\mathbb{E}_x \log D_G^*(x) - \frac{1}{2}\mathbb{E}_z \log(1 - D_G^*(x))$.

For a fixed generator, what is this optimal discriminator? This discriminator's job is to report the probability that a data point is "real", so given two distributions (the distribution of actual data x, and the distribution of generated data x_G), we ask here what probability of "realness" the model should report to have the greatest chance

---

[5] As review, the optimization method of gradient descent is described in Chapter 6.

of being correct. We are optimizing the expression $-\frac{1}{2}\mathbb{E}_x \log D(x) - \frac{1}{2}\mathbb{E}_z \log(1 - D(G(z)))$. From the definition of expectation, we expand the expression:

$$\int_x p_{data}(x) \log D(x)\, dx + \int_z p_z(z) \log 1 - D(G(z))\, dz \qquad (8.34)$$

$$\int_x p_{data}(x) \log D(x) + p_G(x) \log 1 - D(x)\, dx \qquad (8.35)$$

Any function of the form $a \log x + b \log 1 - x$ reaches its maximum value when $x = \frac{a}{a+b}$. Accordingly, our optimal discriminator is

$$D_G^*(x) = \frac{p_{data}(x)}{p_{data}(x) + p_G(x)}. \qquad (8.36)$$

Now, we can continue to computing our maximal criterion $\max_{\theta_D} V(\theta_D, \theta_G)$ by substituting the optimal discriminator:

$$-\frac{1}{2}\mathbb{E}_x \log \frac{p_{data}(x)}{p_{data}(x) + p_G(x)} - \frac{1}{2}\mathbb{E}_z \log\left(\frac{p_G(x)}{p_{data}(x) + p_G(x)}\right) \qquad (8.37)$$

Note that $\frac{p_G(x)}{p_{data}(x)+p_G(x)}$ is just $1 - \frac{p_{data}(x)}{p_{data}(x)+p_G(x)}$.

Ideally, we would want the distribution learned by the generator to exactly match the distribution underlying the data it is learning to mimic. So, we want our criterion to reach a global minimum when $p_G = p_{data}$. When this is true, the optimal discriminator will return a value of $1/2$. Inserting this value into our above criterion expression, we now reach

$$-\frac{1}{2}\mathbb{E}_x \log \frac{1}{2} - \frac{1}{2}\mathbb{E}_z \log\left(\frac{1}{2}\right) = -\frac{1}{2}(\mathbb{E}_x(-\log 2) + \mathbb{E}_z(-\log 2)) = -\frac{1}{2}(-\log 4) \quad (8.38)$$

How do we know that this is the optimal value for our model? We will show now that the criterion is minimized by adding 0 (as $-\log 4 - (\mathbb{E}_x(-\log 2) + \mathbb{E}_z(-\log 2))$) to our criterion expression, which gives us:

$$-\log 4 + KL\left(p_{data}\left|\left|\frac{p_{data} + p_g}{2}\right.\right.\right) + KL\left(p_g\left|\left|\frac{p_{data} + p_g}{2}\right.\right.\right). \qquad (8.39)$$

KL-divergence is always non-negative, so the global minimum is reached only by the solution that $p_g = p_{data}$ (that is, the data generated by the model matches the training data distribution).

So, with the theoretical case for GANs made, actually how effective are GANs at generating material similar to the source distribution? A particular strength of GANs is their ability to generate sharp samples, as opposed to blurry interpolations of training data. This is very important to consider when choosing an approach to a particular musical problem, and is a direct consequence of the optimization goal.

Recall that VAEs aim to minimize the KL-divergence between a model and training distribution. This allows the generation of blurry content in between sharp modes
of the training data. As a concrete example, consider the work of Esling et al. [150]
in constructing variational generative timbre spaces. From the data, we have distinct
modes (instruments). The VAE is very effective at interpolating between the modes,
generating sounds that do not fall into either category but represent what we might
imagine a hybrid of the two sounds to be. This is great for this particular problem,
but such bluriness isn't appropriate for problems when you want to closely, sharply
model a pattern found in the data. By contrast, GANs excel at this task.

Why is this the case? Goodfellow originally thought this may be due to the asym-
metric nature of KL-divergence that you will show in the exercises at the end of the
chapter. MLE methods minimize KL(data, model), while GAN training procedures
minimize Jensen-Shannon divergence, which is similar to KL(model, data). A model
trained with the KL(model, data) divergence would emphasize learning only modes
which appear in the training data, rather than generating modes which may not appear in the data. Surprisingly, recent evidence suggests that this is not the reason for
the sharp, mode re-creation abilities of GANs – MLE training methods are still effective with the GAN architecture, and GANs actually generate from fewer modes than
promoted by KL(model, data) divergence. This suggests that some other underlying
property of the GAN training process that causes this sharp convergence to a subset
of modes.

Algorithm 7 The GAN training algorithm, using minibatch stochastic gradient
descent

For number of training iterations:

1. For k steps:
   a. Sample minibatch of m noise samples $\{z_1, ..., z_m\}$ from noise prior $p_g(z)$
   b. Sample minibatch of m examples $\{x_1, ..., x_m\}$ from data generating distri-
      bution $p_{data}(x)$
   c. Update the discriminator by ascending its stochastic gradient:

$$\nabla_{\theta_d} \frac{1}{m} \sum_{i=1}^{m} [\log D(x_i) + \log(1 - D(G(z_i)))] \qquad (8.40)$$

2. Sample minibatch of m noise samples $\{z_1, ..., z_m\}$ from noise prior $p_g(z)$
3. Update the generator by descending its stochastic gradient:

$$\nabla_{\theta_g} \frac{1}{m} \sum_{i=1}^{m} [\log(1 - D(G(z_i)))] \qquad (8.41)$$

In his 2016 NeurIPS tutorial, Goodfellow recommends a hyperparameter of $k = 1$
(that is, update the generator each time the discriminator is updated).

8.6.2 MUSIC APPLICATIONS OF GANS

One of the early examples of using GANs is C-RNN-GAN [151] with both the generator and the discriminator being recurrent networks, with two LSTM layers of 350 units each. The discriminator takes into account both past and future using a bidirectional recurrent LSTM. The generation in C-RNN-GAN is done unconditionally.

This work was followed by MidiNet [152]. The model was trained on Hooktheory's TheoryTab database that contains melody with chord progression. The model allows generating melody both unconditionally, and by using chords as conditional input for melody generation. The MidiNet generator and discriminator architecture is CNN with a few convolution layers, followed by fully connected layers. The network can be used for the generation of single or multitrack music. The representation of melody is a one-hot encoding of notes and silence for 8 measures with a time step of sixteenth note. The chords were represented only as minor or major with their root pitch.

This was followed by Dong et al.'s MuseGAN for multi-track MIDI generation [153]. It uses piano roll representation where each independent instrument track can be conceptualized as a binary image. These images can be stacked, creating a input which has dimensions of time (width), pitch (height), and instrument (depth). Similar to the way composers are trained to think "horizontally and vertically" (coarsely speaking, harmonically and counterpunctually/melodically), MuseGAN is structured in a way that can learn relationships across time (both within a single instrument's track and in relation to others), and relationships independent of time (for example, the bass's position and function relative to other voices, or how constituent tracks might join to form a chord). The input to MuseGAN is composed of four random vectors – two inter-track and two intra-vectors, each having a time-independent and time-dependent component. For each track, a shared temporal structure generator and a private temporal structure generator take the time-dependent random vectors as their inputs, and each of them outputs a series of latent vectors, which are further concatenated with the time-independent random vectors and fed to a bar generator for each track, which then collectively create the piano-rolls for each track that eventually comprise a combined multi-track piece. Additional scenarios are described in the paper, such as track-conditional scenario with an additional encoder extracting inter-track features from a user-provided track through.

A different approach to conditional GAN is done in ChordGAN [154]. This application uses chroma features to bias the generation to harmony preserving output. It was demonstrated on style transfer applications translating musical material between the styles of pop, classical, and jazz. ChordGan uses an architectures popularized in image-to-image style transfer known as pix2pix. Input data to ChordGan is represented in a piano roll format, from which chroma vectors are extracted. Using chromagram as an input to the generator G, the model outputs the detailed musical voicing in the target style. The discriminator D receives either the generated voicing or a real piece in the target style, and learns to classify the music as synthetic or authentic, as illustrated in Figure 8.7. The model is trained by extracting chroma structure from the input music and learning to discriminate between true and fake

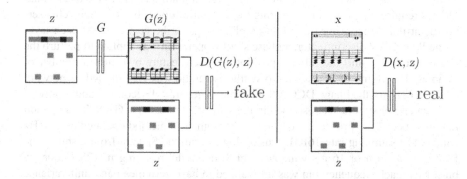

Figure 8.7 ChordGAN generates a realization of a piece from a latent chord representation, then passes this piece *and* its latent representation to a discriminator for training. Similarly, the discriminator will also receive pairs of real pieces with their chord representation to learn correct stylistic realization from information about harmonic progression.

chroma-voicing pairs. The trained generator is then used for rendering output music voices in a target style from chroma vectors as the model input. The success of style transfer was evaluated using a classifier network that was pre-trained to achieve 80% performance on musical data from corresponding styles. Additional novelty of ChordGAN is adding a reconstruction loss function to the discriminator loss. This biases the network to produce realistic music in addition or regardless of the chroma constraint. Since ChordGAN assumes that different styles provide different realizations of voice notes for a given harmonic (chord/chorma) structure, it does not generate long-term structure on its own, but rather operates as an method for inversion of chroma vectors to short-term voicing.

8.6.3 AUDIO APPLICATIONS OF GANS

In the audio domain, GAN has been used for generating and transforming audio, commonly know and Neuro-Synthesis and Voice or Timbre Conversion. Since modeling audio samples directly is data intensive, most of the models operate on some time-frequency representation such as spectrograms or speech specific features, often ingnoring the phase for more robust statistics. We have mentioned previous the use of Neural Networks for spectrogram magnitude inversion as an alternative to Griffin-Lim algorithm (GLA). Below we survey some of the principle works in the general field of synthesis using GANs.

One of the early works that applied Deep Convolutions GAN (DCGAN) from image processing techniques to both audio waveform and spectrograms is WaveGan and SpecGAN, described in [155]. In the waveform domain, instead of 2D image filters, WaveGAN uses longer (length-25), one-dimensional filters and a larger upsampling (stride 4) factor. A special treatment of the different feature layers in the discriminator was required to prevent recognizing the synthetic sounds by so-called "checkerboard" artifacts that occur due to upsampling steps in the generator. At each layer of the WaveGAN discriminator, a phase shuffle operation was applied to perturb the phase (cyclically shift the relative position) of each feature by uniform number of samples. The ability of WaveGAN to synthesize audio was very limited. A network of similar size to the image DCGAN was able to generate 1 second of audio only.

A second type of GAN described in the same paper was SpecGAN. This method requires special pre-processing of the spectrogram. The method operated on a 8kHz bandwidth (sampling rate 16KHz), using log-Magnitude Spectra from a short-time Fourier transform of 16 ms windows and 8 ms stride, resulting in 128 frequency bins. Next each frequency bin was normalized to have zero mean and unit variance and clipped to 3 standard deviations and rescaled to $[1, 1]$. The image-based DCGAN was applied to the resultant spectra, and the output was inverted back to audio using the Griffin-Lim algorithm. The training method was done using Wasserstein GANs. With this formulation, the GAN is not trained to identify examples as real or fake, but instead is trained as a function that assists in computing the Wasserstein distance between the synthetic (generated) and data (true) distributions. The method was able to produce also about 1 second of audio samples.

Wasserstein Distance

The Wasserstein distance, also known as the Kantorovich–Rubinstein metric or Earth Mover's Distance, is a measure of the distance between two probability distributions. The Wasserstein distance measures the minimum cost of transforming one distribution into the other, where the cost is defined as the amount of "work" required to move a unit of mass from one point in the distribution to another. This has immediate application in GAN training, as our goal is to learn the underlying distribution of the data, and thus it would be helpful to have a measure from the current distribution state of the generator to the ideal state.

We can approximate the work to move a little mass from distribution P with size dp a distance of Δx toward a settling location in distribution Q by the product $dp \times \Delta x$.

If we imagine a discrete distribution, and take a column of height h in the distribution P to be made up of h pieces of size dy, then to move the entire column we have the work expression $\sum_{i=0}^{h} dy \Delta x$.

But, in the case of a continuous distribution, each hypothetical column itself has some associated width dx, with the total distribution width represented as

$\sum\limits_{j=0}^{w} dx$, where w is the number of "columns" we broke our distribution into. In fact, both our dy and dx expressions can be variable in size, so we could consider them to be functions of their respective index (i.e., $dy(i)$, $dx(j)$). So, considering the work to move a complete two-dimensional mass to a new distribution, we have complete expression $\sum\limits_{j=0}^{w}\sum\limits_{i=0}^{h} dy(i) \times \Delta x \times dx(j)$ for any given *transport policy* π. We would like to explore all possible Δx choices we can make for each possible portion dy from distribution P that we are moving to distribution Q, and we select the minimal amount of work (optimal transport) amount as the Wasserstein Distance.

For clarity, we will formulate this distance discretely as

$$D_W(P,Q) = \min_{\pi} \sum_{i,j} \pi_{i,j} d(p_i, q_j), \qquad (8.42)$$

where $\pi_{i,j}$ is a indicator variable iterating through all possible transports of a given policy π (i.e., assists in totalling the costs of moving any piece p_i of P to location q_j on Q according to policy π).

We can express this in continuous space as

$$D_W(P,Q) = \inf_{\pi} \int_{M \times M} d\pi_{x,y} d(x,y), \qquad (8.43)$$

where we are searching over all possible transport plans π, integrating for each possible policy over the space $M \times M$ crossing the marginal probabilities of each distribution, each time enacting one pairing of the policy $d\pi$ and adding to our policy distance the amount of work necessary to move that piece.

Unlike other distance metrics such as Euclidean distance, the Wasserstein distance takes into account the underlying structure of the distributions being compared, rather than just their values at individual points. This makes it a powerful tool for comparing distributions that may have different shapes or sizes.

Computing the Wasserstein distance exactly can be difficult in practice since it requires solving an optimization problem over a space of joint probability distributions. One popular algorithm for computing the Wasserstein distance is the Sinkhorn algorithm, which uses an iterative method to approximate the distance between two distributions.

GANSynth [156] used GANs to generate musical timbre by modeling both STFT magnitudes and phases. The motivation for including phases and specifically estimating phase derivatives over time, also know as *Instantaneous Frequency* was to produce more coherent waveforms compared to previous state-of-the-art methods. GANSynth was trained on a NSynth dataset, which contains 300,000 musical notes from 1,000 different instruments. Limiting the training to individual notes from musical instruments instead of general sounds allowed the authors to increase the STFT frame size and to use mel frequency scale to create more separation between the lower harmonic frequencies in order to achieve better phase continuity. Using global conditioning on latent and pitch vectors, GANSynth was shown to perform interpolation between timbres of musical instruments, thus implementing a long sought-after musical task of spectral morphing and timbre hybridization as a way to create novel musical instrument sounds.

Higher quality sound generation was achieved with MelGAN [157], which is a conditional GAN architecture designed to invert mel-spectrograms to audio waveform. MelGAN introduced several architectural changes to the previously published methods. Its generator is a fully convolutional feed-forward network with mel-spectrogram as input and raw waveform as output. Since the mel-spectrogram is at a temporal resolution that is 256 time lower then the waveform samples, the model uses a stack of transposed convolutional layers to upsample the input sequence. To induce long range correlation among the audio samples, residual blocks with dilated convolutions were added after each upsampling layer. *Dilated convolution* is a technique that expands the kernel by inserting holes between its consecutive elements, thus performing the same operation as convolution but skipping over samples so as to cover a larger area of the input. To deal with "checkerboard artifacts" in audio, instead of using phase shuffle as in GANSynth, MelGAN uses a kernel size that is a multiple of stride. Another unique features of MelGAN is using multiple discriminators at different scales and use of a feature matching objective to train the generator. The multi-scale discriminators are designed so that each discriminator learns features for a different frequency range of audio. For example, the discriminator operating on down-sampled audio does not have access to high frequency components and thus is prone to learn low frequency features. The feature matching objective minimizes the L1 distance between the discriminator feature maps of real and synthetic audio, improving the reconstruction quality by inducing similarity loss between synthetic and real features in addition to discrimination error. MelGAN shows superior performance for generation of audio from mel-spectrogram when trained on speech samples, including for unseen speakers. It was also reported to operate well for conditional generation of audio from other encodings, such as Universal Music Translation Network [148] and VQ-VAE. In these cases the architecture was adjusted to fit the encoding as input and the model was retrained on musical data appropriate for the task.

As of a time of this writing, the use of GANs for audio synthesis is an active research topic, with new methods coming out showing improved performance in terms of quality, speed, and complexity of implementation.

8.7 EXERCISES

1. Is KL-divergence a metric? (Hint: one property of a metric is *symmetry*; that is, the distance between A and B is the same as the distance between B and A. Is this true of KL-divergence?)

2. We saw the GAN optimization task as determining the parameters

$$\theta^* = \underset{\theta}{\operatorname{argmax}} \prod_{i=1}^{m} p(x^i|\theta). \tag{8.44}$$

   What mathematical technique can we use so that this objective can be written as a sum instead of a product?

3. Jensen's inequality states:

$$f\left(\sum_{i=1}^{M} \lambda_i x_i\right) \le \sum_{i=1}^{M} \lambda_i f(x_i) \tag{8.45}$$

   where $\lambda_i \ge 0$ and $\sum_i \lambda_i = 1$, for any set of points $\{x_i\}$ and convex function f(x).

   Consider an M-state discrete random variable x, with entropy

$$H(x) = -\sum_{i=1}^{M} p(x_i) \ln p(x_i) \tag{8.46}$$

   Show that the entropy of its distribution $p(x)$ satisfies:

$$H[x] \le \ln M \tag{8.47}$$

4. (a) The basic idea in the Variational Method and Expectation-Maximization is to maximize the ELBO instead of likelihood $P(X|\theta)$. With this "trick", we can find the optimal model. For this problem, we provide a slightly different formulation, where the expectation E is done over $q(z)$ instead of $q(z|x)$. Both versions of ELBO are used in practice, depending on whether the objective is to construct an encoder Q that is more sensitive to input X or not.

   Prove that the log likelihood $\ln p(X|\theta)$ can be decomposed as ELBO + $\text{KL}(q\|p)$, where

$$\text{ELBO} = \mathscr{L}(q,\theta) = \sum_z q(Z) \ln \frac{p(X,Z|\theta)}{q(Z)} \tag{8.48}$$

   and

$$\text{KL}(q\|p) = -\sum_z q(Z) \ln \frac{p(Z|X,\theta)}{q(Z)} \tag{8.49}$$

with q representing the distribution of the latent variables Z and $KL(q||p)$ representing the Kullback-Leibler divergence between the distributions q and p.

Hint: Use definitions of conditional probability (Bayes' rule) so that the sum of the ELBO and KL expressions cancel the dependency of the probability on the variable Z.

(b) ELBO and EM are closely related. One is approximating the likelihood using VAE through differentiable programming (i.e. gradient descent), and the other is an iterative solution. While VAE uses gradient descent to find the approximate distribution q, the EM method uses an old estimate of $p(x|z, \theta)$ as the approximation.

In the EM algorithm, the expectation of the complete-data log likelihood evaluated for some general parameter value θ is given as

$$Q(\theta, \theta^{old}) = \sum_z p(Z|X, \theta^{old}) \ln p(X, Z|\theta) \qquad (8.50)$$

where $p(Z|X, \theta^{old})$ is the posterior distribution of the latent variables estimated in the E step using the current parameter values θ^{old}. Show that the ELBO is the same as $Q(\theta, \theta^{old})$, up to an entropy term in q, for $q = p(z|x, \theta)$.

Hint: entropy is defined as $\sum q \ln q$.

(c) Argue that the best approximate distribution q for a given parameter θ is the posterior distribution $p(Z|X, \theta)$, and use this argument to explain the purpose of the E step in the EM algorithm.

(d) Show that maximizing the ELBO is equivalent to maximizing $Q(\theta, \theta^{old})$.
Hint: Verify which part of the equation depends on the model parameter θ.

5. Suppose that $p(x)$ is some fixed distribution and that we wish to approximate it using a Gaussian distribution $q(x) = \mathcal{N}(x|\mu, \Sigma)$. By writing down the form of the KL divergence $KL(p||q)$ for a Gaussian $q(x)$ and then differentiating, show that minimization of $KL(p||q)$ with respect to μ and Σ leads to the result that μ is given by the expectation of x under $p(x)$ and that Σ is given by the covariance.

Additional questions and programming exercises are found in the **GAN, chroma (MIDI) and pix2pix** notebook at https://github.com/deep-and-shallow/notebooks.

PROJECTS

1. **Composing MultiTrack Music Using MuseGAN**. For this project, you will train a model to generate polyphonic, multitrack, multibar music using a GAN framework. MuseGAN consists of a generator and a critic. The generator tries to fool

the critic with its musical creations, and the critic tries to prevent this from happening by ensuring it is able to tell the difference between the generators forged music and the real thing. For your data, we recommend using Bach Chorales or String Quartets so the instrumentation is consistently in four parts.

Challenge: MuseGAN uses CNN to represent piano-roll as a set of complexly related musical textures. Bach Chorales and String Quartets obey much more strict voice relations in terms of timing and harmony. Consider your own ideas to problems of deciding about when the notes should be triggered (threshold selection is one such a binary decision), and the time and harmonic (chroma) relations across voices. Compare this to other polyphonic representation such as DeepBach or alternative music representation models to CNN.

Suggested reading: MuseGAN: Multi-track Sequential Generative Adversarial Networks for Symbolic Music Generation and Accompaniment [153]

2. **Music Style Transfer**. Music style transfer in the symbolic (MIDI) domain concerns with borrowing some features from musical pieces belonging to one style to modify the another musical piece that belongs to a different styles. Since the distinction of style versus content in music is ill defined, there are several different approaches to try to swap some musical characteristics of one piece to modify another piece. CycleGAN explores mapping two genres of music without specifying what features are mapped from one dataset to another. The representations are derived using CNN that captures different piano-roll structures of music. In this project you may explore changing music representations of the CNN architecture or constraining the mapping to retain certain harmonic (chroma) or other music features while doing the transformation
Suggested reading:
   - Symbolic Music Genre Transfer with CycleGAN [158]
   - ChordGAN: Symbolic Music Style Transfer with Chroma Feature Extraction [154]

3. **Audio Style Transfer**. In image style transfer, models are used to extract the style from a famous painting and apply it to another image, often using GANs. For this project, you will build and train a system capable of performing voice conversion or any other kind of audio style transfer, like converting one music genre to another. One should note that style transfer in audio is ill-defined (unlike images where content and style are usually well understood as visual objects versus texture), and it may encompass anything from changing the expression during performance, to swapping instruments, to generation and control of sound synthesizer, effects or textures (sound design) from learned neural sound model.In this project you are free to explore one of these aspects and discuss the model and its utility for musical creative uses.

Suggested reading:

- MelGAN-VC: Voice Conversion and Audio Style Transfer on arbitrarily long samples using Spectrograms [159]
- Voice Cloning Using Deep Learning[6]
- Audio texture synthesis and style transfer [7]
- Adversarial Audio Synthesis [155]
- Neural Funk[8]

4. **Audio-Guided Machine Improvisation**. Real time one shot learning is required for machine improvisation in a live setting. Existing systems for machine improvisation rely on string matching (LZ, Factor Oracle) to build on-the-fly a dictionary of repeated phrases and reshuffle them to create novel variations. One of the difficulties in using such models are the ability to learn conditional or music-to-music mappings that will guide the output of the generative system to match other concurrently playing musicians.

The goal of this project is to explore the use of VMO for creating an improvised accompaniment from Audio by exploring the use of VMO with audio features instead of MIDI and substituting the librosa features with VAE representations of Audio. Another possible extension is learning cross-modal metric learning (i..e mapping images to computer generated sound / music or mapping midi to audio to create a music concatenative synthesizer).

Suggested Reading:

- Machine Improvisation with Variable Markov Oracle - Toward Guided and Structured Improvisation [160] (MIDI Guided Improvisation)
- Learning Disentangled Representation of Timbre and Pitch using GMM VAE [140]
- Understanding VQ-VAE[9] (scroll down for audio)

---

[6]https://medium.com/the-research-nest/voice-cloning-using-deep-learning-166f1b8d8595

[7]https://dmitryulyanov.github.io/audio-texture-synthesis-and-style-transfer/

[8]https://towardsdatascience.com/neuralfunk-combining-deep-learning-with-sound-design-91935759d628

[9]https://blog.usejournal.com/understanding-vector-quantized-variational-autoencoders-vq-vae-323d710a888a

9 Paying (Musical) Attention

9.1 INTRODUCTION

In our search for powerful models to capture musical structure, we have seen that different treatment has to be given for short-time audio representation versus a long-term musical structure, often better considered in terms of symbolic representation. When we consider the representation of voices as multiple notes spread over different times (or frequency and time distribution), the tools of the trade for neural modeling were CNNs and RNNs. The main constraint for a recurrent model is its capacity of handling long sequences, which had been addressed by adding gating mechanisms in LSTM and GRU models, and later by adding an attention layer in a sequence-to-sequence model. Moreover, due to its recursive character, RNNs are restricted in terms of computation parallelization because every state is obliged to wait for the computation of its previous state. CNNs, used less commonly in modeling long temporal structures, are able to discover local compositional structure in multi-dimensional (multi-channel) sequences by building multiple filters in a hierarchical manner, where each filter becomes a feature detector for some special aspect of the data. From a computational perspective, convolutional networks are amenable to parallelization since the computations are done on every data element independently of other instances at different time steps. In this chapter we introduce a new architecture called Transformer that has been achieving superior performance to CNNs and RNNs in various applications. In a way, the Transformer takes the best of both worlds of the CNN and RNN – it uses the concept of attention in RNN, but without the complicated recurrent part, and it uses the CNN idea of multiple filters to create multiple self-attention heads that capture the repetition structure in the data.

9.2 TRANSFORMERS AND MEMORY MODELS IN RNN

9.2.1 TRANSFORMER

Transformer is a member of a family of deep learning models which, as its name suggests, transforms n d-dimensional objects into a different set of n d'-dimensional objects. While there are many methods which fit this broad description, Transformer models achieve this specifically by learning *queries*, *keys*, and *values* from each datum, giving them the pseudoability to direct attention toward specific objects.

Transformer models have become a popular tool to use in machine learning problems involving text and language for their strengths in sequence modeling and sequence-to-sequence prediction. In this chapter, we will see that Transformer models are similarly well-suited to these problems in music and audio. However, what makes Transformer models particularly interesting is that they are not formulated as sequential models like the previously studied RNNs. In fact, they can be oblivious to

DOI: 10.1201/9781003240198-9

the sequential structure, treating the input as a collection of n objects rather than a sequence of length n. If positional information is of special importance to the model, it must be *embedded*, a topic which we discuss in the following paragraphs.

An important preliminary to understanding Transformer models (and tokenized, sequential modeling in general) is the idea of *embedding*. In many NLP problems, embedding is a representation of some word in the possible vocabulary by creating a vector with weights that, when considering all possible words, represent some information about the contextual properties most regularly found around the word. This context is not encoded in former approaches such as bag-of-words, in which the grammar and usage around the words is lost. This is analogous to viewing an image as a histogram of its pixel intensities or a musical piece as a histogram of the pitches played [161]; while this representation still contains some useful information about the contents of the image, most of its useful structure and relationships between pixels or notes are lost.

In a good embedding, words which are semantically similar will be closer to each other within the vector space (that is, the distance between their vectors will be minimal). This is motivated by the distributional hypothesis from the field of linguistics: "Words that are used and occur in the same contexts tend to purport similar meanings" [162].

Might these same techniques extend to music? Besson and Schn point out that the common ancestor to both language and music is the expression of emotive meanings [163]. Both contain sequential elements the develop and unfold in time; rhythm and temporal ratios appear in the pattern of language, and in the same way that notes construct chords so do phonemes combine to create words. Musician Leonard Bernstein employs the methods of Noam Chomsky in his famous lecture series *The Unanswered Question* [164], relating music to grammar in its contours, cadences, and communicated ideas. In a cognitive sense, both language and music create strong expectancies to listeners or readers; the presence of unexpected words (or notes) generate measurable peaks in brain potential [165].

Word2Vec [166] is an unsupervised model that vectorizes vocabulary in a way that geometrically relates contextual expectations. Instead of assigning tokens to words, Word2Vec learns to predict neighboring words for a given word (Skip-Gram) or predict a center word based on its neighbors (Continuous Bag of Words) over a fixed sized window. Word2Vec was applied to music by Herremans and Chuan [167], showing that the embedded vector space captures tonal relationships from only the context of a musical slice (that is, without any explicit information about the pitch, duration, or intervals contained in the slice).

Without going into too much detail about word2vec, we draw a parallel to the Markov modeling we discussed in the natural language modeling section 2.4.2, as follows. Instead of considering only the past K samples of the language to find a model parameterized by θ that maximizes the likelihood (log-probability) or best predicts the current sample

$$\max_{\theta} \ \log P_\theta(w_n | w_{n-k}, \ldots, w_{n-1}), \tag{9.1}$$

we want to maximize the likelihood of the current position word w_c from its left and right context

$$\max_{\theta} \ \log P_{\theta}(w_c | w_{c-m}, ..., w_{c-1}, w_{c+1}, ..., w_{c+m}). \tag{9.2}$$

The goal of the learning system is to find transformations or embeddings that can take the input words from the context, often originally represented as one-hot vectors, represent them in a lower dimensional vector space that gives real-valued coordinates to each of the words, and finally decode or recover the current word from that embedding. In frameworks such as Keras and PyTorch, the specific networks responsible for taking a one-hot vector input and representing it as a vector are called *embedding layers*. So for example, given words indexed by integers such as 4 and 20, and assuming 2D embedding, the embedding layer will turn each on of them into vectors such, e.g. $[[4], [20]] \longrightarrow [[0.25, 0.1], [0.6, -0.2]]$ In other words, embeddings are ways to learn representation of categorical data based on some semantic similarity, which is most often considered as contextual similarity, as in linguist John Rupert Firth's quote "You shall know a word by the company it keeps". In the same that Word2Vec uses this concept to train the word embedding in one particular way, Transformers use self-attention to learn even more powerful language representation.

Above we described a way to embed information about the meaning of a musical token in relationship to other tokens. However, there is another kind of embedding critical to Transformer: *positional* embedding. In positional embedding, we represent not the meaning of a token, but rather the token's position in a sequence. These can either be learned embeddings, or deterministically defined. In Transformer, these two embeddings (meaning and position) are combined to make a complete token embedding.

Recall one of the challenges associated with RNNs: information from early in the sequence can become lost as the sequence progresses, but this information is often still relevant and important downstream. We discussed some architectural changes that better preserve this information, and this chapter expands on an approach which has exploded in recent years: *attention*.

While the RNN variants we have explored have focused on creating better hidden states which maintain long history, the attention mechanism learns to attend to previous hidden states when relevant. Essentially, the model creates a contextual vector composed of previous hidden states, weighed according to their learned relevance to the current task. We can imagine attention to be the mechanism that guides the model to its most relevant memories at a given time.

Why might attention be important for composing music? Musical form takes shape often at both a macro and micro level. A piece might begin in C major, with two distinct themes presented. It may then modulate to A minor, and perhaps to G major, then back home to C major. Within each of these sections, there is a wealth of melodic and rhythmic figures to enjoy, but at the same time, as a listener, we maintain a sense of the long-term structure which gives us that anticipated relief when we return to the original key. As a listener, we have learned to listen for both immediate patterns (perhaps a melodic figure in the G major section) and consequent responses to patterns we heard earlier in the piece, usually in the form of tonal resolution. As such, it would be important for a neural model to maintain representation of these components simultaneously so that it can learn to create similar complete structure.

The self-attention mechanism is a key defining characteristic of Transformer models which allows the network to make use of preceding or surrounding tokens to model the sequence distribution. There are three key[1] words that we will use to describe the attention mechanism:

1. Query. The query is a learned, dynamically formed vector, usually based on some combination of the input sequence, position, and token embedding of the current token being processed ("reference token").
2. Key. All tokens in the contextual scope map to a key. The "query" from above is "asked" over all of these "keys".
3. Value. Each token in the contextual scope has some associated value vector. The dot product of the query and the key then tells us how much of this value to pass forward in the network.

Taken together, we can consider the inner product of a query with a key to be the significance by which the contextual token deserves attention in making the prediction associated with the current key. The value is then the information associated with that context, which is propagated forward only to the extent of the "attention" granted to it by the query-key pair.

We will adopt the notation of Tay et al. [168] to formally describe in a series of equations the Transformer architecture as explained above, with particular emphasis on multihead attention. First, we generate a query as

$$q = W_q e + b_q, \tag{9.3}$$

where e is the vectorized version of the current input token, W_q and b_q (and subsequent W and b) are learned weights and biases, and q is the query generated from the token e.

After generating a query, we must generate a set of keys to each meld with the query. A key k_t is generated for each contextual vector e_t

$$k_t = W_k e_t + b_k. \tag{9.4}$$

Each combined query + key interaction tells the Transformer model how much of the *value* associated with the key's token to extract. These values v_t are defined by:

$$v_t = W_v e_t + b_v, \tag{9.5}$$

and taken together, the partial value α extracted from each value v_t is determined by the keys as:

$$\alpha_t = \frac{e^{q^\top k_t}}{\sum_{u=0}^{T} e^{q^\top k_u}} \tag{9.6}$$

---

[1]This is one of them.

The dot product between query q and key k is considered an attention matrix, which is responsible for learning alignment scores between tokens within the sequence – that is, it informs the model how a token should gather information from other tokens[2].

The combined value is then

$$v = \sum_{k=0}^{T} \alpha_t v_t. \tag{9.7}$$

The attention mechanism can be imagined as a learned bias used to pool all tokens based on their relevance. However, this learned model comes at a cost: self-attention faces scaling issues due to its quadratic time and memory complexity.

The outputs v of each head can be passed into a dense layer to compute output as a combination of values of attention. To summarize this process, for any reference token, different attention heads (since we are using *multi-head attention*) learn to gather information from surrounding tokens in different ways. This information can then be combined in a dense layer, leveraging multiple learned patterns of attention for the task at hand.

With the attention module complete, standard neural network layers can now be employed, such as feed-forward layers and activations. For example, Vaswani et al. use two feed-forward layers with ReLU activations in their sequence-to-sequence application.

A Sequence-to-Sequence Transformer Example

As a practical example, we will examine an implementation of the Transformer architecture. This example is built in Keras, adapted from an article by Franois Chollet [169]. Interested readers are also directed to a PyTorch analog in "The Annotated Transformer" by Huang et al. [170].

In this example, we will skip the implementation details around dataset preparation, splitting of data into training and validation pools, and calls to model training; instead, we will focus on architecture implementations including encoder and decoder structures.

Let's assume we have some vectorized input data sequence, where the vocabulary size is V, and the input sequence length is s. Because we are doing sequence-to-sequence modeling, at each training step, the model will seek to predict the $n + 1$th target word, using the input sequence and already-produced target sequence items 0 to n. In this way, the input at each training step is actually composed of the input sequence *and* the portion

---

[2]Note that there is typically a scaling term in the numerator and denominator exponents based on the Transformer dimensionality, which we have omitted for illustrative purposes.

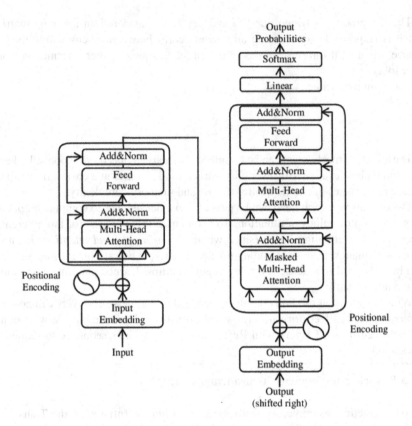

Figure 9.1 The left segment of this figure shows the attention mechanism described above, and its use within the original Transformer architecture proposed by Vaswani et al. in 2017. We note that the inputs and outputs of each multi-headed self-attention module are connected *residually*. *Residual connections* describe neural network layers which combine information from earlier layers directly with the output of layers deeper within the network.

of the output sequence generated prior to the next element. The associated output target is this next element.

The sequence-to-sequence Transformer consists of an Encoder and a Decoder chained together. At this point, we will pause our example to discuss these important components.

9.2.2 TRANSFORMER ENCODERS AND DECODERS

We previously introduced encoders and decoders as a means of reducing the representation of input data to (and reconstructing data from) a latent, lower-dimensional encoding. Transformers can be thought of in a similar fashion; we are trying to model some distribution $p(y|x)$, and we make an assumption that there exists some parameterization θ which through a learning or optimization process can be used to bring out features in x that the model should attend to, forming a latent space $z = f_\theta(x)$. So, we learn encoding $p(y|z)$. In the case of sequential data, the encoder maps a sequence of observations $(x_1, x_2, ..., x_n)$ to a sequence of latent representations $(z_1, z_2, ..., z_n)$, which are passed to the decoder that generates an output sequence $(y_1, y_2, ..., y_m)$. One should note that the length of the output sequence can be different from the length of the input sequence.

In the original formulation of the transfomer [171], attention was used in two fashions: as a way for the decoder to attend to the input, similar to attention in RNN, and as an intra-attention, or self-attention, by letting the input sequence "listen to itself", thus capturing the dependencies across all positions of the input sequences simultaneous rather then sequentially. Compared to RNN, where the number of operations grows with the length of the input data and is impossible to parallelize, in the Transformer the number of operations is constant, albeit at the cost of reduced resolution due to averaging by the attention-weighted positions. This effect was counteracted by using Multi-Head Attention, basically replicating the self-attention with multiple learned weights, which amounts to extracting multiple features in parallel.

We now resume our code example, implementing these Encoder and Decoder structures. The embedding dimensionality refers to the embedding of the input vectors into the queries and keys which will drive the attention mechanism. The dense dimensionality refers to the dimensionality of the feedforward neural network layer that is applied after the self-attention layer, essentially defining the expressivity of the transformation created by the layer which acts upon the weighted values selected from the input.

```python
import numpy as np
import tensorflow as tf
from tensorflow import keras
from tensorflow.keras import layers

class TransformerEncoder(layers.Layer):
    def __init__(self, embed_dim, dense_dim, num_heads, **kwargs):
        super().__init__(**kwargs)
        self.embed_dim = embed_dim
        self.dense_dim = dense_dim
        self.num_heads = num_heads
        self.attention = layers.MultiHeadAttention(
            num_heads=num_heads, key_dim=embed_dim
        )
```

```python
        self.dense_proj = keras.Sequential(
            [layers.Dense(dense_dim, activation="relu"),
             layers.Dense(embed_dim),]
        )
        self.layernorm_1 = layers.LayerNormalization()
        self.layernorm_2 = layers.LayerNormalization()

    def call(self, inputs, mask=None):
        if mask is not None:
            padding_mask = tf.cast(mask[:, tf.newaxis, :],
                                   dtype="int32")
        attention_output = self.attention(
            query=inputs, value=inputs, key=inputs,
            attention_mask=padding_mask)
        proj_input = self.layernorm_1(inputs + attention_output)
        proj_output = self.dense_proj(proj_input)
        return self.layernorm_2(proj_input + proj_output)

class TransformerDecoder(layers.Layer):
    def __init__(self, embed_dim, latent_dim, num_heads, **kwargs):
        super().__init__(**kwargs)
        self.embed_dim = embed_dim
        self.latent_dim = latent_dim
        self.num_heads = num_heads
        self.attention_1 = layers.MultiHeadAttention(
            num_heads=num_heads, key_dim=embed_dim
        )
        self.attention_2 = layers.MultiHeadAttention(
            num_heads=num_heads, key_dim=embed_dim
        )
        self.dense_proj = keras.Sequential(
            [layers.Dense(latent_dim, activation="relu"),
             layers.Dense(embed_dim),]
        )
        self.layernorm_1 = layers.LayerNormalization()
        self.layernorm_2 = layers.LayerNormalization()
        self.layernorm_3 = layers.LayerNormalization()

    def call(self, inputs, encoder_outputs, mask=None):
        causal_mask = self.get_causal_attention_mask(inputs)
        if mask is not None:
            padding_mask = tf.cast(mask[:, tf.newaxis, :],
                                   dtype="int32")
            padding_mask = tf.minimum(padding_mask, causal_mask)

        attention_output_1 = self.attention_1(
            query=inputs, value=inputs, key=inputs,
```

```
                attention_mask=causal_mask)
        out_1 = self.layernorm_1(inputs + attention_output_1)

        attention_output_2 = self.attention_2(
            query=out_1,
            value=encoder_outputs,
            key=encoder_outputs,
            attention_mask=padding_mask,
        )
        out_2 = self.layernorm_2(out_1 + attention_output_2)

        proj_output = self.dense_proj(out_2)
        return self.layernorm_3(out_2 + proj_output)

    def get_causal_attention_mask(self, inputs):
        input_shape = tf.shape(inputs)
        batch_size, sequence_length = input_shape[0],
                                      input_shape[1]
        i = tf.range(sequence_length)[:, tf.newaxis]
        j = tf.range(sequence_length)
        mask = tf.cast(i >= j, dtype="int32")
        mask = tf.reshape(mask, (1, input_shape[1],
                                    input_shape[1]))
        mult = tf.concat(
            [tf.expand_dims(batch_size, -1),
             tf.constant([1, 1], dtype=tf.int32)],
            axis=0, )
        return tf.tile(mask, mult)
```

Let's pay attention to the TransformerEncoder call: we compute the attention output, then further densely encode this output along with the input itself. The various normalization calls apply transformations that maintains the mean activation within each example close to 0 and the activation standard deviation close to 1. The attention_mask is an optional argument to calls of MultiHeadAttention which prevent the attention head from attending to masked keys. This is particularly relevant to the decoder. Because we are modeling sequential problems, one must also consider how causality should be taken into account for Transformer models. In a self-attention layer all of the keys, values and queries are provided at once. In the encoder, there is no constraint that the self-attention must be causal, meaning that it is not restricted to depend only on past (and current) tokens. But, for encoder-decoder frames, if decoders are used in a generative fashion, which is the common use of language models, then rebuilding a sequence is done in an autoregressive manner. In such a case self-attention used in the decoding step must be causal (i.e., depending only on past decoded positions). This causality is achieved by multiplying the attention map with a mask that removes all past positions from an element-wise multiplication of the input values with of the softmax which correspond to illegal connections. Without this mask in place, the decoder could use information from the future, which would result in an impossible model at inference time, when the "future" is truly unavailable.

As a note, a different type of masking is used in decoder-only architectures, where the learning is repeated by randomly masking parts of embedded sequence, so that the goal of the transfomer is to recover the missing part and by doing so, learn the structure across time as a contextual dependency, reminiscent of the prediction of a center word from its surroundings in word2vec.

To analyze the TransformerDecoder call, we see that attention is again applied to the input, and these attention values form the basis for "selection" (via attention mechanism) which aspects of the encoded data is decoded into output.

In RNN as well as in Transformer, the mapping between input an output is done by an inter- or cross-attention mechanism as depicted in Figure 9.2. The cross-attention mechanism in Transformer architecture mixes the features from x and y by performing a dot-product between their embedding sequences after they were mapped to the same dimension. The output length of the decoder is determined by the target sequence y as it plays a role of a query with input x used to produces key and value. Technically, in cross-attention the queries are generated from one embedding and keys and values are generated from another embedding.

One more crucial element to our sequence-to-sequence Transformer is positional embedding, introduced earlier in this chapter:

```
class PositionalEmbedding(layers.Layer):
    def __init__(self, sequence_length, vocab_size, embed_dim,
                 **kwargs):
        super().__init__(**kwargs)
        self.token_embeddings = layers.Embedding(
            input_dim=vocab_size, output_dim=embed_dim
        )
        self.position_embeddings = layers.Embedding(
            input_dim=sequence_length, output_dim=embed_dim
        )
        self.sequence_length = sequence_length
        self.vocab_size = vocab_size
        self.embed_dim = embed_dim
```

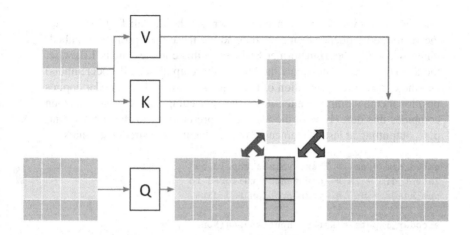

Figure 9.2 Illustration of the cross-attention mechanism. Some input sequence (top left) is transformed by matrix W_V and W_K. These transformations do not need to preserve the original shape of the input. A query transformation W_Q is applied to a separate input sequence (lower left), in this example opting to preserve shape. From the dot product of the query and key, we arrive at a matrix of attention scores. When multiplied by a value matrix, we reach our Transformer output, a matrix of weighted values from one of the input sequences, with weights determined by both that input and the additional query input, hence attention that "cross"es both inputs.

```
def call(self, inputs):
    length = tf.shape(inputs)[-1]
    positions = tf.range(start=0, limit=length, delta=1)
    embedded_tokens = self.token_embeddings(inputs)
    embedded_positions = self.position_embeddings(positions)
    return embedded_tokens + embedded_positions

def compute_mask(self, inputs, mask=None):
    return tf.math.not_equal(inputs, 0)
```

This is used to make the model aware of the element order in the sequence. It works by defining a range from 0 to the length of the input sequence (s), then creating an embedding of the position's index as a vector of dimensionality embed_dim. This can be simply added to the sequence element's token embedding to create a complex representation of both the element's content and position.

We now have everything we need to assemble the model: first, we gather
the vectorized sequence elements, then add to these their positional embeddings. We apply the Transformer Encoder to this complex input. Likewise,
the decoder receives as inputs the "preceding output" (aka decoder_inputs)
and the encoded representation of the sequence inputs. The decoder applies
positional embedding and attention to the "preceding output" sequence, then
combines this densely with the encoded representation of the sequence inputs, outputting at last an element with the size of the desired vocabulary.

```
embed_dim = em  # These values should be
latent_dim = la #  constants, tailored to
num_heads = nu  #  your problem and data.

encoder_inputs = keras.Input(shape=(None,),
                   dtype="int64", name="encoder_inputs")
x = PositionalEmbedding(sequence_length, vocab_size, embed_dim)
                   (encoder_inputs)
encoder_outputs = TransformerEncoder(embed_dim, latent_dim,
                                num_heads)(x)
encoder = keras.Model(encoder_inputs, encoder_outputs)

decoder_inputs = keras.Input(shape=(None,), dtype="int64",
                         name="decoder_inputs")
encoded_seq_inputs = keras.Input(shape=(None, embed_dim),
                            name="decoder_state_inputs")
x = PositionalEmbedding(sequence_length, vocab_size, embed_dim)
                   (decoder_inputs)
x = TransformerDecoder(embed_dim, latent_dim, num_heads)
                   (x, encoded_seq_inputs)
x = layers.Dropout(0.5)(x)
decoder_outputs = layers.Dense(vocab_size, activation="softmax")(x)
decoder = keras.Model([decoder_inputs, encoded_seq_inputs],
                   decoder_outputs)

decoder_outputs = decoder([decoder_inputs, encoder_outputs])
transformer = keras.Model(
    [encoder_inputs, decoder_inputs], decoder_outputs,
    name="transformer"
)
```

Similar to other deep learning models that have encoder and decoder structures,
Transformer models can be used in multiple problem settings. Encoder-only Transformer models can be used for problems like classification. Decoder-only Transformer models can be used for problems like language modeling. Encoder-Decoder
Transformer models can be used for problems like machine translation, often with
multiple multi-head self-attention modules. These can consist of typical multi-head

self-attention blocks which attend to keys and values derived from the same tensor from which queries are learned, found in both the encoder and decoder but also encoder-decoder cross-attention which can allow the decoder to query values from the encoder.

There are three main variants of Transformer:

- The original Transformer from "Attention Is All You Need" (Encoder & Decoder) [171]
- BERT (Encoder only) [172]
- GPT (Decoder only) [173–175]

BERT (Bidirectional Encoder Representations from Transformers) is trained as an Auto-Encoder. It uses Masked Language Model (MLM) to corrupt the input, and the objective of the model is to identify the masked token. It also uses self-attention, where each token in an input sentence looks at the bidirectional context (other tokens on left and right of the considered token).

GPT is trained as an autoregressive model. It is trained with a language modeling objective, where the given sequence of tokens is used to predict the next token (Thus looking at only the past or left side context). It also uses Masked Attention to make it into an auto-regressive model. A simple definition of the Generative Pre-trained Transformer (GPT) model can be done in few hundred lines of code[3].

From GPT-2 and on, the Transformer models started to be used as multi-task learners, where the learning objective was be modified to be task conditional $P(output|input, task)$. For language models, the output, input and task, all are sequences of natural language. This provided the capability of GPT-2 to operate in zero shot task transfer tasks, where model "understands" new instructions without being explicitly trained on them. For example, for English to French translation task the model was given an English sentence followed by the word French and a prompt (:). The model was supposed to understand that it is a translation task and give French counterpart of English sentence.

9.2.3   USE AND APPLICATION OF TRANSFORMERS

In our discussion so far we have hinted at the use of Transformer models as yet another, albeit state-of-the-art, tool for representation learning. Drawing upon the word2vec analogy, we focused on the aspect of contextual (self)similarity as a way to build a representation that draws closely related "meanings" to be close in terms of some similarity measure. That measure, most conveniently but not necessarily formulated in terms of a metric, such as Euclidean distance or dot product, had to be specified in the loss function that we used to train our neural network. Once the learning was completed, the representation could be frozen and reused for other purposes. So, although the Transformer was trained in an unsupervised or semi-supervised way toward a particular task like predicting the next sample, or complete a sequence after

---

[3]https://github.com/karpathy/minGPT/blob/master/mingpt/model.py

some elements were omitted via masking, one of the big advantages of the training was in the use of the network as a means for representation of the data that can be later used for other tasks. Speaking of musical tasks of Transformer models, we will mention their applications both on the symbolic representation (MIDI Transformers) and on audio data (Waveform and Spectral Transformers) in the coming sections. Indeed, the most common application would be generation of continuation of music materials given some initial seed. Other application include creating variations through the BERT-like models that do not specifically deal with continuation but can offer completions or alteration to a sequence if some of the elements are discarded from the input, creating melodic, harmonic, or rhythmical variations. One other important point to consider is the use of the representation for downstream tasks, such as adaptation or quick, so-called one-shot of few-shot transfer learning that reuses some of the Transformer layers for a different purpose than in the original training task. Commonly, the reuse is done at the last output layer. An input that is processed through the whole network then is input into a different final layer, often a fully connected classification layer or a multi-layer perceptron (MLP) that is trained on a new task while freezing the Transformer parameters. This technique, not necessarily restricted to use with Transformers, is commonly known as *transfer learning*. A different task is changing the input to the network, or changing both the input and output layers without altering or retraining the middle layers. Such tasks are commonly called reprogramming, as they reuse an existing network for a different task rather then simply refining or adapting it to a different domain. The reprogramming is often done with some adversarial or malign purpose in mind, as a way for an attacker to reprogram models for tasks that violate the code of ethics of the original network developer. Regardless of this unethical use, and since we are not dealing in this book with neural network attacks and defenses, we would like to mention just that the possibility of reprogramming opens up some creative possibilities and understanding of the network representation and task performance accomplishments.

Accordingly, transfer learning and (adversarial) reprogramming are two closely related techniques used for repurposing well-trained neural network models for new tasks. Neural networks, when trained on a large dataset for a particular task, learn features that can be useful across multiple related tasks. Transfer learning aims at exploiting this learned representation for adapting a pre-trained neural network for an alternate task. Typically, the last few layers of a neural network are modified to map to a new output space, followed by fine-tuning the network parameters on the dataset of the target task. Such techniques are especially useful when there is a limited amount of training data available for the target task. Reprogramming techniques can be viewed as an efficient training method and can be a superior alternative to transfer learning. Particularly, reprogramming might not require the same large amount of new domain data to finetune pre-trained neural networks, including repurposing neural networks across different modalities, such as moving between text and images. This surprising result suggests that there is some universal aspect to the Transformer ability to capture self similarities an repetitions in data that operates across domains and might be a basic trait of artificial (and maybe human) intelligence.

Going back to specifics of Transformer representation, looking at its input and output layers reveals different aspects of data structure that the network is able to extract. The final layer of the Transformer creates an embedding for the whole input sequence. If we think about this as a language model, then the output of the Transformer is effectively an embedding representation for the whole sequence. Summarizing a sentence into a vectors, also know as sentence2vec task, has not been efficiently solved prior to introduction of Transformers. We do need to mention that in the RNN, the last hidden state could be considered as a summarization of the whole input sequence into one vector, also sometimes called a "through vector" as it summarized the idea of the thought of the sentence, which is later used as a seed for generating another similarly meaning sentence when used in a seq2seq fashion, such as in language translation. So despite the limits of the RNN-thought analysis that required inclusion of a gating memory mechanism and later an attention mechanism, it still helps to preserve the idea that Transformer output captures the essence of the data, or for our purposes, "guesses the composer's mind", better than earlier architectures.

Another point worth mentioning is the significance of the first embedding layer that processes the data prior to application of the attention heads and further Transformer layers. As we mentioned earlier, embeddding is required when inputting categorical data, such as one-hot vectors representing note combinations, without having a vectorical representation with underlying metric structure. In other words, the purpose of embedding is to use context to find a space with some natural distance measure or metric that places similar meanings in nearby locations. Accordingly, the embedding itself is a process that extracts essential information or features from the input data, sample by sample, rendering it into vectors where self-similarity or attention can be detected. The first embedding layer is also significant for media data, such as images or sounds. Although often some signal processing knowledge is applied to the signal, such as pre-processing it by spectral or MFCC analysis before inputting into the neural network, these man-made features are often not powerful enough to capture the detailed structure of the data. Work on CNNs in the visual domains had shown layers of such networks, such as the first convolutional layer of AlexNet, effectively learn edge detectors and other spatial frequency patterns reminiscent of early filters in the human visual system. Similar inspection of first linear embedding layers in visual Transformer models like Vision Transformer [176] achieve similar and better filters compared to the CNN first layer. With convolutions without dilation, the receptive field is increased linearly. Using self-attention, the interaction captured between pixels' representations is much more distant, with heads attending to the whole input segment (visual patch) already in the early layers. One can possibly justify the performance gain of Transformer based on the early access to data interactions. Attempts to understand the filtering / feature extraction and interaction aspects of Transformer in audio domains are still in early phases of research, although the empirical quality of results in applying Transformer to various audio and MIDI tasks are suggestive that such architecture are important for music. In the programming exercise of this chapter we address the two aspects of Transformer – we train a predictive sequence model with and without Transformer, and then look at the embedding layer to see how the distribution of tokens changes as a result of using the attention layer.

9.3 MIDI TRANSFORMERS

The application of transformers to symbolic music require steps that are somewhat similar to those in RNN, while also bearing some important distinctions and modeling advantages. Similar to the RNN case, the musical score has to be represented as a sequence of discrete tokens, which are then subject to repetition modeling using the self-attention mechanism. Unlike RNN or CNN that use relative encoding in terms of recurrence relations or local convolution kernel relations, the original Transformer did not explicitly model relative or absolute position information in its structure. In music (as well as in language) relative position is often important. For the core Transformer, which employs neither convolution nor recurrence, incorporating explicit representations of position information is essential since otherwise it becomes invariant to sequence ordering. This core Transformer has been referred to as *regular attention*, in comparison to the more recent *relative attention*.

Both attention mechanisms have been used in deep learning models; regular attention, also known as dot-product attention, is the standard attention mechanism we have introduced, which computes the attention weights between the query and the key vectors by taking the dot product of the two vectors, followed by a softmax operation. The result is a probability distribution over the values, where the attention weights determine how much weight to assign to each value vector when computing the weighted sum.

Relative attention, on the other hand, is a more recent development that takes into account the relative positions of the query and key vectors. In regular attention, the attention weights are determined solely based on the similarity between the query and key vectors. However, in relative attention, additional parameters are introduced to capture the relative positions between the query and key vectors. This allows the attention mechanism to better capture the context and dependencies between the words in a sentence. Relative attention has been shown to outperform regular attention on various NLP tasks, particularly when dealing with long sequences of text. However, it also requires more computational resources and is more complex to implement. Therefore, the choice between regular and relative attention depends on the specific needs and constraints of the task at hand.

Relative-attention-based models have used position encodings by adding sinusoid codes, or adding biased attention weights based on distance between events to incorporate relative time information. Accordingly, in order to capture pairwise relations between musical representations, Music Transformer [177] uses relative positional information based on pairwise distance between two positions. Since the positional encoding in the Transformer takes into account the relations between all positions in the sequence, this creates substantial memory requirements. One of the theoretical contributions of the Music Transformer is an efficient implementation of relative positional encoding. When trained on the Piano-e-Competition dataset that consists of MIDI recorded from performances containing expressive dynamics, the encoding was done using sparse, MIDI-like, event-based representation with 10 milisecond resolution. The MIDI note events were converted into a sequence of events from a vocabulary of 128 NOTE ON events, 128 NOTE OFF events, 100 TIME SHIFT events from 10ms to 1s in 10ms increments, and 32 SET VELOCITY events quantized from 128 possible MIDI velocities. The transformer captured the recurrence relations between notes, timing, and expressive dynamics (velocity) by treating them as a sequence of tokens. This allowed encoding at the scale of 60s ($\sim$ 2000 tokens) compared to a benchmark LSTM [178] that operated at timescales of 15s ($\sim$ 500 tokens).

The Music Transformer was also applied to multi-track musical data of J.S. Bach Chorales. For this musical dataset the score was quantized in time to a sixteenth-note grid, and then serialized by iterating through all the voices within the same time step. This allowed samples to maintain the original timing of the four voices, always advancing four steps across the voices before advancing to the next grid in time. This allowed the model to capture more global timing and produce regular phrasing of the chorales.

Another early application of a Transformer is MuseNet transformer by OpenAI. It uses an autoregressive model similar to GPT-2 that was trained to predict the next token in a sequence. In addition to the standard positional embeddings, MuseNet contains a learned embedding that tracks the passage of time in a given sample. This way, all of the notes that sound at the same time are given the same timing embedding, with an additional embedding for each note in a chord. MuseNet also has two structural embeddings that position the musical sample within the larger musical piece. One embedding divides the larger piece into 128 parts, while the second encoding is a countdown from 127 to 0 as the model approaches the (end) token. The use of several different kinds of embeddings gives the model more structural context. Another novelty of the MuseNet transformer is use of Sparse Attention, explained in the following paragraphs.

A self-attention layer maps input embeddings to an output connectivity matrix that maps indices of output input vectors to earlier instances of the input to which the each output vector attends. Full self-attention for autoregressive models maps every element's attention to all previous positions and its own position. Factorized self-attention instead has several separate attention heads, where each head defines a subset of the indices from the full attention, somewhat reminiscent of strided convolution, with one attention head skipping forward, and the other attending to the blocks between the strides. The methods allowed substantially reducing the complexity of the self-attention model, allowing MuseNet to model longer musical sequences.

MuseNet uses the recomputed and optimized kernels of Sparse Transformer to train a 72-layer network with 24 attention headswith full attention over a context of 4096 tokens. The system can generate 4-minute musical compositions with 10 different instruments, and can combine styles from country to Mozart to the Beatles.

A different architecture was used in Pop Music Transformer that is based on Transformer-XL architecture [179] combined with a novel beat-based music representation called REvamped-MIDI (REMI) [94]. Transformer-XL achieves longer sequence modeling by using a recurrence mechanism, that operated by keeping the outputs of the hidden layers from previous steps and concatenating them with the tokens of the next input. Both are used to calculate the Key and the Value matrices of the current segment at each attention head of the current layer. This gives the network additional information in regard to past without changing the Value matrix. In the training process, each input sequence is divided into "segments of a fixed length, 512 tokens for the Pop Music Transformer. During the training phase, only the weights of the transformer applied to the current segment are updated, while the previous weights are frozen using the so-called stop gradient operation. During inference, all past weight are used, thus extending the effective memory back to the past, with the length depending on the depth (number of layers) in the transformer. Because the length of the sequence being modeled extends beyond the current input frame, Transformer-XL uses relative position encoding to capture information relative to distance between the tokens. Pop Music Transformer used 12 attention layers with 8 attention heads. The length of the input events segment and the recurrence segment are both set to 512. The events are using REMI representation that adds Bar events to mark the bar lines and Position events that point to position in a sixteenth note time grid within the bar. These additional events provide metrical information that maintains more steady beat then using the time-shift events in MIDI derived tokens as in the Music Transformer or MuseNet. To account for performance dynamics and timing deviation REMI also includes Velocity and Tempo events, respectively. To provide more harmonics coherence, REMI adds a set of chord tokens consisting of 12 possible root notes and five chord qualities (major, minor, diminished, augmented, and dominant), making a total of 60 chord tokens. Adding these additional tokens requires pre-processing of the data using various Music Information Retrieval (MIR) tools that are provided in the REMI package[4].

A further improvement to the REMI idea of including musical descriptors as part of the tokens provided to a Transformer, the FIGARO system[5] [180] replaced MIR descriptors with a learned descriptors using a VQ-VAE method that encodes bar-long music segments into a latent vector, which is then discretized to 16 separate codes with a codebook size of 2048. In addition to the learned description, FIGARO provides human expert description that provide global context for future generation. The VQ-VAE model uses a Transformer encoder-decoder model with a 4-layer encoder discretized and fed into a 6-layer Transformer decoder. A linear layer is used before and after vector-quantization to project between model space and latent space. The output of the decoder is the probability of autoregressive prediction for each position in the context conditioned on the past. Other notable works in this domain include Choi [181], MMM [182], MuseMorphose [183], Music Framework [184],

---

[4]https://github.com/YatingMusic/remi

[5]https://github.com/dvruette/figaro

MusicAutobot[6], many still in active research, which use various variants of Transformer to perform tasks such as continuation or inpainting, melody composition based on given chords, harmonization given a melody, creating variations on existing songs, changing and interpolating musical styles and more. One of the basic problems with use of generative models in general, and transformer based generation in particular, is specification of control over the desired musical outcome. Moreover, including multiple instruments and learning dependencies across musical tasks becomes computationally a very demanding task. Schemes to evaluate the usability and creative impact of generative systems, such as Standard System Usability Scale (SUS) (5-point Likert scale) [185], or The Creativity Support Index (CSI) score (5 questions) [186] become important alternatives to evaluating such systems based on user experience, rather then more traditional Mean Opinion Scores (MOS) or statistical perplexity and similarity measures applied to system outputs. To ensure good user experience [187], improvements to responsiveness of the system in terms of speed and flexibility of interaction, together with best-use scenarios, are being developed for iterative composition / production and improvisational applications.

9.3.1   WHERE DO MODELS PLACE MUSICAL ATTENTION?

If you were to analyze a musical score, you might observe connections on a variety of scales. Perhaps the composer has created some common pattern between the harmonic progression of chords underlying a musical phrase, the longer harmonic form of key modulations through a single movement, or even the full-scale relationship of the key signatures of each movement of the work. These relationships occur on different scales of time (location) and interval (duration). Similarly, the composer may introduce some melodic motif which appears throughout the piece with variation; perhaps inverted, re-orchestrated, or otherwise adapted to its current musical context.

As musicians, we could go through with a pencil and identify these connections at multiple points in time, flipping back and forth between pages of a score. Now we ask: does the "memory" of the transformer model provide the same attention to these compositional relationships?

Seeking the answer to this question provides a convenient introduction of a subfield referred to as *Explainable AI* (XAI). Research in XAI aims to make machine learning models more transparent and understandable to humans (typically with a goal to make decisions from these models fair, ethical, and trustworthy). Traditionally, many machine learning models, particularly neural networks, act as black boxes, meaning that it is difficult to understand how they arrive at their decisions. XAI seeks to provide insights and interpretability into the inner workings of these models.

As one such example of XAI, Huang et al. created an open-source tool[7] to visualize musical attention in Transformer models [188]. The authors share four interesting

---

[6]https://github.com/bearpelican/musicautobot

[7]Interested readers are encouraged to experiment with their public visualization application at https://storage.googleapis.com/nips-workshop-visualization/index.html.

observations:

- The attention heads distribute in time, as desired. Some heads look to the beginning of the piece where the key is established, others at cadential landmarks, and many at the immediate past.
- At lower-level network layers, attention is dense (the network attends to many positions), and in higher-level (deeper) network layers, the model attention is more sparse. This is due to the abstract, hierarchical learning of the network; at higher-level layers, the information is already summarized in meaningful ways, so there is less need to "gather" information from all over the composition.
- Regular attention tends to fall in a modal collapse (favoring the beginning of the piece and the immediate past), while relative attention spreads evenly throughout the music. This shortcoming of regular attention leads to repetitive loops in voice predictions.
- The model can attend to characteristic landmarks of an extended motif to learn when and how to change a melodic figure.

9.4   SPECTRAL TRANSFORMERS

In similar manner like the transformers transformed the way language is modeled in NLP, and how by use of tokenization similar breakthroughs happen in symbolic music as surveyed in the previous section, transformer models are also being applied to audio signals, predominantly in speech but also in music. In many ways encoders became a go-to architecture for dealing with sequential data, be it text, sequences of image patches, or sequences of speech or audio segments.

Many new methods that apply transformers to acoustic data appear in the speech processing field, many of which can be found in popular libraries like Hugging-Faces Transformers. One of the early models was Meta's (Facebook) vq-wav2vec. The process starts with a vq-wav2vec tokenization that comprises two convolutional neural networks that produce a representation z_i for each time step i at a rate of 100 Hz. These encodings are passed to a quantization module that replaces the original representation z_i by e_i from a fixed size codebook $e \in R^{V \times d}$ to build a discrete representation comprising of V d-dimensional codes.

Unlike the usual VQ method of clustering that we mentioned earlier in the context of k-means for unit selection in concatentive coding, the method of quantization used in discrete neural representation is based on one-hot encoding using Gumbel-Softmax probabilities assignment. This method enables selecting discrete codebook variables in a fully differentiable way so that a back propagation can be used both for the encoder network and the quantization layers. We will not elaborate on this technique here, but will mention that similar method is used by quantized variational autoencoder which is extensively used in OpenAI's Jukebox system that operates directly on a waveform.

Both vq-wav2vec and Jukebox use a Transformer as the next step after obtaining the discrete representation. The difference is that Jukebox uses a GPT-like

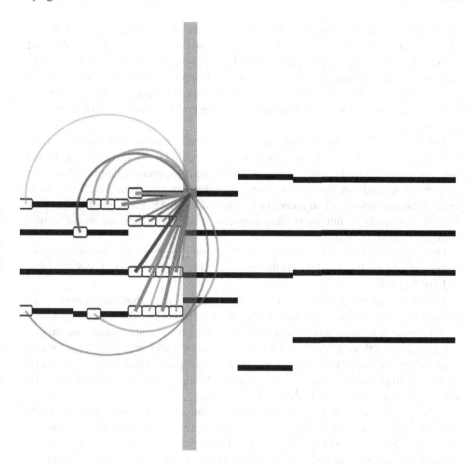

Figure 9.3 A visualization of the attention of Music Transformer on a phrase of a Bach chorale, from the application created by Huang et al. Black lines represent the voices of the Bach chorale, and the pink vertical strip represents the time of analysis, with a bold pink box on the particular voice for which the model would be forming a prediction. The other colored arrows relative widths indicate the weight of attention applied to the particular note. In this case, we can see that the past few notes in the soprano (top) line provide some information; this is perhaps reflective of the elements of voice leading typical of Bach's choral writing. Similarly, weight is found in the first note of the bass and soprano; this position is commonly used by Bach to establish the key, so its importance is clear. As expected, the notes in all voices just prior to the selected note are given attention, and in particular, the strong cadential notes of the bass (bottom) can indicate to the soprano which note provides the proper resolution. By analyzing the attention of the model in this way, we can observe connections between the learned representations and the traditional rules of harmony and voice leading in the style of Bach.

transformer, while wav2vec use a BERT architecture. The main difference between these transformers, when applied to audio, is that GPT learns to predict the next frame, while BERT trains a language model by applying a random mask that covers both past and future context. Since each of the discrete tokens represents around 10 ms of audio it is rather easy to predict a single masked input token using the transformer, so for audio learning the masking spans several tokens (10 tokens in the case of vq-wav2vec).

In both speech and music applications, the transformers are followed by a fine-tuning stage where the self-supervised learning is updated using a specific supervised task, such as feeding it to an acoustic model to perform transcriptions. When used for generative purpose, the final sequence of tokens output from the transformers needs to be converted back to audio. In the case of VQ-VAE, the reconstruction uses WaveNet as a way to interpolate and correctly predict a continuous sound from a sequence of code vectors.

Other uses of transformers that operate directly on spectral representation instead of a raw waveform include AST [189], SpecTNT [190], HTS-AT [191], PaSST [192], and MBT [193].

One of the advantages of using transformers on spectra is that they are operating on larger chunks of audio data compared to waveform, and the input data to the neural networks is already pre-processed to remove phase-related audio information that might be irrelevant for the final task. In case of audio generative applications where audio output is required, neural vocoders or phase reconstruction methods such as Griffith-Lim are applied to the spectral output that was generated by the network in order to convert it to an audio waveform.

Despite evident quality issues in audio synthesis, these new models provide promising alternatives to dedicated synthesis in terms of the versatility of sounds they can produce and ways for novel sound manipulation and editing. One of the main challenges in audio, similar to MIDI, is providing intuitive control over the generated sounds. Currently these model only give access either to global parameters that change the texture or timbre of the whole sounds. In NOTONO application[8], the VQ-VAE-2 architecture was applied to Mel-IF representation proposed in the GANSynth paper for interactive generation of sounds. VQ-VAE-2 is a two-layer hierarchical model that encodes 2D data into 2D integer arrays of top and bottom codemaps. To ensure that the these two codemaps are conditionally dependent, the encoder of the VQ-VAE-2 first downsamples and quantizes the input 2D data into the bottom map. This first representation is then further downsampled and again quantized, yielding the top codemap. In the decoder, the top codemap is first reconstructed using the code vectors of the learned dictionary. This reconstruction is then used as a conditioning information for the decoding of the bottom codemap. NOTONO uses this representation as an input to a tranformer that takes the top codemap as an input and produces an BERT-like bi-directional masking model of the low resolution (slower) sound structures. Then a second transformer is learned by cross-attention.

---

[8]https://sonycslparis.github.io/interactive-spectrogram-inpainting/

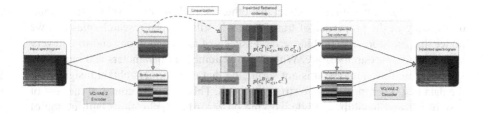

Figure 9.4 The NOTONO inpainting process.

In this scheme, illustrated in the earlier section introducing Transformer, a representation with attention masks from the top set of embeddings is used to highlight the extracted features in a bottom embedding. This is different from self-attention where attention mask is used to highlight its own (single-scale spectral) embedding. The method is used to perform generation of sounds by conditioning them on pitch and instrument type, or perform inpainting operations such as starting from a pre-existing sample, letting the user select and resample specific zones in these codemaps. This can be explained mathematically as a joint sampling from both input and output representations as follows:

Considering that the role of the Transformer applied to the top embedding c^T is to learn the probability of recovering a sample i from its past and an inpainting boolean mask m applied to its future

$$p(c^T) \sim p(c_i^T | c_{<i}^T, m \odot c_{\geq i}^T) . \qquad (9.8)$$

In this setting, the role of the first transformer is to compensate for the masking, while the next step in the learning process is to perform autoregressive modeling of the bottom encoding c^B with conditioning from the top codemap as

$$p(c^B | c^T) = \prod_i p(c_i^B | c_{<i}^B, c^T). \qquad (9.9)$$

Sampling new sounds can now be done by directly sampling from the joint probability of top and bottom codemaps $p(c^T, c^B) = p(c^T)p(c^B|c^T)$. The scheme of inpainting is shown in Figure 9.4.

Cross attention can also be used as a fusion method between multiple modalities, such as image and text, or multi-scale embedding representations such as in VQ-VAE2 spectral (i.e., audio) transformers. Other uses of spectral transformer for non-generative tasks are the previously mentioned AST and HTS-AT models for audio recognition and sound event detection, borrowing architectures from visual transformers (Vision Transformer [ViT] and Shifted Window Transformer [SWin] [194]).

9.5 ATTENTION, MEMORY, AND INFORMATION DYNAMICS

The surprising efficiency of transformers in many complex machine learning tasks gives an interesting perspective on what types of data and information relations such architectures are managing to extract that other methods haven't. Although deep understanding of the properties of transformers is still an open research question, we notice that transformers combine several aspects of modeling in one end-to-end very large and complex architecture. With the huge number of parameters and incredibly long training times, maybe it is not surprising that transformers obtain insights into the data that other models were struggling with. This of course comes at the cost of ease of use and flexibility. While working on zero-shot applications built on top of pre-trained models, we still lack the ability for real-time operations on systems with limited memory and computing power.

Focusing on the relative advantages of the transformer we note that it combines multiple representation layers or attention heads, each one providing direct access and connection across all inputs. Accordingly, transformers overcame difficulties faced by recurrent neural networks (RNNs) that model memory in a sequential manner that decays with time since each step attenuates the previous step by passing the hidden state as the input only to its next neighbor to the right (or to the right and left in bidirectional RNNs). Moreover, Transformers overcome the locality constraint of CNNs since the Query, Value and Key operate on the whole input rather than limit scope to a local neighborhood. As such, it is able to handle sequential data and broader contextual data that a convolutional neural network lacks. Lastly, transformer can effectively utilize parallel processing hardware systems such as GPUs and TPUs, which make it an attractive model to those who own massive computational resource (something that common musicians usually lack).

Given these considerations, we take a look at the components of Transformer models in an attempt to provide alternative leaner architectures that might lack the massive joint estimation of relations across all the data elements, but may still capture some of the representation advantages and contextual / temporal relations that transformers enjoy. Enoder-decoder aspects of Transformer models are important to understanding the different uses of the architecture. These could be also paralleled to different applications of other generative models, depending on the task they are trained to perform, from generation, to continuation, to accompaniment.

The basic transformer operates as a sequence-to-sequence model. The encoder can be seen as a combined embedding and conditioning operation of a decoder that operates in an auto-regressive manner. The encoder and decoder use different types of attention. The encoder attention is global, i.e. it considers all instances of the input data past and present to build its attention map. The decoder uses an auto-regressive attention as it is trained to generate its output sequentially by combining at every step the encoder output with it own generated past. For instance, a sequence of chords can be input into a decoder and a solo improvisation could be provided at the output of the decoder. The decoder will use a shift of one time step to feed the previous generated melody back into the input of the decoder, in parallel with the chord-derived representation from the encoder. This is reminiscent of the way latent codes from the encoder sequence are combined with the past of the decoder output in seq2seq RNN.

In many cases, the input conditioning is not required, as the transformer learns only the structure of the language it is later asked to generate without an external input. The OpenAI GPT family of models provides an arrangement of the transformer block that is capable of doing language modeling. This model discarded the Transformer encoder and used masked self-attention in the input layer that allows only past event to be considered. As mentioned above, the normal self-attention block allows a position to peek at tokens to its right, while masked self-attention prevents the model from looking into the future.

The generation tasks of Transformers often go beyond generation from a random seed or continuation of a short musical starting sequence. Creative musical tasks can be as varied as inpainting or completion of missing musical segments in partially completed musical sketches, creating variations by omitting segments from the input and letting the transformer find new alternatives, or learning to complete musical materials from partial factorized representations, such as completing melodies when only their rhythm is given and so on. In such cases instead of using the next token as a prediction, the transformer learns to deal with random omissions of data, trying to recover missing blocks, very much in the spirit of contextual embedding learning done by GloVe [195] or other word2vec models that use context to recover a missing word. Such masking models are applied only to the decoder in the BERT language model.

Similarly to GPT, Magenta's Music Transformer uses a decoder-only transformer to generate music with expressive timing and dynamics. Music modeling is done similar to language modeling by letting the model learn music in an unsupervised way and then have it sample outputs to create novel compositions. The representation fed into the transformer is handled by an embedding block. Such embedding can be learned separately, or be done as part of the overall end-to-end training. In the programming exercise accompanying this chapter, we use a Transformer to demonstrate the embedding aspect of the encoding when self-attention is used for the next token prediction task.

9.5.1   INFORMATION AND ATTENTION IN TRANSFORMERS

Attention can be interpreted as a means of biasing the allocation of available computational resources toward the most informative components of a signal. This raises the question of what aspect of musical structure is most informative? Apparently, information and attention are closely linked – we pay attention to informative aspects of data and we retrieve information from the environment by paying attention to important aspects of that data. Good representation captures these important aspects, so paying attention and learning representation are ultimately linked as well. An alternative way to think about these problems is as a database lookup problem. Let each feature-data pair be stored in a database as a key-value entry. Information retrieval becomes a problem of finding a relation between an input query and an appropriate database entry by matching the input query to the database key. In other words, if a pair (feature, data) = (key, value) is stored in a database, the key serves as a label for the retrieving the data values for an incoming query. Pairing an input query to database entry is done according to a similarity between the query and the key. This schematic approach to mapping information provides some important insights about the operation of Transformers:

- The problem of representation learning becomes a problem of designing a kernel that matches input data to features/keys.
- Generating data becomes a lookup of entries according to an input query. This can be done by a relatively simple operation such as extracting the top matching key, or by linear weighting of the attention weights.
- Unlike common neural networks, such as CNN or RNN that require a fixed size input, transformer queries can be designed to operate in a manner that is independent of the database size.
- The same query can result in different answers depending on the contents of the database using multiple keys (multiple attention heads).
- Finding relations between different data types is possible by designing appropriate mapping between their keys and queries.

Let us carry this analogy one step further. The attention operation in Equation 9.7 "pools" together multiple data points as values. As such, the attention over the database generates a linear combination of values contained in the database in a regression-like fashion. In fact, this contains the special case of database retrieval where all but one weight is zero. The name attention derives from the fact that the pooling operation pays particular attention to the terms for which the weight is significant. In this context, extraction of the attention weight becomes a similarity kernel $\alpha(q,k)$ relating queries to keys. In particular, considering Euclidean distance, we arrive at what is known as Gaussian kernel

$$\alpha(q,k_i) = exp(-\frac{||q-k_i||^2}{2\sigma^2}) \,.$$

For normalized keys and queries, the exponent can be also expressed in terms of a dot product $-\frac{1}{2}||q-k_i||^2 = q^T k_i - 1$. Since attention weights need normalizing, this kernel can expressed in terms of a softmax of a dot product, resulting in attention weights similar to Equation 9.6.

Moreover, since the entries to our database operation are input tokens e, the dot-product attention is done by a transformation of the input token through matrices W_q, W_k. These matrices are learned by the transformer so that they suitably transform between the input and output spaces, also adding a third learned matrix W_v to transform the input tokens to desired output values.

In previous chapters we discussed labeling data through the process of quantization and principal component analysis. This labeling was limiting the amount of information by selecting classes of similar events, or finding latent representation that capture data distribution. For sequential data we applied information dynamics criteria to select a reduced representation that had the best predictive properties. Such predictive quality was assessed on a global scale by finding long-term repetitions that are approximately similar. The attention mechanism in deep learning is also developed on a global scale. For example, the matrix multiplication in self-attention draws global dependencies of each word in a sentence or each pixel in an image.

9.5.2 ATTENTION, SELF-SIMILARITY, AND VMO

To gain some additional intuition about the operation of transformers in music we may observe interesting similarities between the way self-attention and musical self-similarity concept. This also brings another relation between Transformers and VMO that we will discuss in the following paragraphs.

The self-attention mechanism is a key defining characteristic of Transformer models. The mechanism can be viewed as a graph-like inductive bias that connects all tokens in a sequence with a relevance-based pooling operation. In a way, the encoder self-attention changes a local representation of the musical data into a global vector of connections or transition probabilities into other instances of that data. Let us rewrite that self-attention equation as a regression

$$v = f(q) = \sum_i v_i \frac{\alpha(q, k_i)}{\sum_j \alpha(q, k_j)} \qquad (9.10)$$

where $\alpha(q, k_i)$ is an arbitrary kernel, which in the transformer case is commonly an exponent of a dot product between key and query ($e^{q^T k_i}$). This means that the transformer value function performs a regression calculation (pooling) over all values weighted by the attention value that plays the role of a regression kernel between keys and queries. In statistics, kernel regression is a non-parametric technique to estimate the conditional expectation of a random variable, which in our particular case is done using attention as a kernel that computes similiarity between keys and queries, with the regression done over values. When values and keys are equal, Equation 9.10 is the same as kernel regression. Going further with this observation, we note that if query and key are the same, a dot-product exponential kernel becomes similar to a music self-similarity matrix, a technique often used to discover musical structure such as repeated blocks or motifs in a musical piece. Self-similarity matrix (SSM) representation was championed by Jonathan Foote as a tool for visualization of musical form [196]. An example of such visualization is shown in Figure 9.5.

From here, the link to VMO is rather straightforward. In the VMO library one of the analysis functions is *create_selfsim*. What this function does is use the suffix links in the optimal factor oracle (FO) graph and plotting them as a matrix. There is a one-to-one equivalence between graphs and connections matrices, and SSM can be turned into a binary matrix by finding a suitable threshold that will turn the grayscale image into binary black and white. Going further with this analogy, the regression expression of the transformer can be understood as a prediction of which next segment of the musical data appearing in the value vector should be recopied when a certain query is input in the VMO graph. When the query is repeated, each time using the latest generated musical frame, these calls generate an improvisation by traversing

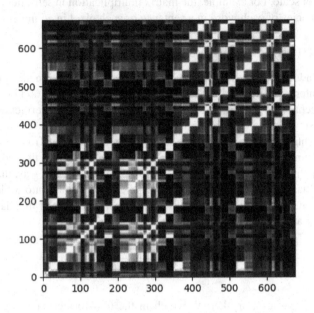

Figure 9.5　Self-similarity visualization of a Glen Gould recording of Bach's Well Tempered Clavier No,1, using Mel-spectrum as a feature.

the FO graph structure along their suffix links. A missing item in this analogy is interpreting the results of the query in a Transformer as a probability for transition along the FO graph. This is where the kernel regression analogy comes in, as the pooling could be done either as averaging over all values or as a randomized selection of the value to be retrieved (recopied) according to similarity between between key and query. So what are the huge advantages versus difficulties of the Transformer versus shallow string matching based methods like VMO? The main and foremost advantage of transformers is its learning of the transformation matrices of input data into the key, query, and value vectors. Unlike SSM or VMO where the kernel distances are computed using a fixed set of feature extractors, Transformers learn the kernels by optimizing the representation for the specific task. Moreover, an advantage as well as an impediment of transformers is its data-hungry nature. To estimate the multiple heads, the many types of feature transformations are estimated using large amounts of data. The enormous success of transformers in natural language processing provides strong evidence that a distributed representation of words through contextual proximity over a long enough data segment can effectively capture significant aspects of language, which in turn can be used for credible generation of synthetic examples that make not only syntactic but also semantic sense. With the advent of

Transformer-XL autoregressive extensions, the span of generative structures has significantly improved. Nonetheless, this seems to be insufficient for capturing musical form that has an implicit, but well established conventions for long term recurrence relations while carrying the listener through a series of developments, buildings of tension, and their resolutions.

One consideration that arises from our discussion is the question of achieving personal originality with larger pre-trained language models. Turning long enough contextual dependencies into a statistical predictor using transformer-derived latent representations, the boundary between what comprises structure versus texture in music is blurred in a manner similar to the question of syntax versus semantics, or rhetoric versus dialectic. When the purpose of a transformer is to solve a particular task by providing an input conditioning that specifies what output is desired, the question of finding intrinsic meaning in the transformer output, both in music or in text, is circumvented. We expect the problem of "meaning" to re-emerge in interactive music applications, where the interaction with a musical agent is expected to carry some level of autonomy and self-expression both in the human and their artificial partner. As we move away from thinking about AI in music as a controllable music instrument, the danger of "stochastic parrots" [197] becomes not only the replication of abusive language[9] but also the lack of meaningful interaction that will hinder rather then foster creativity, musical originality, and self expression.

9.6 EXERCISES

1. Write a list of ten musical terms. Thinking about vector embedding, how would you plot these terms in 2D such that relationships between the words are preserved? Draw such a sample plot. Then use a pretrained word Embedding layer (we recommend the GloVE model in Keras) to embed these ten words into vectors. What size does this vector have? To plot this in 2D, we will need to further reduce the dimension. What techniques do we have available to do so? Applying one of these techniques, reduce the dimension and plot the location of the words. Does this match your expectations? To help create stronger "context" during dimensionality reduction, you can also introduced non-musical terms to help establish proximity between your musical terms in the 2D plot.

Additional questions and programming exercises are found in the **Attention and Transformers** notebook at `https://github.com/deep-and-shallow/notebooks`.

PROJECTS

1. **Hierarchical Token-Semantic Audio Transformer**. HTS-AT is a deep neural network model based on transformer architecture. It achieves the state-of-the-art audio classification on three common audio classification datasets: AudioSet,

---

[9]Such language might be acquired via prevalent biases appearing in language data.

ESC-50, and Speech Command V2. In this project, you need to read the paper of HST-AT[10] and get familiar with the code[11]. The tutorial notebook [12] can help you build the basic idea and usage of HTS-AT on the ESC-50 dataset. Then, you can propose a project on leveraging HTS-AT into other audio or music tasks. Some of ideas on the project (from easy to hard) can be:

    a. Using the pretrained HTS-AT checkpoint (available in the github) in other audio classification datasets and evaluate its performance.

    b. Using the pretrained HTS-AT checkpoint in the sound event detection task, according to the DCASE challenge[13]. This involves some changes on the input and output of HTS-AT.

    c. Using the HTS-AT model in other audio-related tasks, such as cover song identification, music melody extraction, music generation, etc. This involves some changes on the input, output and network layers of HTS-AT. The dataset collection is also one of the challenges.

2. **Composing Polyphonic Melody Using RNN with Attention**. In the notebook programming exercises, we explored use of sequence models for generating a sequence of pitches as a melody. For this project, build a model that predicts the next set of pitches and durations (given a sequence of previous pitches and durations) for polyphonic (multiple voice) music. This model will require a polyphonic input embedding, followed by a stacked LSTM network with an attention mechanism. LSTM layers are stacked by passing the hidden states of the previous layer as input to the next. Stacking layers in this way gives the model freedom to learn more sophisticated features from the data. Attention layers should be added either by considering a sequence-to-sequence attention, or as self-attention added for the next note prediction.

Possible extensions to this LSTM include adding a VAE layer, such as Music-VAE, MeasureVAE and PianoTree (but note that MusicVAE and MeasureVAE are monophonic).

Some useful ideas of polyphonic tokenizers can be found here
- Generate Piano Instrumental Music by Using Deep Learning[14]
- Signal Like Embedding[15]

Suggested reading: Neural Machine Translation by Jointly Learning to Align and Translate [198]

---

[10]https://arxiv.org/abs/2202.00874

[11]https://github.com/RetroCirce/HTS-Audio-Transformer

[12]https://github.com/RetroCirce/HTS-Audio-Transformer/blob/main/htsat_esc_training.ipynb

[13]https://dcase.community/challenge2022/task-sound-event-detection-in-domestic-environments

[14]https://towardsdatascience.com/generate-piano-instrumental-music-by-using-deep-learning-80ac35cdbd2e

[15]https://github.com/MagiCzOOz/signallike-embedding/blob/master/representations.py

3. **Improving Transformer Music Generation**. Transformers can be trained (depending on their architecture) to perform various musical tasks, from continuation, to inpainting (completing missing parts), to generating accompaniment or harmonization - see the relevant lecture on transformers for some examples. The difficulty in learning transformers is the large amount of data required to train the model, which makes it difficult to learn individual styles, and the time it takes to train the model, which makes it impractical for real-time or near real-time applications.

The goal of this project is to explore different transformer architectures and propose some ideas or solutions to the above problems. One possible direction is use of transfer learning to speed up the training procedure, such as text transfer methods explored in this paper Exploring the Limits of Transfer Learning with a Unified Text-to-Text Transformer[16]

Another possible project is to explore the use of FNet for music transformer applications. FNet is a new transformer architecture that is much faster to train, as described here: Mixing Tokens with Fourier Transforms[17]

Suggested reading about music and transformers:

- Music Transformer [107]
- Music Transformer: Generating Music with Long-Term Structure[18]
- Pop Music Transformer: Beat-based Modeling and Generation of Expressive Pop Piano Compositions [108]
- Compound Word Transformer: Learning to Compose Full-Song Music over Dynamic Directed Hypergraphs [96]
- LakhNES: Improving Multi-Instrumental Music Generation with Cross-Domain Pre-Training [199]

---

[16]https://poohi5.medium.com/exploring-the-limits-of-transfer-learning-4a12b7ee3849

[17]https://medium.com/geekculture/mixing-tokens-with-fourier-transforms-a64beaa03692

[18]https://github.com/jason9693/MusicTransformer-pytorch

10 Last Noisy Thoughts, Summary, and Conclusion

10.1 MUSIC COMMUNICATION REVISITED: INFORMATION THEORY OF VAE

As a coda to our journey of modern music AI, we may consider now the broader and almost philosophical questions of how musical brains may imagine and communicate musical ideas through a combination of aspects of learning a representation of musical information and the ability to listen, anticipate, and create new materials by generative modeling, formulated in terms of a communication problem, or transmission of musical information across voices and over time. A key goal of representation learning is to identify and disentangle factors in the data so that it becomes easier to understand and possibly manipulate the data for various tasks. This process can happen in the listener's mind, as a way to make sense of the auditory sensations, which are shared between the audience and the musicians. From all of the possible sound phenomena surrounding us, in music in particular we are interested in learning latent representations of sound that can help uncover the underlying structure of music, both in terms of its temporal organization and across different musical rules, falling within "style conventions and practices. On the creative side, we desire to learn models of music where novel instances in the same "style" can be generated by sampling from latent parameter distributions. These two tasks – finding representations for the purpose of understanding or inference, versus the task of modeling for creative purposes – are not always aligned with each other; one can find good generative models with poor or no explicit representation of musical structure or little ability to control the outcome, and vice versa, we can find meaningful representations that are very limited in terms of their generative abilities. This discrepancy can be especially critical for music since it contains significant temporal structure and dependencies that are hard to "summarize" into a latent variable. The dynamics of music might be such that it leads from one musical phrase to another almost mechanistically, without much "intent" or ability to control its course. This raises the question of how much of the musical "meaning" is indeed transmitted through its evolution. To make such an argument more concrete, let us recall that in previous chapters we have discussed RNNs and auto-regressive models as efficient ways to generate sequential data. Since RNNs are universal function approximations, almost any temporal relations could be captured by such models. Adding latent constraints or conditional variables to RNNs is problematic since the model itself is so powerful that it largely ignores a latent cause, thus largely preventing control of the outcome of the sequence generator. Why is such a situation problematic for music machine learning? On one hand, RNNs have shown great results in generating music that resembles the sequential

DOI: 10.1201/9781003240198-10

statistics of the musical corpus it was trained on. On the other hand, we expect our model to operate as an information processing tool where the latent states capture and allow control of some deeper meaning in music that is communicated between the composer and the listener. Such a model requires a representation that captures both the listener/encoder's understanding of the musical events through inference of the musical hidden causes, and the composer/decoder's ability to realize and render a novel musical creation in full detail from an abstract musical idea or intent (that hidden cause). If we do not have access to a latent representation, the music generative model may produce rather credible "fake" instances of music with little ability to infer why such music was generated, and with little control over production of a particular desired musical idea or communicating musical intent. In order to understand better the significance of latent states in information production and communications, and specifically their usage in variational modeling of music, we resort to two information theoretical interpretations of VAE. The first one is the so-called bits-back interpretation of the encoding-decoding scheme, and the other is the rate-distortion interpretation of the ELBO procedure that is used for estimating the VAE parameters.

10.1.1 BITS-BACK CODING IN VAE

Ordinary coding of data maps each input instance to a unique codeword. According to Shannon's theory, the best encoding of a data is lower bounded by its entropy, so finding the best code requires knowing the correct data distribution in order to assign code words of appropriate length to each data instance. In latent models the distribution of data x depends on the value of a latent variable z. When we consider z as side information that can be transmitted in parallel with the data itself, then the ambiguity of x in terms of its hidden "meaning" that is captured by z can be used efficiently in the decoding process.

Bits-back coding is casting the problem of optimizing VAE into a problem of compression by designing an efficient coding scheme in a situation where the data probabilities depend on an additional auxiliary variable z. To do that, VAE is seen as a way to encode data into two main parts: $p(z)$ that encodes the prior/side musical knowledge about the essential latent or hidden structures of music, and $p(x|z)$ being the realization of the musical detail (musical surface) given that structure. The variational approximation adds an additional auxiliary part that transmits the "meaning" of the data (inference of z, or finding the hidden cause) as determined by the encoder $q(z|x)$.

In such scenario the transmission of x can be done in two steps: encoding of the true latent variable z first, and then encoding of x using the knowledge of z. The expected code length under this coding scheme is given by a sum of the two codes:

$$C(x) = E_{x \sim p(x), z \sim q(z|x)} [-\log p(z) - \log p(x|z)]$$
$$= H(x,z) = H(x) + H(z|x)$$

where $1/\log p(z)$ and $1/\log p(x|z)$ are the Shannon code lengths of z, and x given z, respectively. This adds an additional code penalty $H(z|x)$ to the ideal efficient encoding of the data x in terms of Shannon theory $H(x)$. So why would we want to infer and possibly transmit or share knowledge about abstract musical structures between musician and listener if this amounts to wasting in our mental resources? After all, we were operating so far under an assumption that in the process of learning music one discovers music's complex structures, which can later be used for creating new musical pieces or engaged when actively listening to someone else's composition. Why would we engage in the complex process of inference if this is not the most efficient way to represent musical data?

The solution to this paradox comes from the bits-back argument. What this argument says is that this extra coding length penalty can be remedied by making the inference of z available at the decoder. In such a case z does not need to be transmitted, as it can be inferred from x alone, reducing the coding $C(x)$ back to $H(x)$. The interesting part occurs when we include an imperfect inference that can be thought of as including an imperfect listener into the loop. Since the listener/encoder has only partial knowledge of the musical dynamics, they perform an approximate inference of the true musical "cause" z. Accordingly, encoding of music in the listener's mind has to include an extra "penalty" of inefficient encoding using $q(z|x)$

$$
\begin{aligned}
C_{BitsBack}(x) &= \mathbb{E}_{x\sim p(x),z\sim q(z|x)}[-\log p(z) - \log p(x|z)] \\
&= \mathbb{E}_{x\sim p(x)}[-\log p(x) + D_{KL}(q(z|x)||p(z|x))] \\
&= H(x) + \mathbb{E}_{x\sim p(x)}[D_{KL}(q(z|x)||p(z|x))]
\end{aligned}
$$

Only when $q(z|x) = p(z|x)$, i.e. the listener has perfect knowledge of the latent causes, does the extra coding penalty become zero. It can be said that by randomly selecting codewords according to probability distribution $q(z|x)$ in the decoder, we in fact communicate extra auxiliary information along with the data we are coding. The Bits-Back method provides an encoding scheme, details of which we will not prove here, that claims that the extra information communicated through an auxiliary data is in fact a knowledge that is shared between the encoder and decoder. Giving it a musical interpretation, we will use again the notes versus chords example. In order to encode the notes that we hear in the most efficient way, we need to know their probability. If we assume that the notes originate from chords, then rather then always assigning the notes to the most likely chord, we actually need to account for the ambiguity in chord progressions. Only by embracing such ambiguity we can reliably infer the probabilities for the notes themselves. The shared knowledge of harmony between the composer and the listent will make up for the excess coding penalty of not always being able to do a perfect harmonic analysis, or using the shortest codeword in the process of encoding the notes by using the highest probability $p(notes|chord)$. The beauty of listening to music is in fact entertaining such multiple hypotheses, which can be also considered as the most efficient coding of the musical data through a process of inference of abstract music structures (chords in this example).

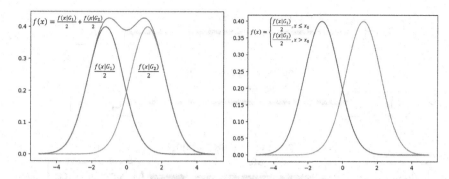

Figure 10.1 This example shows a source model that may produce multiple codewords for a given symbol. The graph on left shows a source with a single binary hidden variable which identifies from which Gaussian, G_1 or G_2, the symbol value x is sampled. Values of x near x_o are likely to have come from either Gaussian. The graph on right shows the resulting coding density effectively used if we were to always pick the shorter codeword. This density wastes coding space because it is wrongly shaped.

The interested reader is referred to the Frey and Hinton's Free Energy Coding articles [200] where they propose a distribution approximation that uses the joint coding length of x and z as an energy function. In the paper they work out a toy example of a Gaussian mixture model and show that the encoding of data by always encoding it in terms of a single maximum-likelihood Gaussian and sending the Gaussian index as side information performs worse than using an ambiguous coding that randomly selects the Gaussians at the decoder. This example is shown in Figure 10.1. So, instead of transmitting the side information and doing what seems to be the most efficient encoding for each sample, it is actually better to embrace the ambiguity about the causes (i.e., which Gaussian most likely generated the data), since the identity of the Gaussian that produces a given symbol is unknown, especially in regions where the Gaussians strongly overlap and the data is likely to have come from either Gaussian. In these cases the source model maps each symbol to two codewords, one for each Gaussian, and is left up to the decoder to randomly decide how the code is interpreted. It turns out that by randomly selecting codewords, the method effectively communicates the extra side information about the hidden source along with the data it is coding. Looking at this differently, the bits communicated in the auxiliary side information will make up for the excess codeword lengths that result from not always using the shortest codeword, thus getting the bits back.

The encoding scheme of the bits-back argument operates when a source code produces multiple codewords, or in other words, when ambiguity exists as to origin of the data with respect to possible origin or cause of the message. In this scheme, the auxiliary data provided in the encoder is recovered by the receiver. By randomly selecting codewords, the bits communicated in the auxiliary data will make up for the excess codeword lengths that result from not always using the shortest codeword.

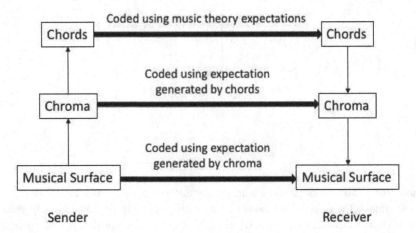

Figure 10.2   An illustration of the relationship between good representations and economical communication from [200].

This approach was used as a tool for discovering efficient perceptual codes [201]. What makes this relevant to music is the idea that codes are communicated between a sender and a receiver, or musician and a listener in our case. An illustration from the original paper is provided in Figure 10.2 for the case of visual communication. If the images are well-modeled in terms of objects and edges, then they can be communicated cheaply by using this representation. The top-down expectations produced by the generative model operating on representations at one level will assign high probabilities to the data actually observed at the next level down, so by using the top-down expectations it is possible to communicate the data efficiently.

For our purposes, since we are not interested in compression per-se, we want to use the Bits-Back argument to understand the tradeoffs between encoding of $p(x|z)$ with or without substantial influence of z. As shown in Equation (10.1), the two-part code view of VAE adds to the minimal representation of the data $H(x)$ an extra code length of $D_{KL}(q(z|x)||p(z|x))$ nats for using a posterior that is not precise. We may understand now why sometimes the latent code z is not appropriately used by considering it at as an inefficiency of VAE as stated by the Bits-Back coding: a long sequence of musical information $x_1, x_2, .., x_n$ that is modeled locally by decoding from distribution $p(x_1, x_2, .., x_n|z)$ without access to z will be captured locally in terms of structural relations that govern the dynamics of musical data regardless of it's intended "meaning" z. In such a case only a small fraction of musical information that is not dependent on the musical rules that tie together $x_1, x_2, .., x_n$ independently of z will be encoded in z. This is why so often we consider the "meaningful" music events to be such that violate the common musical progressions by breaking the "textbook" rules.

The "remedy" to the situation of VAE ignoring z can be two fold – either encoding small portions of music that do not require very powerful decoders, thus breaking the representation into chunks or fine music granularity where the relations between

z and x are strongly manifested, or encoding larger musical structures in approximate ways, such as using lossy encoding that prefers global statistics and discards local statistics. When we learn a lossy compression/representation of data, we can try to construct a decoding distribution just for reconstructing the detailed parts of the data that we don't want the lossy representation to capture. In other words, the lossy encoding should be done in a way that the this encoder is incapable of modeling the detailed information that the lossy representation discards. This tradeoff between lossy latent encoding efficiency versus representation error will be discussed next.

10.1.2   LOSSY ENCODING VIEW OF ELBO

Further intuition of the information aspects of encoding of data by VAE is given in [202] where the authors show that maximization of Evidence Lower Bound (ELBO) in VAE is equivalent to minimization of the information between the data x and the latent state z, expressed in terms of $I(X,Z)$ for the VAE encoder, with an added minimization requirement of the decoder observing a certain level of reconstruction error $D(X,Z)$. Adding a reconstruction error casts the problem into an approximate encoding scheme. Let us consider the steps leading to this equivalence, as follows:

We consider the encoding in terms of variational approximation $q(z|x)$ for the encoder and true probability for the data $p(x)$. Accordingly, the mutual information between the data X and the latent states Z when using the encoder, becomes a measure of for the joint distribution, expressed through the encoder $p_e(x,z) = p(x)q(z|x)$, or through the decoder $p_d(x,z) = p(x|z)q(z)$. We assume that $p_e(x,z) = p_d(x,z)$, so we will use them interchangeably. The reason for explicitly writing the encoder-decoder joint distribution is to notice the two ways of associating the data x with the latent representation z derived using the variational encoder-decoder approximation.

$$I(X,Z) = \int p_e(x,z) \log \frac{p_e(x,z)}{q(z)p(x)} dzdx \tag{10.1}$$

$$= \int p(x)q(z|x) \log \frac{q(z|x)}{q(z)} dzdx = \mathbb{E}_{p(x)}[KL(q(z|x),q(z))] \tag{10.2}$$

Let us now introduce two auxiliary definitions: the reconstruction error

$$D = -\int p(x)q(z|x) \log p(x|z) = -\mathbb{E}_{p(x)}\mathbb{E}_{q(z|x)}[\log p(x|z)] \tag{10.3}$$

which is the average over all inputs $x \sim p(x)$ of the negative log-likelihood of the reconstructed output using latent z's that were encoded by $q(z|x)$, and a rate

$$R = \int p(x)q(z|x) \log \frac{q(z|x)}{p(z)} = \mathbb{E}_{p(x)}[KL(q(z|x),p(z))] \tag{10.4}$$

which is an average KL distance between the encoded z's and the prior $p(z)$. An important observation is that these two factors appear in the ELBO expression

$$-\mathbb{E}_{p(x)}[ELBO] = D+R \tag{10.5}$$

Using some algebraic manipulations it can be shown that

$$R \geq I(X,Z) \tag{10.6}$$

or in summary

$$-ELBO \leq I(X,Z) + D, \tag{10.7}$$

By maximizing ELBO (minimizing -ELBO) we are minimizing an upper bound on the sum of encoding information $I_e(X,Z)$ and reconstruction error. There is a tradeoff between Rate and Distortion in VAE learning that includes a variable weighting factor β between the cost of the reconstruction error at the decoder and the amount of information between the data and the latent prior distribution in the encoder. Neural network models that use this principle include β-VAE that adds a weighting factor β between R and D, so that $ELBO(\beta) = D + \beta R$. A more general approach to using information interpretation of VAE is known as the InfoVAE family of neural networks.

The left vertical line corresponds to the zero encoding rate setting where the encoding distribution $e(z|x)$ is independent of x, thus failing to produce any useful learned representation. In such as case, by using an overly powerful decoder $d(x|z)$ that captures correlations between the components of the data x itself, the distortion can still be made low. Zero distortion can be also achieved in the so-called *auto-encoding limit* where the encoder simply passes the input do the decoder without any compression, thus increasing the cost of the encoding by ignoring any compression or regularization imposed by the prior. In both cases the ELBO objective fails to achieve its purpose. Thus, in order for VAE to operate properly, a delicate balance has to be maintained between the two aspects of ELBO of having a somewhat weaker decoder and a sufficiently effective and informative compression at the encoder.

10.1.3   REDUCING THE MUSICAL REPRESENTATION

The idea of musical reduction is known from various theories of music analysis, such as Schenkerian analysis [203] and later generative grammar approaches like GTTM [204]. These theories consider deeper musical structures, somewhat related to musical theory concept of *Ursatz* that comprises a background abstract layer from which the musical foreground surface[1] emerges. It should be noted that Ursatz is not really predictive and has not been proven to represent music cognition, much like many of the formal grammar theories that are still arguably non-representative of true human cognitive faculties. Nevertheless, it can still considered as a prototype for music reductionist analysis. The GTTM, which is derived from Schenkerian analysis, is a generative model by definition, suggestive of another conceptual parallel to our methods. Of course these techniques are very different from the methods developed in this paper and are brought here only for motivation purposes. As we will observe below, both musical surface and highly compressed representations contain

---

[1]Musical surface is musical data that contains the actual notes and sounds.

little predictive power, while maximal predictability happens in the mid-range of reduction quality. A different aspect of reduced representation that served as motivation, which is closer to aspects of human cognition is the study of Rate–Distortion as a way of extracting useful or meaningful information from noisy signals [56]. The idea of reduced representation also has been recently explored in the context of representation learning in deep neural networks using a framework known as Information Bottleneck [205].

The special case of music is that the deeper background structure serves not only to compress but also to predict musical continuations, or in other words, the concept of *Ursatz* introduces the idea that longer musical progressions or temporal relations, which are hard to perceive on the surface, can be more evidently revealed from the background. Accordingly, the question of reduction in music is closely related to the task of prediction. In deep learning some attempts to consider predictive information through use of a bottleneck or noisy representation in temporal models such as RNNs have recently appeared in the literature [206], [207]. An important distinction between these works and the proposed framework is that we are not introducing rate-limitation or adding noise to the latent codes during the learning process, but rather we are applying bit-reduction to a pre-trained encoder-decoder network in order to reduce the complexity of the latent representation prior to decoding. This allows experimenting with various bit-rate regimes without retraining the network each time. For this purpose we borrow a technique of bit-allocation from Rate–Distortion theory of lossy information processing. The reduced latent representation streams will be later subject to predictive analysis to consider their temporal significance.

10.1.4   BIT-RATE LIMITED ENCODING

As mentioned above, in this study we consider a particular case of reduced representation that is based on Rate–Distortion theory. Rate–Distortion theory offers an optimal solution for finding the most compact (least rate) encoding for a given limit on the distortion or reconstruction error. Equivalently, Distortion–Rate finds the best encoding in terms of least distortion for a given rate. Algorithms for optimal bit allocation according to the Rate–Distortion theory are so-called *bit-allocation methods* that we describe below. By using a rate-limited channel between encoder and decoder of the VAE we are able to control the complexity of the encodings using a bit-allocation algorithm. In our case, we use Rate as the free parameter to find the least Distortion codes, under the assumption that latent codes in VAE are distributed as multi-variate uncorrelated Gaussians. The Rate–Distortion function that provides the lower limit on the achievable rate R as function of the maximal allowed distortion level D, is given by

$$R(D) = \begin{cases} \frac{1}{2} \log_2 \frac{\sigma^2}{D}, & \text{if } 0 \leq D \leq \sigma^2 \\ 0, & \text{if } D > \sigma^2 \end{cases} \tag{10.8}$$

where R is the rate, and D is the distortion value. This Rate–Distortion function can be converted into a Distortion–Rate function $D(R) = \sigma^2 2^{-2R}$ that gives the lower

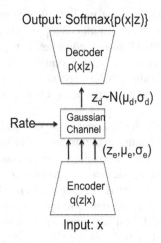

Figure 10.3   Noisy channel between encoder and decoder.

limit on distortion D that is achievable for a given rate R. This ideal lower limit (i.e., least distortion) can be efficiently achieved for a particular type of signals that is known in communication theory as "multivariate Gaussian channel". We adopt this channel model for our experiments without further justification. What is special about this type of channel is that an optimal bit-reduction can be achieved by using the so-called reverse water-filling algorithm [208]. This algorithm starts with a predefined bit-rate R, and successively allocates one bit at a time to the strongest component, repeating the process until all bits in the bit-pool are exhausted. One should note that channels (i.e., latent variables in our case) with variance less then allowed distortion, or channels that run out of bits for a given rate, are given zero bits and thus are eliminated from the transmission.

Schematic representation of the channel inclusion in the auto-encoder architecture is given by Figure 10.3. Encoding the latent components at a rate R changes the mean and variance of the VAE as follows [209]

$$Q(z_d|z_e) = Normal(\mu_d, \sigma_d^2) \tag{10.9}$$

$$\mu_d = z_e + 2^{-2R}(\mu_e - z_e) \tag{10.10}$$

$$\sigma_d^2 = 2^{-4R}(2^{2R} - 1)\sigma_e^2 \tag{10.11}$$

This process requires some explanation: for a given rate R we obtain the bit-rate for each of the latent variable according to the reverse water-filling procedure. This gives us different number of bits for each latent dimension, where the high variance dimensions tend to grab the bits first, often leaving the weak (small variance) latent variables with zero bits. Next we proceed by sampling a value from the encoder distribution according to the original VAE mean and variance parameters, μ_e and σ_e^2. Then, using the rate R and the original mean and variance parameters for each latent variable, we derive a new mean and variance μ_d and σ_d^2. We use these probability parameters to sample a reduced bit-rate value and use it as our new input to the decoder. One can see that latent variables that are allocated zero bits need not be transmitted[2], while channels allocated a very high rate will transmit an (almost) unaltered value of the latent variable that was sampled in the VAE encoder.

Depending on the specific experiment and data-type, the last softmax layer needs to be processed to determine how it translates into specific notes or spectrogram segments. The details of each representation are discussed in the corresponding experimental section. The VAE-based noisy channel is common to all cases, done during the encoding-decoding part prior to the final data reconstruction step.

10.1.5 MUSICAL EXAMPLE: LOSSY ENCODING-DECODING

To demonstrate the effect of lossy encoding, we show here an encoding-decoding example using a pre-trained VAE model on MIDI input. The VAE was trained on a Pop Music database that contained 126 music clips, mostly comprising of chords and melody, divided into chorus and verse sections. The VAE architecture had an input layer comprising of concatention of 16 musical units, each containing notes played at a resolution of sixteenth notes, representing total of four quarter notes or one bar in 4/4 meter. The hidden layer had 500 units, passed respectively to VAE mean and variance networks for variational encoding.

Figure 10.4 shows the VAE output printed in parallel with the input. As an input data we used MIDI file from Naruto Shippuden anime. This song has different style than the music in the Pop Music corpus that was used for VAE training. We see that the texture of the output is significantly different from the chord-melody texture of the input, but the harmonic relations are preserved and the improvisation reproduces music that matches the chords or the overall harmony of the query.

The correspondence between input and output starts deteriorating when using a reduced representation. In this experiment the lossy encoding was done using bit-allocation procedure that effectively eliminates parts of the latent variables z according to their variance. The details of these methods are beyond the scope of this chapter and can be found in [210]. Figure 10.5 shows the results of reducing the bit-rate of the encoder to 256 bits per frame. Musical analysis of the resulting output shows that the output music breaks away in some cases from the harmony of the query. For example, in measures four through nine shown in Figure 10.5, the improvisation shown on top plays a quick chord progression G-A-D, while the query on bottom plays D in the left hand and melody closer to G. Harmonic collisions continue in third and fourth bars, merging together to meet on the A minor chord in bar five. Additional bit-reduction results and the uncontrolled random generation are provided online[3]. We can say that further reducing the rate not only makes the output different

---

[2]More precisely, the value that the decoder needs is mean value of that latent variable that is independent of the particular instance being transmitted. This mean value can be obtained a-priori and thus can be "hard coded" into the decoder ahead of time, with no need to transmit it.

[3]https://github.com/sdubnov/qbdi.

Figure 10.4 Output of VAE that was trained on Pop Music database, using Naruto Shippuden midi file as an input.

Figure 10.5 Generation by VAE from a bit-reduced encoding starting at same measure number four as in the previous figure.

from input but also tends to improvise on fewer chords, eventually converging to improvisation on C chord, which is the tonality of the piece.

10.2 THE BIG PICTURE: DEEP MUSIC INFORMATION DYNAMICS

In order to allow for a quantitative formal analysis of what's going on in the "musical mind" [34], we develop an information dynamics approach to modeling of creative cognition that assumes that the imagination of the composer, the improviser, or the listener actively operates in combination of several objectives: a representation forming activity that involves both processing of immediate music sensations and cognitive anticipations of the musical future. In terms of information processing, the encoding step is done by learning and extracting salient features from the sound that allow efficient representation of the musical signal. This approach shares its view about perception with the so-called Bayesian Brain framework that considers perception as a process of inference that connects sensation with perception through a process of entrainment and learning. The anticipatory aspect of music understanding and imagination is informed by a different, albeit related brain theory of predictive coding that is based on the idea that instead of representing the sensations directly, it is often preferable to represent the prediction error. In other words, it is beneficial to consider the difference between a sensory input and a prediction that the brain forms by trying to guess the evolution of the perceptual features in time. In computational terms, while the first process can be viewed as a process that deals with recognition of isolated sound events, it is the second aspect of prediction that is responsible for sensations of surprise, tension, and resolution that emerge through violation or validation of expectations, making sense of larger musical form and following a musical narrative.

The Bayesian brain and predictive coding ideas can be formulated in terms of information theory by considering the relation between four factors: the musical past X, its present instance Y, and their internal, reduced mental representations, denoted by latent variables Z and T, respectively, The relationship between these four factors X, Y, Z, and T is illustrated in Figure 10.6.

The goal of such a model is to find a hidden reduced representation Z that efficiently captures the salient aspects of X, which in turn can be used to predict Y. In other words, the triplet X, Y, Z obeys Markov relation $p(X, Y, Z) = p(Y|X)p(X|Z)p(Z)$. Using the Markov relations $Z - X - Y$, one can formulate the goal of a music machine learning system [211] in terms of finding an optimal trade-off between simplicity of representation and its prediction ability. Such learning is looking for a representation that minimizes the discrepancy, or statistical difference, between signal prediction using complete information about the past X, versus its prediction capability when using a simplified encoding of the past Z. The overall quality of such error, averaged over all possible encoding pairs X, Z of the musical surface and its latent code, is given by [212]

$$\langle D_{KL}(p(Y|X)||p(Y|Z))\rangle_{p(X,Z)} = I(X,Y|Z) = I(X,Y) - I(Z,Y) , \qquad (10.12)$$

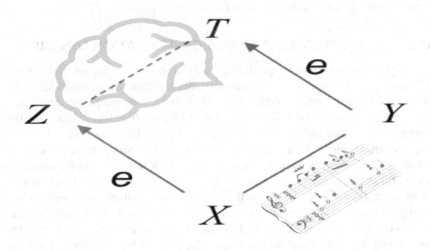

Figure 10.6 Schematic representation of the musical stimulus evolving over time from the past X to present Y, and their mental representations Z and T. Understanding music requires both encoding of music sensations and prediction of the next mental state and imagining its sensory future.

where $D_{KL}(\cdot,\cdot)$ is the Kullback-Liebler (KL) divergence between two distributions, and $I(\cdot,\cdot)$ is the mutual information between their random variables. Since $I(X,Y)$ are independent of Z, minimizing the KL divergence happens when $I(Z,Y)$ is maximized, with zero KL obtained when $I(Z,Y) = I(X,Y)$. In other words, one may postulate that a goal of a musical machine learning system, and possibly of human musical entrainment or learning, is finding a latent representation Z that "explains out" most of the Musical Information Dynamics $I(X,Y)$. This principle is expressed as minimization of $I(X,Y|Z)$. i.e. finding a latent reduced Z, so that there will be very little residual information passing between the past X and the present Y of the musical surface itself.

10.2.1   ADDING SIMPLICITY REQUIREMENT OF THE LATENT REPRESENTATION

The above formulation says that one needs to be looking for a meaningful latent representation Z, but we still do not know what such Z looks like, so minimizing KL could be trivially satisfied by taking $Z = X$. To avoid such a trivial solution, a constraint on Z is added, requiring it to be the most compact or simplest latent "explanation" that is derived from X, with best predictive properties. In information theoretical terms, we can write this criteria as the minimization of $I(X,Z)$. Combining the two goals, we arrive at the target function for our learning system

$$\max_{P(Z|X)} \{I(Z,Y) - \lambda I(X,Z)\} \qquad (10.13)$$

This formulation bears close resemblance to the idea of the Information Bottleneck (IB) [205]. The formulation of IB principle says that a goal of a learning system is to find the most compact representation Z of X that still provides most information about a different variable Y. Accordingly, predictive IB looks for the most compact representation of the past that carries maximial information about the musical future. Additionally, the fidelity of representation of the musical surface X by its reduced representation Z has to be accounted. This is done by adding a distortion $D(X,Z)$ that captures the reconstruction quality of X when decoding it from Z.

To summarize, one may formulate the following criteria that combine competing goals of three learning factors $I(X,Z)$, $I(Y,Z)$, and $D(X,Z)$:

- finding the most compact representation of present X that is most informative about the future Y (i.e., time information), and
- finding the most compact representation of X from which X can be recovered with minimal distortion $D(X,Z)$ (i.e., reconstruction quality).

We identify the first criteria as predictive information, and the second as representation learning. These different aspect of musical processing can be summarized in Figure 10.7.

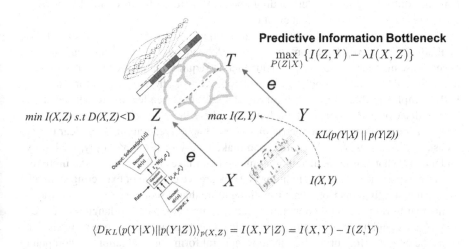

$$\langle D_{KL}(p(Y|X)||p(Y|Z))\rangle_{p(X,Z)} = I(X,Y|Z) = I(X,Y) - I(Z,Y)$$

Figure 10.7 Formulation of deep music information dynamics in terms of lossy encoding and predictive information. For demonstration purposes, the encoding step is represented by lossy autoencoder and predictive information by VMO's information rate. The different mathematical objectives of such musical learning model are marked next to the different processing steps, summarized into a predictive information bottleneck objective marked on the upper left corner of the figure.

10.3 THE FUTURE OF AI IN MUSIC AND MAN-MACHINE CREATIVE INTERACTION

This book combines several topics to provide a broad look at the problem of music creation with AI, from the technical question of representing and extracting meaningful information from music and audio data, to questions of anticipation and surprisal as the musical data evolves in time, to the role of noise as a driving force of generative models in sound and music, and even aspects of imagination and attention as they are modeled by modern neural networks models. But the ultimate motivation and goal of this book is providing an account of techniques and teaching the basic tools and skills to allow building novel musical AI systems that will ultimately change the way we compose music, boost our creativity as humans, and allow novel creativity in tandem with smart musical machines.

Looking from the historical perspective, the use of machines for creating music evolved from the rule-based and Markov approaches of the Illiac Suite (Hiller and Isaacson, 1979) [213], to communication theory inspired machine improvisation using Variable Markov models, to the more recent deep learning methods where the question of representation and generation are combined through complex networks of features and rules, all of which are learned from exposure to massive amounts of musical data. One of the unique and challenging aspects of creative music computing is the fact that music is organized on many levels of abstraction, from sound features to acoustic units, from units to motif sequences, and from motifs to larger and longer repetition structures, captured by multiple threads of attention. Such systems not only bring new understanding about the nature of music but also provide novel perspective about our own creation.

There is strong research interest about the question of if, or to what extent, AI methods are creative. Traditionally, AI was defined by Herbert Simon as the science of having machines solve problems that do require intelligence when solved by humans [214]. Going beyond problem solving, AI now allows us to explore increasingly complex problems in search for novel solutions, often leading to our own new human discovery. But unlike other domains, where the value of such discovery can be evaluated against concrete metric of success, music creativity lacks a clear utility measure. Despite the fact that music can make us cry or fill us with joy, we hardly understand what is it in the listening to music that makes it to be one of the more rewarding experiences available to humans. How are we capable of extracting so much that is meaningful to us from what is nothing more than a sequence of acoustic waveforms that have no concrete denotation and meaning compared to language or even animal calls, and has no attribution to physical events of auditory scene analysis that might be essential for survival. In its most general form, the evaluations of computer generated or human-computer art involve the subjective notion of aesthetics [215]. To understand how in music we are able to derive richly structured experiences from these superficially unstructured acoustic signals requires novel insights both into our musical perception and cognition that comprise the aesthetics of music.

In parallel, music practitioners want to explore how machines can be used in a way that adds to a meaningful music experience. AI methods allow the exploration of musical styles, their combination for achieving novel musical ideas, and the transformation of abstract music representation through latent spaces for forming altogether new musical concepts and ways interacting with them. There is, however, an open debate on whether the musical novelty achieved by such systems could considered creative on its own account, or a reflection of creativity of the human who designed or interacts with them. In other words, this question asks whether the methods themselves are creative, or if it is the engineering of the generative algorithms that brings the essential creativity component into the human-machine interaction. This question is part of the open problems that this books only starts to touch. Evaluation methods for answering such questions have been developed, such as the FACE/IDEA models [216], where not only the creative output (e.g., generated music) is examined but also the processes and the level of intervention of the agent constructing the algorithm are examined to determine how creative a system is. Such evaluation models are still poorly understood as their significance depends on very diverse implementations and different settings, such as systems that generate music from scratch, assist composers, interact with musicians, expressively perform, and so on. From a composer's or improviser's perspective, the understanding of what makes machines creative is combined with question of how humans may operate or derive creative value from interaction with such machines. The challenges of such research and evaluation are summarized in a novel field of research called "music meta-creation".

According to Boden [217], there are three types of creativity: (i) explorational, (ii) transformational, and (iii) combinational. The first two notions can, and have been, automated through computational means, and many fine examples exist. The third is less well understood, and is largely beyond the scope and ccurrent conceptions of computational creativity. An alternative distinction [218] is between generative and adaptive creativity. Generative creativity, such as natural evolution, is a profoundly creative force, that requires long time and external environmental pressure to converge to novel solution. In contrast, adaptive creativity is more immediate as it improves the actor's condition through an intentional cognitive act. The distinction is important because in music, as well as in other human processes, the creative act might occur with no apparent overall value to the creative product, such as in entire movements in art or music. Such processes, occurring on the social level, could be considered generative as they represent a co-evolution of the environment together with that of its agents by changing the aesthetic and social norms to provide novel value to yet unseen or unheard forms of music. Thus, creative outcomes can be considered as a combination of both generative and adaptive creative processes. Computational creativity, or meta-creation, as a field that explores the automation of creative processes, must deal with those two aspects in parallel. When one aims to endow machines with creative behaviors, the investigation has to consider both our current state of understanding creativity and its future potential. Accordingly, as a field it investigates:

- Creativity as It Is. It is striving to understand and simulate human creativity. What is creativity? If we can understand this complex notion, can we simulate it? As such, when such a cognitive modeling approach is chosen, it is also part of cognitive science.

- Creativity as It Could Be. The field is also devoted to exploring processes of which we know humans alone to be incapable. The outcomes of those artificial processes might nonetheless be considered novel and valuable, that is, creative.

In attempt to address the complexity of such evaluation, one needs to consider multiple factors that will make such system creative both now and into the future. Some of the categories for evaluation and planning further research and developments in the field of music and AI have to take into account the following system-engineering aspects:

- Quality: Does the system achieve the task it sets out to achieve? Is it any good at it? Is the system human-competitive at the task?
- Creativity: Is the system demonstrating creativity? What type? How does the system fare against humans?
- Believability. For some research projects, the process implemented is meant to behave in ways that are anthropomorphic (or as a simulation of some computational model of a natural agent). How successful at such imitation is the system?
- Complexity. The algorithmic properties of the system are often of interest. What class of complexity is the creative task defined within? Does the system produce a richness of behavior?
- Robustness. Can the system operate in a robust fashion on all input, or is it meant to react to a small set of input data?
- Reliability. Can the system guarantee a reliable quality of output independently of the input? Has the output of the system been cherry-picked?

A different aspect of creativity was addressed in the context of co-creative human-machine interaction for improvisation [219]. In addition to the novelty / effectiveness criteria, cyberhuman co-creativity is strongly felt when two features of improvisation linked to emergence [220] and non-linear dynamics [221] are identified: (1) emergence of cohesive behaviors that are not reducible to, nor explainable by, the mere individual processes of agents; (2) appearance of nonlinear regimes of structure formation, leading to rich musical co-evolution of forms. By producing emergent information structures as a result of cyber-human interaction, one might achieve an epistemological leap [222] beyond the difficulty of conceding creativity to artificial systems, and assess that creativity is not a state anyway, but rather a dynamical effect of interaction in a complex system, showing radical novelty as a marker of emergence [223]. By building on this epistemological boost, one would be able to model deep interactions that in turn will trigger co-creative behaviors.

We hope that this book may provide the much needed mix of providing the basic tools, technical and musical concepts, and guidelines for conducting research into Music and AI, combined together with a broader and deeper view into the challenges of musical creation using intelligent machines. Some of the more challenging aspects of our understanding of existing music are entwined with new realizations about our own ways of musical thinking and learning. Pushing the envelope of our musical understanding is essential in order to build musical systems according to meta-creation usability and co-creativity emergence criteria, which holds the promise of achieving novel and yet unexpected ways of creation. The future of musical experiences will deal not only with unprecedented levels of complexity in structure and aesthetics but also will need to answer some profound questions about the role of music in our lives, understanding our creative intent, and considering how such understanding can play a role in bettering of the human musical condition.

A Introduction to Neural Network Frameworks: Keras, Tensorflow, Pytorch

Throughout this book and the accompanying exercises, we have shared examples of code drawing from a variety of neural network frameworks. In this Appendix, we will briefly introduce these programming tools, as well as some common pitfalls and recommended practices.

The three libraries imported in this book are Keras, TensorFlow, and PyTorch.

- Keras is an open-source neural network library written in Python. It is designed to be user-friendly, flexible, and modular, which makes it easy for users to build and experiment with different types of neural networks. Keras has a high-level API that allows users to quickly build and train neural networks using pre-built layers and models. This makes it a popular choice for beginners who are just getting started with neural networks.
- TensorFlow is another open-source machine learning library that was developed by Google Brain. It is also written in Python and is designed for large-scale machine learning projects. In fact, Keras was built on top of a TensorFlow backend, allowing for abstraction of certain implementation details while still maintaining access to powerful features of TensorFlow. TensorFlow has a low-level API that allows users to build custom models and operations, as well as a high-level API that is similar to Keras. TensorFlow has become one of the most popular deep learning libraries because of its scalability, flexibility, and robustness.
- PyTorch is another popular deep learning library that was developed by Facebook (now Meta). It is also written in Python and is known for its dynamic computation graph, which allows users to build and modify neural networks on the fly. PyTorch has a user-friendly API that is similar to Keras, which makes it easy for beginners to get started. PyTorch is also known for its ease of debugging, which makes it a popular choice for researchers who are developing new deep learning models.

A note on libraries: As you may have seen from the programming examples and notebooks, Python libraries are changing all the time, and many scripts we write draw on multiple such libraries. Sometimes a change made to one version of a library affects others which depend on it. For this reason, it's important for users to be aware of which versions of a library they should install to run a program, and we try to provide this information when possible.

It is a frequent problem that we have to run many programs with conflicting dependencies; while one program might want to use TensorFlow version 1, another

DOI: 10.1201/9781003240198-A

may need TensorFlow version 2. As a possible tool, virtual environments provide a way for us to manage which libraries our python interpreter "sees" when we execute the program. These can be created and managed through the virtualenv package, or alternatively through the Anaconda environment manager. There are plenty of other virtual environment tools that exist, and most serve the same purpose. In these setups, we have our default (base) environment, and then we can additionally create virtual environments. These virtual environments are blank slates until one installs the desired libraries within the environment. It is recommended practice to make a virtual environment to run your code, then install your associated libraries to this virtual environment before running the program. This will help you to avoid package conflicts between programming examples, problems, and projects.

In general, we recommend readers consult documentation of any library used in case of errors introduced during implementation.

B Summary of Programming Examples and Exercises

Accompanying this book are a set of programming examples and exercises, available at https://github.com/deep-and-shallow/notebooks and formatted as Jupyter notebooks. Here, we provide a brief description of each notebook and a recommended chapter of content for which the notebook could be paired.

- Chapter 1: **Introduction to Music Representation** lets readers convert the same music through a variety of representations and visualizations (MIDI, Piano Roll, Audio) and observe the strengths, weaknesses, and challenges associated with such representations and conversions.
- Chapter 2: **Probability** invites readers to implement Mozart's Dice Game and experiment with random number generation to create music from noise.
- Chapter 3: **Markov Chain and LZify** guides readers in exploring Markov Models to generate pop music chord progressions, then provides an exercise in implementing and using the Lempel-Ziv algorithm to parse, analyze, and generate a musical melody.
- Chapter 4: **Discrete Fourier Transform** lets readers construct and use the DFT matrix to quickly compute the Fourier transform of audio signals.
- Chapter 4: **Spectrograms STFT and Griffin Lim** will introduce readers to generation of Short-Time Fourier Transform plots, and readers can implement the Griffin Lim algorithm to reconstruct phase when discarded from frequency representations of signals. Readers are invited to record their own short audio samples for these exercises.
- Chapter 4: **Speech Formants & LPC** lets readers play with the source-filter model of human voice, investigating the combinations of frequencies to create vowel sounds.
- Chapter 5: **VMO Audio Oracle** uses the VMO model to construct a recombinant model from a given saxophone target recording. Then, readers will use the VMO query function to "drive" this model using another sound file. The query sound file will contain an accompaniment part of a song, so the result will be a new saxophone improvisation over that song.
- Chapter 6: **PCA with Linear Autoencoder** walks readers through training an autoencoder for the purpose of comparing its output to that of PCA, using basic sinusoidal audio input as the training data.
- Chapter 7: **Generating Music with RNN** helps readers to practice using Keras to create a generative model based on the music created by the stochastic Mozart Dice Game.

DOI: 10.1201/9781003240198-B

- Chapter 7: **Parallel CNN – RNN** explores the use of CNN-RNN for genre classification, comparing its performance to similar CNN-only or RNN-only models.
- Chapter 8: **GAN, chroma (MIDI) and pix2pix** explores a style transfer application that tries to change the musical texture of a piece while maintaining the harmonic structure. In order to do so, readers train a pix2pix type of model that learns the relations between chroma and the musical texture (distribution of notes). For this purpose readers extract chroma from MIDI data and learn a generator that complements the notes from a given texture.
- Chapter 9: **Attention and Transformers** introduces readers to the effects of attention in the Transformer model, visualizing the effects of models with and without attention on the weight applied to various aspects of input, drawing on examples from both NLP and symbolic music.

C Software Packages for Music and Audio Representation and Analysis

In this Appendix, we will briefly introduce some of the programming frameworks that are used for loading, processing and analysis of audio and symbolic music data, often as a first step before proceeding with statistical modeling using deep or shallow methods. Some of these packages are used in the programming exercises accompanying this book as a first step in preparing the data for fitting into AI models.

LIBROSA

Librosa is a python package for audio analysis, designed mostly for music information retrieval. It includes a range of commonly used functions, broadly falling into four categories: audio and time-series operations, spectrogram calculation, time and frequency conversion, and pitch operations. Audio and time-series operations include functions for reading audio from disk (load), resampling a signal at a desired rate (resample), stereo to mono conversion (to_mono), time-domain bounded auto-correlation (autocorrelate), zero-crossing detection (zero_crossings), and estimate of the dominant frequency of STFT bins (piptrack) and pitch tracking (yin). Spectrogram operations include the short-time Fourier transform (stft), inverse STFT (istft), and instantaneous frequency spectrogram (ifgram), and constant-Q transform (cqt). It provides also mapping between different time representations: seconds, frames, or samples; and frequency representations: hertz, constantQ basis index, Fourier basis index, Mel basis index, MIDI note number, or note in scientific pitch notation. Since many of the spectral manipulation operations are performed on STFT magnitude, it offers phase recovery from magnitude spectrum using Griffin-Lim algorithm (griffinlim). The beat module provides functions to estimate the global tempo and positions of beat events. Higher level structural analyses are provided using recurrence or self-similarity plots (segment.recurrence_matrix). The decompose module factors spectrograms, or general feature arrays, into components and activations. By default, this is done with with non-negative matrix factorization (NMF), but any sklearn.decomposition-type object will work. Additionally, it provides several signal transformation and signal generation functions.

DOI: 10.1201/9781003240198-C

PRETTY MIDI

Pretty Midi provides functions for representing and handling MIDI data. At the top is the PrettyMIDI class, which contains global information such as tempo changes and the MIDI resolution. It also contains a list of Instrument class instances, with each Instrument specified by a MIDI program number that correspond to names of General MIDI instruments convention. Instrument class instances contain three lists for Note, PitchBend, and ControlChange. The Note class is a container for MIDI notes, with velocity, pitch, and start and end time attributes. PitchBend and ControlChange classes contain attributes for the bend or control change's time and value.

Functions for performing analysis are defined in PrettyMIDI class and their a corresponding Instrument class. Some of the implemented functions include extracting MIDI tempo change events (get_tempo_changes), tempo estimate according to inner-onset intervals (estimate_tempo), beats for every quarter note for 3/4 or 4/4 time signature and every third denominator note for 6/8 or 6/16 time (get_beats), lust of MIDI note onsets (start_times) and downbeats (get_downbeats). A particularly useful and intuitive representation is a piano roll (get_piano_roll) that returns a matrix representation of MIDI notes, with each column spaced apart by fixed amount of seconds as provided by the user. Called "sampling frequency" this should not be consfused with audio sampling, but it is rather a conversion of MIDI events from tempo dependent "ticks relative to the previous event, to absolute time in seconds. Another useful aggregation is in terms of pitch classes independent of the octave, also known as MIDI chroma (get_chroma). Manipulating and synthesizing MIDI file from a piano roll matrix is not provided in the original package, as this requires some fine tuning of the user to determine the best sampling rate and other properties that are missing in order to invert the matrix representation to MIDI. These inversion functions (examples/reverse_pianoroll) are provided as examples on a private github by Chris Raffael (one of the Pretty Midi authors)[1]. See also https://github.com/craffel/pretty-midi/blob/main/Tutorial.ipynb for basic functions summarized in a Jupyter notebook.

MUSIC21

Music21[2] is a Python-based toolkit for computer-aided musicology. The core music21 object is the Stream object with its subclasses (Score, Part, Measure) designed as containers for music21 objects such as Note, Chord, Clef and TimeSignature objects. Streams can store other Streams, permitting a wide variety of nested, ordered, and timed structures. Elements within Streams are accessed with methods such as getElementById(), similar to Document Object Model (DOM) for retrieving elements in XML and HTML documents. One of the most important music21 classes is a Note class that has both a .pitch attribute, which contains a Pitch object, and

---

[1] https://github.com/craffel/pretty-midi

[2] The 21 in the title comes from the designation for MIT's classes in Music, Course 21M.

a .duration attribute, which contains a Duration object. One of the convenient utitlities of Music21 is that Streams can be easily visualized in Lilypond music notation software or with other programs that support MusicXML (such Musescore, Finale or Sibelius). Other important objects are Chords that combine multiple Pitch objects on a single stem and Interval Object that calculates distance in semitones between two notes, with or without taking octave into account. Another important object is the Durations object that represents a span of musical time for Note and all Music21Objects, such as TimeSignature objects. Containers such as Stream and Score also have durations which are equal to the position of the ending of the last object in the Stream. Other notable tools in music21 are Chordify which is a process of making chords out of non-chords. Chordify is used for reducing a complex score with multiple parts to a succession of chords, which can be further queried for various chord properties, such as checking for presence of a specific chord in a polyphonic score. TinyNotation is a lightweight notation syntax, Calling a converter.parse function on a simple text string preceded by a "tinyNotation:" tag results in a stream. Part subclass that is meant for designating music that is considered a single part.

JCHORD

jchord is a Python package for working with chord progressions. It has object representations for notes, chords, and progressions designed for the Western 12-tone system. One of the notable utilities of the package is its ability to convert between different naming conventions for chords, and can convert back and forth between objects and names. Also it provides simple command line tools for converting between progression represented as a string in .txt, .xlsx or .midi format to an output file in .txt, .xlsx, .midi or .pdf formats allows a quick and easy viewing or sonification of strings representing sequences of chords. Another useful functionality is that jchord can parse MIDI files to sequence of block chord by approximate grouping of notes into chords allowing some imperfections.

MINGUS

Mingus is a music theory and notation package for Python with MIDI file and playback support. It can also be used to create sheet music with LilyPond. Musical object include notes, intervals, chords, scales, keys and meters. Chords include natural diatonic triads, seventh chords, augmented chords, suspended chords, sixths, ninths, elevenths, thirteenths, altered chords, and special: "5", "NC", "hendrix" and absolute chords represented from shorthand (min7, m/M7, etc.). mingus also supports inversions, slashed chords and polychords, and referoing to chords by their diatonic function (tonic, subtonic, etc. or I, ii, iii, IV, etc.). Substitution algorithms, diatonic scales and their modes (ionian, mixolydian, etc.), minor (natural, harmonic and melodic) and chromatic or whole note scales are represented. The library can recognize intervals, scales and hundreds of chords from lists of notes. and their harmonic functions. To compose music with Mingus a Composition class is used to organize Tracks, to which notes are added.

MUSPY

MusPy is an open source Python library for management of symbolic music datasets for deep learning research by providing interfaces between music data and PyTorch and TensorFlow. It supports working with common symbolic music formats such as MIDI, MusicXML and ABC, and interfaces to other symbolic music libraries such as music21, mido, pretty_midi and Pypianoroll.It also provides evaluation tools for music generation systems, including audio rendering, score and piano-roll visualizations and objective metrics.

D Free Music and Audio-Editing Software

AUDACITY

Audacity[1] is a free and open-source digital audio editor. Users can import or record audio in Audacity. Download Audacity and learn more at https://www.audacityteam.org/.

LMMS

LMMS (originally named Linux MultiMedia Studio, but now available on multiple platforms) is a free, open-source digital audio workstation with an array of features to synthesize and mix sounds. Download LMMS and learn more at lmms.io.

MUSESCORE

MuseScore is a free music notation software suite and growing online community for writing and sharing music. MuseScore can be used to notate and export scores as PDF or MIDI.

MAGENTA

Magenta[2] is an open-source Google project built in TensorFlow to explore the role of machine learning as a tool in the creative process.

Readers are encouraged to visit their demo page[3] to play with existing tools and find inspiration for further ML projects. For those interested in technical details, the Magenta blogposts are an excellent starting point with references to and explanations of associated research works.

---

[1] Audacity software is copyright 1999-2021 Audacity Team. Web site: https://audacityteam.org/. It is free software distributed under the terms of the GNU General Public License. The name Audacity is a registered trademark.

[2] https://magenta.tensorflow.org/

[3] https://magenta.tensorflow.org/demos

E Datasets

This appendix contains a non-exhaustive list of musical datasets mentioned in examples or recommended for study.

- JSB Chorus contains Bach music as part of Music21 toolkit
- VGMIDI contains Video game music `https://github.com/lucasnfe/vgmidi`
- Lakh MIDI Dataset contains multiple styles `http://colinraffel.com/projects/lmd/`
- Maestro Competition Dataset contains classical music from Yamaha Piano e-competition `https://magenta.tensorflow.org/datasets/maestro`
- ADL Piano MIDI dataset `https://github.com/lucasnfe/adl-piano-midi`
- POP909 `https://github.com/music-xlab/POP909-Dataset`
- GiantMIDI-Piano `https://github.com/bytedance/GiantMIDI-Piano`
- BitMidi `https://bitmidi.com/`
- Classical Archives `https://www.classicalarchives.com/`
- FreeMidi `https://freemidi.org/MusicXML`
- TheoryTab Dataset `https://www.hooktheory.com/theorytab`
- Wikifonia `http://marg.snu.ac.kr/chord_generation/` (CSV format)
- Nottingham Music Dataset `http://habc.sourceforge.net/NMD/`
- Henrik Norbecks ABC tune `http://www.norbeck.nu/abc/`
- MusicNet `https://zenodo.org/record/5120004#.YpbPI-5ByUl`
- MAESTRO `https://g.co/magenta/maestrodataset`
- Piano-Midi `https://www.piano-midi.de/`
- Groove MIDI `https://magenta.tensorflow.org/datasets/groove`
- ASAP `https://github.com/fosfrancesco/asap-dataset`
- Charlie Parker Omnibook dataset `https://members.loria.fr/KDeguernel/omnibook/`
- TRIOS – Score-aligned Multitrack Recordings `https://zenodo.org/records/6797837`
- Jazz Aligned Harmony dataset `https://github.com/MTG/JAAH`
- Moodetector – some with lyrics `http://mir.dei.uc.pt/downloads.html`
- DEAM – Emotional Analysis of Music `http://cvml.unige.ch/databases/DEAM/`
- EMusic – Music Clips with Valence and Arousal EMusic `http://metacreation.net/project/emusic/`
- EMO soundscapes `http://metacreation.net/emo-soundscapes/`
- List of datasets related to MIR `https://www.audiocontentanalysis.org/data-sets/`
- NES-MDB – multi-track MIDI and aligned audio `https://github.com/chrisdonahue/nesmdb`

- Lakh midi dataset `https://colinraffel.com/projects/lmd/`
- Jazzomat project (with links to a database) `https://jazzomat.hfm-weimar.de/`
- Bach Chorals (midi files) `http://www.kunstderfuge.com/bach/chorales.htm`
- Domestic audio tagging `http://www.cs.tut.fi/sgn/arg/dcase2016/task-audio-tagging`
- Annotated audio events `https://research.google.com/audioset/`
- TROMPA_MER: an open dataset for personalized music emotion recognition `https://trompa-mtg.upf.edu/vis-mtg-mer/`
- Emotion in Music dataset `http://cvml.unige.ch/databases/emoMusic/`
- ISMIR Datasets `https://www.ismir.net/resources/datasets/`
- 4Q Audio Emotion Dataset: `https://www.kaggle.com/datasets/imsparsh/4q-audio-emotion-dataset-russell`
- Multi-modal Emotion Dataset: `https://www.kaggle.com/datasets/imsparsh/multimodal-mirex-emotion-dataset`
- Emotion in Music: `https://cvml.unige.ch/databases/emoMusic/`
- Ryerson Audio-Visual Database of Emotional Speech and Song (RAVDESS): `https://www.kaggle.com/datasets/uwrfkaggler/ravdess-emotional-speech-audio`
- LAION-Audio-630K Dataset large-scale audio-text dataset `https://github.com/LAION-AI/audio-dataset/`
- AudioSet `https://research.google.com/audioset/`
- Orchestral dataset containing pairs of piano and corresponding orchestration in MIDI or MusicXML `https://qsdfo.github.io/LOP/database`
- Open Enhanced Wikifonia Leadsheet Dataset `https://github.com/00sapo/OpenEWLD`

F Figure Attributions

Figure 4.4 (DFT Matrix) is licensed under the Creative Commons Attribution-Share Alike 4.0 International license by Wikimedia Commons user Darnling.

The Dirac Delta function illustration in Chapter 4 is licensed under the Creative Commons Attribution-Share Alike 3.0 Unported, 2.5 Generic, 2.0 Generic and 1.0 Generic license.

Figure 7.8 is licensed under the Creative Commons Attribution-Share Alike 4.0 International license by Wikimedia Commons user fdeloche.

Figure 7.9 is licensed under the Creative Commons Attribution-Share Alike 3.0 Unported license by Wikimedia Commons user Michael Plotke. The image file originally appears in GIF format.

Figure 1.4 is licensed under the Creative Commons Attribution 4.0 International License, available at https://creativecommons.org/licenses/by/4.0/legalcode. The original figure was created by Kosuke Itoh, Honami Sakata, Ingrid L. Kwee and Tsutomu Nakada in the article *Musical pitch classes have rainbow hues in pitch class-color synesthesia*.

Figure 1.11 is licensed under the Creative Commons Attribution-Share Alike 4.0 International License, available at https://creativecommons.org/licenses/by-sa/4.0/legalcode. The original figure was created by Goran_tek-en.

Figure 2.4 is licensed under the Creative Commons Attribution 4.0 International license, courtesy of musictheory.net (https://www.musictheory.net).

Figure 4.10 is licensed under the Creative Commons Attribution-Share Alike 4.0 International license, courtesy of Emflazie on Wikimedia Commons.

Figure 4.12 is licensed under the Creative Commons Attribution 2.0 Generic license, courtesy of ish ishwar on Wikimedia Commons.

Figure 5.2 is licensed under the Creative Commons Attribution-Share Alike 4.0 International, 3.0 Unported, 2.5 Generic, 2.0 Generic and 1.0 Generic license, courtesy of Chire on Wikimedia Commons.

Figure 7.6 is an adaptation by Ke Chen of a figure created by Wen-Yi Hsiao, Jen-Yu Liu, Yin-Cheng Yeh, and Yi-Hsuan Yang, licensed under the Creative Commons Attribution 4.0 International (CC BY 4.0) license.

Figure 7.10 is licensed under the Creative Commons Attribution (CC BY) license, courtesy of Haibo Geng, Ying Hu, and Hao Huang.

Figure 7.11 is licensed under the Creative Commons Attribution 4.0 International license, courtesy of Eunjeong Koh and Shlomo Dubnov.

Figure 9.1 is by Yuening Jia - DOI:10.1088/1742-6596/1314/1/012186, CC BY-SA 3.0, https://commons.wikimedia.org/w/index.php?curid=121340680

Figure 9.4 is licensed under the Creative Commons Attribution 4.0 International (CC BY 4.0) by Théis Bazin, Gaëtan Hadjeres, Philippe Esling, and Mikhail Malt.

References

1. Torben Poulsen. Loudness of tone pulses in a free field. *The Journal of the Acoustical Society of America*, 69(6):1786–1790, 1981.
2. Yoiti Suzuki and Hisashi Takeshima. Equal-loudness-level contours for pure tones. *The Journal of the Acoustical Society of America*, 116(2):918–933, 2004.
3. Stanley Smith Stevens, John Volkmann, and Edwin Broomell Newman. A scale for the measurement of the psychological magnitude pitch. *The journal of the acoustical society of america*, 8(3):185–190, 1937.
4. Roger B Dannenberg. The interpretation of midi velocity. In *ICMC*, 2006.
5. Donald Byrd, Roger D Boyle, Ulf Berggren, David Bainbridge, et al. *Beyond MIDI: the Handbook of Musical Codes*. MIT Press, 1997.
6. Josh Gardner, Ian Simon, Ethan Manilow, Curtis Hawthorne, and Jesse Engel. Mt3: Multi-task multitrack music transcription. *arXiv preprint arXiv:2111.03017*, 2021.
7. E. Narmour. *The Analysis and Cognition of Basic Melodic Structures: The Implication-Realization Model*. University of Chicago Press, 1990.
8. L. B. Meyer. *Emotion and Meaning in Music*. University of Chicago Press, 1956.
9. S. Dubnov. Spectral anticipations. *Computer Music Journal*, 30(2):63–83, 2006.
10. S. McAdams, S. Dubnov, and R. Reynolds. Structural and affective aspects of music from statistical audio signal analysis. *Journal of the American Society for Information Science and Technology*, 57(11):1526–1536, 2006.
11. G. A. Wiggins, K. Potter, and M.T. Pearce. Towards greater objectivity in music theory: Information-dynamic analysis of minimalist music. *Musicae Scientiae*, 11(2):295–322, 2007.
12. Samer Abdallah and Mark Plumbley. Information dynamics: Patterns of expectation and surprise in the perception of music. *Connect. Sci*, 21(2-3):89–117, 2009.
13. D. E. Berlyne. *Aesthetics and Psychobiology*. AppletonCenturyCrofts, 1971.
14. Milan Kundera. Xenakis, "prophète de l'insensibilité'". *Regards sur Iannis Xenakis*, pages 21–24, 1981.
15. Douglas W. Gallez. Satie's "entr'acte:" a model of film music. *Cinema Journal*, 16(1):36–50, 1976.
16. James Pritchett. *The Music of John Cage*. Cambridge University Press, Cambridge, 1996.
17. Matthew Weiner. *Brian Eno and the Ambient Series, 1978 - 1982*. Stylus Magazine.
18. Ze. Pequeno. *Autechre: Interview*. Tiny Mix Tapes.
19. Andy Farnell. *An Introduction to Procedural Audio and its Application in Computer Games*. Audio Mostly Conference, 2007.
20. K. Collins. An introduction to procedural music in video games. *Contemporary Music Review*, 28(1):5–15, 2009.
21. J. Bewley. Lejaren a. hiller: Computer music pioneer. *Music Library Exhibit, University of Buffalo PDF available at rapaport/*, 111, 2004.
22. D. Conklin. Music generation from statistical models. In *Proceedings of Symposium on AI and Creativity in the Arts and Sciences*, pages 30–45, 2003.
23. S. Dubnov. Spectral anticipations. *Computer Music Journal*, 30(2):63–83, 2006.
24. Noam Chomsky. *Syntactic Structures*. Mouton, The Hague/Paris, 1957.

25. David Cope. *Experiments in Musical Intelligence*. A-R Editions, 1996.
26. Adriano Baratè, Goffredo Haus, and Luca Andrea Ludovico. Petri nets applicability to music analysis and composition. In *ICMC*, 2007.
27. Myriam Desainte-Catherine Jaime Arias and Shlomo Dubnov. Automatic construction of interactive machine improvisation scenarios from audio recordings. In *4th International Workshop on Musical Metacreation*, 2016.
28. David Cope. *Virtual Music: Computer Synthesis of Musical Style*. MIT Press, 2004.
29. George E. Lewis. Too many notes: Computers, complexity, and culture in voyager. *Leonardo Music Journal*, 10:33–39, 2000.
30. C. Krumhansl. *Cognitive Foundations of Musical Pitch*. Oxford University Press, 1990.
31. Cluade E. Shannon. Prediction and entropy of printed english. *Bell Sys. Tech. J*, 3:50–64, 1950.
32. Belinda Thom and Roger B. Dannenberg. Predicting chords in jazz. In *ICMC*, 1995.
33. Claude E. Shannon and Warren Weaver. The mathematical theory of communication. university of illinois. *Urbana*, 117, 1949.
34. Gérard Assayag, Shlomo Dubnov, and Olivier Delerue. Guessing the composer's mind: Applying universal prediction to musical style. In *ICMC*, 1999.
35. J. Ziv and A. Lempel. A universal algorithm for sequential data compression. *IEEE Transactions on Information Theory*, 23(3):337–343, 1977.
36. Stylistic randomness: about composing ntrope suite. 4.
37. Gerard; El-Yaniv Ran Dubnov, Shlomo; Assayag. Universal classification applied to musical sequences. In *Proceedings of the International Computer Music Conference, ICMC98*, 1998.
38. Shlomo Dubnov and Gérard Assayag. Memex and composer duets: computer aided composition using style modeling and mixing.
39. Thomas M. Cover and Joy Thomas. *Elements of Information Theory*. Wiley, 1991.
40. Jacob Ziv and Abraham Lempel. A universal algorithm for sequential data compression. *IEEE Transactions on Information Theory*, 23(3):337–343, 1977.
41. M. Feder, N. Merhav, and M. Gutman. Universal prediction of individual sequences. *IEEE Transactions on Information Theory*, 38:1258–1270, 1992.
42. Grard Assayag, Camilo Rueda, Mikael Laurson, Carlos Agon, and Olivier Delerue. Computer-assisted composition at ircam: From patchwork to openmusic. *Computer Music Journal*, 23(3):59–72, 1999.
43. Roy P. Ghedini F., Pachet F. *Creating Music and Texts with Flow Machines*. Multidisciplinary Contributions to the Science of Creative Thinking. Creativity in the Twenty First Century. Springer, Singapore, 2016.
44. Y. Singer, D. Ron, and N. Tishby. The power of amnesia: Learning probabilistic automata with variable memory length. *Machine Learning*, 25:117–149, 1996.
45. Cyril Allauzen, Maxime Crochemore, and Mathieu Raffinot. Factor oracle: A new structure for pattern matching. In *International Conference on Current Trends in Theory and Practice of Computer Science*, pages 295–310. Springer, 1999.
46. Arnaud Lefebvre, Thierry Lecroq, and Joël Alexandre. An improved algorithm for finding longest repeats with a modified factor oracle. *Journal of Automata, Languages and Combinatorics*, 8(4):647–657, 2003.
47. S. Dubnov, G. Assayag, and A. Cont. Audio oracle analysis of musical information rate. In Palo Alto, editor, *The Fifth IEEE International Conference on Semantic Computing*, 2011.

48. A. Lefebvre and T. Lecroq. *Compror: Compression with a Factor Oracle.* Proceedings of the Data Compression Conference. 2001.
49. Paul Vitányi and Ming Li. On prediction by data compression. In *European Conference on Machine Learning*, pages 14–30. Springer, 1997.
50. J. Ziv and A. Lempel. Compression of individual sequences via variable-rate coding. *IEEE Transactions on Information Theory*, 24(5):530–536, 1978.
51. N. Marhav and M. Feder. Relations between entropy and error probability. *IEEE Transactions on Information Theory*, 40:259–266, 1994.
52. George Tzanetakis, Georg Essl, and Perry Cook. Audio analysis using the discrete wavelet transform. In *Proc. Conf. in Acoustics and Music Theory Applications*, volume 66. Citeseer, 2001.
53. Olivier Lartillot, Shlomo Dubnov, Gérard Assayag, and Gill Bejerano. Automatic modeling of musical style. In *ICMC*, 2001.
54. Shlomo Dubnov, Gérard Assayag, OLG Bejerano, and Olivier Lartillot. A system for computer music generation by learning and improvisation in a particular style. *IEEE Computer*, 10(38):1–15, 2003.
55. S. Dubnov, G. Assayag, O. Lartillot, and G. Bejerano. Using machine-learning methods for musical style modeling. *IEEE Computers*, 36(10):73–80, October 2003.
56. Chris R. Sims. Rate–distortion theory and human perception. *Cognition*, 152:181–198, 2016.
57. H. B. Barlow. Possible principles underlying the transformations of sensory messages. In *Sensory Communication*, pages 217–234, 1961.
58. Karl Friston. The history of the future of the bayesian brain. *NeuroImage*, 62(2):1230–1233, 2012.
59. Richard G. Lyons. *Understanding Digital Signal Processing, 3/E*. Pearson Education India, 1997.
60. Steven W. Smith et al. The scientist and engineer's guide to digital signal processing, 1997.
61. Alan V. Oppenheim. *Discrete-time Signal Processing*. Pearson Education India, 1999.
62. Daniel Griffin and Jae Lim. Signal estimation from modified short-time fourier transform. *IEEE Transactions on Acoustics, Speech, and Signal Processing*, 32(2):236–243, 1984.
63. Aaron van den Oord, Sander Dieleman, Heiga Zen, Karen Simonyan, Oriol Vinyals, Alex Graves, Nal Kalchbrenner, Andrew Senior, and Koray Kavukcuoglu. Wavenet: A generative model for raw audio. *arXiv preprint arXiv:1609.03499*, 2016.
64. Soroush Mehri, Kundan Kumar, Ishaan Gulrajani, Rithesh Kumar, Shubham Jain, Jose Sotelo, Aaron Courville, and Yoshua Bengio. Samplernn: An unconditional end-to-end neural audio generation model. *arXiv preprint arXiv:1612.07837*, 2016.
65. Ryan Prenger, Rafael Valle, and Bryan Catanzaro. Waveglow: A flow-based generative network for speech synthesis. In *ICASSP 2019-2019 IEEE International Conference on Acoustics, Speech and Signal Processing (ICASSP)*, pages 3617–3621. IEEE, 2019.
66. Nanxin Chen, Yu Zhang, Heiga Zen, Ron J. Weiss, Mohammad Norouzi, and William Chan. Wavegrad: Estimating gradients for waveform generation. In *ICLR 2021*.
67. Chris Donahue, Julian McAuley, and Miller Puckette. Synthesizing audio with gans. 2018.
68. Jesse Engel, Lamtharn Hantrakul, Chenjie Gu, and Adam Roberts. Ddsp: Differentiable digital signal processing. *arXiv preprint arXiv:2001.04643*, 2020.

69. Xin Wang, Shinji Takaki, and Junichi Yamagishi. Neural source-filter-based waveform model for statistical parametric speech synthesis. In *ICASSP 2019-2019 IEEE International Conference on Acoustics, Speech and Signal Processing (ICASSP)*, pages 5916–5920. IEEE, 2019.

70. Jean-Marc Valin and Jan Skoglund. Lpcnet: Improving neural speech synthesis through linear prediction. In *ICASSP 2019-2019 IEEE International Conference on Acoustics, Speech and Signal Processing (ICASSP)*, pages 5891–5895. IEEE, 2019.

71. Perry R. Cook. Singing voice synthesis: History, current work, and future directions. *Computer Music Journal*, 20(3):38–46, 1996.

72. Lawrence R. Rabiner. A tutorial on hidden markov models and selected applications in speech recognition. *Proceedings of the IEEE*, 77(2):257–286, 1989.

73. Arnaud Lefebvre and Thierry Lecroq. Compror: on-line lossless data compression with a factor oracle. *Information Processing Letters*, 83(1):1–6, 2002.

74. Cheng-i Wang and Shlomo Dubnov. Guided music synthesis with variable markov oracle. In *The 3rd International Workshop on Musical Metacreation, 10th Artificial Intelligence and Interactive Digital Entertainment Conference*, 2014.

75. Sergei Prokofiev. Visions fugitives. *S. Prokofiev: Collected Works, Vol.*, 1:1915–1917, 1955. Moscow: Muzgiz.

76. K. Burns. Atoms of eve': A Bayesian basis for esthetic analysis of style in sketching. *Artificial Intelligence for Engineering Design, Analysis and Manufacturing*, 20:185–199, 2006.

77. L. Itti and P. Baldi. Bayesian surprise attracts human attention. *Advances in Neural Information Processing Systems.*, 19:1–8, 2005.

78. Martin J. Wainwright and Michael I. Jordan. Graphical models, exponential families, and variational inference. *Foundations and Trends in Machine Learning*, 1(1-2):1–305, 2008.

79. George David Birkhoff. *Aesthetic Measure*. Cambridge, Mass, 1933.

80. M. Bense. *Introduction to the Information-theoretical Aesthetics*. Foundation and Application to the Text Theory, Rowohlt Taschenbuch Verlag (In German), 1969.

81. H. Leder, B. Belke, A. Oeberst, and D. Augustin. A model of aesthetic appreciation and aesthetic judgements. *British Journal of Psychology*, 95(4):489–508, 2004.

82. David E. Rumelhart, Geoffrey E. Hinton, and Ronald J. Williams. Learning representations by back-propagating errors. *Nature*, 323(6088):533–536, 1986.

83. Diederik P. Kingma and Jimmy Ba. Adam: A method for stochastic optimization. *arXiv preprint arXiv:1412.6980*, 2014.

84. Xavier Glorot and Yoshua Bengio. Understanding the difficulty of training deep feed-forward neural networks. In *Proceedings of the Thirteenth International Conference on Artificial Intelligence and Statistics*, pages 249–256. JMLR Workshop and Conference Proceedings, 2010.

85. David Huron. *Sweet Anticipation: Music and the Psychology of Expectation*. MIT Press, 2008.

86. Chris Donahue, Ian Simon, and Sander Dieleman. Piano genie. In *Proceedings of the 24th International Conference on Intelligent User Interfaces*, pages 160–164, 2019.

87. Perfecto Herrera-Boyer, Geoffroy Peeters, and Shlomo Dubnov. Automatic classification of musical instrument sounds. *Journal of New Music Research*, 32(1):3–21, 2003.

88. Geoffroy Peeters, Stephen McAdams, and Perfecto Herrera. Instrument sound description in the context of mpeg-7. In *ICMC: International Computer Music Conference*, pages 166–169, 2000.

89. John Joseph Shynk. *Probability, Random Variables, and Random Processes Theory and Signal Processing Applications*. John Wiley & Sons, 2013.

90. Michael E. Tipping and Christopher M. Bishop. Probabilistic principal component analysis. *Journal of the Royal Statistical Society: Series B (Statistical Methodology)*, 61(3):611–622, 1999.

91. Peter M. Todd. A connectionist approach to algorithmic composition. *Computer Music Journal*, 13(4):27–43, 1989.

92. Nathan Fradet, Jean-Pierre Briot, Fabien Chhel, Amal El Fallah-Seghrouchni, and Nicolas Gutowski. Miditok: A python package for midi file tokenization. In *22nd International Society for Music Information Retrieval Conference*, 2021.

93. Sageev Oore, Ian Simon, Sander Dieleman, Douglas Eck, and Karen Simonyan. This time with feeling: Learning expressive musical performance. *Neural Computing and Applications*, 2018.

94. Yu-Siang Huang and Yi-Hsuan Yang. Pop music transformer: Beat-based modeling and generation of expressive pop piano compositions. In *Proceedings of the 28th ACM International Conference on Multimedia*, 2020.

95. Gatan Hadjeres and Lopold Crestel. The piano inpainting application, 2021.

96. Wen-Yi Hsiao, Jen-Yu Liu, Yin-Cheng Yeh, and Yi-Hsuan Yang. Compound word transformer: Learning to compose full-song music over dynamic directed hypergraphs. In *Proceedings of the AAAI Conference on Artificial Intelligence*, 2021.

97. Mingliang Zeng, Xu Tan, Rui Wang, Zeqian Ju, Tao Qin, and Tie-Yan Liu. Musicbert: Symbolic music understanding with large-scale pre-training, 2021.

98. Yi Ren, Jinzheng He, Xu Tan, Tao Qin, Zhou Zhao, and Tie-Yan Liu. Popmag: Pop music accompaniment generation. In *Proceedings of the 28th ACM International Conference on Multimedia*. Association for Computing Machinery, 2020.

99. Midime: Personalizing a musicvae model with user data. In *Workshop on Machine Learning for Creativity and Design, NeurIPS*, 2019.

100. Li-Chia Yang, Szu-Yu Chou, and Yi-Hsuan Yang. Midinet: A convolutional generative adversarial network for symbolic-domain music generation using 1d and 2d conditions. *CoRR*, abs/1703.10847, 2017.

101. Ian Simon and Sageev Oore. Performance rnn: Generating music with expressive timing and dynamics. https://magenta.tensorflow.org/performance-rnn, 2017.

102. Adam Roberts, Jesse H. Engel, Colin Raffel, Curtis Hawthorne, and Douglas Eck. A hierarchical latent vector model for learning long-term structure in music. In *Proceedings of the 35th International Conference on Machine Learning, ICML*, pages 4361–4370, Stockholm, Sweden, 2018. PMLR.

103. Ashis Pati, Alexander Lerch, and Gatan Hadjeres. Learning to traverse latent spaces for musical score inpaintning. In *20th International Society for Music Information Retrieval Conference (ISMIR)*, Delft, The Netherlands, 2019.

104. Ruihan Yang, Dingsu Wang, Ziyu Wang, Tianyao Chen, Junyan Jiang, and Gus Xia. Deep music analogy via latent representation disentanglement. In *Proceedings of the 20th International Society for Music Information Retrieval Conference, ISMIR*, pages 596–603, Delft, The Netherlands, 2019.

105. Ke Chen, Cheng-i Wang, Taylor Berg-Kirkpatrick, and Shlomo Dubnov. Music sketchnet: Controllable music generation via factorized representations of pitch and rhythm. 2020.

106. Ziyu Wang, Yiyi Zhang, Yixiao Zhang, Junyan Jiang, Ruihan Yang, Gus Xia, and Junbo Zhao. PIANOTREE VAE: structured representation learning for polyphonic music. In *Proceedings of the 21th International Society for Music Information Retrieval Conference, ISMIR 2020*, pages 368–375.

107. Cheng-Zhi Anna Huang, Ashish Vaswani, Jakob Uszkoreit, Ian Simon, Curtis Hawthorne, Noam Shazeer, Andrew M. Dai, Matthew D. Hoffman, Monica Dinculescu, and Douglas Eck. Music transformer: Generating music with long-term structure. In *7th International Conference on Learning Representations, ICLR*, New Orleans, LA, USA.

108. Yu-Siang Huang and Yi-Hsuan Yang. Pop music transformer: Beat-based modeling and generation of expressive pop piano compositions. In *MM '20: The 28th ACM International Conference on Multimedia*, pages 1180–1188. ACM, 2020.

109. Wen-Yi Hsiao, Jen-Yu Liu, Yin-Cheng Yeh, and Yi-Hsuan Yang. Compound word transformer: Learning to compose full-song music over dynamic directed hypergraphs. In *Thirty-Fifth AAAI Conference on Artificial Intelligence, AAAI 2021*, pages 178–186. AAAI Press.

110. Ethan Manilow, Prem Seetharaman, and Justin Salamon. *Open Source Tools & Data for Music Source Separation*. https://source-separation.github.io/tutorial, October 2020.

111. John F. Woodruff, Bryan Pardo, and Roger B Dannenberg. Remixing stereo music with score-informed source separation. In *ISMIR*, pages 314–319, 2006.

112. Olaf Ronneberger, Philipp Fischer, and Thomas Brox. U-net: Convolutional networks for biomedical image segmentation. In *Medical Image Computing and Computer-Assisted Intervention–MICCAI 2015: 18th International Conference, Munich, Germany, October 5-9, 2015, Proceedings, Part III 18*, pages 234–241. Springer, 2015.

113. Haibo Geng, Ying Hu, and Hao Huang. Monaural singing voice and accompaniment separation based on gated nested u-net architecture. *Symmetry*, 12(6):1051, 2020.

114. Qiuqiang Kong, Yin Cao, Haohe Liu, Keunwoo Choi, and Yuxuan Wang. Decoupling magnitude and phase estimation with deep resunet for music source separation. *arXiv preprint arXiv:2109.05418*, 2021.

115. Eunjeong Koh and Shlomo Dubnov. Comparison and analysis of deep audio embeddings for music emotion recognition. *arXiv preprint arXiv:2104.06517*, 2021.

116. Jort F. Gemmeke, Daniel P. W. Ellis, Dylan Freedman, Aren Jansen, Wade Lawrence, R. Channing Moore, Manoj Plakal, and Marvin Ritter. Audio set: An ontology and human-labeled dataset for audio events. In *2017 IEEE International Conference on Acoustics, Speech and Signal Processing (ICASSP)*, pages 776–780. IEEE, 2017.

117. Sami Abu-El-Haija, Nisarg Kothari, Joonseok Lee, Paul Natsev, George Toderici, Balakrishnan Varadarajan, and Sudheendra Vijayanarasimhan. Youtube-8m: A large-scale video classification benchmark. *arXiv preprint arXiv:1609.08675*, 2016.

118. Jason Cramer, Ho-Hsiang Wu, Justin Salamon, and Juan Pablo Bello. Look, listen, and learn more: Design choices for deep audio embeddings. In *ICASSP 2019-2019 IEEE International Conference on Acoustics, Speech and Signal Processing (ICASSP)*, pages 3852–3856. IEEE, 2019.

119. Relja Arandjelovic and Andrew Zisserman. Look, listen and learn. In *Proceedings of the IEEE International Conference on Computer Vision*, pages 609–617, 2017.

120. Karen Simonyan and Andrew Zisserman. Very deep convolutional networks for large-scale image recognition. *arXiv preprint arXiv:1409.1556*, 2014.

References 311

121. Yizhao Ni, Matt McVicar, Raul Santos-Rodriguez, and Tijl De Bie. An end-to-end machine learning system for harmonic analysis of music. *IEEE Transactions on Audio, Speech, and Language Processing*, 20(6):1771–1783, 2012.

122. Alexander Sheh and Daniel PW Ellis. Chord segmentation and recognition using em-trained hidden markov models. 2003.

123. Abdel-rahman Mohamed, Geoffrey Hinton, and Gerald Penn. Understanding how deep belief networks perform acoustic modelling. In *2012 IEEE international conference on acoustics, speech and signal processing (ICASSP)*, pages 4273–4276. IEEE, 2012.

124. Rudi Cilibrasi, Paul Vitányi, and Ronald De Wolf. Algorithmic clustering of music. In *Proceedings of the Fourth International Conference on Web Delivering of Music, 2004. EDELMUSIC 2004.*, pages 110–117. IEEE, 2004.

125. Sreeparna Banerjee. A survey of prospects and problems in hindustani classical raga identification using machine learning techniques. In *Proceedings of the first international conference on intelligent computing and communication*, pages 467–475. Springer, 2017.

126. Geoffrey E. Hinton. To recognize shapes, first learn to generate images. In Paul Cisek, Trevor Drew, and John F. Kalaska, editors, *Computational Neuroscience: Theoretical Insights into Brain Function*, volume 165 of *Progress in Brain Research*, pages 535–547. Elsevier, 2007.

127. Geoffrey E Hinton, Peter Dayan, Brendan J Frey, and Radford M Neal. The "wake-sleep" algorithm for unsupervised neural networks. *Science*, 268(5214):1158–1161, 1995.

128. Andrey Guzhov, Federico Raue, Jrn Hees, and Andreas Dengel. Audioclip: Extending clip to image, text and audio. In *ICASSP 2022-2022 IEEE International Conference on Acoustics, Speech and Signal Processing (ICASSP)*, pages 976–980. IEEE, 2022.

129. Rongjie Huang, Jiawei Huang, Dongchao Yang, Yi Ren, Luping Liu, Mingze Li, Zhen-hui Ye, Jinglin Liu, Xiang Yin, and Zhou Zhao. Make-an-audio: Text-to-audio generation with prompt-enhanced diffusion models. *arXiv preprint arXiv:2301.12661*, 2023.

130. Mark Hasegawa-Johnson, Alan Black, Lucas Ondel, Odette Scharenborg, and Francesco Ciannella. Image2speech: Automatically generating audio descriptions of images. *Casablanca 2017*, page 65, 2017.

131. S. Forsgren and H. Martiros. Riffusion-stable diffusion for real-time music generation. 2022. *URL https://riffusion. com/about.*

132. Peter Dayan, Geoffrey E Hinton, Radford M Neal, and Richard S Zemel. The helmholtz machine. *Neural computation*, 7(5):889–904, 1995.

133. Auto-encoding variational bayes. In *ICLR*, 2014.

134. Ke Chen, Weilin Zhang, Shlomo Dubnov, Gus Xia, and Wei Li. The effect of explicit structure encoding of deep neural networks for symbolic music generation. In *International Workshop on Multilayer Music Representation and Processing, MMRP 2019*. IEEE, 2019.

135. Ke Chen, Cheng-i Wang, Taylor Berg-Kirkpatrick, and Shlomo Dubnov. Music sketch-net: Controllable music generation via factorized representations of pitch and rhythm. In *Proceedings of the 21st International Society for Music Information Retrieval Conference, ISMIR*, 2020.

136. Ke Chen, Gus Xia, and Shlomo Dubnov. Continuous melody generation via disentan-gled short-term representations and structural conditions. In *IEEE 14th International Conference on Semantic Computing, ICSC*, pages 128–135. IEEE, 2020.

137. Gaëtan Hadjeres, François Pachet, and Frank Nielsen. Deepbach: a steerable model for bach chorales generation. In *International conference on machine learning*, pages 1362–1371. PMLR, 2017.

138. Ziyu Wang, Ke Chen, Junyan Jiang, Yiyi Zhang, Maoran Xu, Shuqi Dai, and Gus Xia. POP909: A pop-song dataset for music arrangement generation. In *Proceedings of the 21st International Society for Music Information Retrieval Conference, ISMIR 2020*, pages 38–45, 2020.

139. Hao-Wen Dong, Ke Chen, Julian J. McAuley, and Taylor Berg-Kirkpatrick. Muspy: A toolkit for symbolic music generation. In *Proceedings of the 21st International Society for Music Information Retrieval Conference, ISMIR 2020*, pages 101–108, 2020.

140. Yin-Jyun Luo, Kat Agres, and Dorien Herremans. Learning disentangled representations of timbre and pitch for musical instrument sounds using gaussian mixture variational autoencoders. In *Proceedings of the 20th International Society for Music Information Retrieval Conference, ISMIR*, pages 746–753, 2019.

141. Wei-Ning Hsu, Yu Zhang, and James Glass. Learning latent representations for speech generation and transformation, 2017.

142. Ke Chen, Beici Liang, Xiaoshuan Ma, and Minwei Gu. Learning audio embeddings with user listening data for content-based music recommendation. In *International Conference on Acoustics, Speech and Signal Processing, ICASSP*, pages 3015–3019. IEEE, 2021.

143. Ke Chen, Xingjian Du, Bilei Zhu, Zejun Ma, Taylor Berg-Kirkpatrick, and Shlomo Dubnov. Zero-shot audio source separation through query-based learning from weakly-labeled data. In *Proceedings of the Thirty-Sixth AAAI Conference on Artificial Intelligence, AAAI 2022*. AAAI Press, 2021.

144. Shlomo Dubnov. In fleeting visions: Deep neural music fickle play. In *Proceedings of the 2019 on Creativity and Cognition*, pages 502–507. AAAI Press, 2019.

145. Eunjeong Stella Koh, Shlomo Dubnov, and Dustin Wright. Rethinking recurrent latent variable model for music composition. In *2018 IEEE 20th International Workshop on Multimedia Signal Processing (MMSP)*, pages 1–6, 2018.

146. Ashis Pati and Alexander Lerch. Attribute-based regularization of latent spaces for variational auto-encoders. *Neural Comput. Appl.*, 33(9):4429–4444, 2021.

147. Adrien Bitton, Philippe Esling, and Tatsuya Harada. Vector-quantized timbre representation. *arXiv preprint arXiv:2007.06349*, 2020.

148. Noam Mor, Lior Wolf, Adam Polyak, and Yaniv Taigman. A universal music translation network. *arXiv preprint arXiv:1805.07848*, 2018.

149. Ian Goodfellow. Nips 2016 tutorial: Generative adversarial networks. *arXiv preprint arXiv:1701.00160*, 2016.

150. Philippe Esling, Adrien Bitton, et al. Generative timbre spaces: regularizing variational auto-encoders with perceptual metrics. *arXiv preprint arXiv:1805.08501*, 2018.

151. Olof Mogren. C-rnn-gan: Continuous recurrent neural networks with adversarial training. *arXiv preprint arXiv:1611.09904*, 2016.

152. Li-Chia Yang, Szu-Yu Chou, and Yi-Hsuan Yang. Midinet: A convolutional generative adversarial network for symbolic-domain music generation. *arXiv preprint arXiv:1703.10847*, 2017.

153. Hao-Wen Dong, Wen-Yi Hsiao, Li-Chia Yang, and Yi-Hsuan Yang. Musegan: Multi-track sequential generative adversarial networks for symbolic music generation and accompaniment. In *Proceedings of the AAAI Conference on Artificial Intelligence*, volume 32, 2018.

154. Conan Lu and Shlomo Dubnov. Chordgan: Symbolic music style transfer with chroma feature extraction.

155. Chris Donahue, Julian McAuley, and Miller Puckette. Adversarial audio synthesis. In *International Conference on Learning Representations*, 2018.

156. Jesse Engel, Kumar Krishna Agrawal, Shuo Chen, Ishaan Gulrajani, Chris Donahue, and Adam Roberts. Gansynth: Adversarial neural audio synthesis. 2019.

157. Kundan Kumar, Rithesh Kumar, Thibault de Boissiere, Lucas Gestin, Wei Zhen Teoh, Jose Sotelo, Alexandre de Brebisson, Yoshua Bengio, and Aaron Courville. *MelGAN: Generative Adversarial Networks for Conditional Waveform Synthesis*. Curran Associates Inc., Red Hook, NY, USA, 2019.

158. Gino Brunner, Yuyi Wang, Roger Wattenhofer, and Sumu Zhao. Symbolic music genre transfer with cyclegan. In *2018 ieee 30th international conference on tools with artificial intelligence (ictai)*, pages 786–793. IEEE, 2018.

159. Marco Pasini. Melgan-vc: Voice conversion and audio style transfer on arbitrarily long samples using spectrograms. *arXiv preprint arXiv:1910.03713*, 2019.

160. Cheng-i Wang, Jennifer Hsu, and Shlomo Dubnov. Machine improvisation with variable markov oracle: Toward guided and structured improvisation. *Computers in Entertainment (CIE)*, 14(03), 2016.

161. George Tzanetakis, Andrey Ermolinskyi, and Perry Cook. Pitch histograms in audio and symbolic music information retrieval. *Journal of New Music Research*, 32(2):143–152, 2003.

162. Zellig S. Harris. Distributional structure. *Word*, 10(2-3):146–162, 1954.

163. Mireille Besson and Daniele Schn. Comparison between language and music. *Annals of the New York Academy of Sciences*, 930(1):232–258, 2001.

164. Leonard Bernstein. *The Unanswered Question: Six Talks at Harvard*, volume 33. Harvard University Press, 1976.

165. Vladimir Bostanov and Boris Kotchoubey. Recognition of affective prosody: Continuous wavelet measures of event-related brain potentials to emotional exclamations. *Psychophysiology*, 41(2):259–268, 2004.

166. Tomas Mikolov, Kai Chen, Greg Corrado, and Jeffrey Dean. Efficient estimation of word representations in vector space. *arXiv preprint arXiv:1301.3781*, 2013.

167. Dorien Herremans and Ching-Hua Chuan. Modeling musical context with word2vec. *arXiv preprint arXiv:1706.09088*, 2017.

168. Yi Tay, Mostafa Dehghani, Dara Bahri, and Donald Metzler. Efficient transformers: A survey. *ACM Computing Surveys*, 55(6):1–28, 2022.

169. Francois Chollet. *Deep learning with Python*. Simon and Schuster, 2021.

170. Austin Huang, Suraj Subramanian, Jonathan Sum, Khalid Almubarak, Stella Biderman, and Sasha Rush. The annotated transformer. (2022). *URL http://nlp. seas. harvard. edu/annotated–transformer*, 2022.

171. Ashish Vaswani, Noam Shazeer, Niki Parmar, Jakob Uszkoreit, Llion Jones, Aidan N. Gomez, Łukasz Kaiser, and Illia Polosukhin. Attention is all you need. In *Proceedings of the 31st International Conference on Neural Information Processing Systems*, NIPS'17, page 6000–6010, Red Hook, NY, USA, 2017. Curran Associates Inc.

172. Jacob Devlin, Ming-Wei Chang, Kenton Lee, and Kristina Toutanova. Bert: Pre-training of deep bidirectional transformers for language understanding. *ArXiv*, abs/1810.04805, 2019.

173. Alec Radford and Karthik Narasimhan. Improving language understanding by generative pre-training. 2018.

174. Alec Radford, Jeff Wu, Rewon Child, David Luan, Dario Amodei, and Ilya Sutskever. Language models are unsupervised multitask learners. 2019.

175. Tom B. Brown, Benjamin Mann, Nick Ryder, Melanie Subbiah, Jared Kaplan, Prafulla Dhariwal, Arvind Neelakantan, Pranav Shyam, Girish Sastry, Amanda Askell, Sandhini Agarwal, Ariel Herbert-Voss, Gretchen Krueger, Tom Henighan, Rewon Child, Aditya Ramesh, Daniel M. Ziegler, Jeffrey Wu, Clemens Winter, Christopher Hesse, Mark Chen, Eric Sigler, Mateusz Litwin, Scott Gray, Benjamin Chess, Jack Clark, Christopher Berner, Sam McCandlish, Alec Radford, Ilya Sutskever, and Dario Amodei. Language models are few-shot learners. In *Proceedings of the 34th International Conference on Neural Information Processing Systems*, NIPS'20, Red Hook, NY, USA, 2020. Curran Associates Inc.

176. Alexey Dosovitskiy, Lucas Beyer, Alexander Kolesnikov, Dirk Weissenborn, Xiaohua Zhai, Thomas Unterthiner, Mostafa Dehghani, Matthias Minderer, Georg Heigold, Sylvain Gelly, et al. An image is worth 16x16 words: Transformers for image recognition at scale. *arXiv preprint arXiv:2010.11929*, 2020.

177. Cheng-Zhi Anna Huang, Ashish Vaswani, Jakob Uszkoreit, Noam Shazeer, Ian Simon, Curtis Hawthorne, Andrew M. Dai, Matthew D. Hoffman, Monica Dinculescu, and Douglas Eck. Music transformer, 2018.

178. Sageev Oore, Ian Simon, Sander Dieleman, Douglas Eck, and Karen Simonyan. This time with feeling: Learning expressive musical performance. *Neural Computing and Applications*, 32:955–967, 2020.

179. Zihang Dai, Zhilin Yang, Yiming Yang, Jaime G. Carbonell, Quoc V. Le, and Ruslan Salakhutdinov. Transformer-xl: Attentive language models beyond a fixed-length context. *ArXiv*, abs/1901.02860, 2019.

180. Dimitri von Rtte, Luca Biggio, Yannic Kilcher, and Thomas Hofmann. Figaro: Generating symbolic music with fine-grained artistic control, 2022.

181. Hawthorne C. Simon I. Dinculescu M. Choi, K. and J Engel. Encoding musical style with transformer autoencoders. In *Proceedings of the 37t International Conference on Machine Learning*. PMLR, 2020.

182. Jeffrey Ens and Philippe Pasquier. MMM: Exploring conditional multi-track music generation with the transformer. *CoRR*.

183. Shih-Lun Wu and Yi-Hsuan Yang. Musemorphose: Full-song and fine-grained music style transfer with just one transformer VAE. *CoRR*.

184. Shuqi Dai, Zeyu Jin, Celso Gomes, and Roger B. Dannenberg. Controllable deep melody generation via hierarchical music structure representation. *arXiv preprint arXiv:2109.00663*, 2021.

185. John Brooke.

186. Latulipe C. Cherry E. Quantifying the creativity support of digital tools through the creativity support index. *ACM Transactions on Computer-Human Interaction (TOCHI)*, 21(4):1–25, 2014.

187. William Albert and Thomas Tullis. *Measuring the User Experience: Collecting, Analyzing, and Presenting Usability Metrics*. Newnes, 2013.

188. Anna Huang, Monica Dinculescu, Ashish Vaswani, and Douglas Eck. Visualizing music selfattention. In *Proc. NeurIPS Workshop on Interpretability and Robustness in Audio, Speech, and Language*, 2018.

189. Yuan Gong, Yu-An Chung, and James Glass. Ast: Audio spectrogram transformer. In *Interspeech 2021*.

190. Wei-Tsung Lu, Ju-Chiang Wang, Minz Won, Keunwoo Choi, and Xuchen Song. Spectnt: a time-frequency transformer for music audio. In *International Society for Music Information Retrieval (ISMIR)*, 2021.

191. Ke Chen, Xingjian Du, Bilei Zhu, Zejun Ma, Taylor Berg-Kirkpatrick, and Shlomo Dubnov. Hts-at: A hierarchical token-semantic audio transformer for sound classification and detection. In *IEEE International Conference on Acoustics, Speech and Signal Processing (ICASSP)*, pages 646–650, 2022.

192. Khaled Koutini, Jan Schlüter, Hamid Eghbal-zadeh, and Gerhard Widmer. Efficient training of audio transformers with patchout. *arXiv preprint arXiv:2110.05069*, 2021.

193. Arsha Nagrani, Shan Yang, Anurag Arnab, Aren Jansen, Cordelia Schmid, and Chen Sun. Attention bottlenecks for multimodal fusion. *Advances in Neural Information Processing Systems*, 34:14200–14213, 2021.

194. Ze Liu, Yutong Lin, Yue Cao, Han Hu, Yixuan Wei, Zheng Zhang, Stephen Lin, and Baining Guo. Swin transformer: Hierarchical vision transformer using shifted windows. In *Proceedings of the IEEE/CVF International Conference on Computer Vision*, pages 10012–10022, 2021.

195. Jeffrey Pennington, Richard Socher, and Christopher D Manning. Glove: Global vectors for word representation. In *Proceedings of the 2014 Conference on Empirical Methods in Natural Language Processing (EMNLP)*, pages 1532–1543, 2014.

196. Jonathan Foote. Visualizing music and audio using self-similarity. 1999.

197. Emily M. Bender, Timnit Gebru, Angelina McMillan-Major, and Shmargaret Shmitchell. On the dangers of stochastic parrots: Can language models be too big? In *Proceedings of the 2021 ACM Conference on Fairness, Accountability, and Transparency*, pages 610–623, 2021.

198. Dzmitry Bahdanau, Kyunghyun Cho, and Yoshua Bengio. Neural machine translation by jointly learning to align and translate. *arXiv preprint arXiv:1409.0473*, 2014.

199. Chris Donahue, Huanru Henry Mao, Yiting Ethan Li, Garrison W Cottrell, and Julian McAuley. Lakhnes: Improving multi-instrumental music generation with cross-domain pre-training. *arXiv preprint arXiv:1907.04868*, 2019.

200. B. J. Frey and G. E. Hinton. Free energy coding. In *Proceedings of the Conference on Data Compression*, DCC '96, page 73, USA, 1996. IEEE Computer Society.

201. Brendan J. Frey, Peter Dayan, and Geoffrey E. Hinton. *A Simple Algorithm That Discovers Efficient Perceptual Codes*, page 296–315. Cambridge University Press, USA, 1997.

202. Alexander A. Alemi, Ben Poole, Ian Fischer, Joshua V. Dillon, Rif A. Saurous, and Kevin Murphy. An information-theoretic analysis of deep latent-variable models. *CoRR*, abs/1711.00464, 2017.

203. Alan Marsden. Schenkerian analysis by computer: A proof of concept. *Journal of New Music Research*, 39(3):269–289, 2010.

204. F. Lerdahl and R. S. Jackendoff. *A Generative Theory Oftonal Music*. MIT Press, 1996.

205. Naftali Tishby and Noga Zaslavsky. Deep learning and the information bottleneck principle. 2015.

206. Alexander Amir Alemi. Variational predictive information bottleneck. In *AABI*, 2019.

207. Zhe Dong, Deniz Oktay, Ben Poole, and Alexander A. Alemi. On predictive information in rnns, 2020.

208. Thomas M. Cover and Joy A. Thomas. *Elements of Information Theory, 2nd Edition (Wiley Series in Telecommunications and Signal Processing)*. Wiley-Interscience, July 2006.

209. Toby Berger. *Rate Distortion Theory; a Mathematical Basis for Data Compression.* Prentice-Hall Englewood Cliffs, N.J., 1971.

210. Shlomo Dubnov. Query-based deep improvisation. In *International Conference on Computational Creativity, ICCC2019, Workshop on Musical Meta-Creation*, University of North Carolina, Charlotte, USA, 2019.

211. David J. Elliott. Musicing, listening, and musical understanding. *Contributions to Music Education*, (20):64–83, 1993.

212. K. Chen, K. Huang and Dubnov, S. Deep music information dynamics. *Journal of Creative Music Systems*, 1(1), 2022.

213. Lejaren Arthur Hiller and Leonard M. Isaacson. *Experimental Music; Composition with an Electronic Computer.* Greenwood Publishing Group Inc., USA, 1979.

214. Herbert A. Simon. The new science of management decision. 1960.

215. George Dickie. EVALUATING ART. *The British Journal of Aesthetics*, 25(1):3–16, 01 1985.

216. Simon Colton, John Charnley, and Alison Pease. Computational creativity theory: The face and idea descriptive models. In *Proceedings of the 2nd International Conference on Computational Creativity, ICCC 2011*, Proceedings of the 2nd International Conference on Computational Creativity, ICCC 2011, pages 90–95, December 2011. International Conference on Computational Creativity 2011, ICCC 2011; Conference date: 27-04-2011 Through 29-04-2011.

217. Margaret A. Boden. *The Creative Mind: Myths and Mechanisms.* Basic Books, Inc., USA, 1991.

218. Oliver Roland Bown. Generative and adaptive creativity: A unified approach to creativity in nature, humans and machines. 2012.

219. Shlomo Dubnov, Gerard Assayag, and Vignesh Gokul. Creative improvised interaction with generative musical systems. In *2022 IEEE 5th International Conference on Multimedia Information Processing and Retrieval (MIPR)*, pages 121–126, 2022.

220. C. Canonne and N. Garnier. A model for collective free improvisation. In *Mathematics and Computation in Music. Third International Conference MCM*, IRCAM, Paris, France, June 15-17, 2011.

221. P. Mouawad and S. Dubnov. On modeling affect in audio with non-linear symbolic dynamics. *Advances in Science, Technology and Engineering Systems Journal*, 2(3):1727–1740, 2017.

222. G. Bachelard. *La formation de l'esprit scientifique.* (reprint. Paris PUF coll. Quadrige, 2013), Paris, Alcan, 1934.

223. P. A. Corning. The re-emergence of "emergence": A venerable concept in search of a theory. *Complexity*, 7(6):18–30, 2002.

Index

Note: Locators in *italics* represent figures and **bold** indicate tables in the text.

Printed in the United States
by Baker & Taylor Publisher Services